W9-BPK-511

# THE
# MICHELIN
## GUIDE

## NEW YORK CITY

2018

MICHELIN

# THE MICHELIN GUIDE'S COMMITMENTS

Whether they are in Japan, the USA, China or Europe, our inspectors apply the same criteria to judge the quality of each and every establishment that they visit. The MICHELIN guide commands a **worldwide reputation** thanks to the commitments we make to our readers—and we reiterate these below:

Our inspectors make **anonymous visits** to restaurants to gauge the quality of cuisine offered to the everyday customer. They pay their own bill and make no indication of their presence. These visits are supplemented by comprehensive monitoring of information—our readers' comments are one valuable source, and are always taken into consideration.

Our choice of establishments is a completely **independent** one, made for the benefit of our readers alone. Decisions are discussed by inspectors and editor, with the most important considered at the global level. Inclusion in the Guide is always free of charge.

The Guide offers a **selection** of the best restaurants in each category of comfort and price. A recommendation in the Guide is an honor in itself, and defines the establishment among the "best of the best."

All practical information, the classifications, and awards are revised and updated every year to ensure the most **reliable information** possible.

The standards and criteria for the classifications are the same in all countries covered by the MICHELIN guides. Our system is used worldwide and easy to apply when selecting a restaurant.

As part of Michelin's ongoing commitment to improving **travel and mobility**, we do everything possible to make vacations and eating out a pleasure.

# THE MICHELIN GUIDE'S SYMBOLS

## AVERAGE PRICES

| | |
|---|---|
| ⬡ | Under $25 |
| $$ | $25 to $50 |
| $$$ | $50 to $75 |
| $$$$ | Over $75 |

## FACILITIES & SERVICES

| | |
|---|---|
| 🍇 | Notable wine list |
| 🍹 | Notable cocktail list |
| 🍺 | Notable beer list |
| 🍶 | Notable sake list |
| ♿ | Wheelchair accessible |
| ⛱ | Outdoor dining |
| 🍽 | Private dining room |
| 🥐 | Breakfast |
| 🍳 | Brunch |
| 🥢 | Dim sum |
| 🚗 | Valet parking |
| 💵 | Cash only |

## RESTAURANT CLASSIFICATIONS BY COMFORT
**More pleasant if in red**

| | |
|---|---|
| 🍱 | Small plates |
| ⵣ | Comfortable |
| ⵣⵣ | Quite comfortable |
| ⵣⵣⵣ | Very comfortable |
| ⵣⵣⵣⵣ | Top class comfortable |
| ⵣⵣⵣⵣⵣ | Luxury in the traditional style |

## STARS

Our famous one ❀, two ❀❀ and three ❀❀❀ stars identify establishments serving the highest quality cuisine – taking into account the quality of ingredients, the mastery of techniques and flavors, the levels of creativity and, of course, consistency.

❀❀❀ Exceptional cuisine, worth a special journey

❀❀ Excellent cuisine, worth a detour

❀ High quality cooking, worth a stop

## BIB GOURMAND

Inspectors' favorites for good value.

## MICHELIN PLATE

Good cooking.
Fresh ingredients, carefully
prepared: simply a good meal.

# DEAR READER,

**It's** been an exciting year for the entire team at the MICHELIN guides in North America, and it is with great pride that we present you with our 2018 edition to New York City. Over the past year our inspectors have extended their reach to include a variety of establishments and multiplied their anonymous visits to restaurants in our selection in order to accurately reflect the rich culinary diversity this great city has to offer.

**As** part of the Guide's highly confidential and meticulous evaluation process, our inspectors have methodically eaten their way through the entire city with a mission to marshal the finest in each category for your enjoyment. While they are expertly trained professionals in the food industry, the Guides remain consumer-driven and provide comprehensive choices to accommodate your every comfort, taste, and budget. By dining and drinking as "everyday" customers, they are able to experience and evaluate the same level of service and cuisine as any other guest. This past year has seen some unique advancements in New York City's dining scene. Some of these can be found in each neighborhood introduction, complete with photography depicting our favored choices.

**Our** company's founders, Édouard and André Michelin, published the first MICHELIN guide in 1900, to provide motorists with useful information about where they could service and repair their cars as well as find a good quality meal. In 1926, the star-rating system was introduced, whereby outstanding establishments are awarded for excellence in cuisine. Over the decades we have made many new enhancements to the Guide, and the local team here in New York City eagerly carries on these traditions.

**As** we take consumer feedback seriously, please feel free to contact us at: michelin.guides@michelin.com. You may also follow our Inspectors on Twitter (@MichelinGuideNY) and Instagram (@michelininspectors) as they chow their way around town. We thank you for your patronage and truly hope that the MICHELIN guide will remain your preferred reference to New York City's restaurants.

# CONTENTS

## ■ INDEXES

# MANHATTAN

# CHELSEA

Chelsea is a charming residential neighborhood combining modern high-rises and sleek lofts with classic townhouses and retail stores aplenty. To that end, this nabe is a shopper's paradise, offering everything from computer marts and high fashion boutiques, to **Chelsea Market**—the city's culinary epicenter. And let's not forget the art: this neighborhood's once-dilapidated warehouses and abandoned lofts are currently home to over 200 prominent galleries as well as the artists who contribute to them. Naturally, it is a burgeoning cultural scene. To feed its well-educated, art-enthusiast residents, and out-of-towners on pilgrimage here, Chelsea teems with casual cafeterias. Those old-world Puerto Rican luncheonettes that used to dot Ninth Avenue have now given way to mega-hip temples of fusion cooking—where diners are accommodated in stylish digs

Chelsea

HUDSON RIVER

MIDTOWN WEST

HUDSON YARDS

M 34 St-Hudson Yards

GARMENT DISTRICT 1

HUDSON RIVER

PIER 63 PARK

PIER 62

CHELSEA WATERSIDE PARK

CHELSEA PARK

MADISON SQUARE GARDEN

34 St-Penn Sta

PENN STATION

M 34 St-Penn Sta

MACY'S

CHELSEA PIERS

The Red Cat 🍴○

Tía Pol 🍴●

🍴○ Trestle on Tenth

🍴● Jun-Men Ramen Bar

🍴○ El Quinto Pino

FASHION INSTITUTE OF TECHNOLOGY

M 28 St

🍴○ Cookshop

🍴○ Blossom

❀ Ushiwakamaru

23 St

M 23 St

🍴○ Foragers City Table

MIDTOWN SOUTH

❀ Del Posto

CHELSEA HISTORIC DISTRICT

Salinas 🍴○

23 St

HIGH LINE PARK

● La Sirena ❀

CHELSEA MARKET

FLATIRON

MEATPACKING

WHITNEY MUSEUM

Gansevoort St.

18 St M

🍴○ Legend Bar & Restaurant

❀ Rouge Tomate

🍴○ da ● Umberto

M 14 St

14 St M

UNION SQUARE

GREENWICH & WEST VILLAGE

UNION SQUARE

14 St-Union Sq M

GRAMERCY, FLATIRON & UNION SQUARE

and the cocktail menu packs a potent punch. Carousers party until last call at such high-energy hangouts as **1 OAK**, launched by greenmarket-obsessed chef, Alex Guarnaschelli's Butter Group. Patrons of this hot spot may then jump ship to the likes of **Marquee**, but also remain loyal to such late-night stalwarts

as **Robert's Steakhouse at Scores New York**. Nestled inside the infamous Penthouse Executive Club, it's really all about the "meat" at this fortress of flesh, where suits seem far more interested in the likes of char-grilled steaks on their plates than the ladies perched on their laps.

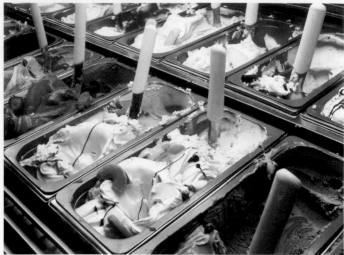

Located above Manhattan's mean streets and atop an elevated freight railroad, **The High Line** is a lengthy public space with a large presence in Chelsea. Populated by yuppies and young families, and punctuated by acres of indigenous greenery as well as surprisingly stunning views of the Hudson, this city-center oasis also offers unique respites for refreshment. For instance, **Bubby's High Line** is perpetually packed for its impressive repertoire of food and drink. Envision a number of young locals ordering off a kid's menu, or late-night revelers devouring a "midnight brunch" and you will begin to understand what this neighborhood is all about. Too rushed to dwell over dessert? Their retail store sells pastries and ice cream sandwiches to-go, after which a shot of single-origin drip espresso at **Blue Bottle Coffee Café** is not just fitting, but fundamental. As history would have it, the last functional freight train that passed through The High Line had cars filled with meat. Ergo, it seems only natural that **La Sonrisa Empanadas** proffers pastry pockets stuffed with ropa vieja, pulled pork, and other eats to ease the summer heat. Nearby, **Terroir at The Porch** is an open-air, full-service café with small plates, wine, and beer to boot.

**I**n 1997, the 1898 Nabisco factory reopened as **Chelsea Market**, a fabled culinary bazaar whose brick-lined walkways are cramped with stores selling everything—from lemons to lingerie. Carb-addicts begin their circuitous excursion here at **Amy's Bread**, where artisan-crafted loaves are as precious as crown jewels. Then they might linger at **Bar Suzette** for scores of fluffy crêpes. Meanwhile, the calorie-counters collect at **Beyond Sushi** for healthy renditions of this Japanese staple, wrapped here in black rice and topped with tofu. Seal such stellar bites with a cooling kiss from **L'Arte del Gelato**. Sound like bliss? It is.

**F**rom Asian signatures to everyday Italian, **Buon Italia** will not only help stock your pantry for a night in with nonna, but also sates those inevitable hunger pangs while you're at it—a stand upfront sells cooked foods and sandwiches to crowds on the run. Other welcome members to this epicurean community include **Dickson's Farmstand Meats** for house-made pâté; **Sarabeth's** or **Fat Witch Bakery** for holiday goodies; **Creamline** for comfort food classics; and **Ronnybrook** for dairy products. Keep trekking northward before sealing the (evening) deal at **La Piscine** (located on the rooftop of Hôtel Americano) with a snack of any kind and a sip (or several) of vino!

# BLOSSOM 🍴

*Vegan*

XX | 🍽

Unpretentious and welcoming, this is a vegan favorite with spot-on spicing and delicious surprises. The cream-colored interior is dim with dark velvet curtains and votive candles reflected in round mirrors. A thematically appropriate "living wall" resides in one corner of the space. The vibe may seem moody come evening, but the staff is always warm and affable.

A black-eye pea cake composed with crushed potatoes is pan-fried to render a golden breadcrumb exterior; while a Moroccan tagine bobbing with chickpeas, a host of vegetables including carrots, turnips and zucchini, and topped with crispy tofu strips is all heart and soul. Come dessert, try the hand-churned cashew ice cream or a lemony cheesecake with a mixed berry reduction and coconut-cookie crust.

- 187 Ninth Ave. (bet. 21st & 22nd Sts.)
- 23 St (Eighth Ave.)
- (212) 627-1144 — **WEB:** www.blossomnyc.com
- Lunch & dinner daily                    PRICE: $$

# COOKSHOP 🍴

*American*

XX | ♿ 🍴 🍱 🥗

It's a delight just to enter this beautiful neighborhood mainstay, with its airy, impeccably clean, and sunlight-flooded dining room. The plant-filled space is furnished with ethically-sourced American oak tables as well as a wall of banquettes; and the bar is perfect for solo dining. And all this charm awaits you even before you sink your teeth into Cookshop's ultra-delicious food.

Chef de Cuisine Andrew Corrigan's contemporary, product-driven, and Mediterranean-inspired menu focuses on local sourcing, and includes dishes like ricotta gnudi with brown butter-apple sauce; grain salad with sesame, pomegranate and poached egg; or grilled bigeye tuna with dried fig anchoiade. Breakfast is served during the week, while weekends offer a full brunch menu.

- 156 Tenth Ave. (at 20th St.)
- 23 St (Eighth Ave.)
- (212) 924-4440 — **WEB:** www.cookshopny.com
- Lunch & dinner daily                    PRICE: $$

# DA UMBERTO 🍴

*Italian*

XX | 🐝 🛋

There is a finely tuned harmony to dining at such classic New York restaurants as this one. The Italian menu is familiar and unpretentious, the kitchen is adept, and ingredients are superb. But, what truly sets it apart is an ability to serve exactly what you crave without seeming trite or predictable. Even the look is a perfectly conjured mix of warm neutrals, with a sleek yet informal Northern Italian style and impeccably timed servers.

Start with the traditional antipasto and then proceed to one of the daily specials like veal Milanese or a lavish dish of garganelli with mushrooms and black truffles. When the dessert cart rolls around, expect an array of excellent house-made sweets like pristine berries under whisked-to-order zabaglione.

■ 107 W. 17th St. (bet. Sixth & Seventh Aves.)

🚇 18 St

✆ (212) 989-0303 — **WEB:** www.daumbertonyc.com

■ Lunch Mon – Fri   Dinner Mon – Sat          **PRICE: $$$$**

# EL QUINTO PINO 🍴

*Spanish*

XX | 🍴

This convivial tapas spot, compliments of Chef/co-owners Alex Raij and Eder Montero, is small but oh-so-warm and friendly. A bustling bar greets you upon entry; behind that lies a sweet little dining space with large windows, mismatched chairs, and a huge woven mural. Service is engaging and attentive. The food may hit the table swiftly, but nonetheless, the multiple courses are very well paced.

This kitchen has a talent for frying to perfection, but the highlight of the menu is arguably their lineup of warm, crusty bocadillos (sandwiches). The menu offers a full range of Spanish tapas that include regional touches from areas like Andalusia, Asturias or Menorca—and clever combinations like the garlic shrimp with ginger and jalapeño or delicious shrimp po' boy.

■ 401 W. 24th St. (bet. Ninth & Tenth Aves.)

🚇 23 St (Eighth Ave.)

✆ (212) 206-6900 — **WEB:** www.elquintopinonyc.com

■ Lunch Sat – Sun   Dinner nightly          **PRICE: $$**

# DEL POSTO ✿

*Italian*

XxxX | 器 ⊡

Most dishes from Executive Chef Melissa Rodriguez at the uniquely opulent and fashionable Del Posto are gorgeously crafted, but it is her playful interpretation of Italian cuisine that makes this kitchen creative. Of course, with neighbors like the High Line, Whitney Museum and Chelsea Market, not only is its location most desirable, but a sense of luxury is clear in their beautifully dressed tables, polished marble, and silk-draped windows.

Balconies sit above the striking bar with live piano music pouring through the room. Despite the formality, there is a warm buzz among diners as the impressive suited staff attends to them. The arrival of a refreshed menu still highlights canapés and top-notch classics like vitello tonnato, but indulge in such updated creations as a warm fennel and radicchio salad tossed with balsamic and raisins. Next-level pastas like farfalle with roasted beets and smoked ricotta reflect influences from up north. Then gnocchi studded with halibut and finished with caviar is an all-round delight, as is the highly enjoyable chocolate budino with coconut sorbet.

A worthy exception to the all-Italian wine list is a superb offering of some 300 champagnes.

◼ 85 Tenth Ave. (at 16th St.)
▣ 14 St - 8 Av
✆ (212) 497-8090 — **WEB:** www.delposto.com
◼ Lunch Mon – Fri   Dinner nightly          PRICE: $$$$

# FORAGERS CITY TABLE 🍴

## Contemporary

XX | ♿ 🛏            **MAP:** B2

This restaurant-cum-market is an offshoot of an independent grocer in DUMBO, though its kitchen philosophy seems to have arrived via California. The dining room radiates functionality through large and unencumbered windows as well as basic hardwood tables. It's staffed and patronized by the sort of local-loving sycophants who consider it an honor to dine here—and it actually is.

The kitchen team will impress you with their skilled cooking featuring local produce from the market's own farm in Columbia County. Heirloom tomatoes are whirled into a lush gazpacho; artisanal dried pasta produced in Brooklyn from organic grain is deliciously dressed; and roasted chicken with Hudson Valley corn polenta is comfort food extraordinaire.

▪ 300 W. 22nd St. (at Eighth Ave.)
▪ 23 St (Eighth Ave.)
📞 (212) 243-8888 — **WEB:** www.foragerscitygrocer.com
▪ Lunch Sat – Sun  Dinner nightly        **PRICE:** $$

# JUN-MEN RAMEN BAR 🍴

## Japanese

XX                               **MAP:** B2

This cool West Chelsea ramen shop is a hot ticket—and with less than two dozen seats, a short wait can be expected at lunchtime. Slick and bright, the grey and white space is accentuated by the stainless steel implements of the open kitchen, where two hot tub-sized stock pots of pork broth bubble away.

That marrow-rich broth is the foundation for a succulent bowlful of toothsome straight noodles topped with simmered bamboo shoots, delightfully fatty chasu, shoyu tamago with a liquid gold yolk, and a splash of fermented garlic oil for good measure. Spicy miso and kimchi are delicious variations on the theme, while small plates offer tastes like pork buns, fried sweet potatoes, and yellowtail crudo dressed with pickled mango and kimchi.

▪ 249 Ninth Ave. (bet 25th & 26th Sts.)
▪ 23 St (Eighth Ave.)
📞 (646) 852-6787 — **WEB:** www.junmenramen.com
▪ Lunch & dinner Mon – Sat         **PRICE:** 🐷

# LA SIRENA ❀
*Italian*

XxX | 🍇 🍹 ♿ 🏛 🖵 🛋

**MAP:** B3

Here come empire-builders Chef Mario Batali and partner Joe Bastianich to rev up the Chelsea scene even further with this revamped Maritime Hotel dining room. La Sirena is anchored by a pretty lounge, where the custom mosaic-tiled floor endures a nightly stampede of stilettos; a wall of glass overlooking an expansive patio allows the sunset to glint off the bar.

Having honed his skills at Casa Mono, Chef Anthony Sasso displays his tapas expertise at this gleaming bar, featuring a separate menu devoted solely to these small plates as well as a unique selection of Spanish wines. But for proper dining, seek out the cached dining rooms where sleek leather furnishings and fine service offer hushed comfort.

Pastas like lasagne al pesto e patate or tonnarelli neri with seafood are a highlight and best enjoyed as the bis portion, split between you and your guest. Then panelle, mint, and pomegranate molasses combine for a Sicilian-inspired backdrop to succulent lamb chops. When asked if you would like bread, your answer should be enthusiastically affirmative—the freshly baked semolina rolls are fabulous. Campari-soaked babà is an unconventional but delightful pastry nicely paired with basil gelato.

◼ 88 Ninth Ave. (bet. 16th & 17th Sts.)
🚇 14 St - 8 Av
📞 (212) 977-6096 — **WEB:** www.lasirena-nyc.com
◼ Lunch Sat – Sun   Dinner nightly

**PRICE:** $$$

# LEGEND BAR & RESTAURANT ¶O

## Chinese

XX

**MAP:** B3

While Legend may offer a variety of Asian fare, just stick to the Sichuan specialties and be thoroughly rewarded. Find one of the many highlights in supremely flavorful and tender Chong Qing spicy chicken, loaded with viciously good dried chilies. The house duck is a traditional presentation of roasted and crisped meat with wraps as well as a host of accoutrements, including crushed peanuts, fragrant herbs, scallions, and tasty plum sauce. Bok choy with black mushrooms is a crunchy, simply delicious departure from the intensity of other dishes you may face here.

The dining room has a certain hip and chic feel that fosters a lively happy hour scene. Colorful fabrics, striped walls, and statues of deities make for an attractive space.

■ 88 Seventh Ave. (bet. 15th & 16th Sts.)
🚇 14 St (Seventh Ave.)
✆ (212) 929-1778 — **WEB:** www.legendbarrestaurant.com
■ Lunch & dinner daily                          **PRICE:** $$

# THE RED CAT ¶O

## American

XX | 🍸 🍹

**MAP:** B2

If crowds indicate quality (and downtown they often do) then this clear favorite is still going strong, after almost 20 years. Loyal customers as diverse as the city itself flood this long bar and richly colored room for lunch, dinner, or just for a finely mixed cocktail and snack. Flowers give the space a touch of luxury; Moorish lanterns add warmth.

The pleasures here are the straightforward items, which arrive courtesy of Chef/owner Jimmy Bradley. Begin with umami-rich and visually stunning roasted broccoli, finished with slivered almonds and parmesan shavings, before moving on to a crisped tranche of salmon crowned with peekytoe crab in creamy saffron aïoli. Finish in style with a perfectly composed pistachio semifreddo draped with dark chocolate sauce.

■ 227 Tenth Ave. (bet. 23rd & 24th Sts.)
🚇 23 St (Eighth Ave.)
✆ (212) 242-1122 — **WEB:** www.theredcat.com
■ Lunch & dinner daily                          **PRICE:** $$

# ROUGE TOMATE ❀

*Contemporary*

XX | 🍴 🍸 🖥 ✍

**MAP:** C3

Located in a cozy brownstone (and previous home to the Gracie family, of Gracie Mansion), Rouge Tomate has reopened without missing a single beat. This iteration is warmer and less clinical—in a soulful space that is a fraction of its former footprint. Its philosophy of sustainability manifests in an appealing design that incorporates wood salvaged from hurricane Sandy devastation, with bright red votives as if to conjure the original spot.

Perhaps the most important continuation is this kitchen's dedication to S.P.E. (*Sanitas Per Escam*) or "health through food." Of course, this translates as cooking that optimizes nutrition, sustainability, and a diner's well-being, while also remaining thoroughly delicious. The result is a menu of ethically raised meats, seasonal produce, and minimal dairy to pair with mocktails, fresh juices, biodynamic wines, and so much more. This may sound steeped in principles, but rest assured as everything churned out of the kitchen is downright delicious.

High points include expertly prepared skate with snail ragout over braised greens, as well as a divine lemongrass parfait topped with mango sorbet, kiwi, and praline crumbles.

▮ 126 W. 18th St. (bet. Sixth & Seventh Aves.)

🚇 18 St

☎ (646) 395-3978 — **WEB:** www.rougetomatechelsea.com

▮ Lunch Sat – Sun   Dinner Tue – Sun

**PRICE: $$$**

# SALINAS ¶○

*Spanish*

✗✗ | 🍸 ♿ 🏖                                    **MAP:** B2

What's not to love here? Even if the lip-smacking tapas menu didn't draw customers in droves, a sexy décor dressed with oodles of fresh roses and the warm glow of candlelight would do the trick. A slender hallway opens up into a narrow dining hall featuring dark walls; tufted velvet banquettes; and a backyard dining area topped by a retractable roof.

The Spanish cuisine, skillfully rendered by chef and San Sebastian native, Luis Bollo, arrives as intricate tapas or hearty large plates, depending on your appetite. Tuck into arroz brut a la plancha, a tender, griddled cake of short grain brown rice, studded with savory merguez, peas, and raisins; or baked fideuà sauced with squid ink and topped with shaved sepia, garlicky aïoli and watercress sprouts.

▨ 136 Ninth Ave. (bet. 18th & 19th Sts.)
🚇 18 St
✆ (212) 776-1990 — **WEB:** www.salinasnyc.com
▨ Dinner nightly                              **PRICE:** $$$

# TÍA POL ¶○

*Spanish*

✗ | 🍽 🛋                                       **MAP:** A2

You'll think you've died and gone to Barcelona. This cozy little tapas den kicks up to boisterous levels in its bustling and festive front area, where servers uncork bottles and the wine flows as guests cue up for tables in the front or back dining room. The wait is all part of the fun, of course, and service is as cheery, efficient and casual as you'd hope it to be.

Originally opened in 2004, owners Heather Belz & Mani Dawes offer a scrumptious array of small plates like creamy black rice plated with shaved cuttlefish and pale green parsley purée; or a thick wedge of potato-studded tortilla Española, laced with delicious garlicky aïoli. Don't miss the skirt steak, a must-try when it hits the specials menu.

▨ 205 Tenth Ave. (bet. 22nd & 23rd Sts.)
🚇 23 St (Eighth Ave.)
✆ (212) 675-8805 — **WEB:** www.tiapol.com
▨ Lunch Tue – Sun   Dinner nightly            **PRICE:** ⊜

# TRESTLE ON TENTH ¶○

*Contemporary*

XX | 🍴 🍴 🍴

**MAP:** B2

West Chelsea's non-stop canteen is favored by a steady stream of gallerists, fashionistas, and tourists out for a jaunt along the High Line. Despite the glitz of this ascendant neighborhood, the look here is cozy, sociable, and downright humble. Pastas may veer from the Central European theme but are nonetheless delicious. Try the tagliatelle tossed in a buttery broth of clams, parsley, and garlic. Calf's liver here is outrageously funky and just as delicious, tender and supremely fresh beneath carmelized onions and a sweet wine reduction. The Nusstorte is a symphony of cruncy walnuts, sticky caramel, and Madagascan vanilla ice cream. Chase it all down with a Swiss wine or craft beer.

Rocket Pig is the restaurant's highly popular offshoot next door.

■ 242 Tenth Ave. (at 24th St.)
🚇 23 St (Eighth Ave.)
✆ (212) 645-5659 — **WEB:** www.trestleontenth.com
■ Lunch & dinner daily

**PRICE: $$**

**Share the journey with us!**
@MichelinGuideNY
@MichelinInspectors

# USHIWAKAMARU ❀

*Japanese*

XX | ⚘ ⚐

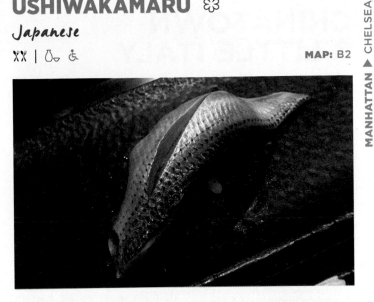

Now firmly settled into its Chelsea home in a former tavern, Ushiwakamaru may no longer have that underground feel of a sushi-ya that only the most dedicated aficionados know about. However, it remains home to luxe sushi and excellent fish.

The brief menu lists wallet-friendly à la carte specials, small plates, and cooked items like sautéed lobster and asparagus, but you may choose to ignore all that. Chef Hideo Kuribara's true focus is on the very impressive omakase, served as a choice of 14 or 20 superb courses. A bowl of pickled cucumber stimulates the appetite as a series of cold dishes arrive, with highlights like chopped horse mackerel with green onion and shiso leaf. Then move on to sashimi that proves just how incredibly fresh the fish here is.

Delve into perfectly cut octopus simply dressed with salt, pepper, and a squeeze of lemon; or needlefish served with a bowl of grated ginger, green onion slivers, and soy for dipping. Each morsel of nigiri is crafted at the dining counter and presented on a ceramic slab, ready to be plucked with your fingers. Expect large, cool mouthfuls of Japanese sea urchin, lightly torched fatty tuna with truffle salt, and rich shad brushed with soy.

▨ 362 W. 23rd St. (bet. Eighth & Ninth Aves.)

🚇 23rd St (Eighth Ave.)

✆ (917) 639-3940 — WEB: www.ushiwakamarunewyork.com

▨ Dinner Mon – Sat                    PRICE: $$$$

# CHINATOWN & LITTLE ITALY

As different as chow mein and chicken cacciatore, these two neighborhoods are nonetheless neighbors and remain as thick as thieves. In recent years, their borders have become increasingly blurred, with Chinatown gulping up most of Little Italy. It is said that New York cradles the maximum number of Chinese immigrants in the country, and settlers from Hong Kong and mainland China each brought with them their own distinct regional cuisines.

## EAT THE STREETS

Chowing in Chinatown can be delectable and delightfully affordable. Elbow your way through these cramped streets to find a flurry of markets, bubble tea cafés, bakeries, and more. Freshly steamed pouches of chicken, seafood, and pork are all the rage at **Vanessa's Dumpling House**, a neighborhood fixture with a long counter and longer queue of hungry visitors. There is lots more deliciousness to be had in this 'hood—from feasting on freshly pulled noodles; ducking into a parlor for a scoop of black sesame ice cream; or breezing past a market window with crocodile meat on display—claws included! **New Kam Man** is a bustling bazaar offering everything from woks to wontons; and Vietnamese mecca, **Tan Tin-Hung**,

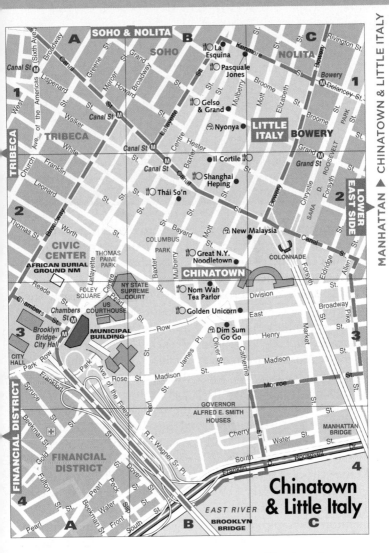

is a mini but "super" market
proffering the best selection
of authentic ingredients in
town—red perilla, *rau ram*,
and *culantro* are ready for
your home kitchen. For more
instant gratification, be sure
to binge on salty eats from
**New Beef King**. Imagine
a spicy blend of jerky and
barbecue—this neat and
mod spot has it all. Over on

Mulberry Street, **Asia Market Corp.** is a sight for sore eyes as shelves spill over with Malaysian, Indonesian, and Thai specialties. The space is tight, but the range of imported goods is nothing less than right. Find celebrity chefs at these Asian storefronts, haggling over flipping fish and quality produce, before sneaking under the Manhattan Bridge for a crusty *bánh mì*. Moving on to chilies and curry pastes, **Bangkok Center Grocery** boasts every ingredient necessary for a Thai-themed feast—not to mention their publications and friendly owner! Fans of Cantonese cuisine join the line outside **Big Wong King**, where comfort food classics (congee and roast duck) are as outstanding as the setting is ordinary. **Amazing 66** is a brightly lit, bi-level darling with two dining rooms. Here dishes arrive almost as swiftly as the crowds go in and out, making it a spot where taste and efficiency are of superlative quality. Then dim sum is obligatory and weekend brunch a longtime tradition at **Jing Fong**. Take the escalator up a floor to arrive at this mainstay, where the service is gruff but the Hong Kong-style treats are very tasty. For a more snug vibe, head to **Tai Pan Bakery** for pastries. The exquisitely light sponge cake at **Kam Hing Coffee Shop** has made it a worthy competitor in the "Best bakeries around town" contest; just as artisan bakeshop, **Fay Da**, has been serving its Chinese treats with a modern twist to the community for near-infinity. Klezmer meets Cantonese at the **Egg Rolls and Egg**

**Creams Festival**, an annual summer street celebration honoring the neighboring Chinese and Jewish communities of Chinatown and the Lower East Side. Every year during Chinese New Year, partygoers pack these streets, with dragons dancing down the avenues accompanied by costumed revelers and firecrackers.

## LITTLE ITALY

The Little Italy of Scorsese's gritty *Mean Streets* is slowly vanishing into what may now be more aptly called "Micro Italy." The onetime stronghold of a large Italian-American population has dwindled today to a mere corridor—Mulberry Street between Canal and Broome. But, the spirit of its origins still pulses in century-old markets, cramped delis, gelato shops, and mom-and-pop trattorias. Seasoned palates love **Piemonte Ravioli** for homemade sauces, as well as dried and fresh pastas—available in all shapes with a variety of fillings. **Alleva Dairy** (known for its ricotta) is the oldest Italian cheese store in the country; while **Di Palo's Fine Foods** boasts imported *salumi* and cheeses. Primo for pastries and espresso, fans never forget to frequent **Ferrara Bakery and Cafe** on Grand Street. Of course, during warmer months, Mulberry Street becomes a pedestrian zone with one big alfresco party—the **Feast of San Gennaro** is particularly raucous. While these days you can get better Italian food elsewhere in the city, tourists and old-timers still gather to treasure and bathe in the nostalgia of this nabe.

# DIM SUM GO GO 🐼

## Chinese

🍴 | 🥢

**MAP:** B3

This wildly popular joint is still packed to the gills most days, and for good reason: the Cantonese fare and dim sum served here is as good as the food you'll find in those super-authentic places in far-flung Queens. Even better, they take reservations—and dim sum orders are taken by the staff, thereby ensuring that the food stays fresh. However, guests should avoid shared tables during the weekend rush as service can verge on chaotic.

If the price seems a bit higher than its competitors, you'll find it's worth it for dishes like sweet shrimp, rolled in rice paper and laced with dark soy sauce. Plump snow pea leaf dumplings are spiked with vibrant ginger, garlic, and may be tailed by rich duck dumplings or an irresistibly flaky roast pork pie.

■ 5 East Broadway (at Chatham Sq.)
🚇 Canal St (Lafayette St.)
📞 (212) 732-0797 — **WEB:** N/A
■ Lunch & dinner daily

**PRICE: $$**

# GELSO & GRAND 🍴

## Italian

🍴 | ♿ 🏮 🍽 🥖

**MAP:** B1

It may be located smack in the middle of tourist-trappy Little Italy, but Gelso & Grand is a special place for creative and contemporary Italian food. The space is attractively industrial, with small tables and large windows that fling open for prime people-watching in warm weather. It may also be a bit pricey for the neighborhood, but that difference goes straight into the quality local ingredients and skillful cooking.

Begin with a pretty fan of tuna carpaccio garnished with tomato jam, candied ginger chips, and buttery green olives. Wood-oven fired pizzas are popular, but don't skip out on house pasta such as the roasted lasagna, layered with breaded eggplant fried golden brown, melted mozzarella, chunky Bolognese, and creamy tomato sauce.

■ 186 Grand St. (at Mulberry St.)
🚇 Spring St
📞 (212) 226-1600 — **WEB:** www.gelsoandgrand.com
■ Lunch & dinner daily

**PRICE: $$**

# GOLDEN UNICORN 🍴

## Chinese

✶ | 🖵 ⚔              **MAP:** B3

This age-old dim sum parlor, spread over many floors in an office building, is one of the few Cantonese spots that actually has the space and volume to necessitate its parade of steaming carts brimming with treats. While Golden Unicorn's system is very efficient and part of the spectacle, arrive early to nab a seat by the kitchen for better variety and hotter items.

A helpful brigade of suited men and women roam the space to offer the likes of exquisitely soft roast pork buns, or congee with preserved egg and shredded pork. Buzzing with locals and visitors, it is also a favorite among families who appreciate the kid-friendly scene as much as the delectable, steamed pea shoot and shrimp dumplings, pork siu mai, and rice rolls stuffed with shrimp.

◾ 18 East Broadway (at Catherine St.)
🚇 Canal St (Lafayette St.)
✆ (212) 941-0911 — **WEB:** www.goldenunicornrestaurant.com
◾ Lunch & dinner daily                    **PRICE:** $$

# GREAT N.Y. NOODLETOWN 🍴

## Chinese

✶ | 🖳 💵              **MAP:** B2

When heading to Great N.Y. Noodletown, invite plenty of dining companions to share those heaping plates of roasted meats and rice and noodle soups served at this bargain favorite. Locals stream in until the 4:00 A.M. closing bell for their great Cantonese fare—food is clearly the focus here, over the brusque service and unfussy atmosphere. Guests' gazes quickly pass over the imitation wooden chairs to rest on the crispy skin of suckling pig and ducks hanging in the window.

These dishes are huge, so forgo the rice and opt instead for deliciously chewy noodles and barbecue meats. Incredible shrimp wontons, so delicate and thin, and the complex, homemade e-fu noodles demonstrate technique and quality to a standout level that is rarely rivaled.

◾ 28 Bowery (at Bayard St.)
🚇 Canal St (Lafayette St.)
✆ (212) 349-0923 — **WEB:** N/A
◾ Lunch & dinner daily                    **PRICE:** ⊜

# IL CORTILE 🍴

*Italian*

XX | 🏠 ⊙

Beyond this quaint and charming façade lies one of Little Italy's famed mainstays, ever-popular with dreamy eyed dates seeking the stuff of Billy Joel lyrics. The expansive space does indeed suggest a nostalgic romance, with its series of Mediterranean-themed rooms, though the most celebrated is the pleasant garden atrium (il cortile is Italian for courtyard), with a glass-paneled ceiling and abundant greenery.

A skilled line of chefs present a wide array of familiar starters and entrées, from eggplant rollatini to chicken Francese; as well as a range of pastas, such as spaghettini puttanesca or risotto con funghi. Several decades of sharing family recipes and bringing men to one bent knee continues to earn Il Cortile a longtime following.

■ 125 Mulberry St. (bet. Canal & Hester Sts.)
🚇 Canal St (Lafayette St.)
🖋 (212) 226-6060 — **WEB:** www.ilcortile.com
■ Lunch & dinner daily

PRICE: $$

# LA ESQUINA 🍴

*Mexican*

X | 🏠 ⟋

When La Esquina opened it was a breath of bright air, offering enjoyably fresh cuisine that stood tall among the paltry selection of Manhattan Mexican. Thankfully, the city's south-of-the-border dining scene has evolved since then. However, this idol remains a fun and worthy option. More playground than restaurant, the multi-faceted setting takes up an iconic downtown corner and draws a hip crowd to its grab and go taqueria, 30-seat café, and subterranean dining room-cum-bar. The spirit here is alive and kicking, with classic renditions of tortilla soup; mole negro enchiladas filled with excellently seasoned chicken; as well as carne asada starring black Angus sirloin with mojo de ajo.

A baby sib in Brooklyn continues to thrive thanks to its retro vibe.

■ 114 Kenmare St. (bet. Cleveland Pl. & Lafayette St.)
🚇 Spring St (Lafayette St.)
🖋 (646) 613-7100 — **WEB:** www.esquinanyc.com
■ Lunch & dinner daily

PRICE: $$

# NEW MALAYSIA 😄

*Malaysian*

✗

Mad for Malaysian? Head to this lively dive, sequestered in a Chinatown arcade. Proffering some of the best Malaysian treats in town, including all the classics, New Malaysia sees a deluge of regulars who pour in for a massive offering of exceptional dishes. Round tables cram a room furnished with little more than a service counter. Still, the aromas wafting from flaky roti canai and Melaka crispy coconut shrimp keep you focused on the food.

Capturing the essence of this region are brusque servers who speedily deliver abundant and authentic bowls of spicy-sour asam laksa fragrant with lemongrass; kang-kung belacan, greens with dried shrimp and chili; and nasi lemak, the national treasure starring coconut rice, chicken curry, and dried anchovies.

▪ 46-48 Bowery (bet. Bayard & Canal Sts.)
▪ Canal St (Lafayette St.)
☎ (212) 964-0284 — **WEB:** N/A
▪ Lunch & dinner daily

**PRICE:** 💰

# NOM WAH TEA PARLOR 🍴

*Chinese*

✗ | 🥢

**MAP:** B3

First things first: you don't go to Nom Wah Tea Parlor for the décor or the service. The latter is polite and ultra-speedy, but otherwise forgettable. And the décor offers little more than pleather booths and a diner-style counter. None of this matters, for once the kitchen starts dropping its lip-smacking Chinese-American fare down with aplomb, you'll be in dim sum heaven.

Begin with soft and tender shrimp-and-snow pea leaf dumplings, before moving on to unique bean curd skin rolls tucked with savory Chinese pork. Downright terrific pan-fried dumplings are filled with pink shrimp and fragrant chives. Don't leave without sampling the restaurant's "Original Egg Roll," which is basically a massive umami bomb, easily split between four people.

▪ 13 Doyers St. (bet. Bowery & Pell St.)
▪ Canal St (Lafayette St.)
☎ (212) 962-6047 — **WEB:** www.nomwah.com
▪ Lunch & dinner daily

**PRICE:** 💰

# NYONYA 😳
*Malaysian*

✗ | ⬛$

Nyonya flaunts a comfy setting composed of brick walls and basic wood tables, but really, everyone's here for their outstanding Malaysian food. Speedy servers steer diners through the varied menu—and perhaps even away from such delicacies as prawn mee, an exceptionally spiced and sour shrimp broth with noodles, pork, vegetables and bean sprouts floating in its goodness.

Asians and other locals know to stick to such faithful and deeply satisfying dishes as nasi lemak, which is a delightful combo of coconut rice, pickled veggies, crispy anchovies, curried chicken and hard-boiled egg. Mee siam spotlights noodles stir-fried with tofu and shrimp in a chili sauce that puts all others to shame, while coconut batter-fried jumbo prawns are nothing short of—omg—wow!

🟦 199 Grand St. (bet. Mott & Mulberry Sts.)
🚇 Canal St (Lafayette St.)
✆ (212) 334-3669 — **WEB:** www.ilovenyonya.com
🟦 Lunch & dinner daily                    **PRICE:** $$

# PASQUALE JONES 🍴

*Italian*

✗✗

This stylish Italian charmer is a neighborhood restaurant fit for the modern age. Expect blistered Neapolitan-style pizzas straight from the wood oven; excellent handmade pastas; and vegetable-focused small plates.

The space is snug, so try to nab reservations ahead—a challenging feat given its popularity. For a thoroughly 21st century bit of hospitality, request a text message when a counter seat opens. Plump diver scallops arrive seared to golden, sporting crisp fennel slivers, crushed hazelnut and juicy mandarin orange, while al dente rigatoni is tossed in a ricotta sauce dotted with pork sausage. For dessert, the seasonal option may feature lime curd topped with mascarpone ice cream, smoky meringue, and hazelnut cookie crumble.

🟦 187 Mulberry St. (at Kenmare St.)
🚇 Bowery
✆ N/A — **WEB:** www.pasqualejones.com
🟦 Lunch Fri – Sun   Dinner nightly          **PRICE:** $$

# SHANGHAI HEPING 🍴

## Chinese

🍴                                 **MAP:** B2

When faced with the long, no-frills menu, there should read a caution sign to not miss out on the crab and pork soup dumplings. The plump, juicy filling and flavorful broth held in each delicate wrapper with soy-ginger seasoning explain the afternoon crowd lunching out of takeout boxes on the entrance in.

Large bamboo steamer baskets line most tables, and the seared pan-fried pork dumplings are not to miss either. Cold appetizers also shine, like dark soy- and sugar-cooked bamboo shoots with wheat gluten, or thinly sliced stir-fried eel with chives. There are larger, steaming hot plates to choose from like Shanghai rice cakes with beef. The "Eight Jewel Rice" dessert matches a mound of sticky rice with red bean paste, red dates, and golden raisin "jewels."

🟦  104 Mott St. (bet. Canal & Hester Sts.)
🚇  Canal St (Lafayette St.)
✆  (212) 925-1118 — **WEB:** N/A
🟦  Lunch & dinner daily                  **PRICE:** $$

# THÁI SO'N 🍴

## Vietnamese

🍴                                 **MAP:** B2

Thái So'n is by far the best of the bunch in this Vietnamese quarter of Chinatown. It's neither massive nor fancy, but it's bright, clean, and perpetually in business. One peek at the specials on the walls (maybe golden-fried squid strewn with sea salt) will have you begging for a seat in the crammed room.

Speedy servers scoot between groups of City Hall suits and Asian locals as they order the likes of cha gio, pork spring rolls with nuoc cham; or goi cuon, fantastic summer rolls filled with poached shrimp and vermicelli. Naturally, pho choices are abundant, but the real star of the show is pho tai—where raw beef shavings are cooked to tender perfection when combined with a scalding hot, savory broth replete with herbs, sprouts, and chewy noodles.

🟦  89 Baxter St. (bet. Bayard & Canal Sts.)
🚇  Canal St (Lafayette St.)
✆  (212) 732-2822 — **WEB:** N/A
🟦  Lunch & dinner daily                  **PRICE:** ⌘

# EAST VILLAGE

Long regarded as the capital of cool, the East Village was once a shadier incarnation of Tompkins Square Park and second home to squatters and rioters. However, the neighborhood today is safer, cleaner, and far more habitable. And while cheap walk-ups filled with struggling artists outspoken spirit for which this neighborhood is known, the East Village flaunts a distinct personality and vibrant dining landscape.

## CHEAP EATS

Budget-friendly bites abound in these parts. Family-run **Veselka**, located in the heart

or aspiring models may be a thing of the past, the area's marked gentrification hasn't led to any sort of dip in self-expression or creativity. In fact, reflecting the independent and of this 'hood has been serving traditional Ukrainian specialties for over 60 years, and is a fitting homage to the area's former Eastern European population. After a night of bar-hopping or other mischief, grab a restorative bite of salt and fat at **Crif Dogs**, where deep-fried hot dogs are doled out until 4:00 A.M (every Friday and Saturday). Along these streets, find a number of food-related endeavors that are the product of laser-focused culinary inspiration. **Bánh mi zòn** for instance is a smash for crackling-skinned Vietnamese pork sandwiches. **Superiority Burger** is a hot spot loved for its lip-smacking vegan take on the classic burger; while **Luke's Lobster** has expanded into an international network presenting rolls stuffed with crustaceans straight from Maine. For ramen, Japanese-import **Ippudo** churns out steaming bowlfuls to its boisterous patrons. Meanwhile,

**Brodo** (the brainchild of Hearth Chef/owner Marco Canora) is a trendsetting "window" that dispenses comforting cups of broths, available in three sizes and types—the Hearth broth, Organic Chicken, and Gingered Grass-fed beef. Others may join the constant queue of students looking for a crusty slice of white from **Artichoke Basille's Pizza** on 14th Street. And while on the topic of cravings of all stripes, the sensory assault around St. Mark's Place offers an immersion in Asian savors that is delightfully kitschy and incredibly worthwhile. Discover a taste of Korea by way of **Korilla**, a food truck sensation brought stateside by Chef Edward Song. Located on the first floor of a brick structure just off Cooper Square, this

## A SWEET SIDE

**B**adass attitude and savory dishes aside, the East Village also has a very sweet side. **Moishe's Bake Shop** is a Kosher delight where challah, rugelach, and marble sponge cake have been on the menu since 1978. In operation since 1894, **Veniero's Pasticceria & Caffé** brings yet another taste of the Old World to these newly minted locals. This Italian idol draws long lines, especially around holiday time, for baked goods. And, don't forget to make these sweets just a bit more beautiful with a shipment of flowers from Fleurs Bella. There can never be a dearth of caffeine in the city, and

mostly take-out barbecue spot is beloved for pearly-white tofu coated with crimson-red, fire-hot *gochujang* and crowned by leafy bok choy. If that doesn't have you salivating, duck into **Boka** for spicy Korean fried chicken. Or, follow the scent of *takoyaki* frying and sizzling *okonomiyaki* at **Otafuku**. Hungry hordes know to look for the red paper lanterns that hang outside haunts like **Yakitori Taisho**; while taste buds are always tingling at divey *izakayas* such as **Village Yokocho**. And yet, among this area's sultry sake dens, none rival the outrageous offering at subterranean **Decibel**— complete with eats and beats.

chic-geeks love **Hi-Collar**—a nifty, Japanese-esque coffee house bedecked with a brass counter and back wall accented by rice paper screens. Stay late and you may even be served some sake. Chef-cum-celebrity, David Chang's dessert darling **Momofuku Milk Bar** also rents space here and serves clever variations on dessert. Birthday cake truffles, "Compost" cookies, and soft-serve have sweet teeth swooning (and returning). **Big Gay Ice Cream** may have started life as a modest truck on the move, but is now a top-seller for signatures like the Dorothy—a swirl of vanilla, *dulce de leche*, and crushed Nilla wafers. The craft cocktail movement has taken firm root in this "village" of trend, where many subtly (and even undisclosed) locations offer an epicurean approach to mixology. **Death & Co.** is a dimly lit, hot-as-hell spot that is packed to the gills, but when in need of a more intimate scene, make your way to the wooden phone

booth inside **Crif Dogs** to access **PDT**—Please Don't Tell—where Benton's Old-Fashioned crafted from bacon-smoked Bourbon may just be every cocktail critic's dream come true. Cached behind a wall in a Japanese restaurant, **Angel's Share's** snazzy bartenders shake and stir for a civilized crowd, while **Mayahuel's** creations lead to south-of-the-border-style fun. Finally, polished **Pouring Ribbons**, devoted to vintage Chartreuse, continues to be praised in the nabe as a sanctuary of sorts among those in-the-know.

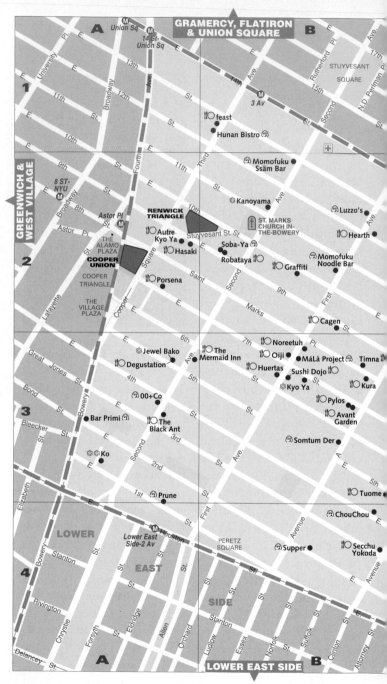

GREENWICH & WEST VILLAGE

Union Sq
14 St-Union Sq
University Pl.
13th
Broadway
12th
11th
10th
9th
8th St-NYU
Astor Pl
8th
Astor Pl.
Lafayette
THE ALAMO PLAZA
COOPER UNION
COOPER TRIANGLE
THE VILLAGE PLAZA
Great Jones
Bond
Bleecker
Bowery
Elizabeth

Fourth Ave.
3 Av
feast
Hunan Bistro
Momofuku Ssäm Bar
Kanoyama
RENWICK TRIANGLE
Autre Kyo Ya
Hasaki
Porsena
Stuyvesant St.
ST. MARKS CHURCH IN-THE-BOWERY
Soba-Ya
Robataya
Graffiti
Momofuku Noodle Bar
Luzzo's
Hearth
Cagen
Jewel Bako
Degustation
The Mermaid Inn
00+Co
Bar Primi
The Black Ant
Ko
Prune
Noreetuh
Oiji
Huertas
Kyo Ya
MáLà Project
Sushi Dojo
Pylos
Avant Garden
Somtum Der
Timna
Kura
Tuome
ChouChou
Secchu Yokoda
Supper

STUYVESANT SQUARE
Rutherford Pl.
17th
15th
N.D. Perlman Pl.
Second Ave.
First Ave.

LOWER EAST SIDE-2 Av
LOWER EAST SIDE
Stanton
Rivington
Chrystie
Delancey
Forsyth
Eldridge
Allen
Orchard
Ludlow
Essex
Norfolk
Suffolk
Clinton
Attorney St.
PERETZ SQUARE
Houston
Stanton

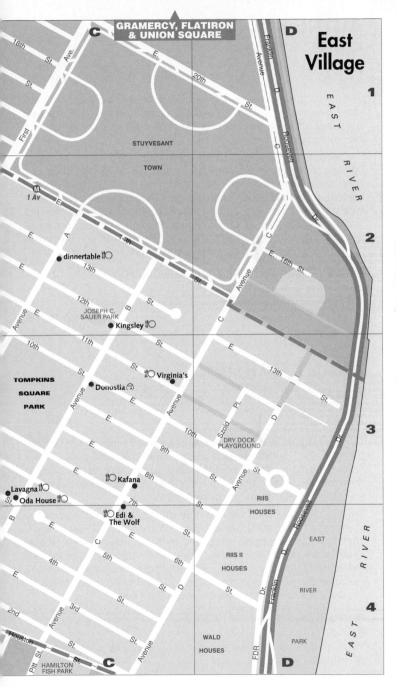

GRAMERCY, FLATIRON & UNION SQUARE

C

D

# East Village

EAST RIVER

STUYVESANT

TOWN

1 Av

● dinnertable ⛤

JOSEPH C.
SAUER PARK

● Kingsley ⛤

TOMPKINS

SQUARE

PARK

⛤ Virginia's

● Donostia

DRY DOCK
PLAYGROUND

⛤ Kafana

RIIS

HOUSES

Lavagna ⛤
● Oda House ⛤

⛤ Edi &
The Wolf

EAST

RIVER

RIIS II

HOUSES

RIVER

HAMILTON
FISH PARK

WALD

HOUSES

FDR

PARK

EAST RIVER

# AUTRE KYO YA 🍴◯

*Fusion*

XX | ♿ 🏠 📠

**MAP:** A2

If you love the popular Japanese kaiseki house Kyo Ya, then you'll really love this hip sibling, Autre Kyo Ya. The inside of the restaurant is warm and homey, and while it's less sophisticated than the elder, it's a lot more fun.

The space is lined with cozy banquettes, a bar, and plenty of nooks for intimate conversation. But the real highlight here is the food, a unique collection of Japanese dishes amped up with French influences and cooking techniques—think pâté de Campagne; a crispy cauliflower with spicy peanut sauce; and Berkshire pork belly Kamadaki rice pot in a garlic-ginger sauce. Other highlights include chilled corn soup, bobbing with tender edamame and laced with leek oil; and the terrific goma tofu "cocktail" in a bonito-seaweed broth.

◾ 10 Stuyvesant St. (bet. Third Ave. & 9th St.)
🚇 Astor Pl
📞 (212) 598-0454 — **WEB:** www.autrekyoya.com
◾ Lunch Sat – Sun   Dinner Tue – Sun          **PRICE: $$**

# AVANT GARDEN 🍴◯

*Vegan*

X

**MAP:** B3

This tight but artsy little jewel box of a restaurant, courtesy of Ravi DeRossi, aims to give vegan food some well-deserved polish. Avant Garden's dynamic menu couldn't have arrived at a better time, as New York diners are hungry for more upscale meatless options. This is excellent food that just happens to be vegan.

Try the cold, salt-baked sweet potato with puréed watercress, crispy jicama and Meyer lemon; or avocado, paired with white asparagus, crunchy radishes, strawberries, and garlicky grilled ramps. Sheets of pasta are tossed with pesto, tomatoes, French string beans and Kalamata olives. Their thick slices of toast topped with cremini mushrooms, sweet onion marmalade, toasted walnuts and herbs de Provence are destined to become a signature item.

◾ 130 E. Seventh St. (bet. Avenue A & First Ave.)
🚇 1 Av
📞 (646) 922-7948 — **WEB:** www.avantgardennyc.com
◾ Dinner nightly          **PRICE: $$$**

# BAR PRIMI 😋

## *Italian*

XX | 🍴 🛋           **MAP:** A3

Chef Sal Lamboglia and Chef/owner Andrew Carmellini clearly know what they wanted to do in this kitchen: make excellent Italian (and Italian-American) food with a delicious twist here and surprise ingredient there. The result is a restaurant we would all want to have just around the corner. Great wine, a friendly service team, and two floors of comfortable seating make it easy for guests to pile in, night after night.

Start with meatballs, a far cry from the generic kind, stuffed with Fontina and braised until tender in a chunky tomato sugo. Pasta here rivals Italy, especially the spaghetti with small, briny clams and spicy 'njuda crumbles topped with breadcrumbs and parsley. Daily specials are also a delight, as is the simply delicious hazelnut gelato.

▨ 325 Bowery (at 2nd St.)
▨ Bleecker St
✆ (212) 220-9100 — **WEB:** www.barprimi.com
▨ Lunch & dinner daily         **PRICE:** $$

# THE BLACK ANT 🍴

## *Mexican*

XX | 🛋           **MAP:** A3

Bringing a dose of Mexico City chic to the area, this restaurant takes its name from the ancient Mesoamerican fable of an ant and incorporates that imagery throughout the setting. Black-and-white checkerboard flooring, wall tiles bearing the insect's motif, and a very cool giant ant mural reinforce the theme. The menu is an unrestricted look at this nation's cuisine. It is only fitting that specialties here include the Climbing Ant cocktail with tequila, Aperol, and mole bitters; guacamole seasoned with crushed ant salt; and grasshopper-crusted shrimp tacos. Bug-free creations are just as appealing, as in tacos with battered and fried cod cheek, aïoli, and cabbage-mango slaw.

For a more traditional but moodier experience, stop by Ofrenda in the West Village.

▨ 60 Second Ave. (bet. 3rd & 4th Sts.)
▨ 2 Av
✆ (212) 598-0300 — **WEB:** www.blackantnyc.com
▨ Lunch Sat – Sun    Dinner nightly      **PRICE:** $$

# CAGEN 🍴

## *Japanese*

XX

**MAP:** B2

Unless you're only interested in staring into your date's eyes, sit at the elm counter rather than at a table—that way, you'll get to witness the skill and dexterity on display here. Chef Toshio Tomita spent many years at Nobu and the influence of his alma mater is obvious.

There are a number of menu options available—from omakase to à la carte—but one sure thing is that sashimi will be a highlight, whether that's the king salmon with chimichurri, or the fluke with crispy chili and garlic. The soba is also good—you may find authentic slurping a little difficult but be sure to mix the sobayu (the water in which the noodles were cooked) with the tsuyu dipping sauce for a flavorsome little drink at the end.

◼ 414 E. 9th St. (bet. Avenue A & First Ave.)
🚇 Astor Pl
✆ (212) 358-8800 — **WEB:** www.cagenrestaurant.com
◼ Dinner Tue – Sun                    **PRICE: $$$$**

# CHOUCHOU 😊

## *Moroccan*

X

**MAP:** B4

There are two schools of thought when it comes to menu design: one is the encyclopedic, all-inclusive tome, and then there is ChouChou.

This East Village hangout, complete with romantic hanging lanterns, is best described as hyper-focused. In fact, the tightly edited menu is divided into just two categories: tagines and couscous. Choose from six couscous preparations ranging from lamb and chicken to lobster, while four tagines tempt from their iconic conical vessels. Once decided, an array of tangy salads and sides arrive. Lifted tableside, the delightful fragrance contained within these tagines immediately seduces, as the silky lamb and spiced couscous delight in all their classic Mediterranean goodness. Moroccan pastries end meals on a sweet note.

◼ 215 E. 4th St. (bet. Avenues A & B)
🚇 1 Av
✆ (646) 869-1423 — **WEB:** www.couchounyc.com
◼ Dinner Tue – Sun                    **PRICE: $$**

# DEGUSTATION 🍴

*Contemporary*

✗✗                                                **MAP:** A3

This cozy tapas bar packs a big punch thanks to the winning combination of Chef Nicholas Licata and proprietor Jack Lamb. At the center of the action is an open kitchen with surround counter seating—from here you can watch the fast-moving, amicable chefs work up their delicious magic.

Chef Licata's fare is stylish and inventive, with one eye on Spain and the other meandering around the Mediterranean. Crispy chicken croquetas are paired with smoky aïoli; while a bowl of milky burrata is bathed with bright green herbs and served atop cubes of toasty bread. Paella arrives bursting with blue prawns, chorizo, and irresistible socarrat; and a classic dessert of torrija (basically a fancier version of French toast) is crowned with creamy cajeta and sea salt.

▪ 239 E. 5th St. (bet. Second & Third Aves.)
▪ Astor Pl
✆ (212) 979-1012 — **WEB:** www.degustation-nyc.com
▪ Dinner nightly                                **PRICE: $$$**

# DINNERTABLE 🍴

*Contemporary*

✗                                                **MAP:** C2

Tucked behind The Garret East, this 20-seat gem is nothing if not incognito. But upon discovery, enter to find a polished bar with silver banquettes and mosaic surfaces. Then make way through the packed room to arrive at speakeasy-like dinnertable—a wee space furnished with just a few seats and that ubiquitous counter.

The talented kitchen behind this concept has created a menu of surprisingly elegant small plates. An uni paella ball is seared to crisp delight, while bluefin and avocado are paired with yuzu for a perfect contrast in taste and texture. Then charred striped bass joins together with roasted cabbage, broccoli, and a lemon oil. Stick with this kitchen's Asian influences and close out with a matcha sundae drizzled with miso-caramel sauce.

▪ 206 Avenue A (bet. 12th & 13th Sts.)
▪ 1 Av
✆ N/A — **WEB:** www.dinnertable.nyc
▪ Dinner Tue – Sat                              **PRICE: $$**

# DONOSTIA ☺

*Spanish*

✗

You'll want to bring friends and graze your way through these Basque delights oh-so-slowly. Offering traditional tapas and pintxos, the menu at Donostia features small plates like delicate, cold water-brined boquerón, drizzled with grapeseed oil and vinegar; or tender razor clams, laced with white bean purée, piment d'Espelette and lemon zest. The traditional tortilla with thinly sliced potatoes and mayonnaise is yet another big hit.

The minute you walk through the door, the dining room feels abuzz with excitement. A narrow row of tables tucked under the antique map of "Donostia" welcomes groups. Lone diners can snag a small perch facing Tompkins Square Park for people-watching, while others may head to the back to see dishes being plated as they eat.

■ 155 Avenue B (bet. 9th & 10th Sts.)

▣ 1 Av

𝒫 (646) 256-9773 — **WEB:** www.donostianyc.com

■ Dinner nightly                                **PRICE: $$**

# 00 + CO ☺

*Vegan*

✗ | ☂

There are wine bars and then there is this amazing concept from plant-based food guru, Matthew Kenney. But lets just dwell on this space for a moment. Outfitted with tall, communal tables, backlit wine shelves, and beautiful artwork, the scene inside is both sexy and urbane.

With his unique vision behind 00 + Co, the chef contends he is "crafting the future of food." There is no dairy or meat here; and by the taste of things, no one's missing it either. A long, tantalizing lineup of low-gluten pizza and "not pizza" dominate the menu, along with occasional specials like a wickedly good sweet potato cavatelli. A vegan cheese plate might feature creamy truffled cashew or almond ricotta. All washed down with exquisite organic wine? Food nirvana, indeed.

■ 65 Second Ave. (bet 3rd & 4th Sts.)

▣ Bleecker St

𝒫 (212) 777-1608 — **WEB:** www.matthewkenneycuisine.com

■ Lunch Sat – Sun   Dinner nightly              **PRICE: $$**

# EDI & THE WOLF ⅋○
*Austrian*

❌ | 🍸 🏠 🛋️                                    **MAP:** C4

This is as much an Austrian heuriger (wine tavern) that one can find in New York. While the menu has some modern and creative elements, the décor is comprised of wood planks and thick coils of rope for an attractively barn-like feel. That cozy and disheveled character makes you forget where you are—same goes for the superb list of German and Austrian wines. On warm days, head to the equally pleasing and tiny back patio.

Most everyone knows to go for the schnitzel, served with potato salad, cucumbers, and lingonberries. Still, you won't go wrong with a host of rustic small plates like crisped Brussels sprouts tossed in pork ragout with scallions and pickled mustard seeds, or perhaps roasted beets with pickled walnuts, walnut milk, and dill.

■ 102 Avenue C (bet. 6th & 7th Sts.)
🚇 1 Av
✆ (212) 598-1040 — **WEB:** www.ediandthewolf.com
■ Lunch Sat – Sun   Dinner nightly          **PRICE:** $$

# FEAST ⅋○
*Contemporary*

❌ | 🛋️                                        **MAP:** B1

This straightforward but promisingly named East Village stalwart is a rustic and textbook amalgam of wood, brick, and tiles. And the kitchen consistently offers several prix-fixe menus, served family-style. These might be based on specials from the farmer's market or even incllude a nose-to-tail meal of lamb, including merguez stew, as well as lasagna layering shank, broccoli rabe, and goat cheese. If you're not up for a whole feast, dine à la carte on meaty, ocean-fresh oysters capped by cocktail sauce aspic; or a nouveau take on incredibly tender chicken and "dumplings" flaunting liver-stuffed pan-fried gnocchi and wisps of crisped skin.

End with the awe-inspiring Valrhona chocolate pudding—leaving a single dark chocolate cookie crumb behind is impossible.

■ 102 Third Ave. (bet. 12th & 13th Sts.)
🚇 3 Av
✆ (212) 529-8880 — **WEB:** www.eatfeastnyc.com
■ Lunch Sat – Sun   Dinner nightly          **PRICE:** $$

# GRAFFITI ▯○

*Contemporary*

**MAP:** B2

This cool cub brought to you by Chef/owner Jehangir Mehta seems to be a perpetual hit among various diners. And if that's not enough, baby boy is quite the dreamboat. Dressed with tightly packed communal tables and beaded ceiling lights, petite Graffiti may be dimly lit, but an exposed brick wall glossed with a metallic finish and hugging framed mirrors is all brightness.

Feeding a pack of 20 on newspaper-wrapped tables are Indian-inspired sweet and savory small plates. Highlights may include squares of watermelon and feta cubes cooled by a vibrant mint sorbet; and soft, pillowy eggplant buns spiked with toasty cumin. Adventurous palates however are bound to find much to admire in such inventive items as the green mango paneer or zucchini-hummus pizza.

- 224 E. 10th St. (bet. First & Second Aves.)
- 1 Av
- (212) 464-7743 — **WEB:** www.graffitinyc.com
- Dinner Tue – Sun

**PRICE:** $$

# HASAKI ▯○

*Japanese*

**MAP:** A2

Since the mid-eighties, this local darling has been doing a solid business thanks to its high quality ingredients, skilled kitchen, and excellent value. For around $20, the soba lunch set will warm the heart of any frugal fan of Japanese cuisine. This generous feast features a bowl of green tea noodles in hot, crystal-clear dashi stocked with wilted water spinach and fish cake, accompanied by lean tuna chirashi, yellowtail, and kanpyo. The ten-don, a jumbo shrimp tempura served over rice, is just as enticing. The à la carte offerings draw crowds seeking delish sushi as well as a host of tasty cooked preparations; a Twilight menu is nice for early birds.

The dining room has a clean and spare look, with seating available at a number of wood tables or sizable counter.

- 210 E. 9th St. (bet. Second & Third Aves.)
- Astor Pl
- (212) 473-3327 — **WEB:** www.hasakinyc.com
- Lunch Wed – Sun   Dinner nightly

**PRICE:** $$

# HEARTH ⅈО

*Italian*

XX | 🍇 ☞

**MAP:** B2

Duck your head into beloved Hearth, its loyal patrons buzzing about as happy as ever, and you might not even notice that the kitchen has moved on to some new and exciting things. It's still delicious Italian, yes, but now the ingredients are more carefully sourced, on the healthy side, and with a deep commitment to GMO-free grains, less butter, and no processed oils.

The renewed focus on vegetables, grains and brodi is a winning combination. The kitchen lights up in the vegetable arena, braising Sorana beans to perfection with sage, garlic, and mackerel "bottarga"; or topping carrot and beet tartare with cured egg yolk, chervil and breadcrumbs. Meat lovers, take heart—Hearth's beloved braised rabbit, ribollita and "Variety Burger" are all still available.

◾ 403 E. 12th St. (at First Ave.)

▣ 1 Av

✆ (646) 602-1300 — **WEB:** www.restauranthearth.com

◾ Lunch Sat – Sun   Dinner nightly          **PRICE:** $$$

# HUERTAS ⅈО

*Spanish*

XX

**MAP:** B3

Huertas is lovely—even lovelier than you might expect for its gritty location. The casual space is deep, with a long bar pouring cider or sherry, dedicated counter where a host of cured meats including jamón is sliced, and larger tables in the back.

The Basque-leaning menu showcases pintxos like stuffed and batter-fried squash blossoms, duck croquetas, and skewers of white anchovies with olives and pickled peppers. The selection of conservas promises the type of fare that only the Spanish can do, as in zamburiñas in a complex tomato sauce with lemon, herbs, and bread topped with a heavy drizzle of mayo. A handful of larger platos round out the menu with dishes like deep-fried porgy with toasted garlic, pickled chilies, and manzanilla olives.

◾ 107 First Ave. (bet. 6th & 7th Sts.)

▣ Astor Pl

✆ (212) 228-4490 — **WEB:** www.huertasnyc.com

◾ Lunch Sat – Sun   Dinner nightly          **PRICE:** $$$

# HUNAN BISTRO 🐶
## Chinese

🍴 | 📷                                          **MAP:** B1

Delicious, lip-scorching Hunan fare makes its way to the East Village and everyone's just a little bit happier for it. Tucked into a narrow space with dark wood paneling, industrial lighting and large planters, Hunan Bistro offers swift, but warm and helpful service—and an all-together welcoming dining space for exploring this intriguing cuisine.

Dinner might kick off with razor-thin slices of pig ear, tossed with a confetti of green onions and glistening with smoky chili oil; or crunchy, sour pickled cabbage topped with red chilies and cilantro. Next up? Toothsome dan dan noodles beneath a thatch of ground pork with loads of chili oil, black vinegar and Sichuan pepper; or perfectly cooked, shell-on crawfish laced in a wildly good chili sauce.

■ 96 Third Ave. (bet. 12th & 13th Sts.)
🚇 3 Av
℘ (212) 388-9855 — **WEB:** N/A
■ Lunch & dinner daily                        **PRICE:** $$

# KAFANA 🍴〇
## Eastern European

🍴 | 💲                                          **MAP:** C3

If the Eastern European intelligentsia needed somewhere to plan a revolution or maybe just talk politics, they would meet here. Walls papered with Cyrillic newspapers set a deliciously covert scene, yet overall, the effect is inviting.

The menu highlights Serbian fare that is hard to find in Manhattan. That said, some specialties will seem familiar, like zeljanica, a buttery wedge of classic phyllo pie folded with chopped spinach, garlic, herbs, and feta. Unique dishes feature dried prunes stuffed with crumbly cheese, rolled in chicken liver and bacon. Also try gently dredged and fried spearing fish, piled on butcher paper with urbenes dip. Ćevapi are the catchall for sausages from the same area and here they highlight finely ground pork with herbs.

■ 116 Avenue C (bet. 7th & 8th Sts.)
🚇 1 Av
℘ (212) 353-8000 — **WEB:** www.kafananyc.com
■ Lunch Sat-Sun   Dinner nightly             **PRICE:** $$

# JEWEL BAKO ✿

*Japanese*

✗ | 👜

Only a discretely marked door and tiny glass windows signal the entrance to this beloved sushi bijou. Once inside, you'll find a deeply elegant scene highlighting sloped bamboo slats that frame a row of beautifully plated, close-knit tables. There's a gorgeous blonde wood sushi bar in the back, while gentle jazz music plays in the background. The overall effect is very appealing and particularly serene. Service is excellent and begins at the door, with the reserved host carefully attending to your belongings. The waiters have an eagle eye for detail, managing to be so unobtrusive that you're able to enjoy intimate conversation.

You can choose from multiple options—pick from a wide variety of fish à la carte or leave it up to the talented chef by going with the fixed-price omakase. Either way, you're in for a culinary treat. The quality and seriousness of the kitchen remains excellent with each passing year, turning out exquisite dishes like seasonal lobster sashimi laced with ponzu—its head and innards later presented in a savory miso soup. The sashimi that follows is equally astounding, from the slicing technique to the fish quality, much of it seasonal and flown in directly from Japan.

▩ 239 E. 5th St. (bet. Second & Third Aves.)

🅿 Astor Pl

🖉 (212) 979-1012 — **WEB:** www.jewelbakosushi.com

▩ Dinner Mon – Sat                                        **PRICE: $$$**

# KANOYAMA 🏵

*Japanese*

✗

**MAP:** B2

The spotlight shines here on the seriously talented Chef Nobuyuki Shikanai and commands the rear room's attention as he performs his magic before the few coveted seats along his omakase counter. Beyond this, the space has a row of tables where you might observe a group indulging in a tuna rib that appears large enough to have come from a cow: first sliced raw, then cooked to enjoy this incredibly fresh fish both ways.

Ancillary rooms almost feel like a sushi-ya within a sushi-ya. The service team is swift and friendly even as they work in the shadow of their master.

Kanoyama's omakase is a profoundly personal experience, as Chef Shikanai slices, cuts, and brushes, dabs, and perfects each morsel before presenting it to you with cupped hands, to be taken with your fingers. Pieces are precisely crafted yet delicate and beautiful in that traditional Edomae style. Overall, the meal is a progression from light, firm fish to vivid, buttery salmon and toro with exciting stops along the way, like cherry trout hakozushi (box-pressed) or jackfish with grains of Icelandic sea salt and a drizzle of lemon. Finish with an extraordinary block of cake-like tamago topped with a silken yolk.

■ 175 Second Ave. (at 11th St.)

🚇 3 Av

📞 (212) 777-5266 — **WEB:** www.kanoyama.com

■ Dinner nightly

**PRICE: $$$**

# KINGSLEY 🍴

## *Contemporary*

XX | 🍸 👤 🏠 🍷                                    **MAP:** C2

The crowds are clamoring for a table at this East Village charmer, and for good reason: Kingsley's splurge-worthy cuisine is sophisticated, surprising, and delicious. And the cozy space makes for a rare oasis amid the neighborhood's raucous dining scene.

Featuring an interesting juxtaposition of flavors and textures while being reminiscent of classic fare, dinner here might begin with a ridiculously fresh summer bean salad starring cranberries, rattlesnake, and Romano beans paired with bacon marmalade, crème fraîche and sautéed spicy greens. Soft, chewy wild rice noodles are topped with stir-fried mushrooms and Asian greens, just as a heavenly Wagyu Basses-Côtes steak arrives with velvety Fairy Tale eggplant, grilled potato, and a streak of chimichurri.

🔲 190 Avenue B (bet. 11th & 12th Sts.)
🔳 1 Av
📞 (212) 674-4500 — **WEB:** www.kingsleynyc.com
🔲 Lunch Sat – Sun   Dinner Tue – Sun          **PRICE:** $$$

# KURA 🍴

## *Japanese*

X                                                **MAP:** B3

From first glance, Kura is everything that a personal, well-run, and very authentic Japanese restaurant should be. Inside, the master dons a traditional samue and greets each guest who approaches the L-shaped counter, as he begins to prepare the next course. Also find a few tables in the front of the room where groups manage to squeeze in.

The menu offers four different levels of omakase, beginning with the likes of braised fava beans; a whole stuffed squid brushed with a sweet-salty reduction; as well as rice topped with nori and ikura. Settle into the ten-piece nigiri, presented as an array of hyper-seasonal fish dabbed with soy, gently torched, or wrapped in cured cherry leaf. Finish with a familiar and delicious cube of chilled tamago and miso soup.

🔲 130 St. Marks Pl. (bet. Avenue A & First Ave.)
🔳 Astor Pl
📞 (212) 228-1010 — **WEB:** N/A
🔲 Dinner Mon – Sat                            **PRICE:** $$$$

# KO ✿ ✿
*Contemporary*

✕✕ | 器 | 🍽️

Once you've worked out that the little peach motif actually indicates the entrance, you'll find yourself taking a seat at what the theatrical world would call a thrust stage. This extraordinarily handsome three-sided counter is wrapped around an open kitchen where the evening's performance takes place. Each element just works so well here: from the judicious lighting that makes everything feel more sensual, to the music (never too intrusive but far from anodyne) and the delightful team of servers who appear ninja-style from nowhere to be at your side when you need something. Counters are usually such elbow-y affairs, but this one is so wide and everyone is so spread out that you could barely touch your neighbor with a stick.

There is no à la carte for you to waste time examining. The multi-course set menu has been expertly honed, practiced and refined. Completed dishes are handed over by the chefs, who may have perfected the bad boy/girl looks of the modern urban cook, but speak with unalloyed pride when they describe what you're about to eat.

Each perfectly formed dish delivers flavors that are refined yet assured, innovative yet expertly balanced; clever yet ridiculously easy to eat.

▪ 8 Extra Pl. (at 1st St.)
🚇 2 Av
✆ (212) 500-0831 — **WEB:** www.momofuku.com
▪ Lunch Fri – Sun   Dinner Tue – Sat          **PRICE: $$$$**

# KYO YA ✿

*Japanese*

✗✗ | ⌂

Tucked away down a discreet flight of steps in an unremarkable East Village building, it's easy to cruise right past Kyo Ya. But what a shame it would be to miss this brilliant jewel. If the mostly Japanese crowd doesn't tell you you're onto something special, the relentless charm and hospitality of the staff will win you over completely.

This is a cozy and intimate room with lots of polished wood and displays of lovely Japanese ceramics. A row of counter seats cuts down the middle of the space, along with a smattering of small tables. A six-seat counter at the back is reserved for those having the kaiseki menu.

Kyo Ya's dishes are delicate, exquisite, and perfectly balanced. And as if that isn't enough, most of them use authentic, imported ingredients, which are not commonly found in domestic kitchens. A ten-course kaiseki, for example, might unveil a soft ball of fresh edamame tofu in a delicate, clear fish broth flavored with junsai as well as sweet and earthy spaghetti squash. Then chewy kuruma-fu is served in a winter melon soup bobbing with spicy pink peppercorns, mizuna and kinira ohitashi. A finish of crispy shishito pepper tempura and cherry tomato make it downright excellent.

▪ 94 E. 7th St. (bet First Ave. & Avenue A)

▣ Astor Pl

✆ (212) 982-4140 — **WEB:** N/A

▪ Dinner Tue-Sun

PRICE: $$$

# LAVAGNA 🍽

## Italian

✗ | 🏮 🛥                                              **MAP:** C3

The little menu at this neighborhood fixture proves that quality trumps size. Lavagna's kitchen is snug, but still manages to make ample use of a wood-burning oven to bake everything from delicate pizzette to whole roasted fish. Pastas are always a treat, while other tasty options can include pan-fried smoked scamorza paired with a roasted red pepper-topped crostini, juicy rack of lamb, or a slice of spot-on crostata filled with seasonal fruit and dressed with caramel sauce.

Framed mirrors, a pressed-tin ceiling, and candlelight produce a mood that is almost as warm as the genuinely gracious service, which ensures that regulars receive the royal treatment. That said, everyone who steps through these doors will feel welcome and well taken care of.

■ 545 E. 5th St. (bet. Avenues A & B)
🚇 2 Av
✆ (212) 979-1005 — **WEB:** www.lavagnanyc.com
■ Lunch Sat – Sun   Dinner nightly                 **PRICE: $$**

# LUZZO'S 😀

## Pizza

✗                                                   **MAP:** B2

Ovest Pizzoteca, Da Mikele, Luzzo's and Luzzo's BK: you can't throw a stone without hitting one of the talented Michele Iuliano's restaurants these days, and for good reason. Nestled in the East Village, this original outpost of Luzzo's boasts a colorful exterior, treasured, century-old coal-burning oven that pushes out not only ace pizzas, but also Neapolitan classics like frusta, la quadrata and pizza fritta. The term pizzeria just doesn't do this lovely spot justice.

And judging by the patient crowds lined up outside, the neighborhood knows a good thing when they see it. Once inside, guests are treated to a charming interior of exposed brick, mismatched chairs, and kitschy knickknacks. Soft Italian music plays beneath the happy hum of friends and family chatting.

■ 211-13 First Ave. (bet. 12th & 13th Sts.)
🚇 1 Av
✆ (212) 473-7447 — **WEB:** www.luzzospizza.com
■ Lunch & dinner daily                              **PRICE: $$**

# MÁLÀ PROJECT 🐶
*Chinese*

✗

Add this delicious venture to the growing list of Chinese restaurants that are finally giving Manhattanites a chance to feast on spice levels once reserved for the outer boroughs. Inside MáLà Project's two rooms, find seating that includes a long, group-friendly communal table tucked into a nook, exposed brick walls, beautiful floors, and big green leafy plants.

Dinner could go in any number of delicious directions, but a MáLà dry pot might be the most fun. Diners are given a choice of ingredients—meat, poultry, seafood, vegetables, rice—and then asked for their desired degree of spiciness. A pot of lamb, bok choi, wood ear mushrooms, shrimp balls, and chicken gizzards make their way into a wok with a fragrant "secret sauce" and complex spice oil.

▓ 122 First Ave. (bet. 7th St. & St. Marks Pl.)
🚇 1 Av
✆ (212) 353-8880 — **WEB:** www.malaproject.nyc
▓ Lunch & dinner daily                              **PRICE: $$**

# THE MERMAID INN 🍴
*Seafood*

✗ | 🏮 🛶

This laid-back and inviting seafood spot has been a neighborhood favorite for over a decade now, spawning locations in Greenwich Village and the Upper West Side. A steady stream of guests lines the bar early in the week for Monday's five to seven happy hour with freshly shucked oysters, snack-sized fish tacos, and other specially priced bites. For a hearty plate after your nosh, try blackened catfish dotted with crawfish butter alongside hushpuppies, or the lobster roll with Old Bay fries. On Sunday nights, look out for lobsterpalooza—a whole lobster accompanied by grilled corn on the cob and steamed potatoes.

At the end of your meal there's no need to deliberate over dessert. A demitasse of perfect chocolate pudding is presented compliments of the house.

▓ 96 Second Ave. (bet. 5th & 6th Sts.)
🚇 Astor Pl
✆ (212) 674-5870 — **WEB:** www.themermaidnyc.com
▓ Lunch Sat – Sun   Dinner nightly                 **PRICE: $$**

# MOMOFUKU NOODLE BAR 😊

## *Asian*

✗

**MAP:** B2

This elder member of David Chang's culinary empire is hipper and hotter than ever. A honey-toned temple of updated comfort food, decked with wood counters and a sparkling open kitchen, the service here may be brisk. But rest assured, as the menu is gutsy and molded with Asian street food in mind.

Those steamed buns have amassed a gargantuan following thanks to decadent fillings like moist pork loin kissed with Hollandaise and chives. Additionally, that bowl of springy noodles doused in a spicy ginger-scallion sauce is just one instance of the crew's signature work. Korean fried chicken with seasonal greens is fit for a king; while more modest items, including desserts like candy apple truffle, are beautifully crafted and rightfully elevated to global fame.

■ 171 First Ave. (bet. 10th & 11th Sts.)

🚇 1 Av

✆ (212) 777-7773 — **WEB:** www.momofuku.com

■ Lunch & dinner daily                **PRICE: $$**

# MOMOFUKU SSÄM BAR 😊

## *Contemporary*

✗ | ♿ 🛋

**MAP:** B2

You can't go wrong with anything porcine at Founder David Chang's East Village stalwart, so kick off with a steamed pork belly bun or slices of nutty Broadbent ham to get you in the mood for more meat eating. Having something wrapped, in homage to the name, is also a wise choice but consider too the platters, whether that's rotisserie duck or spiced beef brisket—they arrive on metal trays which adds some penitentiary chic to proceedings.

The place has a laid-back vibe, although newbies may have to cajole the servers into offering guidance on what—and how much—to order. At least the prices mean you can do so with giddy abandon. Take care if you're on a date as the zeal with which you devour your food may be a little off-putting to potential mates.

■ 207 Second Ave. (at 13th St.)

🚇 3 Av

✆ (212) 254-3500 — **WEB:** www.momofuku.com

■ Lunch & dinner daily                **PRICE: $$**

# NOREETUH 🍴

*Fusion*

✗ | 🎍 🥢                                    **MAP:** B3

For a taste of something different, make a beeline to this unique Hawaiian-flavored spot. Headed by a trio of Per Se veterans, Noreetuh features an intimate setting of two slender dining rooms adorned with hexagonal mirrors and shelving units used to store bottles from the impressive wine list.

Bigeye tuna poke strewn with seaweed, diced macadamia nuts, and pickled jalapeños is just one of the delicious highlights on offer, while plump shrimp seasoned with crushed garlic and arranged over a bed of sticky rice and baby romaine makes for another fine choice. For dessert, the signature take on bread pudding boasts caramelized slices of custard-soaked King's Hawaiian bread with rum raisins and a knockout scoop of pineapple ice cream.

▪ 128 First Ave. (bet. 7th St. & St. Marks Pl.)
▪ Astor Pl
✆ (646) 892-3050 — **WEB:** www.noreetuh.com
▪ Lunch Sat – Sun   Dinner Tue – Sun              **PRICE:** $$

# ODA HOUSE 🍴

*Eastern European*

✗                                            **MAP:** C3

For a taste of something different, the inviting Oda House serves up intriguing specialties from Georgia. The vibe is simple and rustic with pumpkin-stained walls, exposed brick, and wood furnishings. Of course, this nation's proximity to Azerbaijan, Turkey, and Armenia results in a vibrant and diverse cuisine.

A liberal use of spices, kebabs, khinkali (oversized meat-and-cheese dumplings), and khachapuri typify the kitchen's preparations. But, more classic dishes may reveal satsivi or boiled chicken served cool in a warmly spiced and seasoned walnut sauce, accompanied by gomi (hominy grits in a mini cauldron studded with rich and stretchy cheese).

Balance out this hearty feast with a bright garden salad perfectly dressed with green ajika sauce.

▪ 76 Avenue B (at 5th St.)
▪ 2 Av
✆ (212) 353-3838 — **WEB:** www.odahouse.com
▪ Lunch Fri – Sun   Dinner nightly                **PRICE:** $$

# OIJI ⅋○
## Korean

✕✕                                                    **MAP:** B3

Oiji's modern take on Korean dining is a reminder that this food is so much more than barbecue. Devoid of smoky tabletops, the dining room is small and attractive, with an open kitchen to sneak peeks at the very talented chefs as they prepare a cuisine rooted in culinary tradition, but with creative and refined touches.

Signature dishes do not disappoint, so try the wonderfully original pine-smoked mackerel, balancing the rich fish with citrus-soy sauce. Cold buckwheat noodles are a cool and contemporary nest of dark and chewy noodles topped with half of a slow-cooked egg, sesame seeds, and loads of scallions. And finally, gochujang chicken showcases nicely braised drumsticks with a variety of wintery vegetables in a spicy, tart, and garlicky sauce.

▪ 119 First Ave. (bet. 7th St & St. Marks Pl.)
▪ Astor Pl
☎ (646) 767-9050 — **WEB:** www.oijinyc.com
▪ Dinner nightly                          **PRICE:** $$


# PORSENA ⅋○
## Italian

✕✕ | ✧                                                **MAP:** A2

Sophisticates of all ages flock to this neighborhood favorite to be enveloped by a warm, welcoming, and upbeat vibe. Euro-chic Porsena also boasts adept servers who can be seen strutting about with appetizing platters of aromatic food.

As always, Chef Sara Jenkins proves herself to be a talent and a pro through presentations that are unfussy yet remain uniquely flavorful and always special. The menu rotates with the seasons, but standbys cannot be missed, like wild escarole salad with crisp leaves wilting in hot anchovy dressing; or huge rounds of anelloni tossed with spicy lamb sausage, peppery mustard greens, and breadcrumbs. If offered, get the lasagna expertly layering pasta sheets with a creamy béchamel and hearty veal-prosciutto ragù.

▪ 21 E. 7th St. (bet. Second & Third Aves.)
▪ Astor Pl
☎ (212) 228-4923 — **WEB:** www.porsena.com
▪ Dinner nightly                          **PRICE:** $$

# PRUNE ☺
## *Contemporary*

X | 🍸 🛋

This beloved neighborhood bistro won locals' hearts many moons ago, but Chef/owner/writer Gabrielle Hamilton's evolving talents keep them loyal. The tiny space packs a big punch—both for its sweet décor, which is surprisingly comfy to linger in, and for the kitchen's adventurous food. From greeting to check, Prune delivers the whole package—and consistently at that. Chef Hamilton's dishes are soulful and unpretentious. Savor tender stewed tripe Lyonnaise in a luxurious broth with carrots, celery and bay leaf; or perfectly poached chicken in a deliciously fatty and restorative stock with ham and oxtail. Guests can also watch the excitement unfold in the open kitchen while nursing a drink.

Nightly specials, listed on the chalkboard, are always worth perusing.

■ 54 E. 1st St. (bet. First & Second Aves.)
🚇 2 Av
✆ (212) 677-6221 — **WEB:** www.prunerestaurant.com
■ Lunch Sat-Sun   Dinner nightly                    **PRICE: $$**

# PYLOS ⁑○
## *Greek*

XX

Restaurateur Christos Valtzoglou has found the winning formula with this longstanding hideaway in the vibrant East Village. Pylos continues to sparkle as brightly as the Aegean Sea on a summer day. And, taking its name from the Greek translation of "made from clay," this contemporary taverna also features a ceiling canopy of suspended terra-cotta pots, dressing up a room with rustic whitewashed walls and lapis-blue insets.

Pale-green stemware and stark white crockery are used to serve Greek wines and a menu of rustic home-style cooking. Gigantes are baked in honey-scented tomato-dill sauce; grilled marinated octopus is drizzled with balsamic reduction; and aginares moussaka is a creamy vegetarian take on the classic made here with artichokes.

■ 128 E. 7th St. (bet. First Ave. & Avenue A)
🚇 Astor Pl
✆ (212) 473-0220 — **WEB:** www.pylosrestaurant.com
■ Lunch Wed – Sun   Dinner nightly                **PRICE: $$**

# ROBATAYA 🍴

*Japanese*

XX

Irasshaimase! This is the kind of intensely authentic place where welcomes are shouted to guests upon entering. At peak times, wait among Japanese expats and young couples lining the sidewalk. Aim straight for the counter to appreciate the theatrics of it all, where orders are acknowledged with more shouts flying from Japanese servers to chefs. The energy is high, but so are the standards for their expertly grilled meats and vegetables.

Kneeling cooks use long wooden paddles to deliver dishes hot off the robata, like gyu tataki, seared beef filet topped with tobiko and scallions on a bed of red onions with ponzu. Technical mastery is clear in a salt-packed sea bream's subtle smoky flavors emphasizing the delicacy of such white, flaky fish.

■ 231 E. 9th St. (bet. Second & Third Aves.)
🚇 Astor Pl
✆ (212) 979-9674 — **WEB:** www.robataya-ny.com
■ Lunch Fri – Sun   Dinner nightly                    **PRICE: $$**

# SECCHU YOKODA 🍴

*Japanese*

X

New York may be a hotbed of great Japanese food, but Secchu Yokota adds a bit of frill and fun to the dining scene with its very personal take on tempura. The diminutive room feels warm, as the handful of guests are seated directly in front of the working chefs and fully open kitchen.

The traditional omakase moves through courses that highlight the chef's training in both Eastern and Western kitchens. To begin, an appetizer may showcase French technique in a sublime English pea soup with jalapeño oil and fennel. Japanese tradition guides the preparation of each delicately fried morsel of seasonal tempura, from shrimp to mushroom caps. Wonderful layers of flavor twirl through the green tea soba noodles with duck breast, finished tableside with a cool dashi.

■ 199 E. 3rd St. (bet. Avenues A & B)
🚇 Essex St
✆ (212) 777-1124 — **WEB:** www.secchuyokota.com
■ Dinner Mon – Sat                              **PRICE: $$$**

# SOBA-YA 😀

## *Japanese*

X

There's a ton of Japanese restaurants that line this stretch of the East Village, so why Soba-Ya? Why not Soba-Ya, its ultra-dedicated patrons would argue—for the buckwheat soba as well as the hearty udon on tap here are consistently off-the-charts good. Co-owner and mini-mogul, Bon Yagi, favors authenticity over flash in his establishments. And here he employs that traditional aesthetic to sweet perfection; along with a graceful, but simply appointed dining space; and quiet, well-timed service.

A meal might begin with uni and grated mountain yam, kissed with wasabi and crispy, toasted nori. Then transition to a seasonal noodle dish like warm soba mingled with plump, pickled oysters, mountain yam, cilantro and tempura root vegetables.

◼ 229 E. 9th St. (bet. Second & Third Aves.)
◼ Astor Pl
✆ (212) 533-6966 — **WEB:** www.sobaya-nyc.com
◼ Lunch & dinner daily                    PRICE: 😋

# SOMTUM DER 😀

## *Thai*

X | ♿                                  **MAP:** B3

Tucked along the fringes of Alphabet City, a little taste of authentic Isaan Thai awaits. Originally based out of Bangkok, the New York outpost of Somtum Der offers a cozy little enclave for the East Village set, stylishly accented with bright pops of red, and a welcome glimpse of the kitchen's somtum station. There, you'll spy large glass jars of peanuts, dried red chilies, and spices—the contents of which are ground by mortar and pestle to produce what some claim is the city's best green papaya salad.

Order big here, for the portions aren't massive and the food is so terrific you'll inevitably want more. The kitchen is happy to kick things up a notch, spice-wise, but you'll need to request the hotter end of the spectrum for greater authenticity.

◼ 85 Avenue A (bet. 5th & 6th Sts.)
◼ 2 Av
✆ (212) 260-8570 — **WEB:** www.somtumder.com
◼ Lunch & dinner daily                    PRICE: $$

# SUPPER 😍
*Italian*

XX | 器 🛋 ⏢ 🥢 💲          **MAP:** B4

This is the kind of fuss-free Italian cooking that true New Yorkers keep in regular rotation. The dark, quirky interior spreads across multiple rooms for a relaxed setting.

There is no better salvo to this style of dining than their complimentary beans soaked in olive oil with chilies, garlic, and parsley. Follow with thick, shareable portions of bruschetta, slathered with chicken liver and bits of sea salt. Their "extraordinary platter of vegetables" is just that, and serves as a reminder that few cuisines can work such wonders with roasted fennel, sautéed escarole, grilled asparagus, and more. Veal Milanese is just as delicious as those fancy midtown joints, but half the price.

The adjacent wine bar is a worthy stop to sip from an incredible list.

■ 156 E. 2nd St. (bet. Avenues A & B)
🚇 1 Av
✆ (212) 477-7600 — **WEB:** www.supperrestaurant.com
■ Lunch Sat – Sun   Dinner nightly          **PRICE:** $$

# SUSHI DOJO 🍴
*Japanese*

X | 🍶          **MAP:** B3

Sushi Dojo is a snug den where the 14-seat counter and smattering of tables stay decidedly packed with Japanese food hunters-in-the-know. In fact, this minimally decorated space still feels a bit cult-like, with diners waiting patiently outside for a chance just to sample the goods.

The chef's choice menu is highly recommended, offering great value for this level of skill and quality. With much of it ariving straight from Japan, the fish is pristine and ultra-seasonal. Counter customers are locked into the omakase (and won't regret it), but diners can also opt for à la carte. Either way, expect the likes of red snapper, fried shrimp head, yellowtail from Australia, blue fin from Greece, buttery Hokkaido scallop, and even a dollop of creamy uni.

■ 110 First Ave. (bet. 6th & 7th Sts.)
🚇 Astor Pl
✆ (646) 692-9398 — **WEB:** www.sushidojonyc.com
■ Dinner Tue – Sat          **PRICE:** $$$

# TIMNA ⚪

## *Middle Eastern*

✗ | 🛋

**MAP:** B3

Diners may end up arguing about which of Timna's appetizing and complex Middle Eastern dishes is the most memorable, but almost everything whipped up by Chef Nir Mesika will have you buzzing. Tucked below street level, this deep and narrow space features plenty of exposed brick, as well as a welcoming bar located up front.

Start with the addictive kubaneh, a Yemenite brioche-and-challah hybrid served with crushed tomato sauce, butter-thick yogurt, and jalapeño salsa. For a refreshing treat, dive in to the Chinatown salad—glass noodles tossed with a pesto of fragrant herbs, palm sugar, and fish sauce, then topped with crispy tempura green beans. Finish the evening with a yuzu tart featuring piña colada-panna cotta and sweet strawberry coulis.

◼ 109 St. Marks Pl. (bet. First Ave. & Avenue A)
🚇 Astor Pl
✆ (646) 964-5181 — **WEB:** www.timna.nyc
◼ Lunch Sat – Sun   Dinner nightly          **PRICE:** $$

# TUOME ⚪

## *Fusion*

✗

**MAP:** B3

This Asian-leaning contemporary gastropub employs classic technique for sublime results. The space itself is quite cozy, with two large wood-framed bay windows offering up plush purple seating, exposed brick walls, and flower arrangements backlit at the bar.

Chef Thomas Chen has worked in the city's top kitchens, and he's a master at weaving together intriguing ingredients. Dinner might begin with a deviled egg reimagined with crispy fried panko, topped with a vivid red garlic chili sauce and micro herbs. Then move on to mouthwatering ripe watermelon, paired with creamy ricotta, faro and a chrysanthemum leaf.

Don't miss the otherworldly chicken liver with sweet maple syrup, toasted milk bread, crunchy pepitas and crispy chicken skin.

◼ 536 E. 5th St. (bet. Avenues A & B)
🚇 2 Av
✆ (646) 833-7811 — **WEB:** www.tuomenyc.com
◼ Dinner Mon – Sat          **PRICE:** $$

# VIRGINIA'S ⑪○

## Contemporary

XX | 🛋

Perfectly East Village in scale, this intimate and ambitious bistro named after Owner Reed Adelson's mother is composed of two slender rooms. These are unified by butterscotch-colored banquettes and whitewashed brick walls hung with vintage menus. Fine stemware and items presented on wooden boards lend an upscale manner to the experience.

The kitchen takes risks while building upon a steady foundation of timeless classics. A crostino of fava bean tapenade and shredded squash is a wonderful seasonal treat—best paired with an icy glass of rosé. Dry-aged and perfectly seasoned duck with maitake mushrooms and cherries is sauced with a vibrant pea pureé, while baby carrots arranged with a taste of sumac and feta offer a light but bright finish.

🔲 647 E. 11 St. (bet. Avenues B & C)

🚇 1 Av

✆ (212) 658-0182 — **WEB:** www.virginiasnyc.com

🔲 Lunch Sat   Dinner Tue – Sat

**PRICE: $$**

Remember, stars ✿
are awarded for cuisine only! Elements
such as service and décor are not a factor.

# FINANCIAL DISTRICT

New York City's Financial District is home to some of the world's largest companies. Previously cramped with suits of all stripes, this buzzing business center is becoming increasingly residential thanks to office buildings being converted into condos and a sprouting culinary scene. Every day like clockwork, Wall Street warriors head to such venerable stalwarts as **Delmonico's** for signature Angus boneless ribeye. If that's too heavy on the heart (or expense account), change course to **Industry Kitchen**, the lunch spot with a waterfront view and authentic wood-fired pizzas.

## NOSTALGIC NIGHTS

At sundown, bring a picnic basket and catch the Shearwater for a memorable sail around the island of Manhattan. Alternatively, step aboard **Honorable William Wall**, the floating clubhouse of

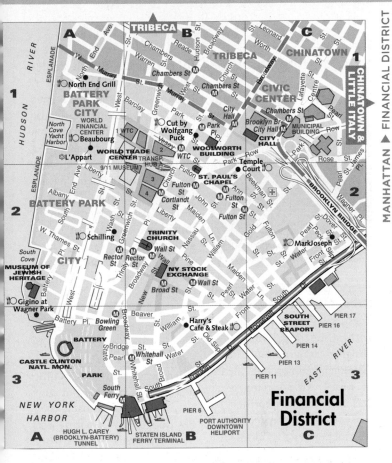

the Manhattan Sailing Club, anchored in the New York harbor from May through October every year. Not only does this stunning platform let you get up, close, and personal with Lady Liberty herself, but it also proffers a perfect view of the evening sailboat races. Of course, don't forget to have a drink while you're at it! Every year as summer approaches, weekend trips to Governor's Island—a lush parkland featuring playing fields and hills—are not just popular but make for a wonderful escape among families and friends alike. Recently recuperated public markets also point to the residential boom in this neighborhood. Case in point: the burgeoning **Staten Island**

**Ferry Whitehall Terminal Greenmarket** (open every Tuesday and Friday) is housed within the large and well-designed Staten Island Ferry Terminal, and deserves plenty of praise for sourcing local and farm-fresh produce to the community from a host of independent vendors.

## BARS & BEVVIES GALORE

**D**espite the destruction wreaked by Superstorm Sandy, restaurants downtown seem to have bounced back into buzzing mode with finance whizzes drowning their worries in martinis, and reviewing portfolios over burgers and beer. One of the neighborhood's largest tourist draws, **South Street Seaport**, is flanked by a collage of fantastic eateries and convivial, family-friendly bars. The legendary **Fraunces Tavern** is a fine specimen on Pearl Street that includes a restaurant and museum paying homage to early American history. While they proffer an impressive selection of brews and cocktails, crowds also gather here for comprehensive brunch- lunch- and dinner-specials. Every self-respecting New Yorker loves happy hour, which is almost always buzzing here with over 140 craft beers and ciders to boot. Thanks to such flourishing destinations, buttoned-up suits have learned to loosen their ties and chill out with locals over the creative libations at **The Dead Rabbit**. And thanks to being voted "The World's Best Bar" in 2016 this delightful watering hole has been drawing city slickers to Water Street as much for the specialty cocktails as for their well-conceived setting and small plates. If the ground floor's sawdust proves too rustic for your taste, head up to **The Parlor** for a whiff of elegance. While here, take a moment to relish some of their homemade punch before perusing the cocktail menu—a work of art in and of itself. Then chase down this kitchen's American bar menu with that classic drink of choice (you guessed right—beer, of coursre) at South Street's **Watermark Bar**. Speaking of bars, revelers may also lounge in style at the **Living Room Bar & Terrace**, accommodated in the sleek **W Hotel,** and accoutered with towering windows set above specially designed seats that afford unobstructed views of the glimmering skyline. By cooking up classic plates in conjunction with a litany of enticing martinis, this spot remains a coveted summer venue for concerts, corporate events, and other such occasions.

## BITES ON-THE-GO

**J**amaican food sensation **Veronica's Kitchen** carries on the food-cart craze in the FiDi with its spectrum of flavorful Caribbean classics. Locals never seem to tire of the food here, and return on the regular for smoky and deliciously tender jerk chicken. Similarly, carb lovers rejoice at **Adrienne's Pizzabar**'s brick oven pies and other Italian delights, after

which **Financier Patisserie** is a dream for tantalizing sweets. Top these off with a steaming cuppa' joe at one of the numerous vendors nearby and heave a satisfied sigh. Even food-focused events like the **Stone Street Oyster Festival** play to this district's strengths—what better way to lift your spirits and celebrate the local Blue Point harvest in September than by slurping up oysters, outdoors on narrow, sinuous, and very charming Stone Street? Located in the shadows of the monumental and glitzy World Trade Center is

**Hudson Eats**—a substantial food court complete with an impressive lineup of nibbles and sips. If visions of a grilled cheese sammie scattered with chunks of fresh lobster come to mind, you have arrived in the right place. Finally, custom pastries, coffee, and cake from **Le District** (in Brookfield Place) deliver much decadence to the local palate by way of unique fillings, frostings, and flavors. Even chocolate lovers are welcome here to gorge on truffles, nougats, toffee, and biscuits.

# BEAUBOURG ⅋○

*French*

✗✗ | ⅋ ⅋ ⅋ ⅋ ⅋

Talk about a room with a view. As part of the French market, Le District, Beaubourg sits on the banks of the Hudson, facing a wide promenade and a beautiful row of yachts. Diners linger over crisp French wine and excellent cheeses, soaking in the scene. It's a picture postcard in the making, but this brasserie is more than just a pretty face.

Start with phenomenal house-made charcuterie—from the velvety foie gras to the dense terrines and creamy pâté de campagne, everything is luscious. The wonderful steak tartare, dressed with anchovy, briny capers, and a tiny, quivering quail egg, arrives with crispy pommes gaufrettes; and entrées like perfectly roasted chicken and delicate Dover sole in lemon butter make for a refined and elegant finish.

■ 225 Liberty St. (at West St.)
▩ World Trade Center
℘ (212) 981-8588 — **WEB:** www.beaubourgnyc.com
■ Lunch & dinner daily
**PRICE: $$$$**

# CUT BY WOLFGANG PUCK ⅋○

*Steakhouse*

✗✗✗ | ⅋ ⅋ ⅋ ⅋

Wolfgang Puck shot to fame after opening L.A.'s Spago in 1982, and it wasn't long before he reached megabrand status. CUT by Wolfgang Puck is by far his most expansive venture, with six outposts spanning the globe. This Manhattan locale is tucked at the base of the swanky downtown Four Seasons Hotel, and sports a fittingly elegant look with deep magenta chairs, floor-to-ceiling marigold draperies and lovely artwork from the chef's private collection.

Kick things off with Puck's signature tuna tartare studded with ginger, avocado, and shallots, then brought to elegant new heights with wasabi aïoli, more avocado, and togarashi crisps. Wagyu arrives charred to caramelized perfection, sporting a gorgeous rosy medium-rare center and graced by béarnaise.

■ 99 Church St. (bet. Barclay St. & Park Pl.)
▩ Chambers St (Church St.)
℘ (646) 880-1995 — **WEB:** www.wolfgangpuck.com
■ Lunch & dinner daily
**PRICE: $$$$**

# GIGINO AT WAGNER PARK 🍴

*Italian*

XX | ♿ 🪑                                    **MAP:** A3

To find food this tasty in a rather touristy neck of the woods is a welcome surprise. A setting that boasts views of the Statue of Liberty, Ellis Island, and Hudson River is unique enough that they could probably get away with less than this very good Italian-ish food.

In warmer months, the best seats are out on the patio amid blinking harbor lights and a gorgeous vista. A tastefully subdued dining room and unpretentious service make it a pleasant place to while away an evening.

This is a kitchen that cuts no corners, especially in the superb potato gnocchi coated in a silky tomato ragù with braised meatballs. Melanzane alla Sorrentina features layers of mozzarella, basil, chunky tomato sauce, and thick slices of fried eggplant.

🟦 20 Battery Pl. (in Wagner Park)
🚇 Bowling Green
☎ (212) 528-2228 — **WEB:** www.gigino-wagnerpark.com
🟦 Lunch & dinner daily                      **PRICE:** $$


# HARRY'S CAFE & STEAK 🍴

*American*

XX | 🍄 🍽 🥢                                **MAP:** B3

The historic Hanover Bank Building is the home to two different restaurants (albeit one kitchen). Enter through Stone Street and find the "cafe." Or enter through Pearl Street and make your way into the casual, cavern-like steakhouse—a bustling space donning a convivial atmosphere with snug rooms, roomy booths, and an elegant vibe. Both are equally charming and polished—and ripe for a business meal.

Start with mushroom bisque, extra rich with a splash of Sherry and dollop of crème fraîche, or Harry's salad chockablock with grilled hearts of palm, peppers, tomatoes, and mushrooms. Other successful entrées include the succulent beef Wellington, where tender baby carrots in a savory wine jus are rendered to melt-in-your-mouth precision.

🟦 1 Hanover Sq. (bet. Pearl & Stone Sts.)
🚇 Wall St (William St.)
☎ (212) 785-9200 — **WEB:** www.harrysnyc.com
🟦 Lunch & dinner Mon – Sat                  **PRICE:** $$

# L'APPART ✿

*French*

XX | 器 ♿

Secreted within Le District is this little French jewel designed to resemble a Parisian apartment—hence its name. In fact, a meal at the charming L'Appart feels less like coming to a restaurant and more like attending a dinner party, albeit one with potentially 28 guests. Thus, you're handed a drink as soon as you walk through the doors and are thereafter introduced to the affable chef, Nicolas Abello.

At this point you'll realize it's worth making the effort to buy into the whole conceit; otherwise the inherent awkwardness of the whole situation could make you want to run for the hills. It helps that the service staff here is genuinely warm and eager to please.

From then on, things settle down into a more recognizable format. Their set menu kicks off with "Nico's snacks" that are artistic little creations to get your tastebuds warmed up. These could include a succulent mouthful of brandade or a crisp cone of creamy ricotta and sweet fig. Then it's into the lineup of French dishes made using all manner of modern techniques; flavors are well-defined and marry well, and the dishes are unapologetically rich—in this apartment "cream" is certainly not a dirty word.

■ 225 Liberty St. (at West St.)

🚇 World Trade Center

✆ (212) 981-8577 — **WEB:** www.lappartnyc.com

■ Dinner Tue – Sat

**PRICE:** $$$$

# MARKJOSEPH 🍴

*Steakhouse*

XX

Well positioned on a historic and touristy stretch to attract diners from near and far, MarkJoseph is more approachable than the clubby competition, but rest assured that these steaks are treated with the utmost care. The dining room looks rather masculine, flaunting chairs with plush fabric and dark brown pinstripes.

This is the kind of place where the namesake salad does away with lettuce, leaving a refreshing combo of poached shrimp, porky bits of lardons, string beans and beefsteak tomatoes. Meticulously chosen, aged, and cooked steak, often served sizzling on platters for two or more, is what distinguishes this dedicated and skilled kitchen. Most meals here may be bookended by seafood platters and unapologetically decadent desserts.

■ 261 Water St. (bet. Peck Slip & Dover St.)
🚇 Fulton St
☏ (212) 277-0020 — **WEB:** www.markjosephsteakhouse.com
■ Lunch Mon – Fri  Dinner nightly              **PRICE: $$$**

# NORTH END GRILL 🍴

*American*

XxX  |  🍸 ♿ 🎪 🍽 🧺

**MAP:** A1

Its contemporary look features that same stunning combination of white umbrella-like fixtures, black-stained walls, and midnight-blue banquettes. However, the reigning chef in the open kitchen reveals a menu shift towards grilled foods, updated comfort favorites, and charcuterie. Start with an artfully arranged terrine layering strips of pig's ear topped with green beans and mustard vinaigrette.

The flavors of wood infuse every element of a thick, blistered pizza decked with potatoes, pancetta, sweet onions, and gently poached eggs. French sensibilities shine in the simply grilled Colorado lamb chops with ribbons of zucchini, baby leeks, and carrots. For dessert, the creamsicle pie bursts with the taste of candied orange, whipped cream, and childhood.

■ 104 North End Ave. (at Murray St.)
🚇 Chambers St (West Broadway)
☏ (646) 747-1600 — **WEB:** www.northendgrillnyc.com
■ Lunch & dinner daily                         **PRICE: $$$**

# SCHILLING 🍴
## Austrian

✗
**MAP:** A2

If anyone's willing to set up shop in unlikely places, it's the talented Eduard Frauneder, who has quietly tucked his newest creation into the Financial District. The 70-seat restaurant, designed by Florian Altenburg, features a striking glass-panel garage door and sleek interior with exposed barn wood and steel columns that make use of the building's original features. In the back, a U-shaped bar pours some terrific Viennese-inspired cocktails.

At Schilling, Frauneder's contemporary take on Austrian cooking hints at sunnier climes, as in wild mushroom ravioli with sorrel sauce, baby shiitake, and courgette fondant. Don't miss tender, perfectly braised lamb shoulder set over pistachio crumble, couscous, harissa, and zippy mustard greens to cut the richness.

▨ 109 Washington St. (bet. Carlisle & Rector Sts.)
▨ Rector St
☎ (212) 406-1200 — **WEB:** www.schillingnyc.com
▨ Lunch Mon – Fri   Dinner nightly           **PRICE: $$$**

# TEMPLE COURT 🍴
## Contemporary

✗✗✗ | 🍸 ♿ 🖵 🖼 ⬚
**MAP:** B2

Tucked inside the Financial District's Beekman Hotel, which marries old-school glamour with modern indulgences, Temple Court is a stunning addition to the neighborhood. This culinary and architectural feat hails from the Colicchio restaurant family, and Chef Bryan Hunt composes dishes that live up to the hype. Think silky foie gras with bright persimmon; diver scallops with leeks and black truffles; rabbit schnitzel with pistachio; or tender lamb with Niçoise olives, Swiss chard and lemon confit.

The lush dining room finds its match in stunning, ceiling-high stained glass windows. But don't leave until you've taken a spin through the adjacent Bar Room, which offers a bevy of serious cocktails and the chance to ogle the impressive nine-level atrium.

▨ 5 Beekman St. (bet. Nassau St. & Theater Alley)
▨ Park Place
☎ (212) 658-1848 — **WEB:** www.templecourtnyc.com
▨ Lunch & dinner daily                        **PRICE: $$$$**

# GRAMERCY, FLATIRON & UNION SQUARE

**A**nchored around the members-only Gramercy Park, this neighborhood of the same name is steeped in history, classic beauty, and tranquility. Even among thoroughbred New Yorkers, most of whom haven't set foot on its private paths, the park's extreme exclusivity is the stuff of legends—because outside of the residents whose homes face the square, Gramercy Park Hotel guests are among the few permitted entrance.

**B**ounded by tourist-y Union Square and the fashionably edgy Flatiron District, Gramercy is a quiet enclave that also boasts of beautiful brownstones, effortlessly chic cafés, artisanal restaurants, and haute hotels. Channel your inner Dowager Countess of Grantham as you nibble on dainty finger sandwiches at the refreshed **Lady Mendl's Tea Salon**, a Victorian-style parlor tucked inside the Inn at Irving Place. Stroll a few blocks only to discover assorted pleasures at Maury Rubin's **City Bakery**, a popular haunt for fresh-baked pastries and—in true New York City style—pretzel croissants. Old-timers love the warm chocolate *babka* from **Breads Bakery** and Mediterranean

delights (think cheese) from **Lamazou**. For those who like a little spice, trek a few blocks north to **Curry Hill**, where restaurants focused on the greasy takeout formula reside alongside such choice ingredient paradises as **Foods of India**. After combing these aromatic shelves, head on over to nearby **Kalustyan's**, an equally celebrated spice emporium showcasing exceptional products like orange blossom water and some thirty-plus varieties of dried whole chilies. Similarly, **Desi Galli** is a quick-serve spot for street food faves— think delicious stuffed bread. Here, pick either a white or wheat *paratha* or *roomali roti* (griddled flatbread) to be filled with the likes of lamb *keema*, spicy *channa* and potato masala, or chicken *tikka*. The vibrant-green mint chutney served on the side is particularly sublime.

## FLATIRON DISTRICT

**N**amed after one of the city's most notable buildings, the Flatiron District is a commercial center-turned-residential mecca. Engulfed with trendy clothing stores and chic restaurants, the

area today is a colorful explosion of culture and shopping. A few blocks to the west is the welcoming Madison Square Park with its own unique history and vibe. Ergo, it is only fitting that visitors are greeted by the original outpost of burger flagship, **Shake Shack**, serving its signature fast food from

an ivy-covered kiosk. While burgers and Chicago-style dogs are all the rage, it is their house-made custard that has patrons fixated and checking the online "custard calendar" weekly for favored flavors. Tourists looking to trend it up should hang with the cool kids at the **Ace Hotel** who take their sip from **Stumptown Coffee Roasters** to savor in the hipster-

hungry aficionados. Another frequented spectacle is **Eataly NYC Flatiron**, founded by Oscar Farinetti but brought stateside by Mario Batali and Joe Bastianich. This *molto* glam marketplace incorporates everything Italiano under one roof, including a dining hall with delicious eats, regional specialties, and aromatic food stalls.

## UNION SQUARE

Nearby Union Square is a formidable historic landmark characterized by a park with tiered plazas that host political protests and rallies. Today it may be best known for its **Greenmarket**—held on Mondays, Wednesdays, Fridays, and Saturdays—heaving with seasonal produce. Beyond the market, find some fine wine to complement your farm-to-table meal from **Union Square Wines and Spirits**, or **Italian Wine Merchants**. Further evidence of this *piazza*'s reputation as a culinary center is the flourishing presence of **Whole Foods** and the city's very first **Trader Joe's** —both set within just blocks of each other.

reigning lobby. The equally nifty **NoMad Hotel** is home to Gotham's first **Sweetgreen** and socialites watching their waistline along with "Silicon Alley" staffers can't get enough of their cold-pressed juices and frozen yogurt. A long way from clean tastes, barbecue addicts remain committed to the **Big Apple Barbecue Block Party** held every June. This weekend-long fiesta features celebrity pit masters showing off their "smoke" skills to

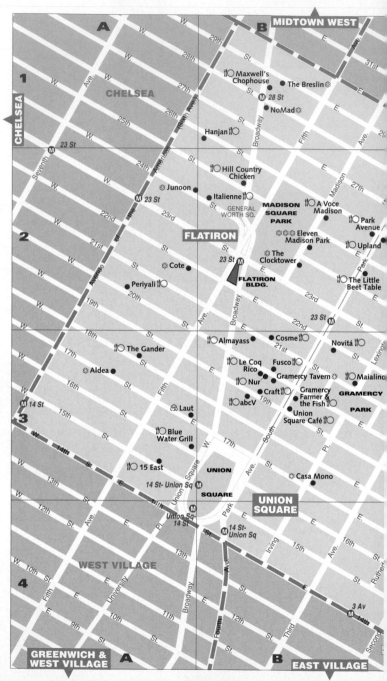

A

B

CHELSEA

1

W. 29th St.

W. 28th St.

W. 27th St.

CHELSEA

W. 26th St.

Seventh Ave.

23 St

W. 25th St.

W. 24th St.

Sixth Avenue

‖○ Maxwell's
Chophouse

● The Breslin ✿

Ⓜ 28 St

● NoMad ✿

Broadway

● Hanjan ‖○

Fifth Ave.

Madison Ave.

31st Ave.

2

W. 23rd St.

Ⓜ 23 St

W. 22nd St.

W. 21st St.

W. 20th St.

Fifth Ave.

W. 19th St.

FLATIRON

Sixth Avenue

✿ Junoon

● Italienne ‖○

GENERAL
WORTH SQ.

‖○ Hill Country
Chicken

MADISON
SQUARE
PARK

✿✿✿ Eleven
Madison Park

✿ The
Clocktower ●

23 St Ⓜ

FLATIRON
BLDG.

Broadway

Madison Ave.

27th

‖○ A Voce
Madison ●

‖○ Park
Avenue /

‖○ Upland

Park Ave.

23rd St.

23 St Ⓜ

‖○ The Little
Beet Table

✿ Cote ●

● Periyali ‖○

3

Ⓜ 14 St

W. 18th St.

W. 17th St.

W. 16th St.

W. 15th St.

W. 14th St.

W. 13th St.

Fifth Ave.

‖○ The Gander ●

✿ Aldea ●

⊕ Laut ●

‖○ Blue
Water Grill

‖○ 15 East ●

‖○ Almayass ● ● Cosme ‖○

22nd St.

‖○ Le Coq
Rico Fusco ‖○

‖○ Nur ● Gramercy Tavern ✿

● Craft ‖○

‖○ abcV ●

Gramercy
Farmer &
the Fish ‖○

Union
Square Café ‖○

Broadway

South Ave.

Union Square W.

UNION
SQUARE

17th St.

14 St- Union Sq Ⓜ

Novitá ‖○

‖○ Maialino

GRAMERCY

PARK

Lexington Ave.

Park Ave.

E. 16th St.

23 St Ⓜ

✿ Casa Mono ●

UNION
SQUARE

Union Sq-
14 St Ⓜ

Ⓜ 14 St-
Union Sq

Park Ave.

Irving Pl.

15th St.

4

W. 12th St.

W. 11th St.

W. 10th St.

Fifth Ave.

University Pl.

WEST VILLAGE

9th St.

10th St.

11th St.

Broadway

13th St.

12th St.

Fourth Ave.

Third Ave.

3 Av Ⓜ 14

16th St.

Rutherford Pl.

Second

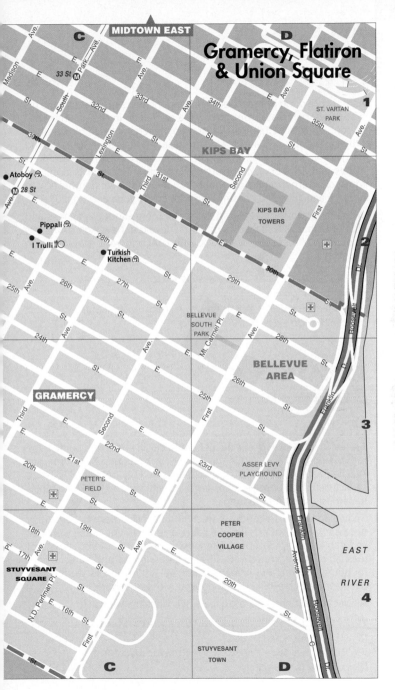

# Gramercy, Flatiron & Union Square

# ABCV ⁑○

## Vegetarian

XX | 🍷 ও 🎋 🛆 ⟅

**MAP:** B3

Another offspring in Jean-Georges Vongerichten's ABC family, and his first vegetarian restaurant, may have been long in the planning but its confidence is writ large: this isn't about vegetables impersonating protein—it's about giving them star billing in their own right. Behind the glass wall, his kitchen uses plenty of modern techniques to produce dishes that are perky, colorful and satisfying. The best options are those of international provenance, such as spinach spaghetti with broccoli and kale; and creamy tofu with crispy yuba and ponzu.

White, bright but dotted with color, the room shouts freshness and vigor; the vibe is fun and hearteningly devoid of New Age smugness or pious worthiness. Just check your coat and your prejudices on your way in.

▨ 38 E. 19th St. (bet. Broadway & Park Ave. South)

🚇 14 St - Union Sq

✆ (212) 475-5829 — **WEB:** www.abchome.com/eat/abcv

▨ Lunch Mon – Fri   Dinner nightly   **PRICE: $$**

# ALMAYASS ⁑○

## Lebanese

XX

**MAP:** B3

Armenian influences steer the Lebanese cuisine here to a unique and rather elegant place. While this family-run operation has numerous Middle Eastern locations, this is their sole U.S. outpost. Polished service befits the upscale room, installed with vivid artwork and tables generously sized for feasting.

Beginning with a selection of fresh and flavorful meze is absolutely necessary. Cold options include kabis, an assortment of spicy pickled vegetables; and moutabbal Almayass, a magenta-colored spread of mashed beets seasoned with sesame paste, lemon, and garlic. Or opt for hot, succulent, and Armenian mantee—little pockets stuffed with beef, earthenware-baked, and doused with tart yogurt.

A selection of Lebanese producers headlines the wine list.

▨ 24 E. 21st St. (bet. Broadway & Park Ave. South)

🚇 23 St (Park Ave. South)

✆ (212) 473-3100 — **WEB:** www.almayassnyc.com

▨ Lunch & dinner daily   **PRICE: $$**

# ALDEA ☙
*Mediterranean*

XX | 🍸 ⬛

A perfect climate and great scenery— it's easy to see the appeal of life on the Mediterranean. George Mendes' cheerful restaurant may not transport you there, but you will leave feeling as though your serotonin levels have received a timely boost. Those who like to eat while deciding what to eat will delight in an appealing petisco or snack—the crisp and refreshing gin and tonic macaron for example— served to kick off the four-course meal.

The menu reflects the seasons and is full of dishes to match that Southern European climate: they are bright, sunny, and you feel they are doing you good. Nothing says the Med more than bacalhau—here served grilled and set over earthy-sweet sunchoke purée, finished tableside with enriched soy sauce. The kitchen is equally adept at more warming, comforting dishes—try the grilled quail with butternut squash and pumpkin seeds. Aim for items that remain truer to their Portuguese heritage rather than Japanese embellishments.

The restaurant comes decorated with birch wood and shades of blue and is spread over two narrow rooms. Thanks to the open kitchen, the first floor has more buzz, but ask for the more intimate mezzanine level if on a date.

⬛ 31 W. 17th St. (bet. Fifth & Sixth Aves.)

🚇 14 St - 6 Av

✆ (212) 675-7223 — **WEB:** www.aldearestaurant.com

⬛ Dinner Tue – Sat                         **PRICE: $$$**

# ATOBOY 🐸

## Korean

✗

**MAP:** C2

Together with his wife, Ellia, Chef Junghyun Park wows diners from start to finish at this Gramercy hot spot with their unapologetic love for Korean food. The fact that they eschew any kind of city pretense in favor of a deeply welcoming atmosphere simply adds to the allure.

With its polished cement floors, posters designed by the owners, and row of communal tables, the interior is clean and industrial, and the enticing menu woos diners with its adventurous—yet approachable—take on Korean food. Here you may find creamy braised eggplant with sweet snow crab, tomato, and lemon; or tender squid stuffed with minced pork, shrimp, and paired with a Korean-leaning chimichurri. Close out with firm, oily mackerel swimming in a flavorful soy-green chili bath and set atop cubes of braised daikon.

■ 43 E. 28th St. (bet. Madison & Park Aves.)
🚇 28 St (Park Ave. South)
✆ (646) 476-7217 — **WEB:** www.atoboynyc.com
■ Dinner nightly
**PRICE:** $$

# A VOCE MADISON 🍴

## Italian

✗✗ | 🕸 ♿ 🏠

**MAP:** B2

Situated between the bustling Flatiron and the leafy expanse of Madison Square Park, this simply elegant restaurant is as appealing to sophisticated tourists seeking a respite from the city as it is for hungry professionals. In fact, with its precise timing, sleek, quiet setting, and roomy, shaded front patio, it's the ideal spot for a proper business lunch.

An appetizer of cappellacci served with both fried and creamy artichokes and dusted with Perigord black truffle is worthy of your attention, while entrées like tender salmon with perfectly crisped skin or octopus-topped linguine with spicy ragù will leave you wanting more. To that end, finish with a semi-sphere of layered chocolate mousse—white, milk and dark—over chocolate pan di spagna.

■ 41 Madison Ave. (entrance on 26th St.)
🚇 28 St (Park Ave. South)
✆ (212) 545-8555 — **WEB:** www.avocerestaurant.com
■ Lunch Mon – Fri   Dinner Mon-Sat
**PRICE:** $$$

# BLUE WATER GRILL 🍴

## Seafood

XX | ⛲ 🍽 🍷　　　　　　　　　　**MAP:** A3

This New York institution has become an iconic part of the Union Square landscape. The stately building is a former bank, with century-old architectural details and marble aplenty. The recently updated interior enhances its classic looks with bright colors, brass accents, and perhaps more importantly, a few more inches of elbow room between tables.

The menu has also been revamped by the talented Chef Chris Meenan, who has added signatures like the lobster Milanese. But the cooking remains true to its name, showcasing food that leans heavily on seafaring classics with an ample raw bar and sushi counter. Fish is always perfectly handled and often rises well above its accompaniments on the plate. Desserts are skillfully prepared and downright delicious.

■ 31 Union Sq. West (at 16th St.)
🚇 14 St - Union Sq
✆ (212) 675-9500 — **WEB:** www.bluewatergrillnyc.com
■ Lunch & dinner daily　　　　　　　**PRICE:** $$$

# COSME 🍴

## Mexican

XX | 🍸 ♿ 🍽 🍷　　　　　　　　　**MAP:** B3

Chef Enrique Olvera's Cosme is dressed in a hip and urbane style that is perfectly suitable for its location. Of course, while the uni tostada is reason enough to visit this contemporary space, the sleek bar up front pouring a litany of stirring cocktails is yet another. Then add in the roomy dining room and soft lighting to its playful and modern Mexican cuisine, and you have quite a winning formula.

One glance at the menu will also tell you why this kitchen is so beloved. A tempting tamal filled with broccoli purée and peppery arugula or crisped-skin duck carnitas served in a cast-iron skillet—this cooking is clever, and, at times, surprisingly delicate. Even desserts, like a pecan tart with salt-and-pepper ice cream, offer remarkable bursts of flavor.

■ 35 E. 21st St. (bet. Broadway & Park Ave. South)
🚇 23 St (Park Ave. South)
✆ (212) 913-9659 — **WEB:** www.cosmenyc.com
■ Lunch & dinner daily　　　　　　　**PRICE:** $$$$

# THE BRESLIN 🏵
*Gastropub*

🍴 | 👤 🛎 🧺 📱

Many a culinary crime has been committed in the name of the Scotch egg. However, if you order one here at April Bloomfield's famed gastropub to enjoy while you scan the menu, you'll be presented with one that is a thing of such beauty it'll induce a tear of national pride in every passing Brit.

The decorative style in this dining room is that of an English pub designed by an amnesiac émigré. It certainly captures the essence of your typical taproom and has touches of whimsy that every good "local" boasts. However, it also has pure New York City DNA running through it and is an integral part of the Ace Hotel to which it is attached.

Come during lunchtime and there's a decently priced set menu, which may include, perhaps with a hint of irony, chicken tikka masala. It's really best to visit for dinner though, when the vibe and the low-level lighting make more sense and the menu is more extensive. Pub food is about bold flavors and familiar combinations, so the lamb burger is a perennial favorite here. But look out for other delights like curried lamb shank or pork shoulder with pancetta, both of which go very well with a pint of Spotted Pig bitter—as indeed does a Scotch egg.

▪ 16 W. 29th St. (bet. Broadway & Fifth Ave.)
▪ 28 St (Broadway)
☏ (212) 679-1939 — **WEB:** www.thebreslin.com
▪ Lunch & dinner daily                    PRICE: $$$

# CASA MONO ✿

*Spanish*

XX | 😳

There's something reassuring about a kitchen that gets in whole beasts and does its own butchery— you just know it understands the essence of what good cooking is all about and that their creations will be borne out of a love of food, not balance sheets.

Here at the small, but perfectly formed Casa Mono, dishes are designed for sharing but are big enough to do so, and there are none of those one-bite-and-it's-gone plates that blight so many places these days. Nor do they arrive in a stampede at your table. Instead, they are sent out in a sensible and well-paced order for the benefit of the diner rather than the convenience of the kitchen. Having said that, with so many appealing items on the menu, it's very easy to over-order.

The kitchen is nominally influenced by the Costa Brava, but rest assured that its reach is far greater than that and the tapas are far more sophisticated than they pretend to be. Creamy eggs with uni is a must; caramelized scallops come with a well-balanced green curry; confit goat will make you question why you don't see more of it on other menus; and the spiced lamb sausages really pack a flavor punch. This is food to cure what ails you.

◼ 52 Irving Pl. (at 17th St.)
🚇 14 St - Union Sq
✆ (212) 253-2773 — **WEB:** www.casamononyc.com
◼ Lunch & dinner daily                    PRICE: $$$

# THE CLOCKTOWER ⍟

*Contemporary*

XxX | 88 ⓰ 🍽 🔥

**MAP:** B2

Nothing shouts "Brit" like a billiards room and there's one to be enjoyed at this swanky dining den of the Edition hotel—a collaboration between restaurateur Stephen Starr and British chef Jason Atherton.

The space shares the same decorative style as sibling Berners Tavern, which is housed inside the London Edition, with high ceilings, handsome wood-paneling, and every inch of wall space covered with framed pictures of the good and great. But whereas the London elder is one huge room, this handsome retreat comes divided into three manageable sections, all attended to by a cadre of affable and attentive service staff.

There's a subtle and contemporary British accent to the menu too. Their version of fish and chips takes the national dish to a whole new level, with sweet English peas and triple-cooked chips, while a chutney made from plum and shallots is served with tender roasted Long Island duck and woodsy chanterelles. However, there are other European influences at play, so you may start with a decadent crab and uni risotto, or perfectly done quail and pigeon pie. Make sure to end this feast by sharing a plump, bronzed apple tarte Tatin for two coupled with vanilla ice cream.

◼ 5 Madison Ave. (bet. 23rd & 24th Sts.)
🚇 23 St (Park Ave. South)
☏ (212) 413-4300 — **WEB:** www.theclocktowernyc.com
◼ Lunch & dinner daily

**PRICE:** $$$

# COTE ✿

*Korean*

XX | 🍸 🍷 ⛯

This Korean steakhouse is a high-minded tribute to owner Simon Kim's home country, and its renowned love for great beef. Make your way past a long, dark hallway to arrive at this well-designed, slate-colored room with such elegant touches as brass accents and crystal glasses. However, those still in doubt of the restaurant's forte should head downstairs to the glass-enclosed aging room filled with hanging slabs of luscious meat.

Begin with banchan that are categorically untraditional, but nonetheless divine. Then dive into crisp Korean "bacon," which is even better than it sounds, served as little shards of jerky-like sweet and smoky pork belly topped with pickled jalapeño. A pedestrian-sounding kimchi stew is elevated with sophisticated anchovy consommé, potatoes, and zucchini; and the marbling on their aged ribeye, cut into cubes for tabletop searing, looks like something Michelangelo may have sculpted. Match this with grilled mushrooms and galbi for a true feast. Come summertime, pair those sizzling steaks with cold noodles—bi-bim somyum—mingled with white radishes in a mild chili paste sauce.

After hours, locals may carve a slot at their impressive bar for more cocktails and fun.

■ 16 W. 22nd St. (bet. Fifth & Sixth Aves.)
🚇 23 St (Broadway)
☎ (212) 401-7986 — **WEB:** www.cotenyc.com
■ Dinner Mon – Sat                                **PRICE:** $$$

# CRAFT ⅋◯

*American*

XX | ⅙ & ⌷                                    **MAP:** B3

It's been years since Tom Colicchio first opened Craft to great acclaim, but the easy charms of the celebrity chef and TV personality's downtown institution haven't waned a bit. The room still bustles most nights of the week with stylish types who appreciate the triple threat of cozy décor, elegant fare and a crackerjack service team.

As the name suggests, guests «craft» a meal from seasonal, perfectly executed dishes featuring pristine ingredients. Dinner might kick off with a cured slice of crudo, served with shaved fennel, radish and micro greens in a Meyer lemon dressing. Don't leave without trying one of Chef Colicchio's legendary pastas, like a gorgeous tangle of capellini with lemon zest, grated cheese, ramps and Calabrian chilies.

■ 43 E. 19th St. (bet. Broadway & Park Ave. South)
▣ 14 St - Union Sq
✆ (212) 780-0880 — **WEB:** www.craftrestaurantsinc.com
■ Lunch Mon – Fri   Dinner nightly                **PRICE: $$$$**

# 15 EAST ⅋◯

*Japanese*

XX | ◡ &                                       **MAP:** A3

A Japanese restaurant divided in two: you can perch at the counter and watch the sushi chefs in action, or you can go next door and sit at a table in a slickly run, narrow room decked out in earthy tones. Either way, you'll be well looked after by an attentive team.

The menu is also divided—between sushi and sashimi from the bar, and hot dishes from the kitchen. There is an impressive selection of the former, with the sashimi being particularly worthy. The hot dishes range from the traditional to the more innovative and adapted. Avoid the over-generously battered tempura and go instead for the soba noodles, made in house and served with a choice of topping such as uni or ikura, or the rich squid ink risotto with cuttlefish.

■ 15 E. 15th St. (bet. Fifth Ave. & Union Sq. West)
▣ 14 St - Union Sq
✆ (212) 647-0015 — **WEB:** www.15eastrestaurant.com
■ Lunch & dinner Mon – Sat                        **PRICE: $$$**

# ELEVEN MADISON PARK ✿✿✿

*Contemporary*

XxxX | 🍴 🍸 🍺 ♿ 🍽️

Chef Daniel Humm's cooking is clever, innovative and even a little whimsical; it is as often robust as it is delicate. This variety and depth is what sets him apart from other chefs, and puts Eleven Madison Park on the vanguard of America's dining evolution. No menu is presented here, but diners are empowered to choose their preferences for a number of courses.

The myriad plates that subsequently appear are dramatic, like the gueridon presentation of asparagus in rosemary broth cooked sousvide in a pig's bladder, but also display extraordinary understanding of technique, as in the dry-aged duck. The latter sports a crisped auburn skin flecked with roughly crushed spices. Baked Alaska for two is a splashy presentation, drizzled with Chartreuse and flambéed tableside.

The restaurant is housed within the sort of grandeur that could only ever have belonged to a financial institution. At two decades in, this imposing arena now flaunts an updated interior that befits the luxurious cuisine. Considerable help comes courtesy of the engaging staff as they explain each dish in loving terms but without ever sounding too virtuous. They also know when to talk and when to leave you to enjoying your meal.

■ 11 Madison Ave. (at 24th St.)
🚉 23 St (Park Ave. South)
✆ (212) 889-0905 — **WEB:** www.elevenmadisonpark.com
■ Lunch Fri – Sun   Dinner nightly          **PRICE: $$$$**

# FUSCO ⁑○

*Italian*

XxX | ⅋ǎ⅋                        **MAP:** B3

The former Veritas space has found new life under the steady hand of lauded chef, Scott Conant. In what might be the chef's most personal project to date, Fusco is named for Conant's grandmother, Carminella Fusco, who hailed from Benevento, Italy. His inspired menu pays delicious homage to her Italian culinary legacy.

Inside the elegant dining room, find whitewashed walls, eye-catching artwork, dramatic chandeliers, and fresh flower arrangements. Conant spins pristine ingredients into his creative Italian cooking— think homemade casoncelli stuffed with succulent braised oxtail, paired with horseradish agliata and roasted sunflower seeds. His legendary stromboli, filled with salami and tender smoked mozzarella, reaches epic heights at Fusco.

◼ 43 E. 20th St. (bet. Broadway & Park Ave. South)

🚇 23 St (Park Ave. South)

✆ (212) 777-5314 — **WEB:** www.fusconewyork.com

◼ Dinner nightly                            **PRICE:** $$$

# THE GANDER ⁑○

*Contemporary*

XX | ♿ ⌷ ⪥                    **MAP:** A3

There are two distinct parts to Chef Jesse Schenker's Flatiron eatery: the Bar Room has become much more than merely a place for drinks and a holding bay for those about to dine. It offers its own something-for-everyone menu and may be considered a destination in its own right. The Dining Room at the back is a large, airy and comfortable space where clusters of oversized lampshades hanging from the high ceiling lend some personality.

The contemporary cooking is ambitious but, while there's an occasional tendency to gild the lily when it comes to presentation, the innovative touches are tempered by an inherent appreciation of what goes with what. There's also no doubting the quality of the ingredients, whether scallops, octopus or duck.

◼ 15 W. 18th St. (bet. Fifth & Sixth Aves.)

🚇 14 St - Union Sq

✆ (212) 229-9500 — **WEB:** www.thegandernyc.com

◼ Lunch daily    Dinner Mon – Sat          **PRICE:** $$

# We built our smartest car yet.
# And then we got a little ridiculous.

**The 2018 Mercedes-AMG E 63 S Sedan.**

DRIVING PERFORMANCE

# GRAMERCY FARMER & THE FISH ¶○

*American*

✗✗ | 🍸 ♿ ⛶ 🍽

**MAP:** B3

The kitchen is always seasonal and dishes incomparably fresh when most of the produce comes from its own farm and seafood from the owner's company.

Yet loving care and creativity abound in cooking that has its own Mid-Atlantic meets New England slant, resulting in creations like a lobster roll enhanced with bone marrow. This is the kind of place to indulge in a daily array of raw seafood, butter-poached king crab, or one of their extraordinary shellfish towers. The menu goes on to offer refined all-American preparations of chicken, pork, and farm-fresh vegetables. Desserts may bear humble names but are deliciously elevated, like the "s'mores" made with graham cracker cookie crumbles, dark chocolate ice cream, and caramel meringue.

🟥 245 Park Ave. South (bet. 19th & 20th Sts.)

🚇 23 St (Park Ave. South)

✆ (646) 998-5991 — **WEB:** www.farmerandthefish.com

🟥 Lunch & dinner daily                    **PRICE: $$$**

# HANJAN ¶○

*Korean*

✗✗

**MAP:** B1

This contemporary take on Korean cuisine continues to thrive and is cherished among locals and visitors alike. A convivial crowd gathers along a cluster of tables in the petite space, where ivory-hued ceramic pieces are set against grey walls.

Small plates arranged as "traditional" and "modern" highlight quality ingredients and stimulating presentations. The signature house-made tofu is unmissable: these chilled scoops of soybean curd are a toasty shade of brown, sprinkled with slivered green onion, sesame seeds, and accompanied by soy sauce and perilla vinaigrette. Lunch is an equally enticing affair, featuring a handful of starters, mains like bi bim bap, as well as popular noodle dishes—perhaps mixing pork belly and vegetables doused in black bean sauce.

🟥 36 W. 26th St. (bet. Broadway & Sixth Ave.)

🚇 28 St (Broadway)

✆ (212) 206-7226 — **WEB:** www.hanjan26.com

🟥 Lunch Mon-Fri   Dinner Mon-Sat              **PRICE: $$**

# GRAMERCY TAVERN ✿
## Contemporary

XxX | 🦀 🍺 ♿ 🍽

**MAP:** B3

In a roll-call of New York's most beloved restaurants of the last couple of decades, Gramercy Tavern would be high on many people's list. It is one of those places that manage the rare trick of being so confident in its abilities that it can be all things to all people. You'll probably leave happy whether you've come on a date or are here to impress the in-laws; whether you're closing a deal or simply lubricating the thought processes behind a deal.

The "Tavern" side is the better one for lunch, especially if there are only two of you and you can sit at the bar—it doesn't take bookings so get here early and join in the grown-up "I'm not really queuing, I'm just standing here" queue outside. The "Dining Room" is for those who like a little more pomp with their pappardelle, and really comes into its own in the evening.

The cooking is the perfect match for the warm and woody surroundings: this is American food sure of its footing and unthreatening in its vocabulary. The main component, be it sea bass or pork loin, is allowed to shine and there is a refreshing lack of over-elaboration on the plate that demonstrates the confidence of the kitchen.

🔲 42 E. 20th St. (bet. Broadway & Park Ave. South)
🚇 23 St (Park Ave. South)
☎ (212) 477-0777 — **WEB:** www.gramercytavern.com
🔲 Lunch & dinner daily

**PRICE: $$$$**

# HILL COUNTRY CHICKEN ⅝○

*American*

🍴 | ♿ 🏠                                                    **MAP:** B2

Gussied up in a happy palette of sunny yellow and sky blue, this 100-seat homage to deep-fried down-home country cooking serves exemplary fried chicken offered in two varieties. The "classic" sports a seasoned, golden-brown skin; "Mama El's" is skinless and cracker-crusted. Both are available by the piece or as part of whimsically named meals, like the "white meat solo coop."

Step up to the counter and feast your eyes on cast-iron skillets of chicken, as well as sides like creamy mashed potatoes, pimento macaroni and cheese, or grilled corn salad with red peppers and green onion. And then there's pie. More than 12 assortments, baked in-house and available by the slice, whole, or blended into a milkshake for a drinkable take on "à la mode."

- 🔲 1123 Broadway (at 25th St.)
- 🚇 23 St (Broadway)
- 📞 (212) 257-6446 — **WEB:** www.hillcountrychicken.com
- 🔲 Lunch & dinner daily                            **PRICE:** 🍴

# ITALIENNE ⅝○

*Mediterranean*

🍴🍴 | 🍸 🍹 ♿ ⬜                                        **MAP:** B2

Two Italians in one: the front room is the more animated and relaxed, with a counter bar and a menu of snacks and sharing plates; in the larger and somewhat rustically decorated dining room at the back you'll find more ambitious cooking and a team of enthusiastic servers.

Here Chef/co-owner Jared Sippel's menu is divided into "Beginnings," "Grains from the field," and "The land and the sea." The influences are Northern Italian with the occasional foray over the border into France. Start by sharing some of their freshly sliced Prosciutto di San Daniele; homemade pastas, like pappardelle with snail ragout, are a welcome departure from the usual; and mains like rabbit with apricot and speck show that the kitchen knows its way around an animal.

- 🔲 19 W. 24th St. (bet. Broadway & Sixth Ave.)
- 🚇 23 St (Sixth Ave.)
- 📞 (212) 600-5139 — **WEB:** www.italiennenyc.com
- 🔲 Dinner Mon – Sat                                **PRICE:** $$$$

# I TRULLI ⅃○

*Italian*

XX | 🍴

Although it's steps off Park Avenue South, you'll likely find yourself checking the street signs to confirm you're still in Manhattan as you enter this Italian gem. While beloved I Trulli threatened closure, it thankfully just moved next door and now boasts a polished look (blue walls, marble bar, linen-swathed tables). Rest assured though as the multi-seasonal walled garden will still have you entirely smitten.

This family run spot has a long history of doling out elevated comfort food. Few things are as reliable as the pasta handmade by Mamma Dora, who has her own perch in the dining room and puts to shame most other versions around. And thanks to said trullo, deliciously charred pizzas are still offered next door at Sottosuolo, a more casual spinoff.

◼ 124 E. 27th St. (bet. Lexington Ave. & Park Ave. South)
🚇 28 St (Park Ave. South)
✆ (212) 481-7372 — **WEB:** www.itrulli.com
◼ Lunch Mon – Fri   Dinner nightly          PRICE: $$$

# LAUT 🅐

*Asian*

X

Laut is a unique Malaysian restaurant that is at once cheerful and authentic, yet never challenging or inaccessible. It is likewise true to its downtown spirit, in a room that features dim lighting and exposed brick adorned with chalk drawings of orchids and water lilies.

The personable staff and menu of Southeast Asian delights are as steady as the constant crowd. Popular choices include roti telur, a thin and slightly crisped yet pliable pancake stuffed with scrambled eggs, onions, and peppers, paired with fragrant coconut chicken curry. The nasi lemak is a dome of coconut rice surrounded with sweet chili shrimp, hard-boiled egg, roasted peanuts, and dried anchovies for mixing into an outrageously good mélange of Malaysian flavors.

◼ 15 E. 17th St. (bet. Broadway & Fifth Ave.)
🚇 14 St - Union Sq
✆ (212) 206-8989 — **WEB:** www.lautnyc.com
◼ Lunch & dinner daily          PRICE: $$

# JUNOON ✿

*Indian*

XxX | 🍇 🍹 ⭐ 🚪

Creative cuisine, attention to detail and a stunning décor set Junoon apart from its upscale Indian associates. Step through the restaurant's ebony wood doors, and you'll find a dramatic, welcoming space adorned with treasures from the subcontinent. The large bar up front, replete with two antique jhoolas (swings) crafted from Burmese teak, delivers sophistication and fun—and by day, lunch is served in the light and airy (Patiala) room.

Dinner guests are treated to the more theatrical room, walking along the length of the space through an ancient wooden arch and carved panels, seemingly afloat in a reflecting pool. This leads to an amber-tinted dining area where tables are luxuriously spaced. The overall effect is exotic, luxe and transporting—not easily forgotten.

The talented kitchen team is particularly adept at bringing out contrasting flavors and textures in vegetarian dishes. A plate of kofta paneer, highlighting soft cottage cheese-like dumplings with a crisp exterior, puddled in a mustard-greens curry studded with English peas and abundant chilies, reaches epic heights when paired with a cheese-filled naan. But for a truly regal affair, opt for the chicken biryani—aromatic, moist and perfectly spiced.

■ 27 W. 24th St. (bet. Fifth & Sixth Aves.)
🚇 23 St (Sixth Ave.)
✆ (212) 490-2100 — **WEB:** www.junoonnyc.com
■ Lunch & dinner daily                                    **PRICE: $$$**

# LE COQ RICO 🍴

*French*

XX | ♿ 🖼 🍽

**MAP:** B3

Chicken takes the spotlight at Le Coq Rico, but these birds go well beyond the basic. Tucked into a gleaming interior at the base of a Beaux-Arts building, the restaurant offers two distinct dining areas—the main room with its stylized décor of whitewashed brick and white oak floors, as well as a glossy counter area overlooking the open kitchen.

There is a list of chicken breeds to choose from including Plymouth Rock, New Hampshire and Rohan Farm Duck. The menu offers plenty to mull over—imagine eggs, soups, and salads of sautéed guinea fowl and artichokes à la Barigoule. Finally, mains like chicken fricassée sided by rice pilaf or Maine lobster served with shellfish jus are just as delightful as a dessert of vanilla-raspberry vacherin.

▪ 30 W. 20th St. (bet. Broadway & Park Ave. South)

🚇 23 St (Park Ave South)

℘ (212) 267-7426 — **WEB:** www.lecoqriconyc.com

▪ Lunch & dinner daily

**PRICE: $$$**

# THE LITTLE BEET TABLE 🍴

*American*

XX | 🍽

**MAP:** B2

A healthy, wholesome, gluten-free, "vegetable forward" menu may sound as appealing as dining with that overly earnest, mildly pious relative you know you should see more often, but in truth there is something irredeemably cute about this more formal offshoot of fast-casual Little Beet.

The menu is divided into four sections—small plates, salads, vegetables and mains—but the sizes of dishes vary considerably so it's best to use price as a guide and assemble your own feast. Highlights include crispy pearl rice with shishito peppers and, of course, anything with beets—especially good here when partnered with caramelized fennel. There is actually more meat on the menu that you might expect—the organic herb-roasted chicken is well worth ordering.

▪ 333 Park Ave. South (bet. 24th & 25th Sts.)

🚇 23 St (Park Ave South)

℘ (212) 466-3330 — **WEB:** www.thelittlebeettable.com

▪ Lunch & dinner daily

**PRICE: $$**

# MAIALINO 🍴

*Italian*

XX | ♿ 🚻 🚇 ♨

Housed inside the legendary Gramercy Park Hotel, Danny Meyer's Maialino is one of the sexiest trattorias in town—buzzing day to night with New Yorkers in all their trendy glory. Reservations are always a good idea here, though you can always try for a seat at the charming bar, with its tasty little salumi and bread stations.

The menu is deliciously simple and hearty: well-sourced food rendered to sweet satisfaction. A starter of tender fried artichokes is paired with lemon aïoli, and al dente bucatini all'Amatriciana arrives with well-rendered pork bits, guanciale, tomato sauce and pecorino. Of course, the Berkshire pork chop, served with tender, braised turnips and a sweet-and-sour plum mostarda, remains a perpetual highlight.

▨ 2 Lexington Ave. (at 21st St.)

🚇 23 St (Park Ave South)

🕿 (212) 777-2410 — **WEB:** www.maialinonyc.com

▨ Lunch & dinner daily　　　　　　**PRICE: $$**

# MAXWELL'S CHOPHOUSE 🍴

*Steakhouse*

XX | 🍸 ♿

Maxwell's is an opulent and gilded steakhouse that instantly feels like a well-bred, New York classic. Zig-zag marble floors, potted palms, and leather banquettes fashion the kind of grand, art deco setting that would make Greta Garbo feel right at home. The cocktail bar is as dedicated as the kitchen, mixing martinis that are almost as destination-worthy as the 32-ounce Porterhouse steaks.

Like any self-respecting chophouse, sides like buttery whipped potatoes, nicely balanced wedge salads, and on-point desserts are traditional and delicious. However, those thick cuts of dry-aged, top-tier steaks are a perfectly rare treat. Meats are cooked with tremendous precision and paired with the likes of a glossy sauce Diane, dotted with soft peppercorns.

▨ 1184 Broadway (bet. 28th & 29th Sts.)

🚇 28 St (Broadway)

🕿 (212) 481-1184 — **WEB:** www.maxwellschophouse.com

▨ Lunch Mon – Fri　Dinner nightly　　　**PRICE: $$$$**

# NOMAD ✿
*Contemporary*

🍴 | 🍸 🍺 ♿ 🛋

MAP: B1

The reputation of the seductively louche NoMad hotel, housed within a strikingly bohemian Beaux-Arts building, owes much to the considerable talents of Will Guidara and Chef Daniel Humm of Eleven Madison Park, as they look after all things relating to food and drink.

The glass-roofed Atrium is the chief pleasure dome but a meal in NoMad's land is a moveable feast and some prefer eating in the more languid surroundings of the Parlour, where there's a little less head swiveling and competitive dressing. Wherever you sit, you'll find the service confident and engaging and the menu hugely appealing.

Don't come expecting the culinary pyrotechnics of Eleven Madison Park: here it's about familiar flavors in more approachable, less intricate dishes, but with the same care and understanding of ingredients. Chicken—which, if we're honest, would be the final meal of choice of many of us—is the undoubted star; they roast a whole bird, pimp it up with foie gras and black truffle and serve it for two. Bone marrow adds depth to beef, while asparagus with bread sauce shows the kitchen is equally adept when subtlety is required. For dessert, look no further than the aptly named "Milk & Honey."

■ 1170 Broadway (at 28th St.)
🚇 28 St (Broadway)
☏ (212) 796-1500 — **WEB:** www.thenomadhotel.com
■ Lunch & dinner daily
**PRICE: $$$$**

# NOVITÁ 🍴

*Italian*

✕✕ | 🚪 ⬤                                         **MAP:** B3

Enjoyable and quietly elegant, Novitá boasts a genuine Italian sensibility both in setting and service. The small size and low ceilings foster a surprisingly serene ambience that is all but disappearing in the city. Prices are not cheap, but the quality is high. The cooking does not necessarily break new ground, but is nonetheless good. Rather than explore the costlier dishes that perhaps feature Kobe beef or black truffles, it's best to stick to the tried-and-true favorites.

Start with a superb combination of pan-fried shiitake caps filled with shrimp and scallions. Then, move on to tiny orechiette mingled with just the right amount of slow-cooked and fiery lamb ragù, broccoli rabe, and grated cheese. The espresso-soaked tiramisu is a perfect pick-me-up.

🟦 102 E. 22nd St. (bet. Lexington Ave. & Park Ave. South)
🚇 23 St (Park Ave South)
📞 (212) 677-2222 — **WEB:** www.novitanyc.com
🟦 Lunch Mon – Fri  Dinner nightly                **PRICE:** $$$

# NUR 🍴

*Middle Eastern*

✕✕                                              **MAP:** B3

Tel Aviv's Meir Adoni has made a big splash with this culturally adroit restaurant. Its appetite-whetting cuisine is nuanced, with plenty of influences from the Middle East and Northern Africa. The menu spotlights recognizable dishes, but there are a number of unfamiliar newcomers that are a must.

Start with fantastic breads, like the kubaneh with its toasty brown exterior and buttery, feathery interior. Palestinian hand-cut beef tartare is given a regional slant with sliced jalapeño and thick, tart yogurt and tahini. The Damascus qatayef are Syrian pancakes, almost like empanadas, filled with spiced lamb and nicely paired with an Aryan chaser, a light and refreshing Turkish yogurt drink. Even desserts, like that grapefruit Campari tart, are rave-worthy.

🟦 34 E. 20th St. (bet. Broadway & Park Ave. South)
🚇 23 St (Park Ave South)
📞 (212) 505-3420 — **WEB:** www.nurnyc.com
🟦 Dinner nightly                                **PRICE:** $$$

# PARK AVENUE 🍴

## Contemporary

XX | 🍴 ♿ 🍴 🛋️                                          **MAP:** B2

For some, walking into a restaurant one knows well is as comforting as a warm embrace; others may feel there's a thin line between familiarity and monotony. The USP of Michael Stillman's Flatiron establishment is that the decorators and designers change the look of the place four times a year to match the seasons, which is no mean feat considering the vastness of this restaurant.

The kitchen sticks to its part of the bargain by also adhering closely to the seasons. Dishes are generally light and easy to eat and the cooks know not to crowd a plate. There are salads aplenty but the best options are those, like the fish dishes, which come with a little dash of Mediterranean color— whatever the weather outside.

🔲 360 Park Ave. South (at 26th St.)
🚇 28 St (Park Ave. South)
📞 (212) 951-7111 — **WEB:** www.parkavenyc.com
🔲 Lunch & dinner daily                                    **PRICE:** $$$

# PERIYALI 🍴

## Greek

XX | 🍴                                                    **MAP:** A2

Relaxing and stylish for grown-ups, Periyali serves the kind of straightforward Greek cooking that remains blissfully unconcerned with trends. Think grilled octopus is boring? Think again, when presented with charcoal-grilled morsels, marinated for two days in red wine and finished with olive oil and parsley sauce. Salmon may not be native to Greece, but it gets its due respect here, wrapped with herbs and baked in phyllo, served alongside stewed okra. A puréed dish of fava kremidaki showcases a terrific blend of textures, colors, and flavors that is the heart and soul of this rustic kitchen.

The dining room echoes the culinary theme with a suspended wall of shimmering decorative fish, abundant flower arrangements, and a back room flooded with natural light.

🔲 35 W. 20th St. (bet. Fifth & Sixth Aves.)
🚇 23 St (Sixth Ave.)
📞 (212) 463-7890 — **WEB:** www.periyali.com
🔲 Lunch Mon – Fri  Dinner nightly                         **PRICE:** $$$

# PIPPALI 😊

*Indian*

✗✗

MAP: C2

Pippali offers a pleasing study on the myriad regional cuisines of India with an array of sensational curries, seafood dishes, and so much more. On-point service makes it a dream destination for date night or dinner with friends, and a muted color scheme in the sleek dining room provides an ideal backdrop for the kitchen's rout of boldly seasoned dishes.

Standards are done right, but focus on their specialties for a unique perspective: melagu chemeen is a must—black pepper-rubbed Chilean sea bass simmered in a coconut-rich red chili curry; while Bombay dabeli unveils soft buns slathered with spicy mashed potatoes and crispy sev. Presentations are careful and unfussy, as found in baingan ka salan replete with peanut, sesame, and of course, more spice.

■ 129 E. 27th St. (bet. Lexington Ave. & Park Ave. South)
🚇 28 St (Park Ave. South)
📞 (212) 689-1999 — **WEB:** www.pippalinyc.com
■ Lunch & dinner daily                    PRICE: $$

# TURKISH KITCHEN 😊

*Turkish*

✗✗ | 🍽 ☞

MAP: C2

Turkish Kitchen showcases all the classics but excels in the preparation of grilled meats. Indulge in yogurtlu karisik, a dish of moist and smoky char-grilled lamb, chicken, and spicy kebabs on a cooling bed of garlic-scented yogurt and pita bread. Pillowy beef dumplings also wade in a pool of that signature sauce topped with paprika-infused oil as well as a dusting of sumac, oregano, and mint. A wide selection of Turkish wines makes a fine accompaniment to a hearty meal.

Dangling globe light fixtures give the entrance to this cavernous, multi-level restaurant with floor-to-ceiling windows a modern glow. Tables are topped with pristine white cloths and set between black and white striped chairs;  cherry-red walls lend a pop of color.

■ 386 Third Ave. (bet. 27th & 28th Sts.)
🚇 28 St (Park Ave. South)
📞 (212) 679-6633 — **WEB:** www.turkishkitchen.com
■ Lunch Sun – Fri   Dinner nightly        PRICE: $$

# UNION SQUARE CAFE ⅃◯

*American*

✗✗✗ | 🍸

**MAP:** B3

Union Square Cafe is to NYC as steel is to skyscrapers, so regulars practically went into mourning when news broke that it was shuttering. But Danny Meyer doesn't disappoint, and when it re-opened nearly a year later in a shiny new locale, everyone breathed a sigh of relief—and promptly made reservations.

Nobody does relaxed elegance like the aforementioned restaurateur, and this two-story space is no exception. Service is exemplary whether you're a local or Broadway star, and the menu is filled with upmarket takes on crowd faves—everything from the ever-popular burger to a silky and savory cauliflower sformato. And with an option like triple-layer espresso chocolate cake with locally roasted espresso ganache on the menu, you'd be crazy to skip dessert.

- 🔲 101 E. 19th St. (at Park Ave. South)
- 🚇 23 St (Park Ave South)
- ✆ (212) 243-4020 — **WEB:** www.unionsquarecafe.com
- 🔲 Lunch & dinner daily       **PRICE:** $$$$

# UPLAND ⅃◯

*Mediterranean*

✗✗ | ♿ ⬚ ✍

**MAP:** B2

The stars must have aligned to bring Chef Justin Smillie, restaurateur Stephen Starr, and design firm Roman and Williams together to form this bright spot along Park Avenue South. Everything seems to click at Upland—the restaurant's interior design is urbane but cozy, with vintage flooring and glowing jars of preserved lemons and backlit wine bottles lining the walls. Earthy and bountiful, it's the perfect backdrop for Smillie's gorgeous Mediterranean-influenced dishes.

A meal in this kitchen's capable hands might reveal a small plate of crispy duck wings, glossy with yuzu sauce; or a plate of estrella, star-shaped tubular pasta with crushed chicken livers, herbs, and pecorino. Finish the feast with a wonderful yuzu soufflé, laced with calamansi curd.

- 🔲 345 Park Ave. South (at 26th St.)
- 🚇 28 St (Park Ave. South)
- ✆ (212) 686-1006 — **WEB:** www.uplandnyc.com
- 🔲 Lunch & dinner daily       **PRICE:** $$$

# GREENWICH & WEST VILLAGE

Once occupied by struggling artists, poets, and edgy bohemia, Greenwich Village today continues to thrive as one of New York City's most artsy hubs. With Washington Square Park and NYU at its core, this area's typically named (not numbered) streets wear an intellectual spirit as seen in its many cafés, indie theaters, and music venues.

## ASSORTED PLEASURES

Mamoun's has been feeding students for decades with some of the best falafel in town. Area residents however have been

known to experience similar gratification at **Taïm**, which features updated renditions of this fried delight. Chase down these savory treats with one of their smoothies or opt for a cup of fair trade coffee at **Kopi Kopi,** known for its Indonesian flair. For those looking to lunch on the run, **Good Stock** is a popular take out soup and chili spot; while **Urban Vegan Kitchen** brings you flavorful food and interesting wines in a casual yet cozy setting. Also captivating the culinary elite are those delicate, very satisfying rice- and lentil-flour crêpes served with character and flair at food truck sensation, **N.Y. Dosas**. For crêpes in their original, faithful form along with other excellent French goodies, stop by **Patisserie Claude**, or unearth a slice of Italy by way of old-time bakeries

parsley and cheese sausage or tray of arancini—even though the staff insist that one must be eaten warm, before leaving the store. Setting aside the dusty floors and minimal décor, **Florence Prime Meat Market** in operation for over 70 years, is every gourmand's go-to spot for

and butchers also settled here. **Faicco's Pork Store** as well as **Ottomanelli & Sons Meat Market** have been tendering their treats for over 100 years now. Take home a round of

Christmas goose, Newport steak, and so much more. And really, what goes best with meat? Cheese, of course, with **Murray's Cheese Shop** initiating hungry neophytes

into the art and understanding of their countless varieties. Completing Italy's culinary terrain in Greenwich Village is **Raffetto's**, whose fresh, handmade pastas never cease to please. From here, hop countries to arrive in London via **A Salt & Battery**, where fish and chips are crafted from the finest ingredients and served with a range of first-rate sides. Think—curry sauce, Heinz baked beans, and mushy peas. Of course, no Village jaunt is complete without pizza, with some of the finest to be found coal-fired and crisp, only by the pie, at **John's of Bleecker Street**. **Joe's** is another gem dishing up thin-crust selections that promise to leave you with a lifetime addiction. Close

this feast with a uniquely textured scoop from **Cones**, available in surprisingly tasty flavor combinations...even watermelon!

## WEST VILLAGE

**L**ocated along the Hudson River and extending all the way down to Hudson Square, the West Village is predominately residential, marked by angular streets, quaint shops, and charming eateries. Once known as "Little Bohemia," numerous old-fashioned but resilient food favorites continue to thrive here and offer a taste of old New York. For a nearly royal treat, stop by **Tea & Sympathy** for high tea, followed by a full Sunday supper of roast beef and Yorkshire pudding. **Dominique Ansel Kitchen** serves up deletable pastries topped with an abundance of French flair, and over on Commerce Street, fans are swooning over **Milk & Cookies**' unapologetically sinful goodies. These are reputedly as sensational as the breakfast and burgers always on offer at **Elephant & Castle**. The influential **James Beard Foundation** is also situated steps away, in a historic 12th Street townhouse that was once home to the illustrious food writer. But, if Tex-Mex is more your speed, then join the raucous twenty-somethings at **Tortilla Flats**. Known as much for Bingo Tuesdays as for their potent margaritas, it's a guaranteed good time

here. Manhattan's love for brunch is a time-tested affair that continues to thrive in this far west stretch. Find evidence of this at **La Bonbonniere**, a pleasant little diner whose brazen and beautiful creations are excelled only by their absurdly cheap prices. Pack a basket of egg specialties and enjoy a picnic among the urban vista of roller skaters and runners at Hudson River Park. While strolling back across bustling Bleecker, let the overpowering aromas of butter and sugar lead you to the original **Magnolia Bakery**. Proffering over 128 treats, this official sweet spot is a darling among tourists and date-night duos. **Li-Lac** is one of the city's oldest chocolate houses dispensing the best chocolate-covered pretzels in town—

take your pick between dark and milk! Beyond bakeries, the bar scene here is always abuzz. Night owls pound through pints at the **Rusty Knot**, while relishing cheap eats and fantastic live music. Equally expert mixologists can be found pouring "long drinks and fancy cocktails" at **Employees Only**; just as bartenders reach inventive heights at **Little Branch**—where an encyclopedic understanding of the craft ensures dizzying results. At the foot of Christopher Street and atop the waterfront, **Pier 45** is a lovely destination for icy cold drinks, hot dogs, and sunbathing.

## MEPA

Everyone from fashionistas, curious locals, and stiletto-clad socialites make the pilgrimage further north to the notoriously chic Meatpacking District. Once home to slaughterhouses, prostitution services, and drug dens, today MePa is packed with moneyed locals and savvy tourists looking to get their snack, sip, and groove on.

Thanks to the huge success of the High Line—an abandoned 1934 elevated railway that is now a 19-block-long park—these once-desolate streets now cradle some of the city's coolest restaurants and hottest nightclubs. As if in defiance of these cautious times, luxury hotels, "starchitect" high-rises, and festive bistros have risen—and these modish minions cannot imagine being elsewhere. But in the midst of all this glitz, find **Upholstery Store**, a precious find (read: repurposed furniture store) serving stirring cocktails. Of course, **The Standard** hotel is the area's social hub with beer and bratwursts running the show every summer at **The Biergarten**. Come fall, hipsters soak up the scene at **Kaffeeklatsch**, a pop-up shop preparing hot beverages for freezing skaters doing the rounds at Standard Plaza; while foodies flock to **Valbella** for Northern Italian food. Finally, obfuscated by this haute hotel, **Hector's Café** is a modest holdout that continues to feed the few remaining meatpackers here—usually all day, everyday.

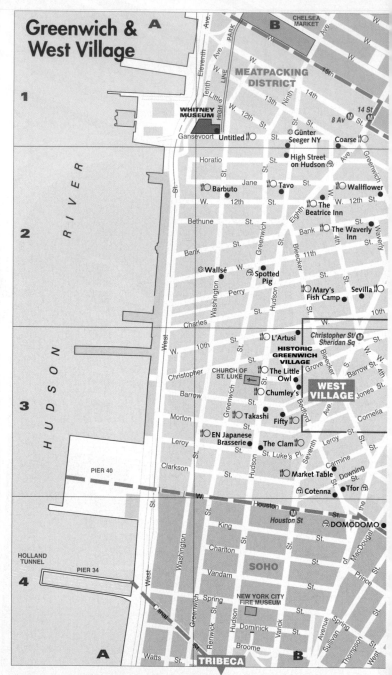

# Greenwich & West Village

**A** **B**

CHELSEA MARKET

**MEATPACKING DISTRICT**

WHITNEY MUSEUM

**1**

Gansevoort — Untitled ‖○
Günter Seeger NY
Coarse ‖○

High Street on Hudson

Barbuto ‖○ — Tavo
Wallflower ‖○

The Beatrice Inn ‖○

The Waverly Inn ‖○

R I V E R

**2**

Wallsé
Spotted Pig
Mary's Fish Camp ‖○
Sevilla ‖○

H U D S O N

Christopher St/ Sheridan Sq

L'Artusi ‖○

**HISTORIC GREENWICH VILLAGE**

CHURCH OF ST. LUKE
The Little Owl ‖○

Chumley's ‖○

**WEST VILLAGE**

**3**

Takashi ‖○
Fifty

EN Japanese Brasserie ‖○
The Clam ‖○

PIER 40

Market Table ‖○

Cotenna ○
Tfor ○

Houston St

**DOMODOMO**

HOLLAND TUNNEL
PIER 34

**SOHO**

NEW YORK CITY FIRE MUSEUM

**4**

**TRIBECA**

**A** **B**

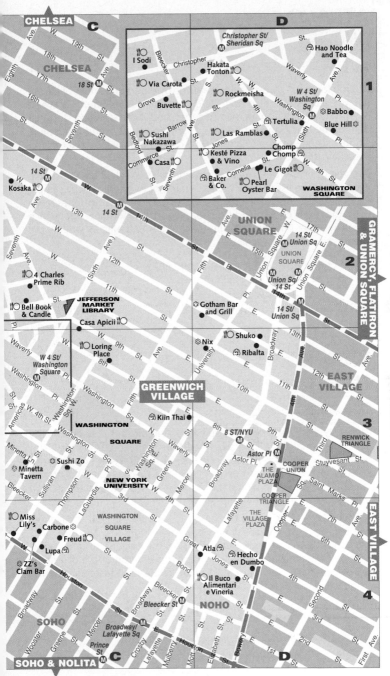

CHELSEA

Eighth Ave.
W. 19th St.
W. 18th St.
18 St Ⓜ
W. 17th St.
W. 16th St.
Seventh Ave.

‖◎ I Sodi
Bleecker St.
Christopher St.
Christopher St/Sheridan Sq Ⓜ
Hakata Tonton ‖◎
W. 10th St.
W. 4 St/ Washington Sq Ⓜ
❀ Hao Noodle and Tea
Waverly Pl.

‖◎ Via Carota
Grove St.
Buvette ‖◎
Barrow St.
W. 11th St.
‖◎ Rockmeisha
Washington Pl.
Tertulia ‖◎
Blue Hill ❀
Babbo ❀

Sushi Nakazawa ‖◎
Bedford St.
Commerce St.
Casa ‖◎
Seventh Ave.
Jones St.
Las Ramblas ‖◎
Chomp Chomp ◎
Le Gigot ‖◎
Cornelia St.
W. 4th St.

Kesté Pizza & Vino ‖◎
Baker & Co. ◎
Pearl Oyster Bar ‖◎

WASHINGTON SQUARE

W. 14th St.
Kosaka ‖◎
W. 13th St.
14 St Ⓜ

UNION SQUARE
W. 17th St.
14 St/ Union Sq Ⓜ
UNION SQUARE
W. 15th St.
Union Square W.
Union Square E.
Union Sq/ 14 St Ⓜ
14 St/ Union Sq Ⓜ
14th St.

Seventh Ave.
W. 12th St.
W. 11th St.
(Sixth) Ave.
Fifth Ave.

‖◎ 4 Charles Prime Rib

‖◎ Bell Book & Candle
JEFFERSON MARKET LIBRARY
Casa Apicii ‖◎
W. 10th St.
W. 9th St.
❀ Gotham Bar and Grill
Broadway
University Pl.

‖◎ Loring Place
E. 9th St.
E. 8th St.
❀ Nix
Shuko ◎
❀ Ribalta
E. 13th St.
E. 12th St.
EAST VILLAGE

Waverly Pl.
W. 4 St/ Washington Square Ⓜ
Washington Pl.
GREENWICH VILLAGE
E. 11th St.
E. 10th St.
4th Ave.

Ave. of the Americas
W. 4th St.
WASHINGTON SQUARE
Washington Sq. S.
◎ Kiin Thai
E. 8th St.
8 ST/NYU Ⓜ
9th St.
RENWICK TRIANGLE

Minetta Ln.
❀ Minetta Tavern
❀ Sushi Zo
NEW YORK UNIVERSITY
Sullivan St.
Thompson St.
LaGuardia Pl.
Greene St.
Mercer St.
Washington Sq. E.
Waverly Pl.
Astor Pl. Ⓜ
Astor Pl.
THE ALAMO PLAZA
COOPER UNION
Stuyvesant St.
COOPER TRIANGLE
Saint Marks Pl.

Bleecker St.
‖◎ Miss Lily's
Carbone ❀
Freud ‖◎
Lupa ❀
WASHINGTON SQUARE VILLAGE
THE VILLAGE PLAZA
Lafayette St.
7th St.
6th St.

❀ ZZ's Clam Bar
Houston St.
Greene St.
Atla ◎
❀ Hecho en Dumbo
Bond St.
Second Ave.
5th St.
4th St.

Broadway
Wooster St.
Mercer St.
Bleecker St.
‖◎ Il Buco Alimentari e Vineria
Bleecker St Ⓜ
NOHO
3rd St.
Bowery

SOHO
Broadway/ Lafayette Sq Ⓜ
Prince St.
Crosby St.
Lafayette St.
Mulberry St.
Elizabeth St.
Mott St.
Houston St.
First Ave.

# ATLA 😊
## *Mexican*

XX | 🍽️

Flatiron favorite Cosme may be doted on by diners and critics alike, but nobody puts Atla in a corner. The delightful little sibling on Lafayette St. stands proudly on its own two feet, and if the dazzling design—defined by black-and-white tiles, tiny wood tables, and a bustling, worldly scene—makes Atla feel like a contemporary Mexican terrace, well that's the point.

First things first: order a mezcal from the massive selection, then settle in to peruse the list of small plates. A party of two could easily sample every delicious morsel on the menu, but Chef Daniela Soto-Innes really rocks the Arctic char tostada; quinoa, yogurt, and tomatoes done pico de gallo-style; farro wheat and quail egg meatballs; as well as the spectacular chicken enchiladas.

- 372 Lafayette St. (at Great Jones St.)
- Astor Pl
- N/A — **WEB:** www.atlanyc.com
- Lunch & dinner daily

PRICE: $$

# BAKER & CO. 😊
## *Italian*

XX | 🍴 🛋️

With only a few years on the downtown circuit, this chic charmer is already a bonafide Village sweetheart. Brought to you by the team behind the wildly popular Emporio and Aurora, Baker & Co. is housed in the beloved and much-missed Zito & Sons Bakery—and the interior features a long, welcoming bar, cozy, wood-lined banquettes, as well as a vibrant red-and-white mosaic floor.

The kitchen smartly relies on the same formula that put their other outposts on the map: honest, unfussy Italian rendered with a deft hand and deep attention to ingredients. Consider the luscious burrata, paired with pencil-thin roasted asparagus, cured fish roe and a drizzle of salsa verde; or the tender branzino with asparagus, toasted hazelnuts, arugula and chili flakes.

- 259 Bleecker St. (bet. Cornelia & Jones Sts.)
- W 4 St - Wash Sq
- (212) 255-1234 — **WEB:** www.bakernco.com
- Lunch & dinner daily

PRICE: $$

# BABBO ✿
*Italian*

XX | 🕸

While a restaurant can rarely be all things to all people, it should certainly adapt to the various needs and moods of its customers. Come for lunch at Babbo, for example, and there'll be Stan Getz playing gently in the background to accompany the quiet clinking of cutlery and the soft murmur of conversation. Turn up for dinner with friends and Led Zeppelin or Tom Petty will be the soundtrack to the far more excitable vibe.

Mario Batali's Village stalwart is a thoroughbred now heading inexorably towards its 20th birthday. The reason for its longevity is pretty apparent as soon as you walk in: the place just feels right, everything they do they have practiced, and every need you have and every request you make will be accommodated. It's also a decidedly handsome space, with the first floor room adorned with fresh flowers and a staircase leading to a bright, raised second level.

The menu offers a comprehensive selection of Italian dishes whose rustic appearance belies their skilled creation. The homemade pasta dishes are an obvious strength and the kitchen can show a remarkably light touch when required, especially with certain classic desserts like panna cotta.

■ 110 Waverly Pl. (bet. MacDougal St. & Sixth Ave.)
🚇 W 4 St - Wash Sq
✆ (212) 777-0303 — **WEB:** www.babbonyc.com
■ Lunch Tue – Sat   Dinner nightly          PRICE: $$$$

# BARBUTO ⅏

*Italian*

XX | ⅋ ⌂ ⌑ ⌔          **MAP:** B2

When New Yorkers dream of living in the West Village, Barbuto has a place in that dream, too. Springtime lunches with garage doors open to the sidewalk, and a feast of refined, simple dishes have earned Jonathan Waxman a devoted following in a neighborhood already full of charming restaurants. Casually professional service and the dimly lit dining room's dose of California cool enhance the experience.

Barbuto's roast chicken deserves its legendary status, but other dishes tempt too. A cavolo nero salad of thinly sliced black kale and crunchy breadcrumbs tossed in a creamy dressing of anchovies and pecorino puts the average kale salad to shame. Linguini is then coated with black pepper, egg, pancetta, and cheese in one indelible plate of carbonara.

◼ 775 Washington St. (at 12th St.)
▣ 14 St - 8 Av
✆ (212) 924-9700 — **WEB:** www.barbutonyc.com
◼ Lunch & dinner daily          **PRICE:** $$

# THE BEATRICE INN ⅏

*Steakhouse*

XX | ⅋ ⍨          **MAP:** B2

Its glitzy and glamorous history makes this one of those restaurants about which everyone has an opinion—regardless of whether they've been here or not. The celebrity cavalcade may have now moved on, but that appealing sense of speakeasy secrecy remains, with its low ceiling and even lower lighting adding to the sense of intimacy and intrigue.

Chef/co-owner Angie Mar has produced a classic chophouse menu, where meat is king. There are plenty of dishes for sharing, whether that's the dry-aged rack of lamb or the applewood-smoked rabbit, but even standard dishes designed for one are on the hefty size. Flavors are big and bold but the richness of the meat is balanced by a judicious use of herbs and fruits. That said, make sure you come hungry.

◼ 285 W. 12th St. (bet. W 4th St. & Eighth Ave.)
▣ 14 St (Seventh Ave.)
✆ (212) 675-2808 — **WEB:** www.thebeatriceinn.com
◼ Dinner Tue – Sun          **PRICE:** $$$$

# BELL BOOK & CANDLE ⅄◯

*American*

XX | 🍸 ᶳ⃛

Funky, relaxed, and locally minded, the idea behind this farm-to-table style of dining might seem overdone if the cooking here wasn't so good. Enter carefully down a steep set of stairs to find low ceilings, large canvas artwork, and comfortable seating that lets you settle in and ponder just how very local the lettuce can be (answer: the rooftop).

In fact, much of the produce here was harvested from their aeroponic rooftop gardens, while the rest is sourced from local purveyors. From start to finish, the American fare is consistently pleasing. Highlights include crispy fried P.E.I. oysters with jalapeño-buttermilk dressing, thick and juicy grilled sausage with house pickles and flatbread, and gooey chocolate brownies with pistachio ice cream.

◼ 141 W. 10th St. (bet. Greenwich Ave. & Waverly Pl.)
🚇 14 St (Seventh Ave.)
☏ (212) 414-2355 — **WEB:** www.bbandcnyc.com
◼ Lunch Sun  Dinner nightly                    PRICE: $$$

# BUVETTE ⅄◯

*French*

X | 🍽 ᶳ⃛

Charming and proudly French, Buvette serves delicious Gallic plates to a notably svelte set. While carb addicts can barely fit into these wee seats, it's worth the squeeze for Chef Jody Williams' famously rustic cooking. Inside, everything comes alive with jazz and chatter. Instagrammable dishes take their cue from French classics and may feature crusty olive oil-drizzled country bread slathered with fluffy scrambled eggs, salty prosciutto, and nutty parmesan. Then await croissants—fresh, buttery, and flaky—served with sweet fruit preserves for a typically French and very decadent treat.

If not up the block at her other spot or across the pond in Paris, you may even find the chef herself holding meetings over a potent, frothy, and flawless cappuccino.

◼ 42 Grove St. (bet. Bedford & Bleecker Sts.)
🚇 Christopher St - Sheridan Sq
☏ (212) 255-3590 — **WEB:** www.buvette.com
◼ Lunch & dinner daily                         PRICE: $$

# BLUE HILL ✿

*American*

✕✕ | 🍸 ⬚

Knowing when to leave something alone, whether you're a painter, singer or cook, requires confidence in your material and your own ability. Here at Blue Hill, Dan Barber's kitchen displays its utter trust in the products at hand not only by not interfering with them too much but also giving them space in which their natural flavors can shine. Think Frank Sinatra, but with sweet corn and tomatoes.

This intimate, sophisticated restaurant is as popular as ever and the youthful team clearly shares Chef Barber's passion and pride. The "farm to fork" mantra may be something of a cliché these days but this restaurant demonstrates that the startlingly obvious equation of great seasonal ingredients = great food remains the cornerstone of every great restaurant. Here, a majority of ingredients come from Stone Barns Center and the eponymous farm in Massachusetts.

Diners decide between a six course "Farmer's Feast" tasting menu or a four-course "Daily Menu" which offers some choice. Dishes are described in refreshingly terse terms to reflect the relative simplicity of what's on the plate, whether that's wreckfish paired with clams, or gnocchi filled with ricotta. This is food that tastes and feels good.

◾ 75 Washington Pl. (bet. Sixth Ave. & Washington Sq. Park)
🚇 W 4 St - Wash Sq
✆ (212) 539-1776 — **WEB:** www.bluehillfarm.com
◾ Dinner nightly

**PRICE:** $$$$

# CARBONE ✿

*Italian*

XX | 🍸 ⬜

With nostalgia at the forefront, Carbone is plain gorgeous. While this big, bold, and beautiful ode to Italian-Americana comes alive at night under the low lights, lunch is equally admired among brash bankers with big appetites and Valentino-donning divas. That same sense of history pervades the entire space, which highlights plush banquettes, impressive ceramics, and glittering chandeliers. Was the striking tiled-floor inspired from a certain restaurant scene in The Godfather? Probably.

Mid-century classics are what this menu is all about, but exalted ingredients, skill, and presentations will excite even the most cynical savant. Stylish servers—who work the floor with a little flirt and lot of flair—remain in character while presenting top antipasti like crusty garlic bread, soppressata, and fresh, particularly divine olive oil-dunked mozzarella. A Caesar salad tossed tableside with carb-worthy croutons and gently pickled white anchovies hits the ball out of the park, just as pale-yellow, ricotta-filled tortellini over an intensely rich and meaty ragù is a laudable delight.

Desserts like a proper cheesecake set atop a cookie-crumb base and laced with lemon curd is New York in all its old-school glory.

▪ 181 Thompson St. (bet. Bleecker & Houston Sts.)
🚇 Houston St
📞 (212) 254-3000 — **WEB:** www.carbonenewyork.com
▪ Lunch Mon-Fri   Dinner nightly          **PRICE: $$$$**

# CASA ¶○
## Brazilian

X | 🛋️                                          **MAP:** C2

Somehow, this warm little Brazilian brasserie has been hiding in plain sight for nearly two decades. The white room's clean décor, votive candles, and jazz music keep it homey yet fashionable enough for the sophisticated downtown locals who regularly seem to populate it.

Come here on a wintery night for a downright perfect bowl of canjinha de galinha, a rustic and flavor-packed chicken soup with string beans, leeks, and rice. Order a bowl of tantalizingly spiced pork, oxtail, and lamb merguez stew and find the accoutrements as tasty as the main dish. Expect an array of creamy black beans, orange segments, farofa (crunchy fried cassava), garlicky spinach, and diabolically hot preserved red peppers. Desserts are appealing and very well priced.

■ 72 Bedford St. (at Commerce St.)
🚇 Christopher St - Sheridan Sq
✆ (212) 366-9410 — **WEB:** www.casarestaurant.com
■ Lunch Sat – Sun   Dinner nightly            **PRICE: $$$**

# CASA APICII ¶○
## Italian

XX | 🍸 🍽️ 🛋️                                    **MAP:** C2

If in the mood for cocktails, start the evening by heading to the second floor of this townhouse, where Bar Fortuna entices with a categorically amazing selection. Then dinner waits at Casa Apicii—a restaurant run by the who's who of NY's dining scene, with resumes that include Daniel and Lincoln.

The main room is loud, but let's just call it "lively" since everyone here seems to be enjoying it. An alabaster fireplace, starburst chandeliers, and plush leather seating fashion an ambience so welcoming that it almost lets you forget about those errors in service. The "mozzarella menu" is a delicious statement of their dedication to both the house-made and an array of imported cheeses. Other highlights include freshly made strozzapreti in an exceptionally rich tomato-based sauce of octopus, pancetta, and bone marrow.

■ 62 W. 9th St. (bet. Fifth & Sixth Aves.)
🚇 Christopher St - Sheridan Sq
✆ (212) 353-8400 — **WEB:** www.casaapicii.com
■ Lunch Sat – Sun   Dinner nightly            **PRICE: $$$$**

# CHOMP CHOMP 😳

## Singaporean

X | 🍴　　　　　　　　　　　　　　　**MAP:** D2

Named for the legendary Chomp Chomp Food Centre in Singapore, this eatery takes its cues from the same nation's delicious street foods. Owned by Simpson Wong, Chomp Chomp's interior features cool, concrete floors and industrialist fixtures, reclaimed school chairs and mirrors, as well as flickering votive candles. Tables are closely packed or communal—the latter making it the ideal place to bring a big group and order one of everything.

Popular items may include succulent, head-on cereal prawns, Hainanese chicken, or savory carrot cake, a dish which bears little resemblance to the sweet American dessert. This version is fried in sweet soy sauce and packed with radish, fish, Chinese sausage and a flutter of chives. Sound odd? It's anything but.

▪ 7 Cornelia St. (bet. Bleecker & W. 4th Sts.)
▪ W 4 St - Wash Sq
☏ (212) 929-2888 — **WEB:** www.chompchompnyc.com
▪ Lunch Sat – Sun　Dinner nightly　　　　**PRICE:** $$

# CHUMLEY'S 🍴○

## Gastropub

XX | 🍹 🍺　　　　　　　　　　　　　**MAP:** B3

There's little resembling the Chumley's of old, save the name, door, and framed book jackets of writers who apparently found their muse in a glass here. The famed watering hole, which had to shutter temporarily a decade ago after a chimney collapse, has risen from the proverbial ashes as a serious contender. This is thanks to Chef Victoria Blamey, who spent time at Atera among other top spots honing her considerable skills. Leather banquettes, French-oak tables, and patterned wallpaper are long on looks, but don't get distracted, since it's all about the (really good) food here.

The dishes may sound familiar—like steak tartare and lobster rolls—but there's nothing ho-hum about this menu. From start to finish, the well-executed items sing.

▪ 86 Bedford St. (bet Barrow & Grove Sts.)
▪ Christopher St - Sheridan Sq
☏ (212) 675-2081 — **WEB:** chumleysnewyork.com
▪ Dinner Mon – Sat　　　　　　　**PRICE:** $$$$

# THE CLAM ℃

*Seafood*

✗✗

Hugging a corner of the West Village, this shellfish charmer is courtesy of Mike Price and Joey Campanaro. The restaurant's huge windows flood the space with daylight, showing off exposed white brick walls and dark wood accents; by night, pretty sconces cast a soft cozy glow. You should be prepared to wait (and yes, it's worth it), but the bustling bar is a fun spot to gather with friends.

The focus at The Clam is, of course, its namesake ingredient, but the menu also features seafood, meat and vegetarian options. Try a delicious tangle of spaghetti and clams in a bright red sauce with glistening greens, chili pepper and scallions; or crispy sweet pea risotto balls served over charred onion-chili crema. The gingerbread ice cream sandwich is unbeatable.

- 420 Hudson St. (at Leroy St.)
- Houston St
- ℰ (212) 242-7420 — **WEB:** www.theclamnyc.com
- Lunch & dinner daily

**PRICE: $$**

# COARSE ℃

*Contemporary*

✗✗ | ♿

Art and food collide at this charming new West Village restaurant courtesy of the talented duo, Vincent Chirico and Marco Arnold, whose food is teeming with depth, flavor, and ingenuity. These chefs showcase their formidable culinary talent alongside the incredible artwork of Amon Focus and Noëmi Manser.

Diners can choose from areas labeled Raw, Garden, Sea, or Land—or just leave it up to the chef, who hand-delivers each plate from the semi-open kitchen into the fun, artsy room. Seafood is a particular strength here, so a night in their capable hands might unveil wildly fresh Long Island fluke with Fuji apple, coriander, and fennel. Also try luscious hamachi, artistically plated with avocado, Fresno chili, and a cool, clear ginger-kissed consommé.

- 306 W. 13th St. (bet. Eighth Ave. & W. 4th St.)
- 14 St - 8 Av
- ℰ (646) 896-1404 — **WEB:** www.coarsenyc.com
- Dinner nightly

**PRICE: $$$**

# COTENNA 😊

## *Italian*

✗

MAP: B3

Cotenna arrives on the New York restaurant scene courtesy of seasoned chef, Roberto Passon, a veteran on the city's food landscape. Tucked inside a tiny spot in a charming nook of the Village, Cotenna makes up for its diminutive size with a big personality, homey décor (wine and prosciutto line the walls) and warm service.

Everything here—from the pastas to the cicchetti, contorni and carpaccio e zuppe—is executed with great care, employs excellent ingredients, and is reasonably priced. Vongole oreganata, that classic Italo-American dish, finds new life with a delicate breadcrumb stuffing and loads of lemon and oregano. And save room for the polpette pomodoro or any of the flat-out delicious pastas—especially the soft, pillowy gnocchi sorrentina.

▧ 21 Bedford St. (bet. Downing & Houston Sts.)
▧ Houston St
✆ (646) 861-0175 — **WEB:** N/A
▧ Lunch & dinner daily                    **PRICE:** $$

# DOMODOMO 😊

## *Japanese*

✗

MAP: B4

Situated just below street level, DOMODOMO is sleek and lovely, with carefully constructed wood furnishings and a long, smooth blonde wood counter. The buzz at the bar is magnetizing, and service is stellar with each sitting, as diners are presented with a small bowl of water and cleansing hand towel.

Sushi is plentiful in New York, of course, but this kitchen ups the ante of their hand rolls with top-notch nori, rice, and fish. The cutting techniques are just as flawless, and while some combinations are familiar and others quirky and inspired, each roll is filled with an array of pristine ingredients. Highlights include spicy salmon with grilled tomato; finely chopped tuna with wasabi; and light, perfectly crisp shrimp tempura with mango salsa.

▧ 138 W. Houston St. (bet. MacDougal & Sullivan Sts.)
▧ Houston St
✆ (646) 707-0301 — **WEB:** www.domodomonyc.com
▧ Dinner nightly                    **PRICE:** $$

# EN JAPANESE BRASSERIE ⅋○

*Japanese*

XXX | ⌂ ⑃ ⟳ ⊟　　　　　　　　　**MAP:** B3

EN doesn't pander to the spicy tuna-loving set, but effectively pays homage to highly seasonal Japanese cooking. In such simple and delicate food, flawless execution is a must so don't hesitate to ask for a recommendation.

Also on offer are three, exceptionally priced kaiseki menus. The informed staff is happy to offer their opinion on items, be it chilled soba with a warm dipping sauce; aburi Tasmanian sea trout in an enticingly flavored pool of garlic and soy sauce; or iwashi rice coupled with crunchy sunomono and floating in a briny bonito broth. Sweet corn kernels are enrobed in nori for a delightful bit of bite.

Lofty ceilings, large windows, and a glass wall lined with shelves of sake attract a young, professional, and fashionable crowd.

■ 435 Hudson St. (at Leroy St.)
▣ Houston St
✆ (212) 647-9196 — **WEB:** www.enjb.com
■ Lunch & dinner daily　　　　　　　　　**PRICE:** $$$

# FIFTY ⅋○

*American*

XX | 🍸 ⊟　　　　　　　　　　　　　**MAP:** B3

Fifty is a formidable newcomer that has not lost a beat in keeping one of the neighborhood's most beloved dining rooms as alive and popular as ever. Even the location conjures up feelings of nostalgia—caddy corner from the Cherry Lane Theater along an iconic West Village alleyway. From inside the long, narrow room, furnished with comfortable banquettes and bistro tables, large windows frame the quaint little street.

The menu may be New American at heart, but Latin notes ensure that the delicious cooking continues to surprise. The chef's vision is clear in a crudo featuring pristine scallops with uni, coconut milk, shiso, and more. Complex flavors abound in goat ribs braised with tomatoes, and set atop farro porridge, avocado, and plantains.

■ 50 Commerce St. (bet. Barrow & Bedford Sts.)
▣ Christopher St - Sheridan Sq
✆ (212) 524-4104 — **WEB:** www.fiftyrestaurantnyc.com
■ Lunch Sat – Sun　Dinner nightly　　　　**PRICE:** $$$

# 4 CHARLES PRIME RIB 🍴

## *Steakhouse*

XX | 🍸

**MAP:** C2

Brendan Sodikoff's lovely newcomer makes the case that New York should be home to more Chicago influencers. It may be a meat-centric spot named for its street address, but the intimate size and modest exterior make this feel like a charming hideaway. The mood of the staff is warm and welcoming.

Some dishes may break with tradition but offer tasty results, like spaghetti carbonara twirled with pecorino and smoky guanciale set beneath a silky fried egg. Others are firmly footed classics, like a phenomenal bone-in Porterhouse for two, served alongside truffle potatoes, creamed spinach, and a whole head of roasted garlic. Bookend your meal with wonderful cocktails and desserts—perhaps a dense wedge of Valrhona dark chocolate pie in an Oreo-cookie crust.

- 4 Charles St. (bet. Greenwich Ave. & Waverly Pl.)
- Christopher St - Sheridan Sq
- (212) 561-5992 — **WEB:** www.nycprimerib.com
- Dinner nightly **PRICE: $$$$**

# FREUD 🍴

## *Austrian*

XX | ♿ 🏠 🖥 🍷

**MAP:** C4

The hospitality is warm and food irresistible at this welcoming spot on LaGuardia Place, flanking NYU's sprawling footprint. Inside, you'll find a décor that's part-rustic part-bistro and the sum is something elegant and familiar. The bar boasts sensational flower arrangements; and the wines by the glass are particularly unique. At Freud, you're meant to linger.

The Austrian-German menu is small but gorgeously executed by Eduard Frauneder. Following suit, the kitchen consistently delivers ingredients and dishes that go beyond nostalgia. And though the desserts ring familiar, Frauneder's versions are an absolute must. This especially after such comforting mains as dark rye späetzle and silky Hemlock hen, served over buckwheat porridge studded with greens.

- 506 La Guardia Pl. (bet. Bleecker & Houston Sts.)
- Bleecker St
- (212) 777-0327 — **WEB:** www.freudnyc.com
- Lunch & dinner daily **PRICE: $$**

# GOTHAM BAR AND GRILL ✿

*American*

XxX | 🍴

"Reliability" may be not be the sexiest adjective with which to describe a restaurant but that is exactly what you can expect from Gotham Bar and Grill. Whether you're hosting family, entertaining clients or just out with friends, this is a restaurant where you know you don't have to worry about it matching up to your hopes and expectations.

The large, warmly lit room comes with just the right amount of glamour to add to any sense of occasion and is helmed by a personable team who make every diner feel like they're in safe hands. This is also the type of establishment that exudes New York from its every pore—and is ideal for those for whom eating out is a visceral pleasure, rather than something to be photographed, posted and blogged.

The cooking walks a pleasing line between comforting and creative and never feels faddish or contrived. In a refreshing break from current mores, dishes are more about flavor than presentation—and their size bears witness to the largesse of the kitchen. The miso-marinated black cod may look daunting when it arrives but is effortlessly easy to eat; the peanut butter sundae balances sweetness and saltiness in a joyful concoction of creaminess.

▪ 12 E. 12th St. (bet. Fifth Ave. & University Pl.)

🚇 14 St - Union Sq

📞 (212) 620-4020 — **WEB:** www.gothambarandgrill.com

▪ Lunch Mon – Fri   Dinner nightly                    **PRICE: $$$**

# GÜNTER SEEGER NY ✿

*Contemporary*

XxX | 🐝 ♿ 🍽️

**MAP:** B1

Downtown New York will always be a place for contemporary fine dining, but Chef Seeger boldly goes against the tide of others offering serious cooking in a casually elegant setting. Here, find a dining room that feels like a part of his own home, decorated with his own artwork, wine collection, floral arrangements, and tiered drum chandeliers covered in rosy fabric. Much of the staff wear a formal mien and the orchestrated service reflects that—as do their uniforms, which are as serious as American Gothic, but still modern.

Local farmers and producers influence the nightly tasting menu with exquisite ingredients that shine in the kitchen's very capable hands. This is the eponymous chef's first foray into NY's dining scene (he is still a household name in his previous home city of Atlanta). And here he crafts a seasonal cuisine that is refined and elegant, yet also restrained and muted. Highlights include a cool and intensely fresh snap pea gazpacho with wild mint and shallots, followed by supremely tender beef tenderloin in a pinot noir-jus reduction.

Desserts like the rote gruütze (red groats) with vanilla cream and green juniper berries make it immediately clear why this is a kitchen of serious standing.

▦ 641 Hudson St. (bet. Gansevoort & Horatio Sts.)

🚇 14 St - 8 Av

📞 (646) 657-0045 — **WEB:** www.gunterseegerny.com

▦ Dinner Mon – Sat                    **PRICE:** $$$$

# HAKATA TONTON 🍴

## Japanese

X

A serious devotion to pork and Japanese spirit is what makes this Kyushu soul food different from anything else around.

The restaurant may have expanded, but the hopping front room still feels tight with close tables, a small counter and service that is, well, pretty bad. Then again, you are all here for the pork, which is impeccable. Hot pots are a must, but they may need to simmer on your tabletop burner for 20 minutes before eating, so go ahead and munch on a grilled pig's foot served in a bowl with yuzu rind and vinegar sauce. Then, dive into that wonderfully savory pork broth bobbing with vegetables, scallions, tofu, dumplings, pork belly, and much more.

The reasonably priced tasting menu is the best way to explore their range of interesting items.

- 61 Grove St. (bet. Bleecker St. & Seventh Ave. South)
- Christopher St - Sheridan Sq
- (212) 242-3699 — **WEB:** N/A
- Dinner nightly                              PRICE: $$

# HAO NOODLE AND TEA 😊

## Chinese

XX | ♿

The full name, Hao Noodle and Tea by Madam Zhu's Kitchen, was directly imported from China—as was the regional menu offering dishes not often seen on American tables. The artsy, young, and vibrant ambience draws as many people in for authentic cooking as it does for afternoon tea.

Be forewarned that the food may not all fit on your tiny table, but the accommodating kitchen is sure to plan your meal accordingly, with well-timed courses arriving and disappearing in synchronicity. Sichuan chili oil makes its creeping, tingling presence known in a wonderfully chewy presentation of spicy bean curd. Chunks of sole are expertly prepared with a crisp exterior coated in savory soy glaze. Superb taste and "Instagrammable" beauty is clear in each dish.

- 401 Sixth Ave. (bet. Greenwich Ave. & Waverly Pl.)
- Christopher St - Sheridan Sq
- (212) 633-8900 — **WEB:** www.madamzhu.com
- Lunch & dinner daily                        PRICE: $$

# HECHO EN DUMBO 😋

## Mexican

✕ | ♿ 🛋                                    **MAP:** D4

Even after happy hour ends and the margaritas are a few dollars more, the crowds continue to flock here for reliably excellent Mexican fare. Weekend waits can be long and that happy hour is one of the area's best, so expect a lively atmosphere. While it may be theoretically possible to fend off the need to order guacamole the moment you enter, give into it. Cool, creamy, and delicious, dotted with white onion, slivers of fiery jalapeño and cilantro, it is the best way to enjoy their fantastic tortilla chips. Then mouthwatering tacos arrive fully loaded with the likes of tender ribeye, cilantro, onions, and a squeeze of lime alongside an array of salsas.

The highlight however may be the open kitchen in the back, serving the "chef's table" its own prix-fixe.

🟫 354 Bowery (bet. 4th & Great Jones Sts.)
🚇 Bleecker St
📞 (212) 937-4245 — **WEB:** www.hechoendumbo.com
🟫 Lunch Sat – Sun   Dinner nightly                    **PRICE:** $$

# HIGH STREET ON HUDSON 😋

## American

✕✕ | 🛋 🛋                                    **MAP:** B2

Fresh off the success of their wildly popular Philadelphia restaurant, High Street on Market, Chef Eli Kulp has opened up this lovely little spot, just steps south of MePa to well-deserved acclaim. Breakfast, lunch and dinner are available, with a focus on grains, sandwiches and wickedly good homemade breads.

This airy and entertaining corner space is bright and welcoming, with a fully open kitchen and small side counter to view the action within. Grilled cheese finds delicious refinement in thick slices of homemade roasted potato bread, aged cheddar and delicious cultured butter. Roasted, perfectly singed broccoli is tossed with herbed mayo and paired with juicy blistered grapes, shaved cucumber, radicchio and spicy, toasted Marcona almonds.

🟫 637 Hudson St. (at Horatio St.)
🚇 14 St - 8 Av
📞 (917) 388-3944 — **WEB:** www.highstreetonhudson.com
🟫 Lunch & dinner daily                    **PRICE:** $$

# IL BUCO ALIMENTARI E VINERIA ᵞᴵ◯
## *Italian*

XX | 🏠 💠 ⚖

This is the kind of cooking and scene that makes us all wish we were Italian. Start with a stroll through the alimentari (located up front) to grab some pickled beans and serious cheeses. Then, head towards the rustic dining area in the back, which oozes warmth and comfort. Note the meticulously conceived copper roof, open kitchen, and other decorative accents that set a picturesque backdrop for a delicious meal. The food here is authoritative and tasty, with a nice representation of Italian cooking from breakfast through dinner. The porchetta panino is timeless, amazing and vies to be the finest around. Skillfully crafted pasta includes textbook-perfect bucatini cacio e pepe. Finish with an affogato, topping a scoop of vanilla gelato with hot espresso.

■ 53 Great Jones St. (bet. Bowery & Lafayette St.)
🚇 Bleecker St
☏ (212) 837-2622 — **WEB:** www.ilbucovineria.com
■ Lunch & dinner daily                    PRICE: $$$

# I SODI ᵞᴵ◯
## *Italian*

XX | 🍸

Manhattan has classic Italian and new Italian, but not many thoughtful Italian restaurants. Tuscany native Rita Sodi is out to change that with this ristorante. She consciously selected every aspect of the design, from the linen napkins to the thick, striated glass windows that hide the modern space from the marauding groups of young people on Christopher Street.

Inside this oasis, Negronis prep palates for al dente rigatoni and hearty, meat-focused dishes like the coniglio in porchetta. This exceptional rabbit preparation combines bacon-wrapped loin with a sweet wine-rosemary- and garlic-sauce. The herbal quality of such savoriness brings out the almost austere nature of the lean rabbit, showing how truly intuitive and innovative Italian cooking can be.

■ 105 Christopher St. (bet. Bleecker & Hudson Sts.)
🚇 Christopher St - Sheridan Sq
☏ (212) 414-5774 — **WEB:** www.isodinyc.com
■ Dinner nightly                    PRICE: $$

# KESTÉ PIZZA & VINO 🍴

*Pizza*

🍴             **MAP:** D2

Mamma mia! New York's love affair with Kesté shows no sign of stopping. This kitchen begins with a puffy, blistered crust that's perfectly salty and tangy, then tops it with ingredients like roasted butternut squash purée, smoked mozzarella and basil. And while its ingredients seem to have taken a small hit in recent years, that crust is still on point.

Co-owner Roberto Caporuscio presides over the American chapter of Associazione Pizzaiuoli Napoletani, and his daughter, Giorgia, oversees the in-house pizza making operations. Diners can choose from more than 22 pizzas (including a few gluten-free options), a roster of calzoni, and nightly pie specials. The restaurant is teeny-tiny, but diners are encouraged to linger, in true Italian hospitality.

◼ 271 Bleecker St. (bet. Cornelia & Jones Sts.)
◻ W 4 St - Wash Sq
📞 (212) 243-1500 — **WEB:** www.kestepizzeria.com
◼ Lunch & dinner daily            PRICE: 💰

# KIIN THAI 😊

*Thai*

🍴🍴 | ♿             **MAP:** C3

Smack in the middle of NYU turf and on a street choking with fast-casual eateries, Kiin Thai cuts an impressive figure design-wise, with its lofty ceilings and light-filled interior. While value-driven lunch specials might on occasion affect quality, the kitchen continues to push out precise renditions of Central and Northern Thai dishes.

Khao soi is a gorgeous orange-hued curry with chewy noodles, tender braised chicken, hard-boiled egg, and the requisite condiments needed to amp the dish up to an incendiary level. Other faves include fish hor mok—a custardy curry with striped sea bass, coconut milk, and duck eggs—topped with herbs and Makrut lime; or the excellent hor nueng gai with chicken, Thai eggplant, and rice, delicately steamed in a banana leaf.

◼ 36 E. 8th St. (bet. Greene St. & University Pl.)
◻ 8 St - NYC
📞 (212) 529-2363 — **WEB:** www.kiinthaieatery.com
◼ Lunch & dinner daily            PRICE: $$

# KOSAKA 🍴○

## Japanese

XX | ♿   **MAP:** C2

Lauded chef Yoshihiko Kousaka, formerly of Jewel Bako, takes the wheel at this wonderful sushi house, partnering with Key Kim and Mihyun Han to offer two shimmering and new omakase menus. The room is sleek and modern, with a handsome Japanese sensibility and a counter for 12, along with three small tables. A relaxed, but deeply attentive service staff rounds out this wonderful little gem.

Much of the fish laid out over the course of the night is imported from Tokyo's Tsukiji Fish Market, though some of it is procured from local purveyors. But each bright, immaculate slice—be it King salmon with smoked soy sauce, scallop with sea grapes and yuzu, or kelp-cured and pressed striped jack—is wildly fresh, cut-to-order, and seasoned with the lightest hand possible.

🔲 220 W. 13th St. (bet. Greenwich & Seventh Aves.)
🚇 14 St (Seventh Ave.)
✆ (212) 727-1709 — **WEB:** www.kosakanyc.com
🔲 Dinner Tue – Sat   **PRICE:** $$$$

# L'ARTUSI 🍴○

## Italian

XX | 🍴 ⬭ 🥂   **MAP:** B3

This polished, airy West Village charmer is a magnet for beautiful people—or maybe it's just that everyone looks gorgeous in L'Artusi's romantically lit room, divvied up into three dining options and a quiet mezzanine, alongside its more traditional dining area. A semi-open kitchen, polished and gleaming with stainless steel, pushes out wickedly good Italian dishes like tender potato gnocchi in a rabbit cacciatore, laced with garlic, sweet tomato, rosemary and sage; or perfectly charred octopus paired with creamy potatoes, spiked with chilies, olives and savory pancetta.

Polish that off with a drink from their generous list of aperitivi or fantastic selection of wines by the glass, and you'll be feeling quite beautiful yourself by dinner's end.

🔲 228 W. 10th St. (bet. Bleecker & Hudson Sts.)
🚇 Christopher St - Sheridan Sq
✆ (212) 255-5757 — **WEB:** www.lartusi.com
🔲 Lunch Sun  Dinner nightly   **PRICE:** $$

# LAS RAMBLAS 🍴

*Spanish*

**MAP:** D1

Sandwiched among a throng of attention-seeking storefronts, mighty little Las Ramblas is easy to spot, just look for the crowd of happy, munching faces. The scene spills out onto the sidewalk when the weather allows.

Named for Barcelona's historic commercial thoroughfare, Las Ramblas is a tapas treat. A copper-plated bar and collection of tiny tables provide a perch for snacking on an array of earnestly prepared items. Check out the wall-mounted blackboard for especiales. Bring friends (it's that kind of place) to fully explore the menu, which serves up delights such as succulent head-on prawns roasted in a terra-cotta dish and sauced with cava vinegar, ginger, and basil; or béchamel creamed spinach topped by a molten cap of Mahón cheese.

■ 170 W. 4th St. (bet. Cornelia & Jones Sts.)
▥ Christopher St - Sheridan Sq
℘ (646) 415-7924 — **WEB:** www.lasramblasnyc.com
■ Lunch Sat – Sun  Dinner nightly          **PRICE:** 🥜

# LE GIGOT 🍴

*French*

**MAP:** D2

At first glance, Le Gigot transports guests to an inviting little family-owned bistro—the kind you'd only find in La Ville-Lumière. The service exceeds expectations with uncharacteristic warmth that brings a welcoming vibe to the nostalgic dining room.

Tasty renditions of classic bistro fare dominate the menu, so expect the cooking to be familiar and pleasing. The petit bouillabaisse begins as a saffron fish broth with a red-peppery North African accent to elevate the traditional fish and seafood dish. Their cassoulet is a beloved Toulousaine version with duck confit, bacon, cannellini beans, herbs, and luscious pork. Finally, brioche pudding conjures all that is simple and good in a dessert, with crème anglaise, berries, and whipped cream.

■ 18 Cornelia St. (bet. Bleecker & W. 4th Sts.)
▥ W 4 St - Wash Sq
℘ (212) 627-3737 — **WEB:** www.legigotrestaurant.com
■ Lunch & dinner Tue – Sun          **PRICE:** $$$

# THE LITTLE OWL 🍴

## *American*

✗ | 🛋

Straddling a picturesque corner of the West Village, with a name that could charm the pants off the grizzliest city diner, The Little Owl has a lot going for it up front. Light pours in from the windows as people stand outside, catching up and chatting with friends. Inside, bright flowers dot the quaint room; and a thoughtful service staff ushers you through your meal.

And then there's Chef Joey Campanaro, who hits his seasonal menu out of the park, weaving top-notch ingredients into comforting creations that are as rustic as they are disciplined. An Italian wedding soup is sourced from local urban gardens and loaded with tender polpettine; while a beautifully seared halibut arrives with fluffy chive-mashed potatoes and a drizzle of lemon crème fraîche.

- 🔲 90 Bedford St. (at Grove St.)
- 🚇 Christopher St - Sheridan Sq
- 📞 (212) 741-4695 — **WEB:** www.thelittleowlnyc.com
- 🔲 Lunch & dinner daily                    **PRICE: $$**

# LORING PLACE 🍴

## *American*

✗✗ | 🍸 ♿ 🛋

Named after the Bronx street that his father grew up in, Loring Place is where Chef Dan Kluger serves up delicious, stylistic, and locally sourced Californian cuisine to a downtown crowd. And yet, none of this comes as a surprise as the chef has showcased his talents for years and been the recipient of much acclaim in the city. Following this, his cooking here is unique and spirited, starting with caramelized cauliflower served with chilies and Meyer lemon jam. Leeks arrive cool and tender, dressed with sherry vinaigrette, set over yogurt, and finished with pear slices. Then duck breast is prepared with rare skill and finesse.

The generously sized room is uncluttered and mid-century chic, with bright orange window frames and boldly striped banquettes.

- 🔲 21 W. 8th St. (bet. MacDougal St. & Fifth Ave.)
- 🚇 8 St - NYU
- 📞 (212) 388-1831 — **WEB:** www.loringplacenyc.com
- 🔲 Lunch Sat – Sun   Dinner nightly         **PRICE: $$$**

# LUPA 🎭
## *Italian*

✗✗                                           **MAP:** C4

Is there anything more lovely than a lazy weekend lunch at Batali and Bastianich's Lupa? You'd be hard-pressed to convince the regulars who flock here in droves day and night for the amicable service, interesting wines, and otherworldly pasta.

Everything on the menu is so lovingly sourced: witness a warm spinach and pancetta salad tossing a perfect mix of vibrant greens with warm, smoky bacon; or starter of plump, marinated sardines laced with oil and coarse salt and served over a bed of miniscule cubes of cucumber and celery. But the star of the show remains the pasta, which may reveal decadent bavette cacio e pepe, a classic dish from Lazio. It's nothing short of sweet satisfaction, dotted with sharp pecorino and freshly ground black pepper.

◾ 170 Thompson St. (bet. Bleecker & Houston Sts.)
🚇 W 4 St - Wash Sq
📞 (212) 982-5089 — **WEB:** www.luparestaurant.com
◾ Lunch & dinner daily                        **PRICE:** $$

# MARKET TABLE 🍴
## *American*

✗✗ | 🐦 🗖 🥢                                **MAP:** B3

Think of this bright little corner as the template for a perfect neighborhood restaurant—one that everyone dreams of having nearby. The vibe is unpretentious yet cool, with a young, attentive service staff. The windowed room feels barnyard-chic, with a chalkboard wall listing wine and cheese offerings beneath reclaimed ceiling beams.

The menu is stocked with the kind of dishes that never disappoint—think bucatini tossed with fried eggplant and creamy burrata in a chunky tomato sauce. The kitchen's knack for making simple food vivid is clear in the impeccably cooked strip loin, served with carrots, haricots verts, and shishitos brought together with smoked chili "pesto." "Take it easy" and choose to end your meal with either a liquid or solid dessert.

◾ 54 Carmine St. (at Bedford St.)
🚇 W 4 St - Wash Sq
📞 (212) 255-2100 — **WEB:** www.markettablenyc.com
◾ Lunch & dinner daily                        **PRICE:** $$

# MARY'S FISH CAMP 🍴○

*Seafood*

🍴

This West Village seafood shack is much more than just a destination for lobster rolls. Located on an irresistibly cute corner and outfitted with large windows, Mary's Fish Camp tempts with creative daily specials. Scrawled on a chalkboard, these may include raw offerings and nostalgic desserts like hot fudge sundaes. Crowds pack into the stainless steel counter and fans spin lazily overhead.

The summery space offers lots of choice, but the lobster roll should not be overlooked. A toasted bun is overflowing with hunks of tender, sweet meat dressed in the perfect proportion of mayonnaise and lemon juice, with a mountain of shoestring fries on the side. Begin the meal with spicy Key West conch chowder and end with a slice of Americana—banana cream pie.

▪ 64 Charles St. (at W. 4th St.)
🚇 Christopher St - Sheridan Sq
📞 (646) 486-2185 — **WEB:** www.marysfishcamp.com
▪ Lunch daily   Dinner Mon – Sat          **PRICE: $$**

# MISS LILY'S 🍴○

*Jamaican*

🍴 | 📶 ⬅

Authentic Jamaican flavors and thumping reggae go hand-in-hand amid Miss Lily's bright orange booths, retro artifacts, and Formica-topped tables. Wide-open windows overlooking buzzy Houston Street merely add to the allure. A well-stocked bar and bins filled with produce set the mood for enjoyable classics brought to you at the hands of glam servers.

Start with jerk chicken that is insanely moist yet nearly black with intense spices, served with a Scotch bonnet sauce that will have your mouth tingling for hours. Then cool down with Melvin's "body good" salad tossing kale, radish, celery, and apples in a citrus-ginger vinaigrette. From the Jamaican Sampler—think curry goat, oxtail stew, and callaloo— to a boozy rum cake, this Caribbean queen reigns supreme.

▪ 132 W. Houston St. (at Sullivan St.)
🚇 Houston St
📞 (646) 588-5375 — **WEB:** www.misslilysnyc.com
▪ Lunch & dinner daily                      **PRICE: $$**

# MINETTA TAVERN ✺

*Gastropub*

While this circa 1937 setting has been restored and refreshed, nothing here changes and that is its beauty. This quintessential New York tavern is still surrounded by dark wood, checkerboard tiled floors, and those framed caricatures. The astute service team handles the crowds and energy as well as ever—they even don the same white-aproned livery seen in Mad Men. It's that kind of place.

The menu's dedication to bistro classics (like oxtail and foie gras terrine) and New York steakhouse staples ensure its longevity. Trust them to prepare a steak tartare that is beyond textbook perfect, comprised here of pristine beef tenderloin, anchovy, capers and more, crowned with a tiny quail's egg. This kitchen has a way with meat that goes far beyond the burger on everyone's lips, thanks to beef that promises the deep, telltale flavors of dry-aging. Their massive pork chop draped in sauce charcutière has an intense crust that is blackened but never burnt, concealing a juicy interior that is no small feat for such a large piece of meat.

The bittersweet chocolate soufflé is, was, and probably always will be crowd-pleasing and delicious, especially when served with a melting scoop of Bourbon-pecan ice cream.

■ 113 MacDougal St. (at Minetta Ln.)
🚇 W 4 St - Wash Sq
✆ (212) 475-3850 — **WEB:** www.minettatavernny.com
■ Lunch Wed – Sun   Dinner nightly                    PRICE: $$$

# NIX ❀
*Vegetarian*

XX | 🍸 ♿ 🍴

Named for the 19th century Supreme Court case that ultimately decided tomatoes are indeed a vegetable, Nix is a bright young starlet backed by some heavy hitters. Chefs John Fraser (of Dovetail's beloved meatless Mondays) and Nicolas Farias are crafting a vegetarian cuisine that makes you wonder if meat might be holding back vegetables— here they shine without it.

The service team is as on-point and well-versed as a letter from the editor (Condé Nast's former Editorial Director is a partner and frequently oversees the dining room). No surprise that it fills with a unique crowd of fashionista foodies that are as visually appealing as those light fixtures sculpted from juniper roots. Green plants and skylights keep everything looking healthy and bright—it's a welcoming scene.

The two à la carte menus offer intriguing vegetarian options or a more concise vegan one, which has many of the same compositions minus the dairy. Playful highlights include crisply charred avocado a la plancha served in a pool of tomato water, salted and spiked with jalapeño, finished with bits of fresh mozzarella. Fuji apple sorbet begins as a fragrant dessert, then pops with the inventive flavors of candied olive and lime.

◾ 72 University Pl. (bet. 10th & 11th Sts.)
🚇 14 St - Union Sq
📞 (212) 498-9393 — **WEB:** www.nixny.com
◾ Lunch & dinner daily

**PRICE: $$$**

# PEARL OYSTER BAR ﹖○

*Seafood*

Ⅹ

It's not hard to find a lobster roll in this city, and for that we can thank Rebecca Charles. This seafood institution—inspired by Charles' childhood summers spent in Maine—has been stuffing sweet lobster meat into split-top rolls since 1997. The two-room setting offers a choice: counter seating or table service. Wood furnishings and white walls are low-key; beachy memorabilia perks up the space.

Start the meal by slurping your way through a classic chilled shellfish platter before tucking into that signature lobster roll, served alongside a tower of shoestring fries. The kitchen shines in daily specials, too, such as the grilled lobster served with corn pudding or pan-roasted wild bass. A hot fudge sundae is an appropriately nostalgic finish.

▧ 18 Cornelia St. (bet. Bleecker & W. 4th Sts.)

▣ W 4 St - Wash Sq

✆ (212) 691-8211 — **WEB:** www.pearloysterbar.com

▧ Lunch & dinner Mon – Sat          PRICE: $$

# RIBALTA ☺

*Italian*

ⅩⅩ

It all starts with the dough. That said, Ribalta's mother version apparently started nearly a century ago and has been kept alive to feed the masses since. Today, it rises for 72 hours before being baked into a crust that is so light and digestible that you might be tempted to go for a second, very authentic Margherita, topped with that perfect balance of tomato sauce, mozzarella, olive oil, and basil. Pasta dishes are just as strong, so sample a duo of wonderfully tender gnocchi, thickly dressed in pesto or an excellent penne rigate con ragù Napolitano loaded with ground pork and beef.

The food may be substantial, but the space feels like La Grande Mela thanks to red leather banquettes, creatively tiled white walls, and planks suspended from the lofty ceiling.

▧ 48 E. 12th St. (bet. Broadway & University Pl.)

▣ 14 St - Union Sq

✆ (212) 777-7781 — **WEB:** www.ribaltapizzarestaurant.com

▧ Lunch & dinner daily          PRICE: $$

# ROCKMEISHA 110

## *Japanese*

Tightly-packed bar height tables fill this tiny izakaya-style restaurant, a quirky canteen with a menu designed for fun. The young crowd sips Sapporo or sake against a soundtrack of old-school rock; and the décor, not far behind, ranges from vinyl records to a framed beer ad featuring Japanese women in bathing suits. The space is cramped yet fun, the atmosphere lively and loose.

An appropriately moist leek omelet shows the kitchen's deft execution of simple dishes. Meaty, deep-fried chicken wings coated in a nose-tingling vinegar-based buffalo sauce are an optimal drinking accompaniment, as is a bowl of chashu ramen with milky pork bone broth, delicate noodles, pork belly, pickled ginger, scallions, and a generous sprinkling of sesame seeds.

■ 11 Barrow St. (bet. Seventh Ave. South & W. 4th St.)
🚇 Christopher St - Sheridan Sq
☏ (212) 675-7775 — **WEB:** N/A
■ Dinner Tue-Sun

**PRICE:** ⊜

# SEVILLA 110

## *Spanish*

Yellowed menus that haven't changed in decades make this old-school Spanish stalwart seem like a relic. Still, no one comes here to be surprised. Rather, they are plowing through their favorite renditions of paella, ranging from vegetable to seafood with chicken and chorizo. The paella Valenciana also adds clams, mussels, and lobster claws. Prices are low, portions are large, and lively crowds are always happy.

Dishes are made to order, so if that arroz con pollo takes 30 minutes to get to your table, know that it will be worthy of the wait. It arrives as a massive amount of saffron-tinged rice and tender bone-in chicken dotted with green onions, pepper strips, chorizo, peas, and lots of garlic. Come dessert, you cannot go wrong with the flan.

■ 62 Charles St. (at W. 4th St.)
🚇 Christopher St - Sheridan Sq
☏ (212) 929-3189 — **WEB:** www.sevillarestaurantandbar.com
■ Lunch & dinner daily

**PRICE:** $$

# SHUKO 🍴

## Japanese

✖✖ | 🍶 🍱

**MAP:** D3

Jimmy Lau and Nick Kim, both Masa alumni, have created a high-end sushi bar for a young and eager crowd. They've nailed the ultra-discreet façade—anyone who's eaten out in Tokyo will know the feeling of walking past a place a couple of times before finding its door. The centerpiece of the windowless room is the three-sided counter fashioned out of white ash—it's a thing of beauty which you'll find unable to resist stroking every now and again.

Drinks aside, you have just one choice to make—to have the omakase or the marginally more expensive kaiseki. Even for Edomae-style sushi, the size is quite diminutive, with the best pieces being those that push a little at the boundaries. The rice could be better but there's no doubting the quality of the fish.

■ 47 E. 12th St. (bet. Broadway & University Pl.)
🚇 14 St - Union Sq
📞 (212) 228-6088 — **WEB:** www.shukonyc.com
■ Dinner Mon – Sat

**PRICE: $$$$**

# SPOTTED PIG 🐷

## Gastropub

✖ | 🍱 🍷

**MAP:** B2

It's impossible to tell if the famously talented April Bloomfield ever imagined the massive draw her restaurant would have, but years ago, when Spotted Pig sashayed its way into the West Village, NY'ers were more than ready to fall in love with the gastropub.

However, it is the cooking that has been the main draw here—even if you are teetering on a wooden stool or knocking elbows with pencil-thin hipsters in this cozy, bi-level space. Outstanding staples like burgers, pan-seared mackerel, or gnudi—ricotta "gnocchi" laced with brown butter, sage and parmesan—have a cultish following; while creamy burrata spread on sourdough with fava and mint, as well as a perfectly roasted poussin served with Sherry vinegar and grilled ramps are favorites for good reason.

■ 314 W. 11th St. (at Greenwich St.)
🚇 Christopher St - Sheridan Sq
📞 (212) 620-0393 — **WEB:** www.thespottedpig.com
■ Lunch & dinner daily

**PRICE: $$$**

# SUSHI NAKAZAWA ¶○

*Japanese*

XX | 器 Ö▽

MAP: C2

Sushi lovers can breathe a sigh of relief—after an oh-so-brief closing, beloved Sushi Nakazawa has emerged sexier, more spacious and more delicious than ever. Even better? It's much easier to «score» a seat now. Updates include an elegant new lounge where a limited selection of sushi is served à la carte, accompanied by some inventive spins on their extensive wine, beer and sake list.

Whether you land in the main dining room or the lounge, the gorgeous fish on offer is of outstanding quality. Indulge in a truly luxurious flight of creamy uni hailing from Maine, Santa Barbara, and Hokkaido; scallop spiked with bold, bright citrusy notes and wrapped in excellent nori; or a perfectly restrained slice of Atlantic bluefin, barely kissed with soy sauce.

■ 23 Commerce St. (bet. Bedford St. & Seventh Ave. South)
🚇 Christopher St - Sheridan Sq
✆ (212) 924-2212 — WEB: www.sushinakazawa.com
■ Dinner Mon – Sat                    PRICE: $$$$

# TAKASHI ¶○

*Japanese*

📶 | Ö▽

MAP: B3

Takashi Inoue honors his Korean ancestry and Osaka upbringing with a delicious array of yakiniku favorites at this cozy space. Tremendous care, planning, and sourcing of specialty cuts went into the design of the menu before the restaurant opened its doors to acclaim. Inside, you'll find high-tech grills gracing the tables and cutesy cartoons depicting beefy cuts, offal and innards on the walls.

The carte is exotic to say the least (testicargot, anyone?), filled with meats, surprises like tripe, or even namagimo—fresh raw liver with sesame oil and roasted rock salt. The kitchen's yakiniku (table-grilling) specialties are presented to you to cook at your own pace and may include items like shio-tan (tongue) marinated in soy, apples, and orange marmalade.

■ 456 Hudson St. (bet. Barrow & Morton Sts.)
🚇 Christopher St - Sheridan Sq
✆ (212) 414-2929 — WEB: www.takashinyc.com
■ Dinner nightly                    PRICE: $$

# SUSHI ZO ✿

*Japanese*

XX

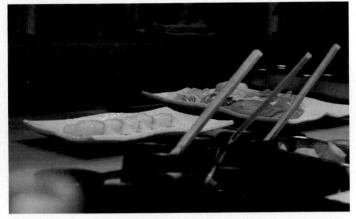

This LA import has sushi that rivals the best in New York but is served with a laid-back vibe that is a welcomed change of pace. Sushi Zo is nonetheless ambitious, serving superlative fish and seafood that is pristine, delicious, and well beyond reproach.

The petite space is serene and showcases a particularly lovely mix of blonde wood and exposed brick, decorated with little more than birch branches. Their nightly omakase menu has only two turns at the counter as well as the handful of tables, so plan well in advance if you want to approach this multi-course feast.

Begin with a plump Kumamoto oyster served with a slightly sweet ponzu sauce and lime zest in the company of spectacular sashimi. Their exquisite nigiri—with bright flavors and skilled torch work—is sure to be the highlight of your meal thanks to halibut with lemon and sea salt, belt fish with wasabi, and shima aji with yuzu juice. Each long slice of perfectly fresh fish drapes off the delicate shari; those generous proportions belie Sushi Zo's origins as a California-based sushi-ya that is unafraid to flout tradition. Finish with a delicate and palate-cleansing fish-bone consommé and sphere of house mochi.

■ 88 W. 3rd St. (bet. Sullivan & Thompson Sts.)

▣ W 4 St - Wash Sq

℘ (646) 405-4826 — **WEB:** www.sushizo.us

■ Dinner Tue – Sat                    PRICE: $$$$

# TAVO 🍴⃝

*Latin American*

XX | 🍸 ⛐ 🏛 🛋       **MAP:** B2

Upscale, thoughtful, and lip-smacking good, Tavo offers pan-Latin fare with a Mexican touch. This however is what one should expect, as the talented kitchen team boasts an impressive resume and are masters at the stove. Beyond the welcoming bar, the décor also reflects the south-of-the-border state of Nuevo León with a warm, modern aesthetic.

Their ceviche Peruano is plain excellent, thanks to ample portions of seafood in a kicky coconut-lemongrass leche de tigre. The kitchen's signature dishes, such as Cuban "lasagna," are as surprising as they are tasty. While it is tempting to order half portions in order to sample a greater variety, don't hold back on the beautifully cooked double-cut rack of lamb in a decadent chocolate-habanero sauce.

■ 615 Hudson St. (bet. Jane & 12th Sts.)
🚇 14 St - 8 Av
📞 (917) 675-6454 — **WEB:** www.tavonyc.com
■ Lunch Sat – Sun    Dinner nightly       **PRICE: $$**

# TERTULIA ⓰

*Spanish*

XX | 🏛 🛋       **MAP:** D1

With a Spanish soul and tastefully raw space, Chef Seamus Mullen's Tertulia is big-hearted and boasts a surprisingly healthy side to its menu. The narrow room decked with a long wood bar and colorful tiles evokes those casual eateries in Spain, complete with a buzzing open kitchen and chalkboards scribbled with cheeses. The bites here are healthy but equally bright with flavor. Tosta matrimonio is a flax-and-quinoa crisp topped with anchovies, slow-roasted tomato, and sheep's milk cheese. Also, try bocata de delicata, a satisfying sandwich of charred delicata squash, roasted red peppers, Swiss chard, and cheddar.

For a sweet fix try the pastel de almendras, a chocolate-covered almond cake with Pedro Ximénez syrup and a side of peanut butter ice cream.

■ 359 Sixth Ave. (bet. Washington Pl. & W. 4th St.)
🚇 W 4 St - Wash Sq
📞 (646) 559-9909 — **WEB:** www.tertulianyc.com
■ Lunch & dinner daily       **PRICE: $$**

# TFOR 🐶

*Italian*

✗✗ | 🍸 🍹                                     **MAP:** B3

There are plenty of Italian restaurants in New York, but Tfor isn't just any old spaghetteria—it's *Sicilian*. And as anyone who hails from Triancria knows, the food from this region deserves a special distinction. Secreted away on a quaint stretch of Bedford Street and outfitted with ultra-modern furnishings, Tfor imports many of its ingredients straight from the island.

Dishes that aren't found anywhere else are a particular highlight here, and a meal isn't complete without sampling one of the tartares (you can't go wrong with the Sicilian tuna, swordfish, or tagliate di carne). Then dive in to homemade pasta with pistachio from Bronte and Mediterranean Imperial prawns, before concluding over a cannolo molto delizioso with candied orange for dessert.

▨ 14 Bedford St. (bet. Downing St. & Sixth Ave.)
🚇 Houston St
✆ (212) 675-9080 — **WEB:** www.tfor-nyc.com
▨ Lunch Sat – Sun   Dinner Tue – Sun                **PRICE:** $$

# UNTITLED 🍴

*American*

✗✗ | ♿ 🚻 🛋                                   **MAP:** B1

Who can outshine a world-renowned museum like the Whitney? Danny Meyer can—especially when his trendy restaurant, Untitled, is housed on site. Located by the entry to the popular High Line, the stunning, modern restaurant is a work of art itself, with floor-to-ceiling windows, sleek red chairs, and a beautiful semi-open kitchen.

Talented Chef Suzanne Cupps oversees the operations here, and the results are anything but ordinary. Witness this vegetable-focused carte reveal the likes of marinated mussels with fava, yellow eye beans and edible flowers; or stradette tossed with broccoli rabe pesto, French beans, and mushrooms. Then throw caution to the wind and close out with a triple-layer peanut butter and blueberry crunch cake.

▨ 99 Gansevoort St. (at Washington St.)
🚇 14 St - 8 Av
✆ (212) 570-3670 — **WEB:** www.untitledatthewhitney.com
▨ Lunch & dinner daily                          **PRICE:** $$

# VIA CAROTA 🍴

*Italian*

XX | 🏠

**MAP:** C1

Occasionally, predictability can be a beautiful thing, especially when it comes to rave-worthy Italian cooking. Via Carota is not so much robotically perfect as it is pleasing—in fact it's the kind of place where dishes can (and should) be piled on. Italian style and artistry combine in this homey space that features bare wood farm tables, sideboards, and whitewashed brick. A no-reservations policy means long waits that are actually worth it, so join those lines.

Diners may start nibbling on deep-fried olives that are plump, piping hot, and stuffed with pork sausage. Then, a luscious (and unmissable) risotto cacio e pepe arrives loaded with pecorino and fresh pepper. For dessert, the simple-sounding flourless chocolate cake is downright excellent.

■ 51 Grove St. (bet. Bleecker St. & Seventh Ave. South)
🚇 Christopher St - Sheridan Sq
📞 (212) 255-1962 — **WEB:** www.viacarota.com
■ Lunch & dinner daily            **PRICE: $$**

# WALLFLOWER 🍴

*French*

XX | 🍹

**MAP:** B2

When a Daniel restaurant veteran opens a casual little cocktail lounge and dining room, the locals will come and never leave. Xavier Herit spent seven years as head bartender at the renowned spot, and his expertise clearly shows in the impressive wine list and complex cocktails—he even crafts a house-made pinot noir syrup for the Scotch-based Père Pinard.

The menu is a true deal in this neighborhood, especially with choices from the raw bar and charcuterie. For heartier fare, try the country pâté or rabbit terrine, both classically prepared and perfectly seasoned. Silky beef short ribs are deeply comforting, garnished with bacon, mushroom, cipollini, and just the right amount of brawny sauce. The coffee-chocolate pot de crème is deliciously intense.

■ 235 W. 12th St. (bet. Greenwich Ave. & W. 4th St.)
🚇 14 St (Seventh Ave.)
📞 (646) 682-9842 — **WEB:** www.wallflowernyc.com
■ Dinner nightly            **PRICE: $$**

# WALLSÉ ✿
*Austrian*

✕✕ | 🍇 🍹

Austrian cuisine is known for being hearty and immeasurably satisfying, but the great strength of Wallsé is that you don't have to have spent the day skiing in Innsbruck to appreciate its cooking because the adept kitchen has a lightness of touch and is not rigidly tied to tradition. There are some foods that just feel right at certain times of the year. When the nights draw in and there's a little chill in the air, there are certain words whose very presence on a menu summon feelings of comfort and warmth—and those words surely include spaetzle, schnitzel, and strudel.

Whether you've chosen the gamey and fork-tender venison cheek goulash or have gone for the tafelspitz, you'll find that the dishes here are harmonious, nicely balanced, easy to eat, and even easier to return to enjoy again and again.

The restaurant is divided into two rooms, both dominated by striking paintings that may even portray the chef himself. The clientele is a largely sophisticated bunch with an inherent understanding of how restaurants work which, in turn, creates an easy, relaxing atmosphere.

The wine list also merits examination, if only to discover there's more to Austrian wine than Grüner Veltliner.

■ 344 W. 11th St. (at Washington St.)
🚇 Christopher St - Sheridan Sq
✆ (212) 352-2300 — **WEB:** www.kurtgutenbrunner.com
■ Dinner Mon – Sat                                    PRICE: $$$

# THE WAVERLY INN 🍴○

*American*

XX | 🛋

Even a good chunk of years into its charmed existence, it's still the case that one feels very lucky to score a table at Graydon Carter's Waverly Inn—though it's not for the privilege of mixing with the A-List crowd so much as the absolutely outstanding food. Of course, the beautifully renovated 1844 townhouse plays a part too. It spent many of its interim years as a tavern, and its red leather booths, ornate fireplaces and lovely, ivy-covered atrium retain a certain sexy, speakeasy appeal.

Everything on the menu is truly sublime: a silky foie gras torchon arrives with bright, juicy melon and pine nut brittle; while creamy Dover sole is delicately browned in butter, then coated in a decadent Hollandaise and served with bright green haricots verts.

■ 16 Bank St. (at Waverly Pl.)

🚇 14 St - 8 Av

📞 (917) 828-1154 — **WEB:** www.waverlynyc.com

■ Lunch Sat – Sun   Dinner nightly

**PRICE: $$$$**

# ZZ'S CLAM BAR ❀
## Seafood

X | 🍸

**MAP:** C4

If you forget about your bank statement, don't arrive faint with hunger, and leave your cynicism at the door—you'll love ZZ's Clam Bar. With just four marble tables and a small counter, this is as intimate as it gets. But you first have to navigate the bouncer at the door who'll only allow admittance with a reservation. This at least ensures that, when you're inside this bijou spot, the door doesn't swing open every minute.

Once in, you're handed a cocktail list—these are, without doubt, some of the best in town and fully justify the lofty prices. The short seafood menu comes with a couple of choices under headings like "crudo," "seared" and "ceviche." Before you do anything else, order the trout roe on toast—it's a beautiful thing and will linger long in the memory.

This is not the place for everyone. Some won't see past some of the more pretentious elements and affectations and the prices can be eye-watering—the Chianina beef carpaccio comes in at over $100. However, judicious ordering before you plunge into the cocktails, like having clams instead of caviar, can at least keep your final bill from escalating too wildly. It also helps that the place is run with considerable charm, patience and care.

▪ 169 Thompson St. (bet. Bleecker & Houston Sts.)
▪ Spring St (Sixth Ave.)
📞 (212) 254-3000 — **WEB:** www.zzsclambar.com
▪ Dinner Tue – Sat  **PRICE: $$$$**

# HARLEM, MORNINGSIDE & WASHINGTON HEIGHTS

This upper Manhattan pocket is best known for its 1920s jazz clubs that put musicians like Charlie Parker and Miles Davis on the map. Home to Columbia University, this capital of African-American, Hispanic, and Caribbean culture lives up to its world-renowned reputation as an incubator of artistic and academic greats. Having officially cast off the age-old stigma of urban blight, these streets are now scattered with terrific soul food joints and authentic African markets that make Harlem a vibrant and enormously desired destination.

## MORNINGSIDE HEIGHTS

Considered an extension of the Upper West Side, park-lined Morningside Heights is frequented for its big and bold breakfasts. Inexpensive eateries are set between quaint brownstones and commercial buildings. When they're not darting to and from classes, resident scholars and ivy-leaguers from Columbia University can be found lounging at the **Hungarian Pastry Shop** with a sweet treat and cup of tea. Special occasions may call for an evening gathering at **Lee Lee's Baked Goods**. Rather

than be misled by its plain-Jane façade, prepare yourself for gratification here by way of the most delicious and decadent rugelach in town. When spring approaches, stroll out on to the terrace and enjoy an apricot-filled treat in the breeze.

## WEST HARLEM

**F**urther north lies Harlem, a sanctuary for the soul and stomach. Fifth Avenue divides this region into two very unique sections: West Harlem, a hub for African-American culture; and East Harlem, a pulsating Spanish district also referred to as "El Barrio." Beloved for its sass and edge, West Harlem is constantly making way for booming gentrification and socio-cultural evolution. One of its most visible borders is **Fairway**, a Tri-State area staple that draws shoppers of all stripes. Pick up one of their goodies to-go or simply savor them while sifting through the extensive literary collection over at the historic Schomburg Center for Research in Black Culture. When the sun sets over the Hudson River, find locals and savvy tourists slipping into

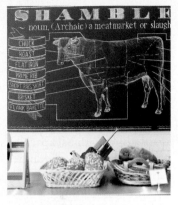

**Patisserie des Ambassades**, where a modern, chic décor does much to lure—for breakfast, lunch, and dinner. Not only do the aromas from fresh-baked croissants, *éclairs au chocolat*, and cream-filled beignets waft down the block, but they also ensure long lines at all times. Every August, **Harlem Week** brings the community together for art, music, and food. Join the fun and take in some of the most soulful tunes in town. Both east and west of Central Harlem, food has always factored heavily into everyday routine, and the choices are as varied as the neighborhood itself. From Mexican and Caribbean, to West African cuisine, there are rich culinary delights to be had. **Lolo's**

**Seafood Shack** cooks up Caribbean-infused steampots and serves them out of a counter; while **Manna's** on Frederick Douglass Boulevard attracts diners to its soul food steam table, where church groups rub shoulders and share stories with backpacking visitors. Fried food junkies fantasize over Chef Charles Gabriel's acclaimed buffet and amazing fried chicken at **Charles Country Pan Fried Chicken**, but for an evening at home, comb the shelves at **Harlem Shambles**, a true-blue butcher shop specializing in quality cuts of meat and poultry that serve to enhance every meal.

## EAST HARLEM

**O**ver in East Harlem, Spanish food enthusiasts and culture pundits never miss a trip to **Amor Cubano** for home-style faves. If smoked and piggy *lechón* served with a side of sultry, live Cuban beats isn't your idea of a good time, there's always that counter of divine Caribbean eats at **Sisters**; or juicy jerk chicken at **Winston & Tee Express Jerk Chicken**. Not pressed for time? Choose to scope the tempting taco truck and taqueria scene along "Little Mexico" on East 116th Street—otherwise known as the nucleus of New York City's Mexican communities.

**A**lmost like a vestige of the Italian population that was once dominant in this district, **Rao's** remains a culinary landmark. Operated from a poky basement and patronized by bigwigs like President Donald Trump or Nicole Kidman, it is one

of the city's most difficult tables to secure. The original benefactors have exclusive rights to a seat here and hand off reservations like rent-controlled apartments. But, rest assured as there is other enticing Italian to be enjoyed at **Patsy's Pizzeria**, another stronghold in East Harlem, famous for its hot coal oven (and occasionally its pizza). Of course **Hot Bread Kitchen**, a tenant of **La Marqueta marketplace**, continues to flourish for their global selection at both breakfast and lunch, and is reputed to be quite the holy haven among carb addicts.

## WASHINGTON HEIGHTS

**S**et along the northern reaches of Uptown, Washington Heights offers ample food choices along its steep streets. From Venezuelan food truck sensation **Patacon Pisao**, to restaurants like **Malecon** preparing authentic *morir soñando*, *mangu*, and *mofongo*, this colorful and lively neighborhood keeps dishing it out. In fact, the Tony award-winning musical *In The Heights* is a tribute to this ebullient district, where Dominican and Puerto Rican communities have taken root. Late-nighters never tire of the Latin beats blasting through the air here, after which a visit to Puerto Rican *piragua* carts selling shaved ice in a rainbow of tropical flavors seems not only nourishing, but also necessary. Locals queue up in lines around the block outside **Elsa La Reina del Chicharrón** for crunchy, deep-fried *chicharrónes*, after which palates may be quenched with *jugos naturales* or natural juices made from cane sugar and fresh fruit for a healthy treat. Hungry hordes can also be found ducking into **La Rosa Fine Foods** for a crowning meal featuring fish, meat, and vegetables. And if in need of some sweet after this abundant savory feast, **Carrot Top Pastries** continues to entice passersby with assorted cookies, colorful cakes, and deliciously moist sweet potato pies. First-rate fish markets and butcher shops also dot these hilly blocks, and less than ten bucks will get you a plate of traditional pernil with rice and beans at any number of diners nearby.

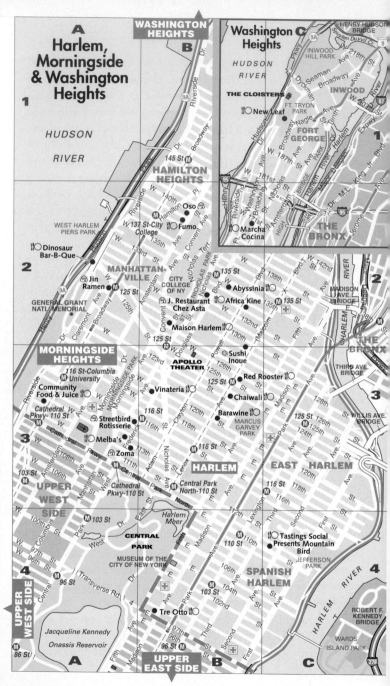

## A
# Harlem, Morningside & Washington Heights

**HUDSON**
**RIVER**

**WASHINGTON HEIGHTS**

## B

## Washington Heights

**HUDSON**
**RIVER**

THE CLOISTERS

¶○ New Leaf

INWOOD HILL PARK

INWOOD

FT. TRYON PARK

FORT GEORGE

THE BRONX

## C

HENRY HUDSON BRIDGE

¶○ Marcha Cocina

145 St
HAMILTON HEIGHTS

Oso ¶○
137 St-City College
¶○ Fumo

WEST HARLEM PIERS PARK

¶○ Dinosaur Bar-B-Que

MANHATTANVILLE

Jin Ramen
125 St

CITY COLLEGE OF NY

135 St

Abyssinia ¶○

Africa Kine ¶○

135 St

GENERAL GRANT NATL. MEMORIAL

J. Restaurant Chez Asta
125 St

Maison Harlem ¶○

MORNINGSIDE HEIGHTS

116 St-Columbia University

Community Food & Juice ¶○

Cathedral Pkwy-110 St

Streetbird Rotisserie

Melba's

Zoma

APOLLO THEATER

Vinateria ¶○

116 St

Sushi Inoue ○

125 St
Red Rooster ¶○

Chaiwali ○

Barawine ¶○

MARCUS GARVEY PARK

HARLEM

EAST HARLEM

THIRD AVE. BRIDGE

116 St

Central Park North-110 St

Harlem Meer

CENTRAL PARK

UPPER WEST SIDE

103 St

96 St

MUSEUM OF THE CITY OF NEW YORK

¶○ Tastings Social Presents Mountain Bird

JEFFERSON PARK

SPANISH HARLEM

ROBERT F. KENNEDY BRIDGE

WARDS ISLAND PARK

103 St

Tre Otto ¶○

96 St

86 St

Jacqueline Kennedy Onassis Reservoir

UPPER WEST SIDE

UPPER EAST SIDE

MADISON AVE. BRIDGE

THE BRONX

WILLIS AVE. BRIDGE

# ABYSSINIA 🍴○
## *Ethiopian*

🍴

Abyssinia's expansion couldn't be better timed, for the local Ethiopian population surrounding its Harlem location has grown by leaps and bounds in recent years. Expanded digs mean no one leaves hungry, including the gluten-intolerant diners lining up for the injera—a sourdough risen flatbread with a uniquely spongy texture that performs the task of cutlery, and is also ideal for sopping up all the amazing flavors from this authentic kitchen.

The dining room is spacious and flooded with natural light; the staff gracious; and the décor simple, clean and functional. This is essentially light, healthy, and spicy cooking, and the best way to experience it is to come with a group and order a slew of entrées to sample. Whatever you do, save room for the delicious slow-cooked beef awaze tibs.

■ 268 W. 135th St. (bet. Adam Clayton Powell Jr. & Frederick Douglass Blvds.)

🚇 135 St (St. Nicholas Ave.)

☏ (212) 281-2673 — **WEB:** www.harlemethiopianfood.com

■ Lunch & dinner daily

**PRICE:** 🍴

# AFRICA KINE 🍴○
## *Senegalese*

🍴

Following the closure of the original location a few years ago, fans of Senegalese cuisine are happy to see the return of this West Harlem café run by a pair of Dakar natives. A giant fork and spoon hanging on the wall are whimsical decorative accents in a room of pale yellow hues and faux marble-topped tables, where placemats double as menus displaying Africa Kine's myriad offerings.

Keep it simple with grilled fish or meat sided by salad, or opt for more succulent items such as peanut butter-enriched lamb mafe or suppa kandja (lamb and fish simmered in an okra and golden palm oil sauce). Note that some dishes are only available on certain nights, and although lunch is a more limited affair, Senegal's national treasure, thiebou djeun, is always on offer.

■ 2267 Seventh Ave. (bet. 133rd & 134th Sts.)

🚇 135 St (Lenox Ave.)

☏ (212) 666-9400 — **WEB:** www.africakine.com

■ Lunch & dinner daily

**PRICE:** 🍴

# BARAWINE Ꝣ○

## Contemporary

XX | 😂 🏠 🖎

**MAP:** B3

Amid the leafy, brownstone-lined Mount Morris Park Historic District, Barawine is an inviting dining room overseen by Fabrice Warin (formerly the sommelier at Orsay). This eye-catching space entices Lenox Avenue passersby to step in, sip and sup, either perched at the bar area's communal table or seated in the quieter, more intimate back dining room. Whitewashed walls attractively double as wine storage throughout.

The crowd-pleasing menu defies classification and embraces many influences. Quinoa salad with tofu and seaweed will please the disciplined, while mac and cheese loaded with béchamel, Gruyère, and diced ham calls out to more indulgent palates. Pan-seared branzino with aromatic herbs and a drizzle of balsamic is a treat for all.

- 200 Lenox Ave. (at 120th St.)
- 116 St (Lenox Ave.)
- (646) 756-4154 — **WEB:** www.barawine.com
- Lunch Sat – Sun   Dinner nightly

PRICE: $$

# CHAIWALI Ꝣ○

## Indian

XX | 🏠 ▭ 🖎

**MAP:** B3

A tea house in theory, Chaiwali's two-floor setting respects the cozy confines of a 19th-century brownstone that has been attractively renovated into an utterly unique locale by owner Anita Trehan. Metal lanterns complement exposed brick walls, a vivid mural adorns the second floor seating area, and the back garden is charmingly discreet. All in all, it's a striking space that adds some zest to Harlem's melting pot.

Indian flavors are reinterpreted here with an eye on contemporary tastes—read kale is prominently featured. Dinner brings more substantial food in mains like smoky mashed eggplant paired with warm, buttery paratha; or spice-dusted crunchy fish with okra "fries" and a streak of tomato-harissa sauce. A cup of the lushly fragrant chai is a must.

- 274 Lenox Ave. (bet. 123rd & 124th Sts.)
- 125 St (Lenox Ave.)
- (646) 688-5414 — **WEB:** www.chaiwali.com
- Lunch Fri – Sun   Dinner nightly

PRICE: $$

# COMMUNITY FOOD & JUICE 🍴○
## American

❌❌ | ♿ 🏠 🛏

**MAP:** A3

As part of Columbia University's sprawl, this address is a godsend for students, faculty, and locals from morning to night. Although it's spacious with plenty of outdoor options, the popular spot doesn't accept reservations—and has the lines to prove it. Executive Chef/partner Neil Kleinberg (also of downtown fave Clinton St. Baking Company) turns out joyful fare, and the weekly blueberry pancake special is just one reason why this place gets so much love.

For lunch, a kale salad with artichoke hearts, pickled carrots, and crispy chickpeas is anything but rote. Come dinnertime, the fish or steak of the day might reveal pan-seared mahi mahi with roasted cauliflower and black truffle beurre blanc, or grilled strip steak brushed with glistening teriyaki.

◾ 2893 Broadway (bet. 112th & 113th Sts.)
🚇 Cathedral Pkwy/110 St (Broadway)
☎ (212) 665-2800 — **WEB:** www.communityrestaurant.com
◾ Lunch & dinner daily                    **PRICE: $$**

# DINOSAUR BAR-B-QUE 🍴○
## Barbecue

❌ | ♿

**MAP:** A2

Huge, loud, and perpetually packed, this way west Harlem barbecue hall draws crowds from near and far. The bar area is rollicking, and for that reason kept separate from the dining quarters. There, wood beams and slats, swirling ceiling fans, and oxblood leather booths fashion a comfortable—and quieter—setting.

The scent of wood smoke wafting through the red brick structure (which coincidentally once served as a meatpacking warehouse) only heightens the diners' carnivorous cravings. Minimize decision making and order the Extreme Sampler: a heaping feast of apple cider-brined smoked chicken, dry-rubbed slow-smoked pork ribs, and lean Creekstone Farms brisket. Add on a creative side or two—perhaps the barbecue fried rice studded with bits of pulled pork?

◾ 700 W. 125th St. (at Twelfth Ave.)
🚇 125 St (Broadway)
☎ (212) 694-1777 — **WEB:** www.dinosaurbarbque.com
◾ Lunch & dinner daily                    **PRICE: $$**

# FUMO 🍴

*Italian*

✕✕ | 🛖 🛋️                                        **MAP:** B2

The setting at Fumo is undeniably chic, with bright white walls, light wood tables, and dark leather furnishings. A wood-fired pizza oven is in the back, while the front offers sidewalk seating under a protective awning. Attractive shelving lined with canned tomatoes frames the bar area and dining room.

The menu offers Italian favorites, executed with a deft hand and solid ingredients. Pizzas are 12-inches and come rosso or bianco, topped with the likes of vodka sauce, wild mushrooms, or charred vegetables. Excellent pastas, like the penne Caprese, are tossed with tomato sauce, fresh basil, and creamy mozzarella. A neatly deboned, beautifully seasoned branzino arrives subtly flavored with fresh herbs and alongside wilted spinach as well as a lemon wedge.

🔲 1600 Amsterdam Ave. (at 139th St.)
🔲 137 St - City College
☏ (646) 692-6675 — **WEB:** www.fumorestaurant.com
🔲 Lunch & dinner daily                       **PRICE:** $$

# JIN RAMEN 😊

*Japanese*

✕                                              **MAP:** A2

All you really need to know is that this is hands-down the best ramen above 59th Street. Sure, decorative elements are simple, and it hardly matters that this gem is hidden behind the 125th Street station's brick escalator. What comes from the kitchen however deserves kudos. The menu is concise but full of classics like pan-fried gyoza served with an addictive sesame seed-flecked dipping sauce. Shio, shoyu, and miso ramen are all delightful, but the tonkatsu ramen is a special treat. This piping-hot, almost creamy, mouthcoating distillation of pork bones is deliciously rich and stocked with fragrant chasu, pickled bamboo shoots, slivered green onion, and a soft-boiled egg.

For added fun, visit Kissaten Jin—an offshot serving homestyle bites and soba made by a master.

🔲 3183 Broadway (bet. 125th St. & Tiemann Pl.)
🔲 125 St (Broadway)
☏ (646) 559-2862 — **WEB:** www.jinramen.com
🔲 Lunch & dinner daily                       **PRICE:** 🍜

# J. RESTAURANT CHEZ ASTA 😊

*Senegalese*

✗ | &

Impressive in its authenticity, this Senegalese café is a rare bird in a neighborhood of vibrant dining choices. Meals here are exquisitely prepared and brim with unique flavors and scents, resulting in a truly transporting experience.

Spotless and comfy, the dining room offers a clutch of wood tables sturdy enough to support the heaping portions of chicken yassa or lemon-marinated chicken cooked with onions; as well as souloukhou, fish and vegetables in a peanut sauce. For a true taste of the country's flavors, go with the thiebou djeun, a one pot wonder of broken rice infused with tomato and Scotch bonnet pepper. It's cooked with fish, cabbage, okra, and cassava, and speckled with xóoñ (those crusty, toothsome bits scraped from the bottom of the pan).

■ 2479 Frederick Douglass Blvd. (bet. 132nd & 133rd Sts.)
■ 135 St (Frederick Douglass Blvd.)
☎ (212) 862-3663 — **WEB:** n/a
■ Lunch & dinner daily　　　　　　　　**PRICE:** ⬭⬭

# MAISON HARLEM 🍴

*French*

✗ | 🏠 ♿

A steady stream of locals, phone-toting tourists, and City College academics filling these well-worn wooden tables proves that this bistro has little trouble attracting a crowd. Floor-to-ceiling windows, dark red banquettes, and quirky touches like vintage Gallic posters or football jerseys tacked to the walls lend a whiff of whimsy.

Maison Harlem's menu plays around with culinary traditions, with results that may include a classic rendition of coq au vin with smoky lardons, browned button mushrooms, and fresh noodles to garnish the wine-braised chicken pieces. Sticking to tradition, ratatouille is a sunny bowlful of diced and stewed summer vegetables. The tarte Tatin layers thick but spoon-tender caramelized apple wedges over outrageously buttery pastry.

■ 341 St. Nicholas Ave. (at 127th St.)
■ 125 St (St. Nicholas Ave.)
☎ (212) 222-9224 — **WEB:** www.maisonharlem.com
■ Lunch & dinner daily　　　　　　　　**PRICE:** $$

# MARCHA COCINA ¶O

## *Latin American*

χ | ⟋

Colors evoke the Caribbean at Marcha, a narrow restaurant known for authentic Spanish tapas. A long bar dominates the sea-blue and sunny-yellow room filled with high tables and a convivial crowd. The music is a touch loud, but the service is refreshingly down-to-earth, and the food impresses beyond what its neighborhood bar-vibe might suggest.

The menu is broad and affordable, which makes a perfect excuse to sample widely. Staples from tender tortilla Española to gambas al ajillo are delicious executions of classic tapas. Ribbons of luscious Spanish ham are on handsome display in the hongos e higos coca, a chewy flatbread also topped with mushrooms, figs, and buttery almonds. It would be blasphemy to skip the dates wrapped in bacon or the thick-cut yucca fries.

- ■ 4055 Broadway (at 171st St.)
- ▣ 168 St
- ✆ (212) 928-8272 — **WEB:** www.marchanyc.com
- ■ Lunch Fri – Sun   Dinner nightly               **PRICE: $$**


# MELBA'S ¶O

## *Southern*

χ | ⟋

With its colorful spirit and lineup of Southern classics, this comfortable spot—as charming and lovely as its namesake owner, born-and-bred Harlemite Melba Wilson—is a perfect reflection of the neighborhood's flavor, culture, and past. It's a place to gather and relax over good food and drinks, from Auntie B's mini-burgers slathered with a smoky sweet sauce to a golden-brown and berry-licious fruit cobbler that's nothing short of heaven on a plate.

Equally enticing is the Southern fried chicken—darkly bronzed, sweet and salty when paired with Melba's iconic eggnog waffles.

Expect other surprises like spring rolls stuffed with black-eyed peas, collards, and cheddar cheese, as well as a healthy minded grilled vegetable Napoleon with buffalo mozzarella.

- ■ 300 W. 114th St. (at Frederick Douglass Blvd.)
- ▣ 116 St (Frederick Douglass Blvd.)
- ✆ (212) 864-7777 — **WEB:** www.melbasrestaurant.com
- ■ Lunch Sat-Sun   Dinner nightly           **PRICE: $$**

# NEW LEAF ⅙○

*American*

✗✗ | ⅃ 🏠 ⌂

Talk about wowing your dinner date. Located in a 1930's slate and fieldstone cottage tucked away in Upper Manhattan's Fort Tryon Park, New Leaf Café was opened as part of the New York Restoration Project. With its stone walls and arched windows, the interior is just lovely. And lunch out on the flagstone terrace is downright stunning—offering unparalleled views of the dramatic Palisades and (if you squint a bit) the George Washington Bridge.

Delicious and modern American food is the name of the game at this kitchen. The menu touches on some usual crowd favorites (think juicy burgers and soft beignets) along with trendy, veggie-based items like avocado smeared on toasted crostini; a bowl of greens and grains; and a falafel burger.

■ 1 Margaret Corbin Dr. (in Fort Tryon Park)
🚇 190 St
✆ (212) 568-5323 — **WEB:** www.newleafrestaurant.com
■ Lunch daily  Dinner Tue – Sun                **PRICE: $$**

# OSO 😊

*Mexican*

✗ | 🏠 ⌂

This chic little Mexican restaurant, whose name means "bear" in Spanish, sits opposite the City College of New York. The charming space is dressed in wood tables, warm lighting, and a Dia de los Muertos mural gracing a corner. One black-tiled dining counter is lined with vintage white metal stools, while another small bar faces the tidy open kitchen where the cooks hand-make tortillas at a steady clip.

The cuisine of Mexico City inspires Oso's menu with a concise, impressive offering of dishes like braised octopus tostada with mandarin salsa, guava- and chipotle-glazed ribs, as well as authentic tacos and antojitos. Come summer, don't miss the wonderful radish salad, served warm with fresh cilantro, serrano peppers, anchovies, and tomato vinaigrette.

■ 1618 Amsterdam Ave. (bet. 139th & 140th Sts.)
🚇 137 St - City College
✆ (646) 858-3139 — **WEB:** www.osoharlem.com
■ Lunch & dinner daily                **PRICE: $$**

# RED ROOSTER 🍴○

*American*

✗✗ | ⚕ 🎐 ⬡ 🛋

**MAP:** B3

So many things make Red Rooster special, not the least of which is Chef Marcus Samuelsson, whose head-spinning achievements include inventive world-renowned cooking, penning cookbooks, and bringing the New Harlem Renaissance to Lenox Avenue. Downstairs, find live music at Ginny's Supper Club. Up front, The Nook serves sweets and sandwiches to-go. And in the center, Red Rooster celebrates Harlem, the African-American diaspora, and great food.

Start with a brilliantly simple wedge of crumbly and buttery corn bread. Then, move on to the likes of highly spiced and "dirty" basmati rice with sweet shrimp and swirls of lemon aïoli; or try their interpretation of South African "bunny chow" served as lamb stew on a sesame bun with a fried egg and fresh ricotta.

■ 310 Lenox Ave. (bet. 125 & 126th Sts.)
🚇 125 St (Lenox Ave.)
✆ (212) 792-9001 — **WEB:** www.redroosterharlem.com
■ Lunch & dinner daily                     PRICE: $$$

# STREETBIRD ROTISSERIE 😬

*Fusion*

✗ | 🛋

**MAP:** A3

Chef Marcus Samuelsson's latest Harlem hot spot is a funky corner devoted to slow-roasted chicken and old-school street-style. Wade through the boisterous, rum punch-fueled crowd and enter this party to find splashes of custom graffiti, eye-popping murals, and lighting fixtures made from cassette tapes, drum sets, and bicycle tires.

Despite this sensory overload, it is impossible not to notice the plump, auburn birds spinning in the glass-fronted oven. Tender, juicy, and exceptionally flavorful, they steal the show and are supported by the chef's signature mash-up of global flavors: green papaya salad, jasmine fried rice, and cornbread. Not feeling the poultry? Opt for the spicy piri-piri catfish with crispy shallots and avocado.

■ 2149 Frederick Douglass Blvd. (at 116th St.)
🚇 116 St (Frederick Douglass Blvd.)
✆ (212) 206-2557 — **WEB:** www.streetbirdnyc.com
■ Lunch & dinner daily                     PRICE: $$

# SUSHI INOUE ❁

*Japanese*

✗✗

**MAP:** B3

For truly outstanding sushi, head to the heart of Harlem, where Chef Shinichi Inoue—formerly of Sushi Azabu—presides over this discreet and unexpected addition to the neighborhood.

Inside the small establishment, bamboo blinds obscuring the scene outside, combined with hushed and genuine hospitality produce a sense of calm and refinement. The Nagasaki-born chef works behind a display of sparkling fillets and a dark counter arranged with 14 washi placemats and sets of lacquered chopsticks. It is here that a concise list of omakase options is prepared increasing in price with the additions of tempura, sashimi and an uni tasting.

Chef Inoue personally looks after every detail of the meal—from the blended soy sauce to the house miso recipe. Pickled ginger placed on your tray ushers in the expertly crafted nigiri, and while the grated wasabi root that sparks most pieces can be a bit aggressive at times, the procession is rather delightful. Highlights include a bite of buttery shima aji from Kyushu island; shiro ika dressed with salt and sudachi; soy-marinated tuna with mustard and toasted sesame seeds; and fatty tuna from Boston—one of the rare pieces not from Japanese waters.

■ 381 Lenox Ave. (at 129th St.)

🚇 125 St (Lenox Ave.)

✆ (646) 766-0555 — **WEB:** www.sushiinoue.com

■ Dinner Tue – Sun

**PRICE:** $$$$

# TASTINGS SOCIAL PRESENTS MOUNTAIN BIRD 🍴

## Contemporary

XX | 🍷　　　　　　　　　　　　　　　**MAP:** C4

The inspiration for Chef Kenichi Tajima and wife Keiko's popular venture no doubt sprung from the popularity of their initial and well-loved incarnation of Mountain Bird. It's clear they were missed, as this hot spot in collaboration with the events organization Tastings Social, stays hopping most nights.

This area has wanted for serious food for a while, and Mountain Bird brings it with style—the dining space, tucked into the ground floor of a red rowhouse, is intimate with a small bar and a smattering of wood tables. As the name implies, the menu bears a whimsical devotion to poultry, featuring dishes like hand-cut ostrich tartare; black truffle chicken wings and duck leg-and-turkey sausage cassoulet; along with a nightly seafood and vegetarian option.

　■　251 E. 110th St. (bet. Second & Third Aves.)
　■　110 St (Lexington Ave.)
　✆　(212) 744-4422 — **WEB:** www.tastingsnyc.com
　■　Lunch Sun　Dinner Tue – Sun　　　　　**PRICE:** $$

# TRE OTTO 🍴

## Italian

XX　　　　　　　　　　　　　　　**MAP:** B4

East Harlem's favorite neighborhood trattoria has triumphantly returned following a move next door. Thanks to proprietors Louis and Lauren Cangiano, the popular surrounds—complete with cheery red walls, exposed brick, and penny-tile floors—are as cozy and welcoming as ever.

Tre Otto's mouthwatering menu boasts home-style dishes made from recipes gathered over time. Antipasti include a luscious salad of shaved fennel and orange segments crowned by tender grilled octopus drizzled with zesty salmoriglio sauce. Freshly made trenette pasta is twirled with pesto Trapanese, a divinely rich combination of tomatoes, almonds, garlic, and basil; while the flavors of pizza, topped with red onions, capers, and tuna, call Sicily's sparkling coastline to mind.

　■　1410 Madison Ave. (bet. 97th & 98th Sts.)
　■　96 St (Lexington Ave.)
　✆　(212) 860-8880 — **WEB:** www.treotto.com
　■　Lunch & dinner daily　　　　　　　**PRICE:** $$

# VINATERÍA 🍴⚪

*Italian*

✕✕ | 🚻 🛶                                          **MAP:** B3

Adding to Harlem and its hidden charms is Vinatería, an Italian darling brimming with wines to accompany each sublime bite. Not only is it cozy, but the attractive slate-toned room etched in chalk with scenes of decanters and menu specials will augment your appetite.

The semi-open kitchen in the back unveils such treasures as house-cured sardines with fiery piquillo peppers and crunchy croutons; or a salad of earthy golden and red beets mingled with yogurt, oranges, arugula, crunchy pistachios, and tossed with a lemon vinaigrette. Herbs plucked from their copper planters may be featured in an impeccably grilled rosemary-marinated pork blade served with rich mashed potatoes; or desserts like citrus-glazed rosemary panna cotta bathed in chamomile grappa.

◾ 2211 Frederick Douglass Blvd. (at 119th St.)
🚇 116 St (Frederick Douglass Blvd.)
📞 (212) 662-8462 — **WEB:** www.vinaterianyc.com
◾ Lunch Sat – Sun   Dinner nightly                **PRICE: $$**

# ZOMA 😊

*Ethiopian*

✕ | 🚻                                              **MAP:** A3

Smart, cool, modern, and always welcoming, Zoma may well be this city's most serious Ethiopian restaurant. The crowded bar emits a golden light from below to showcase its premium spirits, and the ambient dining room is filled with locals from this thriving community.

Attention to detail is clear from the steaming hot towel for cleaning your hands to the carefully folded injera used for scooping up their chopped salads, chunky stews, and saucy vegetables. Unusual starters might include green lentils with a cold and crunchy mix of onions, jalapeños, ginger, white pepper, and mustard seeds. The doro watt—a chicken dish of the Amhara people—is a very traditional stew with a berbere sauce of sun-dried hot peppers and ground spices.

◾ 2084 Frederick Douglass Blvd. (at 113th St.)
🚇 116 St (Frederick Douglass Blvd.)
📞 (212) 662-0620 — **WEB:** www.zomanyc.com
◾ Lunch Sat – Sun   Dinner nightly                **PRICE:** 🍲

# LOWER EAST SIDE

The Lower East Side is one of New York City's most energetic, stylish, and fast-evolving neighborhoods. Bragging a plethora of shopping, eating, and nightlife, this high-energy hub proudly retains the personality of its first wave of hard-working immigrants. But, thanks to a steady stream of artists and entrepreneurs over the last few decades, as well as a real estate uprising, the area faces constant transformation, with an influx of high-rises breaking through trendy boutiques and galleries. And yet, some nooks remain straight-up dodgy as if in defiance of such rapid development; while others feel downright Village-like, in stature and spirit.

## AROUND THE WORLD

Visit the Lower East Side Tenement Museum for a glimpse of the past before trekking its enticing, ethnically diverse streets. Then for a

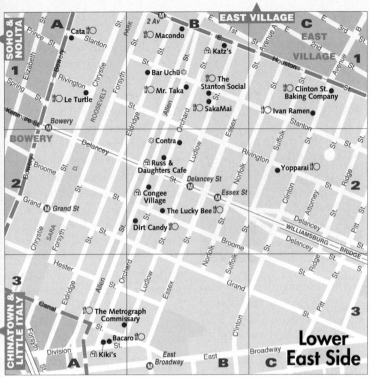

taste of yore, traipse into **Russ & Daughters** for appetizing tidbits including smoked, cured fish and hearty bagels. This nosher's delight was instituted in 1914 but continues to be mobbed even today, especially during the holidays when that "ultimate salmon and caviar" package is nothing short of...you guessed it...ultimate! Also inhabiting these streets are German, Italian, and Chinese residents, whose opposite

cultures have triggered a host of deliciously varied eats and treats. Find signs of this at **Nonna's LES Pizza** where the red, white, and green squares are known to tug at all the right nostalgic strings. **Palà**, which boasts a vast list of gluten-free and vegan selections, is not far behind with homesick hordes craving a host of heartwarming pies. Meanwhile, an afternoon spent at **Gaia Italian Cafè** breezing through magazines

and biting into delicious *dolci* or perfect biscotti will take you back to Rome on a dime. This toasty spot may be mini in size, but cooks up flavors that are bold and bright. **Tiny's Giant Sandwich Shop** is yet another unpretentious but wholly irresistible gem where sandwiches rule the roost and are slung at all times. Ground zero for partygoers, punk rockers, and scholars, this Rivington Street paragon is a rare find, highlighting fresh ingredients and creative presentations. While on the topic of a spirited scene, **New Beer Distributors** is a warehouse-y beer shop in operation since 1968. Housing numerous bottles and cans from the globe over, craft beer aficionados will adore perusing its metal racks for unique (read exotic) varietals. Then, if sweet is what you need, **Economy Candy** is a flourishing emporium of old-time confections. Moving from one timeless pleasure to another are two very different takes on one nostalgic treat. **Morgenstern's Finest Ice Cream** bills itself as a New American ice cream parlor, while **Ice & Vice** boasts highly experimental flavors. Try a scoop of the "opium den" or a pint of smoked dark chocolate as further proof.

## ETHNIC FUN

**B**y the 1950s, the ethnic mosaic that defined this district intensified with a surge of new settlers, but this time they were mainly from Puerto Rico and the Dominican Republic. These communities continue to dot the culinary landscape today, so come to savor such favorites as *mofongo* or *pernil*. Dominican *especiales* and creamy *café con leche* at **El Castillo de Jagua** keep the party pumping from dawn till dusk, while sugar junkies find their fix at **Tache Artisan**

**Chocolate**—launched by pastry chef, Aditi Malhotra. Sample the tequila-infused dark chocolate ganache, which may last just a moment in your mouth, but promises to leave an impression that will remain for a lifetime. Rivington Street is a perfect hybrid of the Old World and New Order. During the day, the mood here is chill with locals who like to linger at cozy coffee houses. Come sunset, these streets start to fill with raucous carousers looking to land upon a scene-y restaurant or popular party spot. Further south, Grand Street is home to well-manicured residential complexes scattered amid shops and catering to a cadre of deep-rooted residents. While here, carb-addicts should be afraid, very afraid, of **Kossar's Bialys** flooded with bagels, babkas, and of course, bialys. Then there's **Doughnut Plant** proffering inventive offerings crafted from age-old recipes. To replicate that classic deli experience at home, pick up pickles to-go from **The Pickle Guys**—settled on Grand Street and stocked with barrel-upon-barrel of these briny treats.

**F**ire escape-fronted Orchard Street is venerated as the original hub of the 'hood. Once dominated by the

resource for three square meals. Of course, it's packed to the rafters during peak hours, so shoppers looking to cool their heels may drop by **il laboratorio del gelato**, located on Ludlow.

## ESSEX STREET MARKET

Every self-respecting foodie makes the pilgrimage to **Essex Street Market**, a treasure trove of gourmet food. Frequented for its top produce merchants, butchers, bakers, and fishmongers all housed under one roof, this public bazaar expounds on their expertise by way of cooking demonstrations and wine tastings that keep crowds coming back. Burned-out browsers however may rest their feet and calm a craving at **Essex** or even **Shopsin's General Store** known for an encyclopedic carte (and cranky owner). Finally, everything from okonomiyaki (at **Osaka Grub**); rice balls (at **Arancini Bros**); or cheese (at **Saxelby Cheesemongers**) make this pleasure palace an enticing destination for gastronomes and curious palates alike.

garment trade with stores selling fabrics and notions, it tells a different tale today with sleek eateries set amid trendy boutiques selling handmade jewelry and designer skateboards. Even tailors remain a cult favorite here, offering cheap, while-you-wait service. At lunchtime, you may find them along with a horde of hungry locals chowing down on mojo beef paratha tacos at Indian fusion hot spot, **Goa Taco**. Concurrently, **Dimes** (the café that exudes Cali-cool on Canal Street) is a reliable

# BACARO ¶IO
*Italian*

X | ☐

Heavy iron candelabras, crumbling stone walls, and communal wooden tables lend a sultry vibe to this underground labyrinth, named for a Venetian bacaro (or counter for casual grazing of snacks and wine). The first floor's marble-topped bar beckons for small bites and a glass of wine, while nooks beneath those low stone ceilings in the downstairs dining room call for a romantic evening over candlelight.

Crafted by Frank DeCarlo, the same chef/owner of Peasant in NoLita, Bacaro's menu highlights the best of Venetian cuisine. Bigoli con sugo d'anatra brings together whole-wheat pasta with tender, pulled duck, a tomato-cream sauce, and shavings of salty parmesan. For dessert, the velvety flourless chocolate cake topped with dried apricots, is as decadent as the setting.

■ 136 Division St. (bet. Ludlow & Orchard Sts.)
🚇 East Broadway
✆ (212) 941-5060 — **WEB:** www.bacaronyc.com
■ Dinner Tue – Sun                                    **PRICE: $$**

# CATA ¶IO
*Spanish*

X | 🍸 ♿

Blue plaid and jean-clad waiters set the casual tone for Cata, a downtown-cool restaurant with a long bar and glass case displaying the day's seafood. Distressed mirrors, vaulted ceilings, and iron accents fill the dark, cavernous space with a certain broody, old-world vibe. Long communal tables are ideal for groups lingering over small plates and an extensive list of gin-based cocktails.

Nibbling should be the strategy here, starting with whole deviled eggs stuffed with tangy-sweet gribiche beneath a single fried oyster. Crispy bite-sized bombas filled with potato, Manchego, and Serrano sit in a nice, mildly spicy tomato sauce. And caramelized torrija with sorbet is likely to be one of the most enjoyable versions of French toast that you've ever had.

■ 245 Bowery (at Stanton St.)
🚇 2 Av
✆ (212) 505-2282 — **WEB:** www.catarestaurant.com
■ Dinner nightly                                      **PRICE: $$**

# BAR UCHŪ ✿

*Contemporary*

XX | 🍇 🍹 🍶

This unexpected culinary diamond lies hidden behind a blonde wood door and right beside a graffiti-covered playground—its only sign is written in Japanese characters. It all feels very LES at Bar Uchū's kaiseki counter. Once inside, the elegance is unmistakable, starting with the warm towels that begin your meal to the paté de fruits that end it.

The intricate beverage program is central to dining here, thoughtfully planned right down to the coasters. There is no open kitchen, but the prime seats are at the bar, where the entertaining bartenders are hand-shaving ice, pouring superb Japanese whiskeys, and filling coups with smoke. Of course, the foremost reason to dine here is for the exceptional kaiseki-style menu.

Behind the kitchen's closed doors, Chef Samuel Clonts has emerged into this spotlight, straight from his training at Chef's Table at Brooklyn Fare. The cuisine is heavily influenced by Japanese craftsmanship and incorporates a host of ingredients, many of which are grown in their rooftop garden. Luxe highlights include a Siberian sturgeon caviar handroll, Miyazaki Wagyu beef, and Hokkaido uni. Finales also astound by way of a soufflé with warm roasted strawberries and matcha ice cream.

■ 217 Eldridge St. (bet. Rivington & Stanton Sts.)
🚇 2 Av
☏ (212) 203-7634 — **WEB:** www.uchu.nyc
■ Dinner Tue – Sat                      **PRICE: $$$$**

# CLINTON ST. BAKING COMPANY ⅔○

*American*

✗ | 🍽 | 🗄 | ⑤          **MAP:** C1

Having finally expanded to include the space next door, the comfort level and service of this brunch-focused bijou has greatly improved. And what started as a bakery is now a legend—one that draws a perpetual crowd waiting for ample rewards. A little bit country and a little bit food lab, this kitchen has achieved such success in NY that the owners now have outposts in Japan and Dubai.

Breakfast for dinner is always a treat, especially when golden-brown Belgian waffles are served with warm maple butter and topped with buttermilk-brined fried chicken for a flawless marriage of sweet and savory. Lighter but still lovely, chicken tortilla soup sees a pile of crunchy fried tortilla strips over hearty broth bobbing with carrots, celery, and shredded chicken.

◾ 4 Clinton St. (at Houston St.)

🚇 2 Av

✆ (646) 602-6263 — **WEB:** www.clintonstreetbaking.com

◾ Lunch daily   Dinner Mon – Sat      **PRICE:** ⊜

# CONGEE VILLAGE 😊

*Chinese*

✗ | 🍴          **MAP:** B2

From the edge of Chinatown comes Congee Village, with its neon-etched sign that shines bright at night. Coveted for its fantastic cooking (check the front window for a slew of accolades), the menu also has a Cantonese focus. Service is basic and the décor kitschy at best, but it's clean, tidy, and tons of fun.

This soothing namesake porridge comes in myriad forms— ladled into a clay pot with bits of crispy roasted duck skin, or mingled with pork liver and white fish to form an intense and rich flavor combination. Pair it with dunkable sticks of puffy deep-fried Chinese crullers for a satisfying contrast in texture. Less adventurous palates may deviate into such solid standards as sautéed short ribs and sweet onions tossed in a smoky black pepper sauce.

◾ 100 Allen St. (bet. Broome & Delancey Sts.)

🚇 Delancey St

✆ (212) 941-1818 — **WEB:** www.congeevillagerestaurants.com

◾ Lunch & dinner daily      **PRICE:** ⊜

# CONTRA ✿

*Contemporary*

✖✖

Minimal, industrial, and in harmony with the cool neighborhood, this is the kind of classic downtown spot that draws trendy millennials from afar. Seating is either intimate or cramped, and the music is lively or loud, all depending on your mood. Enthusiastic servers add to the room's energy.

Offering six courses for under $75, their prix-fixe is renowned not just for its ambition and creativity but also as one of the best values in town. While the menu format may be fixed, dishes change frequently to reflect the young chefs' wide-ranging talents and contemporary flair. The hallmarks of this kitchen are clean flavors and unfussy technique, as in raw shrimp shimmering with brown butter, served with tardivo di Treviso, matcha powder, pink grapefruit, and strips of pickled radish. Then, thin slices of trumpet mushrooms served over a brunoise of Asian pear are accompanied by cilantro and dill in a citrusy lemongrass broth, for perfect balance of flavor and texture. Impressive skill is behind the visual appeal in the fluke fillet, beautifully cooked and set in a creamy pool of almond broth with golden tomato segments.

A few doors down, sibling Wildair serves natural wines with signature snacks.

▪ 138 Orchard St. (bet. Delancey & Rivington Sts.)

▣ 2 Av

✆ (212) 466-4633 — **WEB:** www.contranyc.com

▪ Dinner Tue – Sat                              PRICE: $$$

# DIRT CANDY 🍴

*Vegetarian*

✕✕ | 🍸 ♿ 🛋

**MAP:** B2

East Village foodies and health nuts can't seem to get enough of this culinarily nourishing vegetarian temple. Chef Amanda Cohen and team have comfortably settled into their bigger and bolder digs, where industrial elements meld with white walls and the chic bar proffers both cocktails and consolation seating. Sound too good to be true? It isn't.

Dirt Candy's menu is best described as a bounty of creativity, with options like "Fennel," a hearty salad of raw and pickled shavings with black bean cake and caramelized yogurt spread carta di musica; as well as "Carrots," the orange veggies roasted with jerk spices and served over a carrot waffle with peanut mole sauce. Desserts are every bit as inspired, like a chocolate tart peppered with caramelized onions.

◼ 86 Allen St. (bet. Broome & Grand Sts.)
🚇 Grand St
📞 (212) 228-7732 — **WEB:** www.dirtcandynyc.com
◼ Lunch Sat – Sun   Dinner Tue – Sat          **PRICE:** $$

# IVAN RAMEN 🍴

*Japanese*

✕ | 🍧

**MAP:** C1

This delicious little ramen-ya couldn't have landed on a more fitting spot. It may appear rough around the edges, but the ultra-hip 'hood and its affinity for indie rock beats fit Ivan's scene to a tee. Then consider their sweet staff gliding within the snug space filled with packed seats, and realize how serious a treat this is. Solo diners head to the counter for a view of the action-packed kitchen, while others look for a seat from which to admire that mural of manga cutouts. Find them launching into pickled daikon with XO sauce and sesame seeds for a 'lil crunch and whole 'lotta flavor. Displaying a flare for non-traditional ingredients, paitan ramen with tender chicken confit in a chicken-and-kombu broth makes for a singular, savory, and tasty highlight.

◼ 25 Clinton St. (bet. Houston & Stanton Sts.)
🚇 Delancey St
📞 (646) 678-3859 — **WEB:** www.ivanramen.com
◼ Lunch & dinner daily                        **PRICE:** $$

# KATZ'S 😊
*Deli*

🍴 | 🍳

One of the last-standing, old-time Eastern European spots on the Lower East Side, Katz's is a true NY institution. It's crowded, crazy, and packed with a panoply of characters weirder than a jury duty pool. Tourists, hipsters, blue hairs, and everybody in between flock here, so come on off-hours. Because it's really that good.

Walk inside, get a ticket, and don't lose it (those guys at the front aren't hosts—upset their system and you'll get a verbal beating). Then pick up your food at the counter and bring it to a first-come first-get table; or opt for a slightly less dizzying experience at a waitress-served table.

Nothing's changed in the looks or taste. Matzo ball soup, pastrami sandwiches, potato latkes—everything is what you'd expect, only better.

🔲 205 E. Houston St. (at Ludlow St.)

🚇 2 Av

☎ (212) 254-2246 — **WEB:** www.katzsdelicatessen.com

🔲 Lunch & dinner daily      **PRICE:** 🍝

# KIKI'S 😊
*Greek*

🍴

This is where to find excellent home-style Greek cooking at unbeatable prices. Everything tastes fundamentally right and good, from the perfectly tender braised and grilled octopus to those moist and smoky lamb chops—the aromas alone guarantee that you will dine well here. Start with a superb spanakopita that balances flaky filo with just the right amount of chopped spinach, dotted with onion and feta. Saganaki entices with salty and springy Greek cheese wrapped in filo that manages to stay crisp beneath a rich drenching of honey and sesame seeds.

The tavern-like space feels attractively dark, cozy, fills up quickly, and doesn't take reservations so expect a wait. The servers and staff are a stylish and laid-back mirror image of the neighborhood.

🔲 130 Division St. (at Orchard St.)

🚇 East Broadway

☎ (646) 882-7052 — **WEB:** N/A

🔲 Lunch & dinner daily      **PRICE:** $$

# LE TURTLE ⅋○
## Contemporary

X

**MAP:** A1

Experience and style converge at this beautiful destination and instant favorite of the cool kids in town. The cuisine is not only as attractive as the setting, but sophisticated flavors ensure its success. Kohlrabi bisque is deliciously creamy, with ambitious garnishes like smoked cabbage, pickled mustard seeds, and bits of intensely rich lamb belly to make it savory and very memorable. Straightforward skill is clear in the scored curls of squid served with a refreshing salsa verde, embellished with oroblanco. Every flavor is perfectly complementary in the dense and buttery hazelnut financier, from the chewy caramelized edges to the quenelles of lemon yogurt sorbet and pear purée.

A moderately priced list showcases unique and interesting French wines.

■ 177 Chrystie St. (at Rivington St.)
🚇 Bowery
✆ (646) 918-7189 — **WEB:** www.leturtle.fr
■ Dinner nightly                    **PRICE:** $$

# THE LUCKY BEE ⅋○
## Asian

X | 🥢

**MAP:** B2

This inviting Southeast Asian-inspired restaurant is housed in a quirky retro space accented by bold prints and neon lights. It's a small restaurant, but it practically pulsates with energy. Cocktails are made with local honey to support the NYC Bee Keepers Association, as fun 70s music plays loudly overhead.

Tuck into tender pork and sesame dumplings drizzled with a sharp black vinegar reduction, fermented black beans, and sesame seeds. Or try a bowl of glistening duck larb tossed with mint, basil and raw onions for a crunchy surprise. Don't miss Thai specialties like khao soi, a Northern Thai noodle curry with chicken, pickled mustard greens and a nest of fried noodles in rich coconut broth; or coconut-braised short rib with an excellent green curry.

■ 252 Broome St. (bet. Ludlow & Orchard Sts.)
🚇 Delancey St
✆ (844) 364-4286 — **WEB:** www.luckybeenyc.com
■ Lunch & dinner daily              **PRICE:** $$

# MACONDO ⚟

## Latin American

✗✗ | ⌂

Readers of Gabriel Garcia Marquez will be familiar with this Latin American restaurant's name—Macondo is the fictional setting of 100 Years of Solitude. Here on the Lower East Side (and at the West Village outpost), it is an intimate small plates restaurant with a long bar of counter seating, semi-open kitchen, and exposed brick walls with stocked shelves of Latin pantry ingredients.

Sharing is the strategy here, from the crispy chicken croquettes to the raw kale and manchego salad with crunchy roasted pumpkin seeds and a sweet kick from sticky dried dates, topped with a lemon-chipotle dressing. Be prepared to battle over the last bite of arroz con pollo, a piping-hot cast-iron pan of plump bomba rice, piquant chorizo, tender chicken, and cherry tomatoes.

◾ 157 E. Houston St. (bet. Allen & Eldridge Sts.)
🚇 2 Av
✆ (212) 473-9900 — **WEB:** www.macondonyc.com
◾ Lunch Sat – Sun   Dinner nightly                    **PRICE: $$**

# THE METROGRAPH COMMISSARY ⚟

## American

✗✗ | ⌂

Located on the second floor of The Metrograph theater—a small, independent two-screen movie house in the Lower East Side—The Commisary channels an old Hollywood vibe. Picture retro furniture, potted palms, and plenty of cozy nooks to relax in. The food is simple but sophisticated for the neighborhood, offering a lovely American slant on bistro fare. Even the concessions downstairs are worth perusing for their unusual selection.

The menu is brief but tempting, with small plates of steak tartare, fluke crudo and burrata getting play next to classic salads (think Waldorf and kale Caesars), as well as pleasing entrées like roasted chicken, steak frites and brown butter trout. Comforting sides like mac-and-cheese and steamed broccoli make it a truly American affair.

◾ 7 Ludlow St. (bet. Canal & Hester Sts.)
🚇 East Broadway
✆ (347) 348-0617 — **WEB:** www.metrograph.com
◾ Lunch & dinner daily                                **PRICE: $$**

# MR. TAKA 🍴

*Japanese*

🍴

When the chef of a successful Tokyo ramen-ya opens a spot in NY, success is virtually guaranteed. Mr. Taka may seem small and simple, but the food is fun and distinctive.

The cooking here is a delicious break from tradition, thanks to ramen that ranges in toppings from avocado to the richest slice of pork belly on this side of the Pacific. Of course, all of these garnishes depend on the broth—the spicy miso ramen is made with chicken and bonito, wafting with aromas that are at once spicy, savory, and sweet. These thick ribbons of noodles have a springy, bouncy texture that is never lost within the mounds of bean sprouts, scallions, soft-boiled egg, and much more. Other highlights include a crunchy hijiki salad and piping-hot batons of deep purple sweet potato tempura.

🔲 170 Allen St. (bet. Stanton & Rivington Sts.)
🚇 2 Av
📞 (212) 254-1508 — **WEB:** www.mrtakaramen.com
🔲 Lunch & dinner daily                         PRICE: $$

# RUSS & DAUGHTERS CAFE 😋

*Deli*

XX | 🍴 🛋

From white-jacketed servers to that pristine counter, this updated yet model LES café channels the very spirit and charm of its mothership, set only blocks away. The adept kitchen follows suit, taking the original, appetizing classics and turning them on their heads to form an array of proper and profoundly flavorful dishes.

Regulars perch at the bar to watch the 'tender whip up a cocktail or classic egg cream, while serious diners find a seat and get noshing on hot- and cold-smoked Scottish salmon teamed with everything-bagel chips. The result? A thrilling contrast in flavor and texture. Caramelized chocolate babka French toast is crowned with strawberries for a sweet-savory treat; and "eggs Benny" with salmon, spinach, and challah never fails to peg a bruncher.

🔲 127 Orchard St. (bet. Delancey & Rivington Sts.)
🚇 Delancey St
📞 (212) 475-4881 — **WEB:** www.russanddaughterscafe.com
🔲 Lunch & dinner daily                         PRICE: $$

# SAKAMAI ¶⃝

*Japanese*

XX | 🍶 🍴

MAP: B1

Nestled smack in the middle of the Lower East Side's nightlife hub, this stylish Japanese gastro lounge is a must-do for the adventurous eater. SakaMai's wheelhouse is transforming highbrow ingredients (maybe foie gras, Wagyu beef, luscious uni and caviar) into delicious small plates that pair exceptionally with their formidable Japanese liquor and sake list.

The menu is arranged into a collection of interesting, izakaya-style, shared plates, but there is a $65 tasting menu available as well for those with serious appetites. Dishes often blend Japanese technique with non-traditional ingredients like radicchio or parmesan. Don't miss the yakisaba—box-pressed nigiri topped with smoky, grilled mackerel, crispy lardo Ibérico, and scallions.

■ 157 Ludlow St. (bet. Rivington & Stanton Sts.)
🚇 Delancey St
✆ (646) 590-0684 — **WEB:** www.sakamai.com
■ Dinner nightly          **PRICE:** $$$

# THE STANTON SOCIAL ¶⃝

*Fusion*

XX | 🍸 🍴

MAP: B1

This stylish downtown looker has been going strong for over a decade now. Unlike the hip spots that burn brightly then fade, The Stanton Social still has the stuff—best evidenced, perhaps, by the throngs of beautiful young things that fill its seats every weekend. That said, it's not so cool that you won't find a family with kids squeaking through the door for an early dinner.

Inside the generous space, you'll find sultry purple velvet booths and dark wooden tables. The thumping music and dim lights give it a clubby vibe, as does the bar and lounge upstairs. The food is equally eclectic and playful, with a delicious shareable menu that includes the popular French onion soup dumplings, a "Big Sexy Burger," and Mexican street corn ravioli.

■ 99 Stanton St. (bet. Ludlow & Orchard Sts.)
🚇 2 Av
✆ (212) 995-0099 — **WEB:** www.thestantonsocial.com
■ Lunch Sat – Sun   Dinner nightly          **PRICE:** $$

# YOPPARAI ⅋⃝

*Japanese*

✗ | ⌂

Guests ring a buzzer to gain access to this clandestine izakaya. Inside, you'll find a stylish, serene cubby hole—reservations are a must on popular nights—where every point of your experience has been thoughtfully considered, from the two-person bar stools to the kimono-clad servers with answers at the ready. Two chefs perform their magic in view: one works the grill station while the other tackles sashimi and steamed dishes. A small kitchen in the back pushes out occasional items as well. The menu offers barbecue dishes, robata specials, as well as other seasonal delights. But you'll have the most fun ordering a little of everything—each new presentation is truly an artful revelation.

Housed just down the block, Azasu is the modern and much loved sibling.

▨ 151 Rivington St. (bet. Clinton & Suffolk Sts.)

▨ Delancey St

✆ (212) 777-7253 — **WEB:** www.yopparainyc.com

▨ Dinner Mon – Sat                    **PRICE:** $$$

Look for our symbol 🍸
spotlighting restaurants
with a serious cocktail list.

NO PARKING

NO STANDING

# MIDTOWN EAST

An interesting mix of office buildings, hotels, high-rises, and townhouses, Midtown East is one of the city's most industrious areas. Home to the iconic Chrysler Building and United Nations Headquarters, the vibe here is buzzing with suits, students, and old-timers wandering its streets. Whether it's that reliable diner on the corner, a gourmet supermarket, or fine-dining gem, this neighborhood flaunts it all. Close on the heels of its global theme, **Adana Grill** is a highly enjoyable Turkish takeout spot, where items are grilled to order. The wait is long and entirely worth it. Residents of neighboring Beekman and Sutton Place are proud of their very own cheese shop (**Ideal Cheese**); butcher (**L. Simchick Meats**); bagel and lox shop (**Tal Bagels**); and to complete any dinner party—renowned florist (**Zeze**). While **Dag Hammarskjöld Plaza Greenmarket** is for the most part dwarfed by Union Square, come Wednesdays it presents just the right amount of produce to feed hungry locals. Then sample a bit of chic at Paris-based café **Rose Bakery**,

set inside the very haute and hip Dover Street Market. It may be tucked behind a soaring cement column sheathed in colorful macramé, but turn a corner to find display cases filled with fresh salads and tempting sweets.

## GRAND CENTRAL TERMINAL

**B**uilt by the Vanderbilt family in the 19th century, **Grand Central Terminal** is a 21st century food sanctuary. An ideal day at this titanic and particularly gorgeous train station may begin with a coffee from **Joe's**. Later, stop by one of Manhattan's historic sites, the **Grand Central Oyster Bar & Restaurant**, nestled into the cavernous lower level. This gorgeous seafood respite presents everything from shellfish stews and pristine fish, to an incredible raw bar and more. Then take a turn—of taste—and head to **Neuhaus**, venerable chocolatiers who craft their delicacies from exceptional ingredients. Others may stop by family-owned and renowned **Li-Lac Chocolates** for such nostalgic confections as dark chocolate-covered pretzels or beautifully packaged holiday gift boxes. Of course, no trip to this Terminal is complete without a visit to the "whispering gallery" where low, ceramic-tiled arches allow whispers to sound more like shouts. Just beyond, the loud dining concourse hums with lunch stalls ranging from **Café Spice** for Indian or **Eata Pita** for Middle Eastern.

**Mendy's** is midtown's go-to for everything kosher—think pastrami and brisket mingled in with some Mid-Eastern eats. Then, finish with the sweetest treats—maybe red velvet cupcakes at the Terminal's very own **Magnolia Bakery** outpost. Moving on to the market, Eli Zabar has expanded his empire, and continues to proffer the freshest fruits and vegetables at **Eli Zabar's Farm to Table**. But, for an impressive assortment of pastries and cakes, **Eli Zabar's Bread & Pastry** is your best bet. In addition to its myriad fishmongers, butchers, and bakers, home cooks and top chefs are likely to find the best selection of spices here—at one of the market's better-kept secrets, **Spices and Tease**, specializing in exotic blends and...you guessed it...unique teas. But, if you're among hungry hordes with time to spare, make sure to visit one of the several prized restaurants situated beneath Grand Central's celestial ceiling mural for a stellar night. And finally, if the scene in the Terminal is too

corporate for your liking, then head on over to **Urbanspace Vanderbilt**. This lively food hall may exist in the heart of a commercial center, but it boasts over 20 cutting-edge culinary concepts.

## JAPANTOWN

**T**rek a few blocks east of Lexington to find a very sophisticated Japantown, where *izakaya* and restaurants are scattered among hostess clubs. Salarymen frequent old-world hangouts like **Riki**, **Ariyoshi**, or even rookies like **Lucky Cat**. **BentOn Cafe** is a favored retail outpost, but tenders daily changing bentos at terrific value. Expats with ladies in tow linger over the psuedo-Italian spread at **Aya**, while the yuppie crews opt for a light bite from **Cafe Zaiya** or **Dainobu** (both bustling deli-cum-markets). Just as **Sakagura's** sake collection is impressive and extensive, so is the roster of comforting noodle soups at **Nishida Shoten**. **Hinata Ramen** is an all-time draw for steaming bowls of ramen, while red meat fiends join the lines outside **Katsu-Hama** or **Yakiniku Gen** for delicious grilled eats. Looking to impress your out-of-town guests? Plan a Japanese-themed evening by stocking up on ceramics, cookware, and authentic produce from specialty emporium, **MTC Kitchen**. A few blocks south, younger and quieter Murray Hill has its own distinct vibe. Here, fast-casual finds thrive thanks to thirty-somethings sating late-night cravings. Meanwhile, **The Kitano**, one among a handful of Gotham's Japanese-owned boutique hotels, continues to lure thanks to its sleek vibe, live tunes at **JAZZ at Kitano**, and traditional kaiseki cuisine served at their very own subterranean hot spot, **Hakubai**.

Slightly north, owner and pastry chef, Stephane Pourrez, brings French flair and baked treats to **Éclair** on 53rd Street. Presenting a lineup of pastries, cakes, macarons, and of course, those eponymous eclairs, this sweet midtown spot also houses some of *the* flakiest croissants in town. Steps away indulge in wine and Mediterranean-inspired small plates at petite **Pierre Loti**.

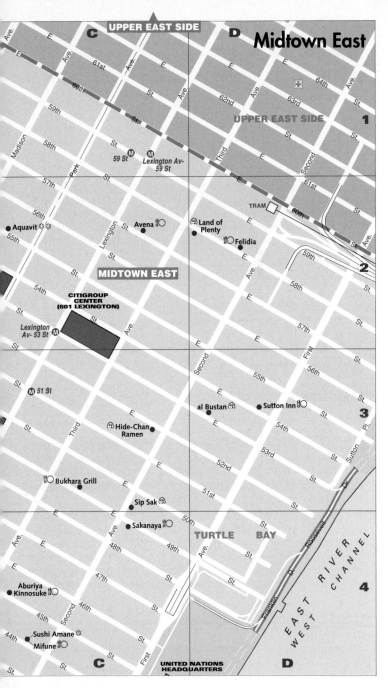

UPPER EAST SIDE

C

D

E Ave.

61st

60th

59th

St.

58th

Madison

57th

Park

St.

59 St Ⓜ Ⓜ Lexington Av-
59 St

56th

● Aquavit ❀❀

55th

Lexington St.

● Avena ‖○

MIDTOWN EAST

54th

**CITIGROUP
CENTER
(601 LEXINGTON)**

St.

Lexington
Av- 53 St Ⓜ

St.

St. Ⓜ 51 St

Third

⊕ Hide-Chan ●
Ramen

‖○ Bukhara Grill

Sip Sak ⊕

● Sakanaya ‖○

Ave.

48th

47th

Aburiya
Kinnosuke ‖○

Second

46th

45th

Sushi Amane ❀

44th

Mifune ‖○

C

UPPER EAST SIDE

64th

63rd

62nd

St.

St.

61st

TRAM ▢ 60th

59th

58th

57th

al Bustan ⊕
●

● Sutton Inn ‖○

54th

53rd

52nd

51st

50th

**TURTLE BAY**

49th

Second

First

Sutton

Sutton Pl.

E A S T   R I V E R

W E S T   C H A N N E L

Roosevelt

Franklin

**UNITED NATIONS
HEADQUARTERS**

D

1

2

3

4

⊕ Land of
Plenty
●

‖○ Felidia

● Land of Plenty

# ABURIYA KINNOSUKE 🍴⃝

*Japanese*

XX | ᗜ⌄                                                    **MAP:** C4

Call it a trip to Tokyo without the tariff. This dark and sophisticated izakaya is tucked down a side street in bustling midtown. Once inside, grab an intimate table for two or join the crowd at the open kitchen counter surrounding the smoky robata grill. The waiters talk up the omakase, but it's worth trusting your own instincts to guide you on a personalized tour through their authentic offerings.

The sukiyaki is a must-try seasonal special of tender marbled beef served in a hot pot bobbing with a beaten egg, tofu, vegetables, and noodles. Other favorites may include smoky bamboo shoots fresh off the robata with shaved bonito; as well as their legendary tsukune, a tender ground chicken meatball brushed with teriyaki and dipped in raw egg.

■ 213 E. 45th St. (bet. Second & Third Aves.)
🚇 Grand Central - 42 St
✆ (212) 867-5454 — **WEB:** www.aburiyakinnosuke.com
■ Lunch Mon – Fri   Dinner nightly                    **PRICE: $$$**

# AL BUSTAN 😊

*Lebanese*

XX | 🍽️                                                    **MAP:** D3

Lebanese specialties are fired up with aplomb at Al Bustan, where a moneyed Middle Eastern crowd dominates the space, along with a steady stream of locals (including diplomats from neighboring UN). Inside, glittering chandeliers hang from a beam-lined ceiling and neat white leather chairs impart an air of elegance.

The expansive menu boasts a slew of meze, house specials, and a knockout dinner prix-fixe. Kick things off with a crunchy fattoush salad; or sambousek jibneh, a baked pastry bubbling with salty feta. You can't go wrong adding a mashawi (mixed grill platter for sharing) to your order; or for that matter, kouzi, a giant round of flaky homemade phyllo stuffed with heavenly spiced rice, peas, carrots and tender gamey lamb.

■ 319 E. 53rd St. (bet. First & Second Aves.)
🚇 Lexington Av - 53 St
✆ (212) 759-5933 — **WEB:** www.albustanny.com
■ Lunch & dinner daily                                **PRICE: $$**

# AGERN ✿

*Scandinavian*

XX | 🦞 🍸 🍺 ⭘ ⟟

Even before disciples of the New Nordic creed started making pilgrimages to Copenhagen's Noma restaurant it was clear that the winds of culinary change were blowing in from that direction. The ethos that has made the cooking in Scandinavia so influential—fierce adherence to seasonality and respect for nature's larder—may not seem particularly ground-breaking but for many a chef and restaurateur it prompted some sort of epiphany. The good news is that, thanks to the great Dane Claus Meyer, you don't need to fly there to find out more.

Agern is hidden at the Vanderbilt Hall end of Grand Central Terminal but has been designed with such understated elegance that you quickly forget where you are. The restaurant also leads into the Nordic-themed "Great Northern Food Hall" so it won't be long before everyone in this part of town is in cable knit sweaters, discussing their own understanding of "hygge."

Ingredients like havgus, söl and ymer may not be familiar to all; nor perhaps will be the liberal use of techniques like pickling, fermenting or smoking. But, under the aegis of Icelandic chef Gunnar Gíslason, the kitchen uses these methods to deliver sharper, more defined and more natural flavors.

■ 89 E. 42nd St. (at Vanderbilt Ave.)

🚇 Grand Central - 42 St

✆ (646) 568-4018 — **WEB:** www.agernrestaurant.com

■ Lunch Mon – Fri   Dinner Mon – Sat         **PRICE:** $$$$

# AQUAVIT ❀❀
*Scandinavian*

XxX | 🍴 ♿ 🛋 

**MAP:** C2

No detail goes unnoticed at this sleek beauty, where black-suited servers in waiting line the dining room, which is intimate without being crowded. The overall design of Aquavit is clean and contemporary—with dark floors, wood tabletops, and high-backed leather chairs. Courses arrive in equally beautiful, but minimalist, dishware like wood boxes, slate platters, and glazed earthenware.

The kitchen does many things well, but what makes it one of the more unique in the city is the chef's ability to take bold Scandinavian flavors like dill, lingonberry, smoke or brine, and soften them into balanced, whimsical and elegant dishes. Take for example, a sheet of raw Colorado Wagyu draped over pickled leeks and carefully strewn with pumpernickel croutons. Then delicately cooked and deliciously crisp Dover sole is plated with crisp apple, parsnip, and excellently seasoned pork cheek ragù for a veritable study in harmonious flavors.

Finally, opt for the namesake aquavit, offered in house-made flavors like anise-caraway-fennel or fig-cardamom, to team with such treats as a "nest" of honey tuile threads cradling three small "eggs" composed of white chocolate and frozen goat cheese. Pure bliss, indeed.

---

■ 65 E. 55th St. (bet. Madison & Park Aves.)
🚇 5 Av - 53 St
📞 (212) 307-7311 — **WEB:** www.aquavit.org
■ Lunch Mon – Fri   Dinner Mon – Sat          **PRICE:** $$$$

# AVENA 🍴⃝
*Italian*

✗✗                                    **MAP:** C2

For a modern take on Northern Italian cooking, Chef Roberto Deiaco, of East 12th Osteria and Armani Ristorante fame, is back with Avena. The mood here is fuss-free—a sentiment that's echoed by white and marble décor. But what the atmosphere lacks in flavor, the food makes up for in leaps and bounds.

The feast begins with the bread basket and its addictive carta di musica, a tissue-thin flatbread brushed with butter and sprinkled with salt and rosemary to represent musical notes. Those familiar with the chef's talents know that fresh pasta reigns supreme, and the ravioli filled with creamy ricotta and quail egg yolk doesn't disappoint. For the carnivore crowd, Colorado lamb loin with a Castelveltrano olive crust is worthy of a standing ovation.

■ 141 E. 57th St. (bet. Lexington & Third Aves.)
▥ Lexington Av - 59 St
℘ (212) 752-5323 — **WEB:** www.avenarestaurant.com
■ Lunch & dinner daily                **PRICE: $$$**

# BUKHARA GRILL 🍴⃝
*Indian*

✗✗ | ⌲                                **MAP:** C3

In NYC's ever-expanding realm of Indian dining, Bukhara Grill has stood the test of time with excellence. Glimpse their expert chefs who seem contentedly trapped behind a glass kitchen wall. Featuring a noisy and yuppie set, this tri-level space is decorated (albeit oddly) with clunky wooden booths, closely set tables, and private rooms.

Peek into the kitchen for a whiff of tandoori treats and Mughlai specialties. Dahi aloo papri (spicy potatoes and chickpeas tossed in yogurt and tamarind) is a predictably perfect starter. The signature, wickedly creamy dal Bukhara will have you coming back for more (tomorrow). Even if the service may range from sweet to clumsy, hand-crafted breads meant to sop up the likes of sarson ka saag remain a crowning glory.

■ 217 E. 49th St. (bet. Second & Third Aves.)
▥ 51 St
℘ (212) 888-2839 — **WEB:** www.bukharany.com
■ Lunch & dinner daily                **PRICE: $$$**

# CAFÉ CHINA ✿
*Chinese*

XX

**MAP:** A1

Blink and you'll miss its inconspicuous façade, but what a shame, for Café China is a little journey into the magnificent pleasures of Sichuan cuisine by way of midtown. Inside find a long, narrow space fitted with seductive portraits of 1930's Shanghai starlets, bright red chairs, bamboo planters and a dominating marble-and-wood bar.

After struggling with their on-again-off-again popularity, this kitchen is back to their A-game, producing Sichuan (and Sichuan-influenced) dishes with aplomb. Their particular strength lies in the elegant and effortless contrast of complex flavors, even when the prep is decidedly simple—as in the delicious steamed eggplant and ginger sautéed duck.

Pickled vegetables achieve harmonious balance between sour and fiery notes; while thinly sliced conch pairs perfectly with tingly chili oil. Sichuan pork dumplings arrive in a delicate wrapper and atop a delicious bath of soy and chili oil. But save space to savor the Chungking chicken, alternately tender and crispy, with abundant dried chilies, scallions and sesame seeds. Spicy cumin lamb, fried to gamey perfection and tossed with sesame seeds, chili peppers and cilantro, is yet another smoky feat.

■ 13 E. 37th St. (bet. Fifth & Madison Aves.)
▨ 34 St - Herald Sq
✆ (212) 213-2810 — **WEB:** www.cafechinanyc.com
■ Lunch & dinner daily

**PRICE:** $$

# CAVIAR RUSSE ✣

*Contemporary*

✗✗✗ | ⬭

No playful pun, no name-check for grandma, no oblique reference to a geographical landmark—whoever christened this restaurant clearly wanted to attract a certain type of customer. This is not the place where you should order by pointing vaguely at the menu—that way lies trouble because you may find yourself having to re-mortgage your apartment to pay for the 250 grams of Osetra caviar you've just inadvertently requested. Best leave that section of the carte to the oligarchs and retired dictators and concentrate on the main menu. Here you will find contemporary dishes of surprising delicacy and precision, with a pleasing bias towards wonderful seafood and shellfish, such as scallops with ricotta gnudi, or delicious bluefin tuna with uni and asparagus.

You get buzzed in at street level, which adds a bit of mystery to proceedings. Up the stairs and you'll find yourself in a lavish little jewel box, with colorful murals on the wall, Murano chandeliers hanging from an ornate ceiling, and semi-circular booths. The only thing missing is James Bond's nemesis drumming his fingers on the table in the corner.

For more plush fun in the sun, there is a seriously posh outpost at The Four Seasons Tower in Miami.

---

■ 538 Madison Ave. (bet. 54th & 55th Sts.)
🚇 5 Av - 53 St
✆ (212) 980-5908 — **WEB:** www.caviarrusse.com
■ Lunch daily  Dinner Mon – Sat     **PRICE: $$$$**

# DON'S BOGAM ☺🍴

*Korean*

XX                                                    **MAP:** A1

At Don's Bogam, the food is fantastic and service indulgent. So, reserve ahead as every seat is filled—from the festive bar up front right down to those two-tops sporting blazing grills. Make no mistake: this is no average K-town joint. Inside, a top-notch venting system lets diners enjoy a smoke-free evening of exceptional grilled meats. Start with fried pork mandu, which are crisp, on-point and extra divine. Wonderfully flaky buchu gochu pajeon is studded with chives for perfect flavor; while pork belly marinated in red wine is smoky and supremely tender.

For the ultimate payoff, opt for the memorable beef platter. It features thinly sliced macun and yangnyeom galbi set beside king trumpet mushrooms that are meaty and mouthwatering in their own right.

◼ 17 E. 32nd St. (bet. Fifth & Madison Aves.)
🚇 33 St
✆ (212) 683-2200 — **WEB:** www.donsbogam.com
◼ Lunch & dinner daily                        **PRICE:** $$

# EL PARADOR 😊

*Mexican*

XX | 🍽                                               **MAP:** B2

This neighborhood mainstay boasts over fifty years of success. With their fantastic menu, killer margaritas, and dedication to hospitality, El Parador is worthy of its status as a beloved destination. The intimate space is decked with ornate wood chairs, red banquettes, and wood plank ceilings, while white brick walls are hung with artwork and artifacts.

The bountiful menu offers favorites like taco trays and nachos in three varieties, as well as a rotating menu of daily specials (be sure to try the fish of the day). Fill up on aguachile de camaron, deliciously classic shrimp ceviche in lime juice and jalapeño; or tender, falling-off-the-bone baby-back ribs served with tequila-chili guajillo salsa, cabbage slaw, and braised camote.

Margaritas are a must, but of course.

◼ 325 E. 34th St. (bet. First & Second Aves.)
🚇 33 St
✆ (212) 679-6812 — **WEB:** www.elparadorcafe.com
◼ Lunch & dinner Mon – Sat                    **PRICE:** $$

# EMPELLÓN ♨️○

*Mexican*

✗✗ | 🍸 ▢

Buttoned-up midtown gets a much-needed shot in the arm compliments of Chef Alex Stupak's lively new flagship for his popular Empellón family. The colorful, multi-level space offers a first floor outfitted with a generous bar area and prime view of the bustling open kitchen. On the mezzanine level, find a more intimate dining space.

The menu bears the chef's signature creative flair, offering a range of small bites, tacos, and shareable large plates. Sample their clever spins on salsa, like a wickedly good smoky cashew salsa that arrives with a sampler salsa starter; or irresistible lamb sweetbread tacos with a flutter of white onion and bright cilantro. Stupak is also a serious pastry chef and it shows in the otherworldly desserts, like the "avocado."

▨ 510 Madison Ave. (entrance on 53rd St.)
▨ 51 St
✆ (212) 858-9365 — **WEB:** www.empellon.com
▨ Lunch & dinner daily                    **PRICE: $$**

# FELIDIA ♨️○

*Italian*

✗✗✗ | 🎱 ▢

Cookbook author, television series host, and restaurateur Lidia Bastianich has been behind her flagship restaurant and greeting customers since 1981. The service is professional yet charming, and the elegant décor inspires dressing up for dinner. Wine connoisseurs will rejoice at the exceptional list, which offers a vast collection of Italian choices.

The family-style lunch prix-fixe is a crowd-pleaser, featuring such signature pastas as cacio e pere ravioli bathed with black pepper and pecorino. Massive portions of scallops, squid, and lobster star in the grigliata drizzled with lemon vinaigrette. Rely on Lidia to deliver a cannoli that lives up to its true potential—narrow tubes filled with lemony ricotta cream spilling into the center of the plate.

▨ 243 E. 58th St. (bet. Second & Third Aves.)
▨ Lexington Av - 59 St
✆ (212) 758-1479 — **WEB:** www.felidia-nyc.com
▨ Lunch Mon – Fri   Dinner nightly         **PRICE: $$$$**

# HANGAWI 😳

*Korean*

XX                                              **MAP:** A1

Beyond an ordinary façade lies this serene, shoes-off retreat with traditional low tables, Korean artifacts, and meditative music. Said footwear is stored in cubbies, seating is the color of bamboo, and clay teapots adorn the back wall. The setting is soothing, but the atmosphere is surprisingly convivial, with groups gabbing over stuffed shiitake mushrooms and green tea.

The ssam bap offers a fun DIY experience with a long platter of fillings. Dark leafy lettuce and thin, herbaceous sesame leaves are topped with creamy slices of avocado, crunchy bean sprouts, pickled daikon, carrot, cucumber, radish, and three rice options—white, brown, and a nutty, purple-tinged multigrain. Topped with miso ssam sauce, each bite is a fresh burst of uplifting textures.

◼ 12 E. 32nd St. (bet. Fifth & Madison Aves.)
◼ 33 St
✆ (212) 213-0077 — **WEB:** www.hangawirestaurant.com
◼ Lunch Mon – Sat   Dinner nightly                **PRICE:** $$

# HATSUHANA ⅟⊘

*Japanese*

XX                                              **MAP:** B3

It's been around since the beginning of time (in NYC Japanese restaurant years) but this is no lesser a destination for excellent sushi. With a retro décor that spans two floors and a business that's run like a machine, Hatsuhana is a go-to for corporate dining.

Though the rave reviews came decades ago, their traditional Edomae sushi still holds its own. Fish is top quality, the army of chefs have solid knife skills, and rice is properly prepared. This reliability draws a host of regulars who develop relationships with the itamae. Stick to the counter and go omakase: the sushi will be surprisingly impressive with accommodations for the spicy tuna set. At lunch, the "Box of Dreams" is an aptly named must-order.

◼ 17 E. 48th St. (bet. Fifth & Madison Aves.)
◼ 47-50 Sts - Rockefeller Ctr
✆ (212) 355-3345 — **WEB:** www.hatsuhana.com
◼ Lunch Mon – Fri   Dinner Mon – Sat            **PRICE:** $$$

# HIDE-CHAN RAMEN 😳

*Japanese*

🍴 **MAP:** C3

Real, genuine tonkotsu-style ramen is happening right here in NY, thanks to Hideto Kawahara, whose ramen-ya roots run deep in Japan. These noodles are cooked exactly as customer-specified and arrive perfect every time—even for the savviest and most discerning salarymen who tend to pour in late Friday nights for the post-work, post-bar scene. But on cold days, arrive early for lunch or risk a line that is sure to snake down the stairs.

In addition to their springy ramen floating in rich, fortifying broth, include other treats like crispy gyoza, traditional takoyaki, and steamed buns. For those who want to shy away from noodles, the dons are surprisingly good. The setting is appropriately informal, while service can be spacey at times.

- ■ 248 E. 52nd St. (bet. Second & Third Aves.)
- 🚇 Lexington Av - 53 St
- 📞 (212) 813-1800 — **WEB:** www.hidechanramen.nyc
- ■ Lunch & dinner daily      **PRICE:** 🍴

# KURUMAZUSHI 🍽️

*Japanese*

🍴🍴 | 🔲      **MAP:** B3

Mimicking Tokyo's tucked-away restaurant style, this sushi destination is located up a dark staircase in a midtown building and through a sliding door. The focal point of the room is the sushi bar, where Chef/owner Toshihiro Uezu meticulously prepares each morsel in a minimal space.

For the full theatrical experience, brace your wallet and settle into the omakase. The undeniable quality of each ingredient is center stage, displayed simply on glazed pottery.

Take a cue from the Japanese and limit conversation: the succession of sashimi and sushi is quick, and all senses should work together without distraction to savor the smooth, buttery fatty tuna, Spanish mackerel (with its lightly blistered skin), pearly white sea bream, and rich unagi.

- ■ 7 E. 47th St., 2nd fl. (bet. Fifth & Madison Aves.)
- 🚇 47-50 Sts - Rockefeller Ctr
- 📞 (212) 317-2802 — **WEB:** www.kurumazushi.com
- ■ Lunch & dinner Mon – Sat      **PRICE:** $$$$

# KAJITSU ❀

*Japanese*

XX | ◷ ▭

It's the way of the modern world that we think of the changing of the seasons more in terms of our wardrobe rather than our food—but a meal at Kajitsu could change that. This Japanese vegan restaurant serves shojin cuisine based on the precepts of Buddhism— if you're in search of an antidote to the plethora of steakhouses in the city, this is it. The traditionally decorated space on the second floor is a sanctuary of peace and tranquility and offers table or counter seating and service that is as charming as it is earnest.

Such is the skill of the kitchen you'll forget in no time about the absence of fish or meat. It's all about balance, harmony and simplicity—and allowing the ingredients' natural flavors to shine, whether it's the delicate onion soup with mizuna and potato, or the visually arresting hassun which could include everything from mountain yam to burdock root.

Your period of contemplation and newfound respect for your fellow man may come to a juddering halt when you find yourself back on Lexington but, for a few moments at least, you'll feel you connected with nature.

■ 125 E. 39th St. (bet. Lexington & Park Aves.)
▦ Grand Central - 42 St
✆ (212) 228-4873 — **WEB:** www.kajitsunyc.com
■ Dinner Tue – Sun

PRICE: $$$

# LA GRENOUILLE ▮○

*French*

 XXX | ⌂                                          **MAP:** B2

La Grenouille is a bastion of old-world glamor and manners with an exorbitant budget for floral arrangements. Although this storied enclave still attracts a devoted following, there's always room for local newbies and blinged-out tourists. Everyone looks good in this lavish space, where red velvet banquettes, polished wood veneer, and softly lit tables bathe the room with rose and apricot hues.

Classic and classy, this French cuisine deserves high praise. Delicate ravioli is stuffed with chopped lobster hinting of tarragon and dressed with creamy, tart beurre blanc; an exquisitely tender-seared beef filet arrives with pommes Darphin and a lick of perfect sauce au poivre; and for dessert, the île flottante is heaven under a cloud of spun caramel.

▮ 3 E. 52nd St. (bet. Fifth & Madison Aves.)
▮ 5 Av - 53 St
☏ (212) 752-1495 — **WEB:** www.la-grenouille.com
▮ Lunch & dinner Tue – Sat                    **PRICE:** $$$$

# LAND OF PLENTY 😊

*Chinese*

XX                                              **MAP:** D2

Why do they call it Land of Plenty? Perhaps it's because of the abundant flavors in Chongqing noodles puddled in a chili oil broth with ground pork, peanuts and sesame seeds; or bean curd bathed in...yes...more chili oil with toasted peanuts and Sichuan peppercorns. Then imagine green snow pea sprouts dusted with salt and garlic, or pork dumplings swimming in a soy- peanut- and chili-bath that's spicy, sweet and salty at once. And know that these are just a few of the plentiful reasons.

Though the focus here is definitely the food, this fiery haven feels more elegant than the other Sichuan spots in midtown. Tucked into a sleek, subterranean space, the décor features marble floors and mosaic-tile walls. A professional service staff helps further set the tone.

▮ 204 E. 58th St. (bet. Second & Third Aves.)
▮ 59 St
☏ (212) 308-8788 — **WEB:** www.landofplenty58.com
▮ Lunch Mon – Fri  Dinner nightly             **PRICE:** $$

# MAPO TOFU 😋

## Chinese

🍴

MAP: A1

"How many?" That's the greeting at this temple of "ma la," where enticing aromas are sure to lure you in. Find yourself among executives and locals slurping up a host of chili oil specialties (don't wear white!). This is the kind of place where dragons go to recharge their breath.

Some may peruse the menu—filled with typos—for daily specials, but most blaze their tongues with Sichuan pickles or chilled noodles tossed in an intense sesame vinaigrette. The place is named after a humble dish, but many items surprise with bold flavors like silky fish fillets swimming in a spicy broth with Napa cabbage, or camphor tea-smoked duck. Peppercorns in stir-fried chicken unite subtle sweetness with intense heat, while sponge squash offers a cooling, textural finale.

◾ 338 Lexington Ave. (bet. 39th & 40th Sts.)
🚇 Grand Central - 42 St
📞 (212) 867-8118 — **WEB:** N/A
◾ Lunch & dinner daily                          **PRICE:** 💰

# MIFUNE 🍴○

## Japanese

XX | 🍸 ♿

MAP: C4

Two superstar chefs arrive in one package with the elegant Mifune and omakase bar, Sushi Amane, which is located downstairs. Chef Hiroki Yoshitake presents delicious, contemporary Japanese cuisine here at Mifune, in a space featuring cement walls, blonde wood, and cozy backlighting.

Alongside tempura, rice dishes, and other delightful entrées, this menu also offers a daily selection of sashimi. Tender smoked butterfish arrives with shaved radish rounds, nasturtium leaves, and a bright chimichurri-like sauce made from garlic, herbs and oil. Then, grilled chicken Yuan-style appears in a mini cast-iron skillet, brushed with an irresistible teriyaki-based sauce, and paired with knobs of tender, buttery potatoes, snap peas, and frizzled leeks.

◾ 245 E. 44th St. (bet. Second & Third Aves.)
🚇 Grand Central - 42 St
📞 (212) 986-2800 — **WEB:** www.mifune-restaurant.com
◾ Dinner Mon – Sat                          **PRICE:** $$$

# NORMA GASTRONOMIA SICILIANA 😊

*Italian*

XX | 🕸 👤 🏠 🖵        **MAP:** A2

To think of these arancini as mere "rice balls" is a slight on Sicilian culture; they are so much more. Nowhere else in the city will you dine on such crisp, classically made beauties, filled with meaty ragù, peas, mozzarella, and tender rice cooked in chicken stock, presented in a pool of excellent, light tomato sauce. Hear the sound of every meatball in midtown suddenly quaking in its red sauce.

The menu goes on to list authentic Sicilian specialties, like rianata pizza of Trapani, that are hard to find elsewhere. The rustic space is filled with old, crackle-glazed platters that probably held the exact style of sinfuly rich anelletti al forno, back in the Old Country. Before you leave, stock up on Sicilian ingredients attractively displayed for sale.

▨ 438 Third Ave. (bet. 30th & 31st Sts.)
🚇 33 St
🖋 (212) 889-0600 — **WEB:** www.normarestaurant.com
▨ Lunch & dinner daily        **PRICE:** $$

# PERA 🍴

*Turkish*

XX | 👤 🖵        **MAP:** A4

For flavorful Turkish food infused with contemporary influence, Pera serves to please. Lunch does big business in this attractive dining room, layered in a chocolate-brown color scheme and packed with corporate types as well as visitors looking for a sleek place to sojourn mid-day. Acoustics can be loud, but with food so fine, you'll want to stay awhile.

Dinner is more low-key but the menu always brims with simple, good quality, and slightly renovated plates like warm hummus with pastirma; lentil and bulgur tartare; or watermelon chunks tossed with salty feta, tomatoes, and olive oil. A forkful of their model and deliciously tender chicken adana with a side of addictively crispy fries has wide appeal and makes for a fitting feast—at all times.

▨ 303 Madison Ave. (bet. 41st & 42nd Sts.)
🚇 Grand Central - 42 St
🖋 (212) 878-6301 — **WEB:** www.peranyc.com
▨ Lunch Mon – Fri   Dinner nightly      **PRICE:** $$

# SAKANAYA ⁏⃘

## Japanese

✗

**MAP:** C4

Sit at the L-shaped counter to best appreciate the skills of Chef Shigeru Nishida as he prepares nigiri with the fluid movements of a seasoned practitioner. You're in his hands for the evening as he offers just two omakase menus—the difference being that the more expensive one comes with an added sashimi course.

The chef sticks to a fairly traditional Edomae style and uses a variety of sources for his fish. Uni may be from Hokkaido but the shrimp is from Canada; tuna from Spain; salmon from Scotland; and the rice hails from California. The menus are good value as they include appetizers, around ten pieces of sushi, chawanmushi, red miso soup and dessert. If, for some bizarre reason, you're still not sated then go next door to the chef's ramen shop, Nishida Sho-ten.

▦ 304 E. 49th St. (bet. First & Second Aves.)
▦ 51 St
✆ (212) 339-0033 — **WEB:** www.sakanayany.com
▦ Lunch Mon – Fri   Dinner Mon – Sat          **PRICE: $$$$**

# 2ND AVENUE DELI ⁏⃘

## Deli

✗

**MAP:** A1

While the décor may be more deli-meets-deco and there's a tad less attitude, this food is every bit as good as it was on Second Avenue. Ignore the kvetching and know that this is a true Jewish deli filled with personality, and one of the best around by far.

The menu remains as it should: kosher, meat-loving, and non-dairy with phenomenal pastrami, pillowy rye, tangy mustard, perfect potato pancakes, and fluffy matzoh balls in comforting broth. Have the best of both worlds with the soup and half-sandwich combination.

Carve a nook during midday rush, when in pour the crowds. The deli also does takeout (popular with the midtown lunch bunch), and delivery (grandma's latkes at your door). Giant platters go equally well to a bris or brunch.

▦ 162 E. 33rd St. (bet. Lexington & Third Aves.)
▦ 33 St
✆ (212) 689-9000 — **WEB:** www.2ndavedeli.com
▦ Lunch & dinner daily                          **PRICE:** ⊜

# SIP SAK 🐶

## Turkish

✗✗                                       **MAP:** C3

Tucked inside a charming, bistro-like setting with pressed-tin ceilings and cool white marble-top tables, this neighborhood favorite just keeps getting better with age. Owner Orhan Yegen runs a tight ship, directing his staff and kitchen as they entice diners with a meze of citrusy olives, delicious hummus, garlicky cacik, and creamy tarama.

Kick things off with a starter of plump shrimp cooked in a downright addictive garlic and parsley sauce; or tuck into an equally earthy Greek salad with a Turkish twist featuring pickled cabbage, crumbled feta, and a poached artichoke heart filled with dilled fava beans. For dinner, skip the seafood and opt for fragrant and hearty lamb meatballs, served over rice pilaf with a grilled tomato and pile of mixed greens.

◼ 928 Second Ave. (bet. 49th & 50th Sts.)
◼ 51 St
𝒫 (212) 583-1900 — **WEB:** www.sip-sak.com
◼ Lunch & dinner daily                    **PRICE:** $$

# SOBA TOTTO 🍴

## Japanese

✗✗ | &♿ ⛶                              **MAP:** B4

It's a jam-packed lunchtime operation here at Soba Totto, where business folks gather and quickly fill the popular space. As the name suggests, everyone arrives in droves for the tasty homemade soba. Dinnertime brings a mellower vibe, and a crowd of beer- and sake-sipping patrons ordering tasty plates of spicy fried chicken and yakitori galore.

Midday features several varieties of lunch sets. Tasty appetizers may unveil a salad of assorted pickles and simmered daikon in a sweet ginger dressing. Skip over the fried seafood in favor of the soba totto gozen set, which includes the wonderful noodles in fragrant dashi; or try one of the many delicious dons topped with tasty tidbits like sea urchin and salmon roe or soy-marinated tuna, grated yam, and egg.

◼ 211 E. 43rd St. (bet. Second & Third Aves.)
◼ Grand Central - 42 St
𝒫 (212) 557-8200 — **WEB:** www.sobatotto.com
◼ Lunch Mon – Fri   Dinner nightly          **PRICE:** $$

# SUSHI AMANE ✿

*Japanese*

XX | &#9855;

MAP: C4

Straight from his work at Tokyo's revered Sushi Saito, Chef Shion Uino has arrived in New York to bring a rare level of skill and experience to Sushi Amane. Do not be misled by the chef's young age—he began his sushi training at 18, which makes him an old timer compared to this cool and serene newcomer of a restaurant.

The handful of tables offer pleasant seating for groups, but the eight-seat sushi counter is the place to sit, right in view of a workspace displaying grated wasabi root and that night's selection from the sea. The chef's expert trimming and slicing is only interrupted by an assistant occasionally replenishing warm bowls of vinegar-seasoned rice.

Cooked bites such as steamed abalone or a clam consommé that tastes of the ocean may be lovely diversions, but the tasting of Hokkaido and Kyushu uni is otherworldly. Still, the real point of dining here is the sushi. Each morsel is beautifully crafted and neither receives nor requires much embellishment. The procession of astoundingly fresh fish may move from gently scored flounder or ruby-red Bluefin tuna to carefully prepared squid and much more. Meals end on a high note with a unique take on tamago that is dense, custardy, and sweet.

&#9632; 245 E. 44th St. (bet. Second & Third Aves.)

&#9633; Grand Central - 42 St

&#8478; (212) 986-2800 — **WEB:** www.mifune-restaurant.com

&#9632; Dinner Mon – Sat

PRICE: $$$$

# SUSHIANN 🍴

*Japanese*

XX | 🍽

Step through the serene, bamboo-filled entrance and into this dedicated sushi den. The mood is respectfully formal yet friendly, thanks to the focused kitchen staff who are happily interacting with guests. Just arrive with a sense of what (and how much) you'd like to eat and insist upon the omakase.

Let the day's catch dictate your meal and take a seat at the counter, where only the glassed-in display of fish and mollusks separates you from this team of skilled, disciplined chefs. The omakase may be wildly varied depending on the day (and your chef), but high standards are always maintained and each morsel is treated with integrity. A final sashimi course may reveal a glistening array of mild giant clam, firm tai, and tuna that melts in the mouth.

◾ 38 E. 51st St. (bet. Madison & Park Aves.)

🚇 51 St

✆ (212) 755-1780 — **WEB:** www.sushiann.net

◾ Lunch Mon – Fri   Dinner Mon – Sat

**PRICE: $$**

# SUTTON INN 🍴

*American*

XX

This charming American bistro flies a bit under the radar, but has all the things you'd want in a neighborhood restaurant. It's exceptionally quaint and cozy; the guests are friendly and often local; and the vibe is perfectly laid-back. And while the space is decidedly unflashy, the refined dishes showcase a delicious interplay between quality ingredients and the notable talents of the kitchen.

Kick things off with a mouthwatering bowl of chilled corn soup, served sweet and creamy and garnished with roasted poblano peppers, Gouda, pico de gallo, and fresh cilantro. Then move on to a lovely fillet of bluefish, roasted to crispy-outside-and-tender-inside perfection, and served over nutty wild rice with snap pea slivers and a mild green curry emulsion.

◾ 347 E. 54th St. (bet. First & Second Aves.)

🚇 Lexington Av - 53 St

✆ (646) 370-3045 — **WEB:** www.suttoninnrestaurant.com

◾ Dinner Mon – Sat

**PRICE: $$$**

# SUSHI GINZA ONODERA 🏵 🏵

*Japanese*

XxX | ⊙⌣ &

Japanese cuisine is often prone to reinterpretation so traditionalists, albeit fiscally unencumbered ones, will like this Edomae sushi restaurant. It certainly looks quite grand in its midtown spot—a location that makes sense as Fifth Avenue and Ginza are pretty similar places. The restaurant is also impressive inside, thanks largely to the 16 seater L-shaped cypress counter that's the focus of the room.

The only real decision you need to make is how many pieces of nigiri you want. Once you've done that and chosen some sake, sit back and watch the chefs make each one with quick, deft movements before placing them individually in front of you. Much of the fish is flown in from Tokyo's Tsukiji market while the white rice is from Niigata Prefecture and is seasoned with two types of red vinegar, hence its dark hue. It's cooked firm, so that each grain is clearly discernible in the mouth—a feature of great sushi.

The nigiri follows the traditional path of starting with lighter fish and progressing through to stronger flavors, with each piece lightly brushed with nikiri. Highlights include salmon roe, succulent aji (horse mackerel) and squid, which comes dressed with a little Hokkaido uni.

▨ 461 Fifth Ave. (bet. 40th & 41st Sts.)
▨ 42 St - Bryant Pk
✆ (212) 390-0925 — **WEB:** https://onodera-group.com/en/
▨ Lunch & dinner Mon – Fri        **PRICE: $$$$**

# SUSHI YASUDA ❀

## *Japanese*

XX | &

There is a Spartan appearance to this sushi temple, where honey-toned bamboo slats are by far the warmest feature. Reservations require confirmation and punctuality, but to sushi-loving diehards, this is just the cost of admission.

Avoid the tables packed with suits (this is midtown, after all) and request a seat at the sleek counter—it's where the magic happens. Your experience here depends entirely on the soft-spoken, attentive, and very focused itamae working before you, as his signature style will guide your meal. Their mission is to ensure that each diner receives a wide variety of fish that has just been cut, formed and dressed moments before it is eaten.

The kitchen lives up to its hype by ignoring new wave trends in favor of serving classically assembled and spectacularly fresh sushi. Every item is handled with the utmost care, especially the progression of sashimi highlighting the ample textures of mackerel, tuna, and salmon. Outstanding clams and scallops are seasoned with a touch of lemon and sea salt flakes to enhance their natural taste; while nigiri featuring Maine and Japanese uni tastings underscore the subtle differences in flavor.

■ 204 E. 43rd St. (bet. Second & Third Aves.)
🚇 Grand Central - 42 St
✆ (212) 972-1001 — **WEB:** www.sushiyasuda.com
■ Lunch Mon – Fri   Dinner Mon – Sat          PRICE: $$$$

# TEMPURA MATSUI ✿

*Japanese*

XX | 🍴

Tempura may be considered a more common pleasure in Japan, but it has been refined to an art form at this home to succulent morsels of fish and vegetables. There is no equal in the city and the kitchen's delicate hand and authenticity is particularly clear in the lightly seasoned batter that sparingly coats each bit of food before it is quickly fried and rendered crisp. The skill here is so great that they could probably get away with serving lesser quality fish, but still, these are often imported from Tsukiji market in Tokyo at their peak of freshness. Don't miss the sweet shrimp wrapped in shiso leaf and butterflied Japanese whiting served with purple sweet potato.

Meals are bookended with premium sashimi and cooked dishes that are just as enticing, like seared butterfish with a tiny radish, spring pea, and onion. Tilefish is prepared with flavors that seem to conjure spring thanks to cherry leaves, uni, and braised broccoli over sticky rice with sesame and goji berries.

The best place to appreciate the kitchen's artistry is from the counter where chefs can be found carefully dipping each little golden nugget of food in and out of boiling oil, then promptly placing it before you.

◾ 222 E. 39th St. (bet. Second & Third Aves.)
🚇 Grand Central - 42 St
📞 (212) 986-8885 — **WEB:** www.tempuramatsui.com
◾ Lunch Tue – Fri   Dinner Tue – Sun        **PRICE: $$$$**

# TSUSHIMA 🍴

*Japanese*

XX | 🍴                                    **MAP:** B4

A shiny black awning marks the entrance to this slightly antiseptic yet considerably authentic sushi bar. A few rooms done in traditional Japanese style provide seating choices at this den, which hums with business groups on the run as well as neighborhood dwellers seeking fantastic value lunches and terrific quality sushi in the evening.

Choose to dine at their sushi counter or at a table in the well-lit dining room, attended to by speedy servers. Then, dive in to generously sized lunch specials featuring perhaps a colorful chirashi, headlining yellowtail, salmon, tamago, and amberjack set deftly over well-seasoned sushi rice. Sticky glazed eel, nicely grilled and plenty fatty, is an absolute must, as is the impressive omakase for dinner.

- 🟫 210 E. 44th St. (bet. Second & Third Aves.)
- 🚇 Grand Central - 42 St
- 📞 (212) 207-1938 — **WEB:** www.tsushimanyc.com
- 🟫 Lunch & dinner daily                     **PRICE:** $$

# WOLFGANG'S 🍴

*Steakhouse*

XX                                        **MAP:** A1

Wolfgang's is no stranger to the bustling New York steakhouse scene. From the lunch hour business crowd to the lively, post-work bar scene, Wolfgang's jams in locals and tourists alike—each coming for the classic fare and precise Manhattans. The service can be gruff at times, but they have a good track record of squeezing you into a table or perch at the bar without a reservation.

Once seated, the bone-in Porterhouse, cooked rare, is the only way to go. It arrives sizzling in its own fat, perfectly seasoned. Save space for a slice of bacon—a must-order appetizer—creamed spinach, and crispy German potatoes with yet more salt and fat (at this point, why not?). Just beware: while dishes are sized to share, they're priced like Maseratis.

- 🟫 4 Park Ave. (at 33rd St.)
- 🚇 33 St
- 📞 (212) 889-3369 — **WEB:** www.wolfgangssteakhouse.net
- 🟫 Lunch & dinner daily                  **PRICE:** $$$$

Look for our symbol 🍇 spotlighting restaurants with a notable wine list.

# MIDTOWN WEST

**M**ore diverse than its counterpart (Midtown East) but still rather gritty in parts, Midtown West presents a unique mix of tree-lined streets and ethnic enclaves amid glitzy glass-walled towers. It is also home to numerous iconic sights, including now well-known **Restaurant Row**—the only street in all five boroughs to be proudly advertised as such. The fact that it resides in an area called Hell's Kitchen and highlights an impressive range of global cuisines is sealing evidence of this nabe's devotion to good food.

## EAT THE STREETS

**A**lso referred to as "Clinton," Hell's Kitchen is a colorful mosaic of workaday immigrants, old-timey residents, and young families. Gone are the Prohibition-era dens, which are now replaced by swanky restaurants, boutique hotels, and hip bars. **Little Brazil**, set only steps from bustling Sixth Avenue, showcases samba and street food every summer on Brazilian Day. And speaking of the same nation, tourist-centric **Churrascaria Plataforma** is an all-you-can-eat Brazilian steakhouse showing off their wares via waiters, armed with skewers of succulent roasted meat. Midtown may be choked by cabs and corporate types on the go, but in true Big Apple-style the residents demand (and streets oblige with) outstanding eats in varying venues. Under the guidance of the Vendy Awards and the blog—Midtown Lunch—

discover a changing lineup of speedy and satisfying street food faves as well as delis stocked with everything from Mexican specialties and dried chilies to farm-fresh produce. Those in a hurry hustle over to **Tehuitzingo** for over 12 types of tacos, but if seeking a more reliable scene, find a seat at **Tulcingo del Valle** where tortas are turned out alongside burritos and burgers. Carnivores also revel over those perfectly pink patties laced with crispy fries at Le Parker Meridien's **burger joint**; however, if barbecue is what floats your boat, trek to the wilds of Eleventh Avenue and into **Daisy May's BBQ USA** for smoky, succulent 'cue. In need of a more rare treat?

**K-town** is a dark horse-like quarter that has been known to sneak up and surprise. Its instant and unapologetically authentic vibe owes largely to the prominence of aromatic barbecue joints, karaoke bars, and of course, grocers hawking everything from fresh tofu to handmade mandu.

**M**acy's is across the street and may sport a frenzied scene, but tucked into its quiet crypt is **De Gustibus**, a cooking school and stage for culinary legends. Trek further along these midtown streets and find that equal attention is tendered to cooking as to arranging storybook mannequins behind the velvet ropes of glossy department

stores. Shop till you drop at Bergdorf; then cool your heels over caviar and croissants at the *très* French and fancy **Petrossian**. Others may opt to stir things up with a martini and tasty small plate served out of the stately **Charlie Palmer at the Knick**, comfortably situated in the Knickerbocker Hotel in Times Square.

**S**witching gears from specialty spots to mega markets, **Gotham West Market** is one of Manhattan's most favored gourmet feats. Settled along Eleventh Avenue, this culinary complex cradles a number of chef-driven stalls and artisanal purveyors offering tapas, charcuterie, sammies, and everything in between. Of special note is the first stateside outpost of **Ivan Ramen Slurp Shop**, where the rockstar chef's global fan base slurp down bowlfuls of these wispy rye noodles bobbing in a sumptuous broth. **City Kitchen** is yet another formidable bazaar featuring a rustic-industrial setting and outfitted with kiosks from **ilili Box**, **Gabriela's Taqueria**, **Luke's Lobster**, **Dough** and more. Of course, cached beneath the graceful Plaza hotel is the tastefully decorated **Plaza**

**Food Hall**. Here, a dizzying array of comestibles is on full-display and makes for a fine attraction—or distraction. Curated by mega-watt personality, Todd English, this 32,000-square-foot space is a perfect meeting spot if you're looking to sip, savor, and shop. Beginning with caviar, lobster rolls, or sushi; and closing with coffee or cupcakes, this veritable tour de force perfectly typifies the city's culinary elite.

## FOOD FIXES

**A** few steps west and Gotham City's eclectic identity reveals yet another facet, where Ninth Avenue unearths a wealth of eats. A wonderful start to any day is practically certified at **Amy's Bread**, where fresh-baked baguettes lend countless restaurant kitchens that extra crumb of culture. But, it is their famously colorful cakes and cookies that tempt passersby off the streets and into the store. Across the way, **Poseidon Bakery** is a winner for Greek sweets. It is also the last place in town that still crafts their own phyllo dough by hand—a taste of the spanakopita will prove it. Then, even though its moniker depicts another district, **Sullivan Street Bakery**'s one and only retail outlet is also housed along this stretch—a location so perilously far west in the Manhattan mindset

that its success is worth its weight in gold. Just as Jim Lahey's luxurious loaves claim a cult-like following, so do the fantastic components (a warm Portuguese-style roll?) at **City Sandwich**. Meanwhile, theater-lovers and Lincoln Tunnel-bound commuters know to drive by **The Counter** and place an order for hand-crafted burgers, proclaimed to be a "must try before you die." New Yorkers in the know never tire of the lure behind **La Boîte**'s spice blends, or the sumptuous cured meats and formaggi found at **Sergimmo Salumeria**. Find more such salty goodness at veteran butcher, **Esposito Meat Market**, proudly purveying every part of the pig alongside piles of offal. Thirsty travelers should keep heading further south of Port Authority Bus Terminal to uncover an enclave rich with restaurants and food marts. Here, foodies start their feasting at **International Grocery** proffering such pleasures as olives, oils, spices, and spreads. But, among their outstanding produce, find the renowned *taramosalata* (as if prepared by the gods atop Mount Olympus themselves). Then consider the fact that it also appears on the menu of many fine-dining destinations nearby, and know that you're in for truly something special.

## TIME WARNER CENTER

**F**inally, no visit to this district is complete without paying homage to the epicurean feat that is the **Time Warner Center**. Presiding and preening over Columbus Circle, high-flying chefs indulge both themselves and their pretty patrons here with ground-breaking success. Discover a range of savory and sweet delights indoors—from **Bouchon Bakery**'s colorful French macarons, to the eye-popping style and sass of **Ascent Lounge**. Located on the fourth floor, **Center Bar** (brought to you by Michael Lomonaco) is a sophisticated perch for enjoying a champagne cocktail while taking in the views of lush Central Park. This is classic New York—only more glossy and glamorous than usual.

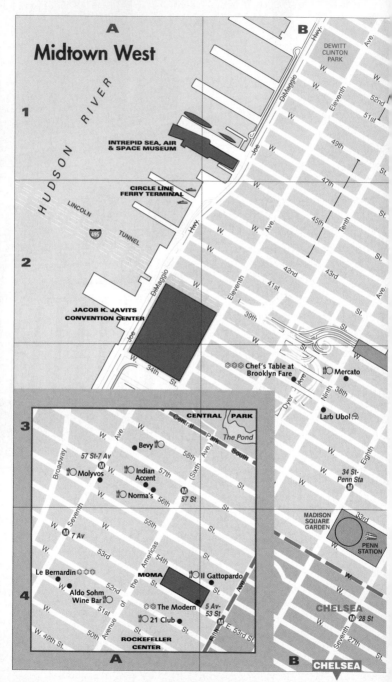

# Midtown West

A

B

**Midtown West**

HUDSON RIVER

DEWITT CLINTON PARK

1

INTREPID SEA, AIR & SPACE MUSEUM

Joe DiMaggio Hwy.

Eleventh Ave.

52nd

51st

W.

49th

CIRCLE LINE FERRY TERMINAL

LINCOLN TUNNEL

495

47th

W. 45th

Tenth Ave.

St.

2

JACOB K. JAVITS CONVENTION CENTER

Eleventh Ave.

42nd 43rd

41st

39th

34th St.

Ninth Ave.

Dyer Ave.

38th

❁❁❁ Chef's Table at Brooklyn Fare

🍴◎ Mercato

● Larb Ubol 🍴

3

CENTRAL PARK

The Pond

Broadway

57 St-7 Av Ⓜ

W. Ave.

● Bevy 🍴◎

Central Park South

58th

W.

🍴◎ Molyvos

🍴◎ Indian Accent

57th

(Sixth) Ave.

St.

Seventh Ave.

W. 56th

🍴◎ Norma's

Ⓜ 57 St

34 St-Penn Sta Ⓜ

Eighth Ave.

W. 55th

St.

Ⓜ 7 Av

W. 53rd

MADISON SQUARE GARDEN

33rd

PENN STATION

Le Bernardin ❁❁

Avenue of the Americas

MOMA

🍴◎ Il Gattopardo

4

Aldo Sohm Wine Bar ●

52nd

❁❁ The Modern

5 Av-53 St Ⓜ

W. 51st

🍴◎ 21 Club

E. 53rd St.

CHELSEA

Ⓜ 28 St

50th

W. 49th St.

ROCKEFELLER CENTER

Seventh

27th

A

B

CHELSEA

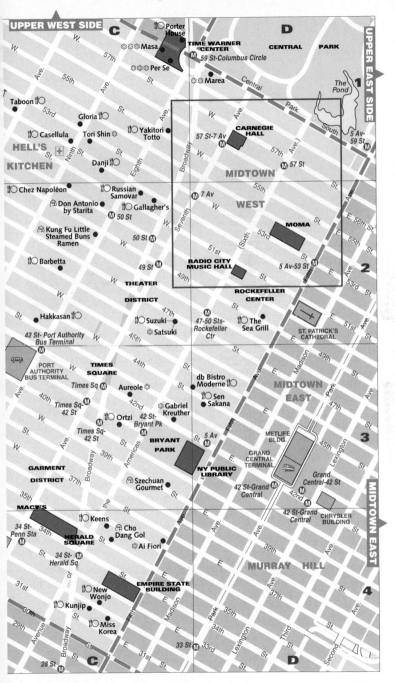

UPPER WEST SIDE

**C**

🍴 Porter House

❄❄❄ Masa

❄❄❄ Per Se

**TIME WARNER CENTER**

Ⓜ 59 St-Columbus Circle

**D**

CENTRAL     PARK

UPPER EAST SIDE

❄❄ Marea

Central

The Pond

Taboon 🍴

W. 53rd

St.

5 Av-59 St Ⓜ

Gloria 🍴

Ninth St.

🍴 Casellula    Tori Shin ❄

🍴 Yakitori Totto

57 St-7 Av Ⓜ

**CARNEGIE HALL**

57th

Ⓜ 57 St

**HELL'S KITCHEN**

Danji 🍴

W.

Broadway

**MIDTOWN**

🍴 Chez Napoléon

🍴 Russian Samovar

Ⓜ 7 Av

W.

55th

St.

**WEST**

Don Antonio by Starita

🍴 Gallagher's

Ⓜ 50 St

Seventh

(Sixth)

**MOMA**

Kung Fu Little Steamed Buns Ramen

50 St Ⓜ

53rd

E. 56th St.

55th

🍴 Barbetta

49 St Ⓜ

51st

**RADIO CITY MUSIC HALL**

5 Av-53 St Ⓜ

53rd

**THEATER**

49th

St.

 Av.

**DISTRICT**

47th

**ROCKEFELLER CENTER**

51st

Hakkasan 🍴

🍴 Suzuki

❄ Satsuki

45th

Ⓜ 47-50 Sts-Rockefeller Ctr

🍴 The Sea Grill

**ST. PATRICK'S CATHEDRAL**

49th

**42 St- Port Authority Bus Terminal**

Ⓜ

W. 44th

St.

Madison

**PORT AUTHORITY BUS TERMINAL**

Ⓜ

**TIMES SQUARE**

Times Sq Ⓜ

Aureole ❄

🍴 db Bistro Moderne

**MIDTOWN EAST**

47th

Times Sq-42 St

42nd

St.

🍴 Sen Sakana

❄ Gabriel Kreuther

Park

40th

W.

St.

Times Sq- 42 St

🍴 Ortzi   42 St- Bryant Pk

5 Av Ⓜ

Lexington

45th

**METLIFE BLDG.**

**GRAND CENTRAL TERMINAL**

Broadway

39th

Americas

**BRYANT PARK**

Fifth

E.

**GARMENT DISTRICT**

37th

the

**NY PUBLIC LIBRARY**

42 St-Grand Central Ⓜ

**Grand Central-42 St**

42nd

42 St-Grand Central

❄ Szechuan Gourmet

St.

35th

**MACY'S**

🍴 Keens

**HERALD SQUARE**

34th

❄ Cho Dang Gol

Ⓜ 42nd

**CHRYSLER BUILDING**

34 St- Penn Sta Ⓜ

St.

 ❄ Ai Fiori

39th

Ⓜ 34 St- Herald Sq

**MURRAY HILL**

37th

31st

🍴 New Wonjo

**EMPIRE STATE BUILDING**

Madison

35th

🍴 Kunjip

30th

Avenue

Broadway

🍴 Miss Korea

Park

34th

Lexington

28th Ⓜ

**C**

31st

33 St Ⓜ 33rd

**D**

Second

MIDTOWN EAST

227

# AI FIORI ❀
*Italian*

XXX | 🍸 🥂 ♿ 🎦 🛎

Elegantly accessed by a sweeping spiral staircase or the Langham Place hotel elevator, Ai Fiori stands proudly above its busy Fifth Avenue address. Walls of windows and espresso-dark polished wood dominate the space. The Carrara marble bar and lounge furnished with silvery tufted banquettes are ideal for solo diners; large florals, brown leather chairs, and square columns adorn the formal dining room. No matter where you sit, servers are attentive, the linens are thick, chargers are monogrammed with a goldleaf "F" and every last detail is very, very lovely.

As one might expect of a Michael White restaurant, pastas here are masterful. Begin with perfectly al dente curls of trofie nero intertwined with a spicy Ligurian crustacean ragù of sepia and scallops. Crowned by spiced mollica, it boasts a perfect play on flavor and texture. Fish courses can be even more enticing. Dine on one of the brightest, freshest fluke crudos known to this city, served atop Meyer lemon breadcrumbs and enhanced by a generous dollop of American sturgeon caviar.

End with a tartiletta di cioccolato, featuring a thin cocoa sable crust and topped with a dark Valrhona chocolate-covered marshmallow, for a delicious and fitting finale.

🔲 400 Fifth Ave. (bet. 36th & 37th Sts.)
🚇 34 St - Herald Sq
📞 (212) 613-8660 — **WEB:** www.aifiorinyc.com
🔲 Lunch Mon– Fri   Dinner nightly          **PRICE: $$$$**

# ALDO SOHM WINE BAR  ⅈ◯

## *Contemporary*

🔲 | 🍧 ⬚  **MAP:** A4

Step through this buffed metal doorway to find an oenophile's fantasy where Zalto stemware is stacked high and each polished glass is ready to be filled by one of the 200 selections brilliantly curated by Le Bernardin's super-star sommelier, Aldo Sohm. Over 40 wines on the list are offered by the glass.

A tailored crowd sits and sips—perhaps on an oversized U-shaped sofa, at a comfy counter, or handful of tall tables. The scene is luxe but also comfortable, featuring crystal fixtures, vivid artwork, and a stylish array of bric-a-brac stacked high to the soaring ceiling. Tapas-sized snacks are designed for sharing with wine consumption in mind and include a plate of cheeses, charcuterie, harissa-roasted carrots, or chicken drumstick prepared coq au vin-style.

🟦 151 W. 51st St. (bet. Sixth & Seventh Aves.)
🚇 50 St (Broadway)
📞 (212) 554-1143 — **WEB:** www.aldosohmwinebar.com
🟦 Lunch Mon – Fri   Dinner Mon – Sat     **PRICE: $$**

# BARBETTA  ⅈ◯

## *Italian*

✗✗✗ | 🍧 🏠 ⬚  **MAP:** C2

It doesn't get more old-world New York than this iconic Restaurant Row institution. Opened in 1906, Barbetta is a testament to proper dining out: men are required to don dinner jackets, outerwear is mandatorily checked, and a brigade of starched servers flit about the hushed and gilded surrounds. Perhaps unsurprisingly, the impossibly romantic patio has been the backdrop for countless marriage proposals.

The kitchen's Northern-influenced specialties are listed on thick cardstock, and each selection is highlighted by the year of its addition to the menu. Linguine with pesto alla Genovese is as scrumptious today as it was in 1914; while luscious rabbit alla Piemontese, dating back to the Clinton era and braised in white wine and lemon, is equally divine.

🟦 321 W. 46th St. (bet. Eighth & Ninth Aves.)
🚇 50 St (Eighth Ave.)
📞 (212) 246-9171 — **WEB:** www.barbettarestaurant.com
🟦 Lunch & dinner Tue – Sat     **PRICE: $$$**

# AUREOLE ✿

*Contemporary*

XxX | 🍸 ♿ ☐

Nestled smack dab in the middle of the melee that constitutes modern-day Times Square, Aureole's message is clear from the moment you enter its serene glass façade: drop your bags (and perhaps your shoulders) and relax—it's time to be pampered by a truly exquisite meal in a truly luxurious setting.

Up front, you'll find the Liberty Room, home to a lively bar that's ideal for an after-work drink or pre-dinner cocktail; and a small collection of handsome, walnut-topped tables comprising a more casual dining area. Toward the back of the restaurant, the formal dining room cuts an impressive, elegant figure with sexy low lighting, crisp white tablecloths, and polished table settings.

Dinner might begin with a beautifully composed and luxurious Hudson Valley foie gras and fig terrine presented alongside a glistening gelée of vin cotto and poached figs. Then move on to tender Nova Scotia halibut crisped to perfection, nestled in a mound of crushed minted peas, and dressed tableside with fish fumet. Desserts are equally sumptuous, including the elegantly prepared apple-Cassis semifreddo sporting a dark chocolate base, piped ribbon of whipped cream, and paired with green apple sorbet.

■ 135 W. 42nd St. (bet. Broadway & Sixth Ave.)
🚇 42 St - Bryant Pk
☏ (212) 319-1660 — **WEB:** www.charliepalmer.com
■ Lunch Mon – Fri   Dinner Mon – Sat          PRICE: $$$$

# BEVY ⑪○

*American*

✗✗✗ | 品 ㅼ

Nestled inside the luxe Park Hyatt hotel, just across from Carnegie Hall, Bevy is a sultry rebuttal to the gray hustle-bustle of midtown. Inside, you'll find a private-feeling dining room, where the magnanimous staff puts customers at ease with effortless service. Next door, a lively lounge offers some pre- or post-dinner fun.

The kitchen doles out an expansive roster of dishes for its well-heeled patrons. While some go for the house specialty (a delicious roast chicken for two), others may opt for more hearty, upscale entrées like Maine lobster, rib eye, or Mangalitsa pork collar. Don't miss the Diver scallops though, served with Romesco sauce and a verdant watercress oil; or seasonal vegetables, highlighted in their own section of the menu.

■ 153 W. 57th St. (bet. Sixth & Seventh Aves.)
🚇 57 St
✆ (212) 897-2188 — **WEB:** www.bevynyc.com
■ Dinner Tue – Sat                          PRICE: $$$

# CASELLULA ⑪○

*American*

▤

Casellula oozes with warmth in both look and feel. Dark wood tables, exposed brick, and flickering votives are a sight for sore eyes, while the delightful staff is so attentive and friendly that you may never want to leave.

Small plates are big here, while medium ones feature tasty sandwiches (crunchy muffulettas stuffed with fontina and cured meats) and shrimp tacos splashed with salsa verde. Pity the lactose intolerant, as cheese (and lots of it) followed by dessert (maybe a pumpkin ice cream "sandwich" pecked with brown butter caramel?) are part and parcel of the special experience at this petite place. Feeling blue? They've got that and much more with over 50 different varieties, perfectly complemented by an excellent and vast wine list.

■ 401 W. 52nd St. (bet. Ninth & Tenth Aves.)
🚇 50 St (Eighth Ave.)
✆ (212) 247-8137 — **WEB:** www.casellula.com
■ Dinner nightly                            PRICE: $$

# CHEF'S TABLE AT BROOKLYN FARE ✿✿✿

*Contemporary*

✕✕✕ | 🍸 ♿

**MAP:** B3

Like a wild mushroom after spring rain, Chef César Ramirez's new home for his incomparable Chef's Table has sprung up in Hell's Kitchen, seemingly overnight. As with the original, the interior is furnished with a long dining counter positioned before the stainless steel and polished copper kitchen to keep the mood celebratory and everyone's eyes on the cooking.

Several tables with banquette seating expand on the former location's comfort and capacity, thereby adding a bit of formality to the otherwise cutting-edge space.

Chef Ramirez may be a visionary, but he refrains from being showy by keeping simplicity and astounding precision at the heart of each dish. The result is a cuisine that is visually arresting, a mosaic of both flavors and textures that coaxes only the best from each morsel of fish. This begins with a tartlet generously filled with sour cream and a precariously balanced mountain of glistening trout roe. Scottish langoustines appear raw, but are in fact warmed just enough to retain their tenderness, finished with translucent radish and a bright blossom. Koshihikari rice gently stirred with foie gras and abalone is enriched by a sea urchin emulsion for a luscious denouement.

🔲 431 W. 37th St. (bet. Ninth & Tenth Aves.)

🚇 34 St - Hudson Yards

✆ (718) 243-0050 — **WEB:** www.brooklynfare.com

🔲 Dinner Tue – Sat

**PRICE:** $$$$

# CHEZ NAPOLÉON 🍴

*French*

🍴                              **MAP:** C2

Oh-so-popular and family-run by the Brunos since 1982, this atmospheric bistro is not to be missed for its unapologetically creamy and butter-dreamy plates of traditional French cuisine. It's not polite to discuss age, but let's just say that Chef/grandmère, Marguerite Bruno, has steadily commanded this kitchen for an impressive tenure.

The scene is magnifique. Take in the creaky wood floors and parchment-colored walls hung with French-themed jigsaw puzzles. Then indulge in chilled silky leeks dressed with the famous house vinaigrette; sautéed veal kidneys in mustard-cream sauce; and steak au poivre with black or green peppercorn sauce. Plan ahead when ordering so you have time (and space) for a classic dessert soufflé sided with crème anglaise.

◼ 365 W. 50th St. (bet. Eighth & Ninth Aves.)
🚇 50 St (Eighth Ave.)
☏ (212) 265-6980 — **WEB:** www.cheznapoleon.com
◼ Lunch Mon – Fri   Dinner Mon – Sat        **PRICE: $$**

# CHO DANG GOL 😊

*Korean*

🍴                              **MAP:** C4

For a change of pace in bustling Koreatown, Cho Dang Gol offers the barbecue-weary an opportunity to explore some of this nation's more rustic cooking. Soft tofu is the specialty of the house and for fitting reason (it's downright delicious). But, bubbling casseroles and spicy stews are equally heartwarming.

The menu also offers favorites like flaky pajeon, satisfying bibimbap, and marinated meats. A sautéed tofu trio with pork belly is stir fried with glassy sweet potato noodles and kimchi, in an excellent sweet and spicy red pepper sauce. The interior has a simple, homey appeal—its cozy dining room simply decorated with close-knit wood tables. The occasional burst of sound drifting down from the upstairs karaoke bar promises a little post-dinner fun.

◼ 55 W. 35th St. (bet. Fifth & Sixth Aves.)
🚇 34 St - Herald Sq
☏ (212) 695-8222 — **WEB:** www.cdgnyc.com
◼ Lunch & dinner daily              **PRICE:** 🪙

# DANJI 🍴

## Korean

🍴 | 🍸

Thanks to tall communal tables that practically fill the dining room, Chef Hooni Kim's Hell's Kitchen hot spot is both festive and bustling. Attractive and smartly designed, its silk panels, pottery, and striking display of spoons are further enhanced by a flattering lighting scheme.

Equally impressive are the menu's myriad small plates, each of them a refreshing take on Korean specialties. Blocks of soft tofu are quickly deep-fried and boldly dressed with gochujang and a ginger-scallion vinaigrette. Poached daikon rings accompanied by bok choy are glazed with a dark and spicy sauce and stacked high for dramatic presentation.

Vegetarian highlights include spicy, crispy dumplings filled with tofu, vegetables, and cellophane noodles.

- 346 W. 52nd St. (bet. Eighth & Ninth Aves.)
- 50 St (Eighth Ave.)
- (212) 586-2880 — **WEB:** www.danjinyc.com
- Lunch & dinner daily                    PRICE: $$

# DB BISTRO MODERNE 🍴

## Contemporary

🍴🍴 | 🎉 ♿ 🚗 🍷

Chef Daniel Boulud's midtown canteen is fashioned by Jeffrey Beers and dons a contemporary demeanor. The front lounge is abuzz with post-work and pre-theater gaggles, while well-behaved crowds in the back are seated in a walnut-paneled space dressed with mirrors and black-and-white photography.

Like its setting, the menu is inventive and unites classic bistro cooking with market-inspired creations. That lush pâté en croute is a buttery pastry encasing layers of creamy country pâté, guinea hen, and foie gras, dressed with huckleberry compote, toasted pine nuts, and pickled enoki mushrooms. Wild rice-crusted fluke presented with Hawaiian blue prawn and sauce Américaine further demonstrates the kitchen's contemporary leanings.

- 55 W. 44th St. (bet. Fifth & Sixth Aves.)
- 5 Av
- (212) 391-2400 — **WEB:** www.dbbistro.com
- Lunch & dinner daily                    PRICE: $$$

# DON ANTONIO BY STARITA 😄

*Pizza*

XX | ら                                    **MAP:** C2

Don Antonio's knows its way around a pie. The namesake outpost, located in Naples, has been running strong since 1901. And if that isn't enough street cred to send you running to Antonio Starita and Roberto Caporuscio's beloved pizzeria, then perhaps the generous buzz surrounding Caporuscio's other New York venture, Kesté, will do the trick.

Don Antonio's signature pie is the Montanara Starita—a lightly fried pizza laced with fresh house-made tomato sauce, smoked mozzarella and basil, then finished in the wood-fired oven. Oh, but who could stop there with treasures like the salsiccia e friarielli pizza to sample. This beauty arrives with sweet, crumbled fennel sausage, smoked mozzarella, bitter rapini greens and a glossy swirl of EVOO.

▪ 309 W. 50th St. (bet. Eighth & Ninth Aves.)
▪ 50 St (Eighth Ave.)
✆ (646) 719-1043 — **WEB:** www.donantoniopizza.com
▪ Lunch & dinner daily                    **PRICE:** $$

# GALLAGHER'S 🍴

*Steakhouse*

XX | 🎴 ら 🖵                              **MAP:** C2

A multi-million dollar renovation hasn't glossed over any of Gallagher's iconic character. Walls covered with photos of horses and jockeys harken back to the seasoned stallion's former proximity to the old Madison Square Garden. The menu's "other soup" is a sly reference held over from Prohibition days; and diners still walk past the window-fronted meat locker where slabs of USDA Prime beef are dry-aged.

Gallagher's fresh sparkle is exhibited by the display kitchen, set behind glass panes. The chefs here turn out contemporary-minded fare like hamachi crudo with a yuzu-jalapeño vinaigrette to go with choice cuts of meat grilled over hickory. The rib steak is a bone-in ribeye that arrives mouthwateringly tender with a side of warm and savory house sauce.

▪ 228 W. 52nd St. (bet. Broadway & Eighth Ave.)
▪ 50 St (Broadway)
✆ (212) 586-5000 — **WEB:** www.gallaghersnysteakhouse.com
▪ Lunch & dinner daily                    **PRICE:** $$$

# GABRIEL KREUTHER ✿

*Contemporary*

XxX | 🍸 🍷 ⚹ ⟷

**MAP:** C3

Proving that the death of fine dining has been grossly exaggerated, Alsace-born Gabriel Kreuther's eponymous midtown restaurant offers artfully designed surroundings, creative and eye-catching food, and service that is formal and quite ceremonial.

It's certainly a striking room, with columns of reclaimed wood juxtaposed with creamy white leather seating and a glass wall offering glimpses of the impressively calm goings-on in the kitchen. The table settings are immaculate too, with delicate glassware, cups and bowls that you can't stop stroking, and surgically thin modern cutlery that you'll either love or hate.

The chef's classical culinary upbringing underpins his modern creations and his Alsatian heritage plays a role too. Alongside kugelhopf, you'll also find sauerkraut—it makes an appearance in one of his more theatrical dishes where it's mixed with sturgeon, garnished with caviar and presented at the table with the lifting of a glass cloche filled with applewood smoke. The desserts, if you can get past their somewhat pretentious monikers ("revisited" or "ethereal" anyone?) show that the pastry section is also given license to push boundaries.

◼ 41 W. 42nd St. (bet. Fifth & Sixth Aves.)
🚇 42 St - Bryant Pk
✆ (212) 257-5826 — **WEB:** www.gknyc.com
◼ Lunch Mon – Fri   Dinner Mon – Sat

**PRICE:** $$$$

# GLORIA 🍴
## *Seafood*

ⵝ

Though dinner at Gloria doesn't come with a side of personal space (read: you'll likely be elbow-to-elbow with your neighbors as you dine), the tiny spot slays its Ninth Avenue competition with a trendy ambience, buzzing bar, and terrific food crafted by Chef Diego Garcia.

The concise, seafood-centric menu, which offers just a handful of savory items and two desserts, reflects the chef's impressive background. Expertly charred octopus or red snapper served in a red wine béarnaise-inspired sauce both hint at Garcia's time at Le Bernardin, while a tres leches cake filled with thick cream is a nod to his Mexican heritage. No matter what you order, be sure to arrive with a fully-charged phone, as these dishes practically beg to be shared on Instagram.

■ 401 W. 53rd St. (bet. Ninth & Tenth Aves.)
🚇 50 St (Eighth Ave.)
☏ (212) 956-0709 — **WEB:** www.gloria-nyc.com
■ Dinner Tue – Sat                          **PRICE: $$**

# HAKKASAN 🍴
## *Chinese*

ⵝⵝⵝ | 🕸 ♿ ⛶ 🚫

If this sensual and sophisticated lair doesn't come to mind when you crave quality Cantonese cooking, it's high time you added it to the list. Behind its front door lies a long, moodily-lit corridor that leads to a massive dining room, which, thanks to cobalt-blue glass, Carrara marble, and mirrors, feels intimate despite its size.

The equally elegant menu underscores mouthwatering dishes like jasmine tea-smoked chicken and stir-fried sugar pea pods with crabmeat and scallops; or bamboo steamers full of scallop siu mai topped with tobiko, King crab noodle rolls, as well as truffle and roasted duck bao. The prix-fixe dim sum, a wallet-friendly delight that synchs perfectly with Hakkasan's luxe tenor, is yet another decadent surprise.

■ 311 W. 43rd St. (bet. Eighth & Ninth Aves.)
🚇 42 St - Port Authority Bus Terminal
☏ (212) 776-1818 — **WEB:** www.hakkasan.com
■ Lunch Sat – Sun  Dinner nightly          **PRICE: $$$$**

# IL GATTOPARDO ¶O

*Italian*

XX | 🏠 🖨 ⚟                                              **MAP:** B4

This leopard's take on Italian dining favors elegance over rusticity. Set within two Beaux Arts townhouses (once home to a Rockefeller family member), the restaurant is an understated sprawl of ivory walls contrasted with dark-stained floors and smoky mirrors.

The smartly attired staff attends to a buttoned-up crowd digging into pricey but pleasing fare like shaved artichoke salad with organic frisée, lemon, olive oil, and bottarga di muggine.

Here, a golden-brown and crisp-skinned baby chicken arrives split into two neat halves, simply grilled with rosemary and lemon, and served with butter roasted potatoes. And like everything else at Il Gattopardo, the cassata Siciliana—with its candied fruit and bright green almond paste—is a dressed-up take on the classic.

■ 13-15 W. 54th St. (bet. Fifth & Sixth Aves.)
🚇 5 Av - 53 St
✆ (212) 246-0412 — **WEB:** www.ilgattopardonyc.com
■ Lunch & dinner daily                            **PRICE:** $$$

# INDIAN ACCENT ¶O

*Indian*

XxX | 🍸 🏠                                              **MAP:** A3

Nestled inside the posh Le Parker Méridien hotel, Indian Accent offers gorgeously plated food with a decidedly modern spin. An outpost of the highly acclaimed original in Delhi, the New York space is sleek and exotic, with purple banquettes, brass details and a shimmering gold-accent wall. The service is polished and professional, with the knowledgeable staff carefully walking you through a customized prix-fixe menu selected from various parts of the carte.

Celebrated chef Manish Mehrotra heads the talented kitchen, serving up impressive starters like freshly griddled phulka paired with jackfruit, green chili sauce, and micro sprouts. Perfectly tender sea bass is then coupled with herbed barley, trout roe, and puddled in creamy coconut sauce.

■ 123 W. 56th St. (bet. Sixth & Seventh Aves.)
🚇 57 St
✆ (212) 842-8070 — **WEB:** www.indianaccent.com
■ Lunch Mon – Sat   Dinner nightly                **PRICE:** $$$

# KEENS ❌🍴

## Steakhouse

❌❌ | 🕸 ⛲

It's not just carnivores who'll appreciate this most classic of steakhouses; Anglophiles, social historians, Scotch lovers and pipe smokers will also find themselves revelling in the immeasurably appealing atmosphere of Keens and its palpable sense of times past. Established in 1885, it suggests a Dickensian Gentleman's club, with its dark wood panelling and low ceiling lined with thousands of clay pipes, although these days the customers are mostly deal-making business types rather than extravagantly whiskered thespians.

Follow their lead and drape your jacket over the back of your chair, roll up your sleeves and attempt to gain control over a Porterhouse steak, dry-aged in-house, or finish their legendary mutton chop in one sitting.

🔲 72 W. 36th St. (bet. Fifth & Sixth Aves.)
🚇 34 St - Herald Sq
📞 (212) 947-3636 — **WEB:** www.keens.com
🔲 Lunch Mon – Fri   Dinner nightly

**PRICE: $$$**

# KUNG FU LITTLE STEAMED BUNS RAMEN 😨

## Chinese

❌

With its lineup of traditionally prepared comfort food, this steamy joint kicks Hell's Kitchen's Chinese competitors to the curb. Set among the bright lights of the Theater District yet more indicative of the noodle houses found south of Canal Street or along Flushing Avenue, the perpetually packed gem offers a so-so ambience but very friendly service.

Hand-pulled and hand-cut noodles are stir-fried with a number of mouthwatering accompaniments; while the dumpling variety is so great it's almost impossible to focus. Herb-spiked pork and shrimp wonton soup is well worth the 20-minute wait, allowing diners plenty of time to devour pan-fried Peking duck bundles and scallion pancakes stuffed with sliced beef; or steamed buns full of mushroom and bok choy.

🔲 811 Eighth Ave. (bet. 48th & 49th Sts.)
🚇 50 St (Eighth Ave.)
📞 (917) 388-2555 — **WEB:** www.kfdelicacy.com
🔲 Lunch & dinner daily

**PRICE:** 🐷🐷

# KUNJIP 🍽️
## Korean

🍴

MAP: C4

The first thing you need to know about this wildly popular restaurant is that it's open 24 hours. The second thing you need to know is that it's actually good. Even better news? An expansion has created additional seating in this two-level dining room, done up in spare, earthy hues and traditional wooden screens. It's classic, clean and simple—the message is clear. At Kunjip, the focus is most decidedly on the food.

Barbecue is always popular, and is done quite well at dinner. The menu, however, reaches much wider with a long list of hearty soups (a big hit with the lunch crowd), stews, and casseroles. Everything is excellent, but a steaming bowl of galbitang—bobbing with tender and fatty short rib, glass noodles and juicy daikon slivers—truly transcends.

◼ 32 W. 32nd St. (bet. Broadway & Fifth Ave.)
🚇 34 St - Herald Sq
✆ (212) 216-9487 — **WEB:** www.kunjip.com
◼ Lunch & dinner daily

PRICE: 🍝

# LARB UBOL 😃
## Thai

🍴

MAP: B3

The larb here really is good enough to be the restaurant's namesake as these spicy, crunchy, salty and herb-y salads sing with flavor. Yet Larb Ubol does much more with equal skill: the sheer size of their massive chicken wings defy nature, yielding enough crisp-skinned and chili-coated meat to satisfy any appetite. Yum moo krob mixes impossibly tender pork with abundant green chilies in a fish sauce dressing for a brilliant counterpoint in flavor; while kai jeow, a Thai-style omelet, is an unexpectedly comforting dish that highlights excellent technique. There may be a choice of three fillings, but the pickled garlic can't be beat.

The space itself is no more than basic; the location is, well, meh. Service is friendly, though not necessarily speedy.

◼ 480 Ninth Ave. (bet. 36th & 37th Sts.)
🚇 34 St - Penn Station
✆ (212) 564-1822 — **WEB:** www.larbubol.com
◼ Lunch & dinner daily

PRICE: 🍝

# LE BERNARDIN ❀❀❀

*Seafood*

XxxX | ❀ ♿ 🛋      **MAP:** A4

When the definitive history of New York City's dining scene is written, Le Bernardin will have a chapter all to itself. Maguy Le Coze and Eric Ripert's midtown icon has been entertaining the city's movers and shakers for over 20 years now and its popularity remains undimmed.

In less experienced hands, the sheer size and scale of this handsome restaurant could make it unwieldy, but the service team is well-drilled and clued-up and as soon as you walk in you are enveloped in its warm embrace. Lunch is busy with those who know what they want and trust this well-oiled machine to deliver it in the time they have available. Come at dinner for a more languid affair.

The menu is divided into headings of "Almost raw," "Barely touched," and "Lightly cooked," but don't be fooled, these dishes have considerable depth. Seafood restaurants have no hiding place when it comes to cooking fish and crustaceans and this kitchen always hits its marks—whether that's poaching halibut, pan-roasting monkfish, baking striped bass, searing tuna or charring octopus. And the fish is always the star on the plate, while the accompanying ingredients, like great backing singers, are there to help it shine.

▪ 155 W. 51st St. (bet. Sixth & Seventh Aves.)
🚇 50 St (Broadway)
📞 (212) 554-1515 — **WEB:** www.le-bernardin.com
▪ Lunch Mon – Fri   Dinner Mon – Sat      **PRICE: $$$$**

# MAREA ❀ ❀
*Seafood*

XxX | 🦪 ⏲

**MAP:** D1

A grown-up restaurant for grown-up people in a grown-up city, Marea couldn't really be found anywhere other than Central Park South. Its urbane clientele ensures the atmosphere remains as sophisticated as ever and the restaurant keeps its side of the deal by providing polished, confident service and a smart, comfortable environment.

Fish and shellfish are the stars of the show and Italian the chosen language. At first glance the menu can appear intimidating, as the choice is considerable—but once you've decided to have four courses (and it would be churlish to have any fewer) then it all falls into place with the prix-fixe.

Nothing starts a meal like crudo and the selection here is impressive, but also consider generously sized antipasti, like creamy white polenta with calamari. Pasta is yet another highlight and leads nicely into the fish course. The quality and condition of the fish are extraordinary, but that would count for little if the kitchen didn't get the cooking process spot on—and it does. Try the wild striped bass and you'll see just how perfect the timings are. Add in an impressive Eurocentric wine list, strong in Italy and Burgundy, and you have all the ingredients for a great meal.

◼ 240 Central Park South (bet. Broadway & Seventh Ave.)
🚇 59 St - Columbus Circle
✆ (212) 582-5100 — **WEB:** www.marea-nyc.com
◼ Lunch & dinner daily

**PRICE: $$$$**

# MASA ✿✿✿

*Japanese*

XX | 🍸 🏺 ♿

To taste what may be the continent's best sushi, experience the quiet, contemplative, and very exclusive ceremony of Chef Masa Takayama's omakase. Everything here carries a certain weight, beginning with the heavy wooden door and carrying through to the bill. The room of course is as unchanging and calming as a river stone, set amid blonde hinoki wood and a gargantuan forsythia tree. Yes, you'll forget it's on the fourth floor of a mall.

Attention to detail is unsurpassed and at times it may seem like a bit much, but a reverential spirit is part of your meal here. Service displays the same smooth grace, with servers at-the-ready carrying their hot towels, fingerbowls, tea, and bits of insight.

Awaken the palate with a sweet chunk of hairy crab meat dressed in citrusy yuzu beneath creamy tomalley. This may be followed by the chef's signature glass coup of minced toro and a very fine—and very generous—pile of Osetra caviar. Maine uni is downright wondrous, served in its shell with caramelized custard and paper-thin, melting sheets of white truffle. The chef's selection of sushi is unrivaled; the rice is firm and temperate, garnishes are subtle, and quality of fish is supreme.

■ 10 Columbus Circle (in the Time Warner Center)
🚇 59 St - Columbus Circle
✆ (212) 823-9807 — **WEB:** www.masanyc.com
■ Lunch Tue – Fri  Dinner Mon – Sat          **PRICE:** $$$$

# MERCATO 🍴○

*Italian*

✗

Italian hospitality with a Pugliese accent is on display at Mercato, a rustic trattoria in the western midtown hinterlands. The space is country-chic, with distressed wood tables, soft, exposed bulbs, and vintage signs. The atmosphere is inviting and the menu is inspired by the classic dishes of Puglia, the birthplace of owner Fabio Camardi.

First get a drink in your hand, then start with fave e cicoria, a straightforward purée of fava beans and garlicky chicory greens. A well-rounded Italian meal must have pasta, so be sure to indulge in the likes of orecchiette with broccoli rabe and garlic, enhanced by anchovies and breadcrumbs. For something deeply satisfying, try the fennel-dusted porchetta with a hearty side of potato and green cabbage mash.

■ 352 W. 39th St. (bet. Eighth & Ninth Aves.)
🏢 42 St - Port Authority Bus Terminal
✆ (212) 643-2000 — **WEB:** www.mercatonyc.com
■ Lunch & dinner daily                    PRICE: $$

# MISS KOREA 🍴○

*Korean*

✗✗ | ▭

24-hour access to delicious Korean food? Yes please, Miss Korea. Located in the heart of K-Town, this popular restaurant is guaranteed to have a line out the door during peak dinner hours, but once inside you'll find a fairly serene décor, with each of its floors dedicated to a unique aspect of Korean culture.

The first floor offers the most robust menu; the second floor is more intimate, with Zen-like private dining rooms and a set menu featuring Imperial cuisine. Each floor is packed with blonde wooden tables fixed with grills. However, make sure to go for the outstanding clay pot galbi highlighting tender USDA Prime beef short ribs marinated on the bone for 24 hours, then cut tableside and grilled to heavenly perfection on the spot.

■ 10 W. 32nd St. (bet. Broadway & Fifth Ave.)
🏢 34 St - Herald Sq
✆ (212) 594-4963 — **WEB:** www.misskoreabbq.com
■ Lunch & dinner daily                    PRICE: $$

# THE MODERN ⌘⌘

*Contemporary*

XxX | ⌘ | ♿ | 🚇                    **MAP:** A4

It goes without saying that The Modern has one of the city's most prized locations, designed to capture the iconic feel of the MoMA in which it is seamlessly housed. Art enthusiasts have always appreciated its timeless and glorious surrounds; and thanks to an ambitious nip-tuck, they are sure to notice the improved acoustics, which facilitate quiet conversation and match the calm of the view over the sculpture garden. The state-of-the-art kitchen allows the team to grow into its full creative potential—both in the dining room and at the buzzy bar. But for a truly special experience, book the chef's table (complete with a multi-course tasting menu) inside the kitchen.

Chef Abram Bissell and crew are wowing these globe-trotting patrons with excellent food and warm, well-timed service. Appealing dishes showcase clean flavors and may include roasted cauliflower with crab butter, almond-cauliflower purée, and crabmeat. Delicate balance and top ingredients are at the height of tender lobster "marinated with truffles" and served in a luscious sauce with radishes and herbs.

For dessert, rhubarb bread pudding is crowned with vanilla-mascarpone mousse for a bit of flourish and whole lot of fun.

▪ 9 W. 53rd St. (bet. Fifth & Sixth Aves.)
🚇 5 Av - 53 St
✆ (212) 333-1220 — **WEB:** www.themodernnyc.com
▪ Lunch Mon – Fri   Dinner Mon – Sat          **PRICE: $$$$**

# MOLYVOS ⍢○

*Greek*

XX

Yes, it's true: the city has upped its Greek game in recent years. But Molyvos has more than earned its OG status—having served fresh, Mediterranean cuisine to a loyal uptown crowd for nearly twenty years. The secret to its longevity lies in the kitchen's beautifully simple and enjoyable food, smart, polished service, and casually elegant setting (tables covered in white cloth and a spare, rustic aesthetic).

Executive Chef Carlos Carreto and collaborating partner, Diane Kochilas (whose books are on sale in the restaurant), oversee this terrific menu. Among a host of delicious sounding (and tasting) options is the octopus carpaccio spotlighting a tender terrine topped with arugula, capers and sumac-and fennel pollen-dusted red onion slivers.

■ 871 Seventh Ave. (bet. 55th & 56th Sts.)
🚇 57 St - 7 Av
✆ (212) 582-7500 — **WEB:** www.molyvos.com
■ Lunch & dinner daily                          PRICE: $$

# NEW WONJO ⍢○

*Korean*

XX

New Wonjo offers a delightful respite in this jam-packed quarter of K-town. The modest space is spread over two floors and is mighty popular for barbecue-seeking groups. The fact that these grills still use charcoal only adds to the overall lure. And no matter the time, one can expect to find hordes of diners huddling around platters of marinated beef short ribs (kalbi) or thinly sliced pork belly (samgyupsal).

Non-barbecue delights include mandoo, chap chae and cochu pa jeon. But, keep room to savor soups like ban gye tang—a soothing ginseng-infused broth bobbing with sticky rice- garlic- and jujubes-stuffed chicken. Gobdol bi bim bap with minced beef, a runny egg, and other spicy condiments is wonderfully flavorful but only incendiary upon request.

■ 23 W. 32nd St. (bet. Broadway & Fifth Ave.)
🚇 34 St - Herald Sq
✆ (212) 695-5815 — **WEB:** www.newwonjo.com
■ Lunch & dinner daily                          PRICE: $$

# NORMA'S 🍴

*American*

✗✗ | 🚽 🛶            **MAP:** A3

Serving heaping platters of breakfast well into the afternoon, Norma's may have been inspired by the humble diner but rest assured that she is no greasy spoon. Tables at this Le Parker Méridien dining room are bound to be filled with business types already dealing over the first meal of the day. Upscale touches include tables wide enough to accommodate a laptop beside your plate, a polished staff, and gratis smoothie shots.

The menu adds personality with whimsically titled dishes like "Very Berry Brioche French Toast" or "Normalita's Huevos Rancheros." The Crunchy French Toast's outrageously over-the-top sweetness begins with a layering of crisped rice, gilded with a sprinkling of powdered sugar, ramekin of caramel sauce, and individual bottle of maple syrup.

- 119 W. 56th St. (bet. Sixth & Seventh Aves.)
- 57 St
- ☏ (212) 708-7460 — **WEB:** www.normasnyc.com
- Lunch daily            **PRICE:** $$

# ORTZI 🍴

*Spanish*

✗ | ♿ 🚽            **MAP:** C3

The Basque region of Spain takes center stage at this delicious tapas restaurant courtesy of talented chef, Jose Garces. Located inside midtown's LUMA Hotel, the space offers a cozy dining room, as well as a popular bar and lounge area that makes a clutch spot for people-watching.

Along with rustic braises and cazuelas filled with stews, this region favors its beloved seafood—and the raw crudo preparations are not to be missed. Gambas a la planxa, served straight from the grill—head and tail still intact—with a wedge of lemon and drizzle of salsa verde, are perfectly fresh; while braised boneless pork ribs, balanced nicely between sweet and savory, are served over a bed of black beans, crema, pickled onion, and topped with a nest of fried onion sticks.

- 120 W. 41st St. (bet. Broadway & Sixth Ave.)
- 42 St - Bryant Pk
- ☏ (212) 730-8900 — **WEB:** www.ortzirestaurant.com
- Lunch & dinner daily        **PRICE:** $$$

# PER SE ❀ ❀ ❀

*Contemporary*

XxXxX | 🍸 ♿ 🖨  

**MAP:** C1

There is no missing this entrance on the Time Warner Center's fourth floor, where an outdoor patio bordered with potted plants and creeping ivy draw the eye to that iconic blue door. While the patio entry is indoors and the greenery is as faux as the idea that a garden can bloom next to a mall escalator, that Cal-French aesthetic invites with wondrous effect.

Arrive in the dining room to face one of the city's best views of Columbus Circle and Central Park. An upscale sense of calm—the kind that only money can buy—soaks the atmosphere inside. And dining here is so relaxing, whisper-quiet, and insanely expensive that it almost feels like a luxuriating day in the spa. A synchronized brigade of servers ensures that your every need is met.

Chef Thomas Keller's cuisine is at once timeless and of the moment, raising the bar with meals that express artistry, seasonality, and sourcing that can seem hyperbolic—they know which Vermont cow gave the milk for your butter. Scallop-edged pierogies are so delicate that the purple tinge of braised cabbage shows from within, making an artful contrast to the surrounding Brussels sprout leaves, candied chestnut, and black truffle butter. Trios of dessert and house chocolates somehow get better with every meal.

◼ 10 Columbus Circle (in the Time Warner Center)
🚇 59 St - Columbus Circle
📞 (212) 823-9335 — **WEB:** www.perseny.com
◼ Lunch Fri – Sun   Dinner nightly

**PRICE:** $$$$

# PORTER HOUSE ¶O

*Steakhouse*

XxX | 88 & ⌖                                    **MAP:** C1

Michael Lomonaco's flagship steakhouse offers unparalleled views of Central Park from its Time Warner Center perch. Here, tables are well-spaced and allow for fine dining, but look for those few intimate booths located in the front bar area—they make for a great escape on busy nights.

The views certainly distinguish this handsome retreat from the pack, as do its carefully selected aged meats, quality fish, and expert sides. The kitchen puts out a tasty helping of sweet and spicy onion rings, buttermilk-battered and deep-fried in portions designed for linebackers. The beautifully marbled ribeye is aged for more than 45 days and would be delicious simply seared, though a chili rub adds an aggressive spice. Cool down with a lightly dressed purslane salad.

▪ 10 Columbus Circle (in the Time Warner Center)
▪ 59 St - Columbus Circle
✆ (212) 823-9500 — **WEB:** www.porterhousenewyork.com
▪ Lunch & dinner daily                          **PRICE: $$$$**

# RUSSIAN SAMOVAR ¶O

*Russian*

XX | ⌖ ⬓                                        **MAP:** C2

Which came first: the vodka or the celebs? It's hard to say when it comes to this hot spot, which caters to hockey players, Russian intelligentsia, and vodka aficionados alike. Our bets are on that beautiful vodka selection, available in all kinds of flavors, qualities, and sizes (shot, carafe, or bottle).

Nestled into the bustling Theater District, Russian Samovar is both quirky and elegant—with low lighting, glass panels, and musicians tickling the piano and violin. The staff is attentive, sweet, and can walk you through delicious fare like fresh salmon-caviar blini, prepared tableside; pelmeni, tender veal dumplings served with sour cream and honey mustard; or milk-cured Baltic herring, paired with pickled onions, potatoes, and carrots.

▪ 256 W. 52nd St. (bet. Broadway & Eighth Ave.)
▪ 50 St (Broadway)
✆ (212) 757-0168 — **WEB:** www.russiansamovar.com
▪ Lunch Tue – Sun   Dinner nightly              **PRICE: $$**

# SATSUKI ⌘

*Japanese*

XX | ⌓ ⅆ

The unique nature of this marvel begins with its layout. Descend to the lower level and first encounter the opulent Three Pillars bar. Then comes the elegant Suzuki dining room, and finally reach your goal at Satsuki. This omakase-only counter seats no more than ten guests in an utterly tranquil shrine dedicated to upscale Japanese cuisine.

Meals begin with the presentation of a wooden box, displaying the seafood that will soon become your meal. Each component of this sushi is prepared with paramount care, right down to the blend of vinegars that season the rice. The selection of fish may sound familiar—shrimp, cuts of tuna, uni—but demonstrate the careful craftsmanship of Chef Toshio Suzuki, who spent an age honing his skills at Sushi Zen. A trio of sashimi is served with three distinct sauces for dipping. This is followed by a simmered dish, like braised monkfish liver with sesame salt. When the parade of sushi arrives, each morsel strives to outdo the last. Meals culminate as the chefs coax layers of flavor from petals of Hokkaido uni with a hint of wasabi, wonderfully mild needlefish, and fatty tuna from Spain.

Handrolls in crisp nori make for a superb conclusion.

■ 114 W. 47th St. (bet. Sixth & Seventh Aves.)
🚇 47-50 Sts - Rockefeller Ctr
✆ (212) 278-0010 — **WEB:** www.suzukinyc.com
■ Dinner Mon – Sat                              PRICE: $$$$

# THE SEA GRILL ✲⭘

## Seafood

XxX | ♿ 🏮 ⬚ **MAP: D2**

This seafood-centric grill looks onto the iconic Rockefeller Center ice-skating rink and is framed by a wall of windows. Inside, find a cool aqua-accented space that inspires dressing up. Yes, tourists flock here after a spin on the ice, but it is also popular among business crowds—especially at lunch when the bar is bustling with sharp suits munching on lobster tail with a martini on the side.

The food itself is light and fresh. In-season you may find soft-shelled crab, served alongside a seaweed salad with citrus-marinated hearts of palm. The Northeast supplies many local seafood choices, such as the Block Island golden snapper a la plancha, with tangy cherry-tomato vinaigrette. Dependable and familiar classics like jumbo lump crab cakes are also on offer.

◼ 19 W. 49th St. (bet. Fifth & Sixth Aves.)
🚇 47-50 Sts - Rockefeller Ctr
☏ (212) 332-7610 — **WEB:** www.patinagroup.com
◼ Lunch & dinner Mon – Sat               **PRICE: $$$**

# SEN SAKANA ✲⭘

## Fusion

XxX | 🍷 ♿ ⬚ **MAP: D3**

Understanding this distinctive cuisine requires a bit of history: the 19th century brought large-scale immigration from Japan to Peru, and Nikkei cuisine is its glorious outcome. New York's best place to better understand this style of cooking is this highly anticipated multi-million dollar spot, comprised of a lounge, dining room, and sushi counter.

The name meaning "one-thousand fish" in Japanese is inspired by the seafood-abundant Peruvian coast; and the menu unveils dishes that seamlessly glide between both cultures' ingredients. The result? Delicious openers like cucumber batons with soy sauce and crispy quinoa, or a lovely ceviche of corvina in lime-y leche de tigre. A selection of skewers from the robata include succulent tsukune and much more.

◼ 28 W. 44th St. (bet. Fifth & Sixth Aves.)
🚇 5 Av
☏ (212) 221-9560 — **WEB:** www.sensakana.com
◼ Lunch Mon – Fri   Dinner nightly         **PRICE: $$$**

# SUZUKI 🍴○

*Japanese*

XX | ○ ㅎ

In typical Japanese fashion, Suzuki nails minimalist chic. The simple elegance doesn't end with its high design. Also noticeably uncluttered is the dining room, so if you're looking for a "scene," venture elsewhere.

The carte here spins to the season and is a study in fine-dining. Artful creations include a vegetarian variety, but those in the know may pass on that menu, order Chef Takashi Yamamoto's version of kaiseki, and let him show off his skills. Wanmori impresses with its exceptional consommé and delicate dumpling; top-quality sashimi is nicely plated; and baby ayu tempura elevates the Saikyo miso-marinated grilled rainbow trout. Kurobuta pork belly served Yamato-style with eggplant and red paprika is delicious despite its less-than-dazzling appearance.

▪ 114 W. 47th St. (bet. Sixth & Seventh Aves.)
▪ 47-50 Sts - Rockefeller Ctr
✆ (212) 278-0010 — **WEB:** www.suzukinyc.com
▪ Lunch Mon – Fri  Dinner Mon – Sat                    PRICE: $$$$

# SZECHUAN GOURMET 🙂

*Chinese*

X

Come lunchtime, midtown office workers with a jones for the tingly heat of Sichuan peppercorns or the burn of bright red chili oil know exactly where to go. A queue for tables is nearly obligatory, but the pace settles down in the evening and on weekends. Inside, red lanterns and pink linens accent the bustling room and servers attend to tables where specialties are piled high.

Though the menu is vast, you can't go wrong by tearing into the best scallion pancakes in town; or cool, hand-shredded chicken draped in a creamy sesame paste and chili oil. Smoked tofu shreds tossed with Asian celery and toasted sesame oil; or wok-tossed jumbo prawns with a crispy shell of peppercorns and spiced salt are the reason for those long lines.

▪ 21 W. 39th St. (bet. Fifth & Sixth Aves.)
▪ 42 St - Bryant Pk
✆ (212) 921-0233 — **WEB:** N/A
▪ Lunch Mon – Fri  Dinner nightly                    PRICE: $$

# TABOON ⅋⃝

*Middle Eastern*

XX | 🍴 🛋️                                      **MAP:** C1

Taboon's namesake brick-walled, wood-fired oven is burning a bit brighter these days since Chef Efi Nahon has returned to Hell's Kitchen's finest Middle Eastern dining room. That oven not only provides a heartwarming welcome and sets the whitewashed interior aglow, but it is also responsible for baking an incredible plank of bread that is alone worth a trip here.

Bring friends because this midtown marvel's menu is best enjoyed by grazing the list of zesty meze like house-made scallop and crab sausage shakshooka with poached quail egg, or a wild mushroom bread pudding with creamy taleggio and romesco. Vegetables aren't spared the flames either, as evident in a luscious and healthy pile of roasted broccolini splashed with orange oil.

- 773 Tenth Ave. (at 52nd St.)
- 50 St (Eighth Ave.)
- ☎ (212) 713-0271 — **WEB:** www.taboononline.com
- Lunch Sun  Dinner nightly                **PRICE:** $$

# 21 CLUB ⅋⃝

*American*

XX | ♿ 🖼️                                      **MAP:** A4

This fabled institution has been in business for over 85 years, and there's nothing slowing it down. Once a speakeasy, 21 Club has wined and dined everyone, from movie stars and music moguls to moneyed locals. Add to that its lantern-holding jockeys, townhouse exterior, leather- and wood-paneled dining room, and know this is a classic through and through. Gentlemen, don't forget to don your jackets here.

The menu is a perfect accompaniment to the setting featuring "Clayton's jumbo lump crab meat" dabbed with mustard and topped with cucumber; or splendid oxtail ravioli in a rich bone marrow-brown butter sauce. The Dutch apple pie with cheddar crumble and sarsaparilla ice cream offers a delightful contrast in taste, texture, and will guarantee your favor.

- 21 W. 52nd St. (bet. Fifth & Sixth Aves.)
- 5 Av - 53 St
- ☎ (212) 582-7200 — **WEB:** www.21club.com
- Lunch Mon – Fri  Dinner Mon – Sat        **PRICE:** $$$

# TORI SHIN ✿

*Japanese*

XX | 🍴

**MAP:** C1

Chefs Shu Ikeda and Atsushi Kono continue to honor the art of grilling at this popular and much loved destination.

A small bar pouring sake, shochu, and Japanese whiskey welcomes patrons into the multi-level dining room, featuring myriad table seating options that include a mezzanine with gold leaf walls. However, nothing compares to the entertainment of sitting at the counter, in front of the chefs fanning charcoal. This may be a serious and sophisticated restaurant, but the warm service as well as the upbeat atmosphere keep it approachable.

The focus is on organically raised chicken parts sizzling over the binchotan-fired grill, where embers are coaxed or cooled with extreme care. A varied selection of skewers is the high point of dining here, so be sure to try crisped wing, seared heart, and creamy liver—all of which need nothing more than a few grains of salt to impart true flavor. The omakase is a worthy progression that might include kara-age, chicken and duck tsukune, blistered shishito peppers, and bowls of springy ramen.

If you're here with friends, go à la carte as it's an ideal way to sample a host of options, which may also unveil favorites like chicken cha-shu.

▪ 362 W. 53rd St. (bet. Eighth & Ninth Aves.)
🚇 50 St (Eighth Ave.)
✆ (212) 757-0108 — **WEB:** www.torishinny.com
▪ Dinner nightly

**PRICE: $$$**

# YAKITORI TOTTO 🍴

## *Japanese*

🍴 | 🍽

**MAP:** C1

To say that this yakitori-ya nails authenticity is an epic understatement. Its discreet signage and second-floor location feels more Tokyo than Manhattan; J-pop dominates the playlist and the crowd is a reassuring mix of native-speakers and in-the-know foodies. Best of all is the aroma from sizzling skewers, deftly prepared over a charcoal fire. Kitchen classics are also popular, but the house specializes in grilled chicken parts like soriresu (chicken oyster) highlighting a layer of succulent skin. Equally tasty are charred shiitakes and niku yaki, dense rice wrapped in a thin shaving of pork belly and grilled until golden.

For dessert, annin tofu showcases silky apricot kernel "tofu" appealingly garnished with frozen raspberry and mint.

▩ 251 W. 55th St. (bet. Broadway & Eighth Ave.)
▩ 57 St - 7 Av
✆ (212) 245-4555 — **WEB:** www.tottonyc.com
▩ Lunch Mon – Fri   Dinner nightly                    **PRICE:** $$

Avoid the search for
parking. Look for valet 🚗.

# SOHO & NOLITA

SoHo (or the area South of Houston) and Nolita (North of Little Italy) prove not only that New York City has a penchant for prime shopping and divine dining, but that the downtown scene lives on now more than ever.

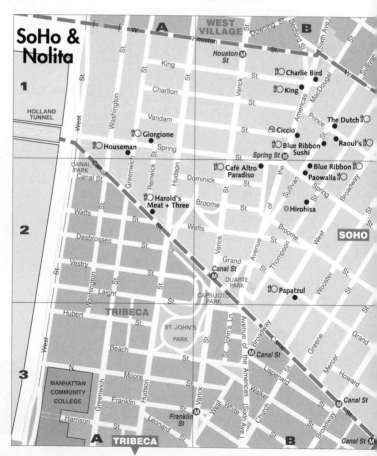

**SoHo & Nolita**

HOLLAND TUNNEL

CANAL PARK

SOHO

DUARTE PARK

CAPSUOTO PARK

ST. JOHN'S PARK

TRIBECA

MANHATTAN COMMUNITY COLLEGE

WEST VILLAGE

🍴 Charlie Bird

🍴 King

Ⓜ Houston St

Ⓜ Spring St

Ⓜ Canal St

Ⓜ Canal St

Ⓜ Franklin St

Ⓜ Canal St

🍴 Giorgione

🍴 Houseman

🍴 Café Altro Paradiso

🍴 Harold's Meat + Three

Ⓐ Ciccio

The Dutch

🍴 Blue Ribbon Sushi

Raoul's

Blue Ribbon 🍴

Paowalla 🍴

Ⓐ Hirohisa

🍴 Papatzul

## SHOPPING CENTRAL

**H**alfway through the 20th century, SoHo's cast-iron structures gave way to grand hotels, theaters, and commercial establishments. Thanks to such large-scale development, housing costs soared and artists absconded to adjoining Chelsea. And yet, these streets remain true to their promise of sun-drenched restaurants and sleek cafés filled with wine-sipping sophisticates, supermodels, and tourists. Locals fortunate enough to live in SoHo's

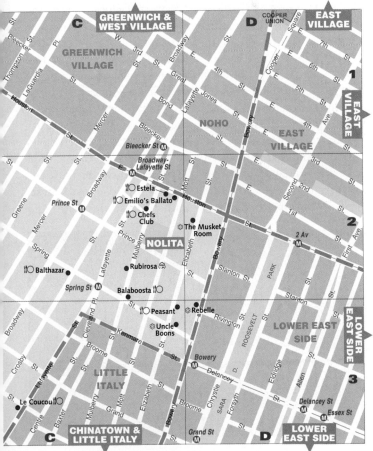

pricey condos know to stock up on cheese and meats from **Despaña**—they may even prepare a traditional tortilla Española for you with advance notice. **Broome Street Bar** is beloved for burgers (served on pitas) as well as desserts, which must be followed by a fantastic selection of sips at **Despaña Vinos y Mas**—the wine boutique next door. Scatttered with specialty shops and stores, these residents are here to stay, and entertaining guests is bound to be a breeze—after a visit to **Pino's Prime Meat Market** complete with quality options. The butchers here know the drill and are happy to engage rookies as they break down some of the best

game in town. On the flip side, vegetarians take great pride in **The Butcher's Daughter**, a meat-free emporium with the sole purpose of treating, cutting, and carving regionally sourced and sustainable produce.

When yearning for regional Italian specialties, sample the brick oven-baked prosciutto rolls at old-time treasure, **Parisi Bakery**; or the signature square pizza along with Sicilian arancini at **Prince St. Pizza**. Sugar junkies find their fix at **Vosges Haut-Chocolat**, where sweets reach new heights of innovation. Try the "Absinthe truffles" filled with Chinese star anise, fennel, dark chocolate, and

absinthe for a truly decadent experience. Then head on over to **MarieBelle**, another renowned cocoa queen, as it combines exotic ingredients and precise methods to create precious "chocolate jewels." For the Big Apple's most cherished cheeses, coffees, and other condiments, the original Broadway location of **Dean & Deluca** is always packed with locals, food lovers, and hungry office workers. And of course, for bagels in their best form, **Black Seed Bagels** on Elizabeth Street is a perpetual dream. Others may wait till the clock strikes happy hour, before sampling the stellar selection of sips at **City Winery**. Located over on Hudson Square and equipped with grapes, barrels, storage, and expertise, this is a bona fide destination for oenophiles to make their own private-label wine. But if sweet is your favorite way to seal a meal, then follow your nose to **Little Cupcake Bakeshop** on Prince Street or **Maman** (a café on Center Street) for comforting French baked goodies. Meanwhile, home shoppers frequent **Global Table** for its international accessories with simple lines and vivid finishes. Avoid hunger pangs inevitable after a shopping spree by visiting **Smile to Go**, a quiet spot set blocks from buzzing Canal Street that serves big breakfasts and light lunch bites.

## NIGHTS OUT IN NOLITA

**N**olita may have been an integral part of Little Italy back in the day, but today it is its own distinctive district and explodes with swanky boutiques, sleek restaurants, and hip bars. Located farther east than tourist-heavy SoHo, this neighborhood is also home to slightly cooler (read

cosmopolitan) groups. Not unlike its name, Nolita's eclectic residents shun the typical nine-to-five drill and reject SoHo's scene-y hangouts in favor of more intimate spots that invariably begin with the word "café."

**A**t the top of this list is **Café Habana**, offering that ubiquitous diner vibe and four square meals a day— breakfasts may include sunny-side-up eggs topped with salsa verde and salsa ranchera. Amazing Mexico City-style corn on the cob is also available for takeout next door at **Café Habana To Go**; while **Cafe Gitane** is an exquisite hipster hangout, well-tread at all times for wonderful French-Moroccan cooking, as well as a litany of stirring cocktails. The ethos in Nolita is simple yet resolute— to do a single thing very well. This may have been inspired by **Lombardi's** on Spring Street, which claims to be America's very first pizzeria (founded in 1905). The fact that they still serve these coal oven-fired delicacies by the pie (not the slice) clearly hasn't been bad for business, and lines continue to snake out the door if not the block at all hours. Hopping cuisines from Italy to Israel, **Hoomoos Asli** draws a trail of twenty- and thirty-somethings for fluffy pitas packed with crispy falafel and outstanding hummus. The décor and service here may be rudimentary at best, but serious effort goes into the food as well as that refreshing side of tart lemonade.

$T$op off this plethora of eats at the aromatic and always-alluring **Dominique Ansel Bakery**. Formerly an executive pastry chef at Daniel, the chef here is now fulfilling his own dessert dreams with a spectrum of specialty cakes, tarts, cookies, and pastries. For a taste of this sweet bliss, follow instructions and eat the made-to-order "Magic Soufflé" piping hot. Desserts are best matched with coffee, so head on over to **La Colombe**—a Philadelphia-

based roaster located nearby on Lafayette Street. If date-night duos aren't closing the deal here over one of their eco-friendly blends, then find them sweetening things up at **Rice to Riches** bringing comfort food to this edgy nook in bowls of creamy rice pudding. The fact that these treats are appended with quirky names like "Sex Drugs and Rocky Road" or "Fluent in French Toast" only adds to this sugar den's supreme appeal.

**C**heesecake addicts take note that **Eileen's Special Cheesecake** bears the moniker "special" for good reason. Embellished with fruit toppings and fun flavors like amaretto or coconut custard, Eileen's divine creations continue to control the downtown scene, chasing those Junior's fans back to Brooklyn. Of course, one of the greater challenges that this neighborhood poses is the decision of where to end the day—or night. But, savvy locals know full well that tucked into these vibrant streets are scores of snug bars, each with its own sleek city feel. Originally a speakeasy during the Prohibition era, today **Fanelli Café** is one of the city's oldest establishments offering an array of simple pub grub, beers and cocktails. But, revelers looking to

end the night with a bit of sweet should head to **Sweet & Vicious**, which pours concoctions that promise to leave you starry-eyed. And

between these countless dinners and drinks, Nolita also caters to New York City's culinary elite by virtue of its numerous wholesale kitchen supply stores, all settled and thriving along the Bowery.

# BALABOOSTA 🍴○

*Mediterranean*

XX | 🍷

MAP: C2

It's hard to walk by and avoid falling in love with this thoroughly charming Mediterranean favorite and its keen (if wandering) eye on Sephardic cuisine.

A small bar serves cocktails and organic wines while the dining room is full of bare tables, exposed brick walls, and shelves lined with bottles and books. Like the main arena, this kitchen bears a bright, friendly vibe. Here, smoke and fire take center stage in the shrimp cazuela, a tagine of plump shrimp, chickpeas, preserved lemons, and fiery jalapeño. Tender striped bass with crispy skin is a thoroughly comforting dish, served on a bed of sautéed mushrooms, buttery spinach and chewy black gnocchi, drizzled with crab bisque. Linger over kanafeh, syrup-soaked shredded filo dough stuffed with cheese.

■ 214 Mulberry St. (bet. Prince & Spring Sts.)
🚇 Spring St (Lafayette St.)
✆ (212) 966-7366 — **WEB:** www.balaboostanyc.com
■ Lunch & dinner daily                    PRICE: $$

# BALTHAZAR 🍴○

*French*

XX | 👤 🍽 🍷

MAP: C2

As ageless as its beautiful patrons, the brassy and mirrored Balthazar should be called "quintessentially SoHo" because it invented the term. One of the benchmark brasseries from serial restaurateur Keith McNally, the attractive space is housed in a former tannery. Those whiffs of leather have been replaced by red awnings, scents of pastries, and an excellent oyster-filled raw bar completing its Parisian transformation.

It seems as though every other table is topped with their bestselling steak frites—hardly a value but expertly prepared and served with a heaping side of fries. On the delicate side, sautéed skate is served with sweet raisins and tart capers; while silky beef tartare with shallots, herbs, and Worcestershire spreads just like butta.

■ 80 Spring St. (bet. Broadway & Crosby St.)
🚇 Spring St (Lafayette St.)
✆ (212) 965-1414 — **WEB:** www.balthazarny.com
■ Lunch & dinner daily                    PRICE: $$$

# BLUE RIBBON ♚○

*Contemporary*

XX

Blue Ribbon stays open until the wee hours, serving somewhat simple but particularly memorable food to SoHo's stylish set. Moreover, this unaffectedly warm and very classic bistro boasts zero pretense and deserves all praise that comes its way. Its décor may have stayed the same through the years—think timeless—but those bar seats remain a hot ticket.

This "chef's canteen" as it is typically hailed is well-tread for masterpieces like fresh shucked oysters; smoked trout salad tossed with sour cream and zippy horseradish; or matzo ball soup—enjoyable, aromatic, and full of root vegetables. Fried chicken with mashed potatoes takes home the gold medal for comfort classics, while banana-walnut bread pudding with caramel sauce is the very essence of decadence.

■ 97 Sullivan St. (bet. Prince & Spring Sts.)
■ Spring St (Sixth Ave.)
☏ (212) 274-0404 — **WEB:** www.blueribbonrestaurants.com
■ Dinner nightly                          **PRICE: $$$**

# BLUE RIBBON SUSHI ♚○

*Contemporary*

XX

Set just below street level and down the block from its eldest sibling, Blue Ribbon Sushi is an inviting spot to watch the masters at work. A sushi bar dominates the space, with colorful sake bottles and premium spirits on display. The low, wood-covered ceilings and polished tables provide an intimate setting, while the counter is a prime perch for a solo diner.

The staff may point to Americanized options, but it's best to trust the expert chefs and go with the omakase. The menu divides itself into Taiheiyo ("Pacific") offerings, like the kohada spotted sardine, or a sweet and briny giant clam; and Taiseiyo ("Atlantic"), perhaps featuring fluke fin or a spicy lobster knuckle. Maki tempts with the karai kaibashire, with spicy minced scallop and smelt roe.

■ 119 Sullivan St. (bet. Prince & Spring Sts.)
■ Spring St (Sixth Ave.)
☏ (212) 343-0404 — **WEB:** www.blueribbonrestaurants.com
■ Lunch & dinner daily                    **PRICE: $$$**

# CAFÉ ALTRO PARADISO 🍴

*Italian*

✗✗ | ⬡ ♿ ⌂ 🖥️

Sommelier Thomas Carter and Chef Ignacio Mattos, aka Team Estela, work their magic again—this time at a chic Italian café that's warm, welcoming and completely packed. What's their secret? At Café Altro Paradiso, a buzzing bar and inviting dining room help set the scene; but the real draw is Mattos' honest, straightforward and delicious Italian cooking.

Kick things off with a wildly fresh crudo dressed with olive oil, caper berry slivers, parsley and a squeeze of lemon; or a bright fennel salad with Castelvetrano olives and diced provolone. Homemade lasagnette is delicious, tucked with silky trumpet mushrooms, leeks and parmesan. Chicken Milanese is rustic and ample, accompanied by lemon, Dijon, and a salad of radicchio, farro and pine nuts.

- 234 Spring St. (bet. Sixth Ave. & Varick St.)
- Spring St (Lafayette St.)
- ☎ (646) 952-0828 — **WEB:** www.altroparadiso.com
- Lunch Tue – Sat   Dinner nightly          **PRICE: $$**

# CHARLIE BIRD 🍴

*Italian*

✗✗ | ⬡ ⌂ 🖥️ 🛋️

Of all the out-of-the-way restaurants that dot this stretch of SoHo, none are hipper than Charlie Bird. You'll be greeted by a blast of music upon entry, where a long bar leads to a brick-lined dining space with leather seats. From there, things just take off: along with a clever menu, upbeat service, and a thoughtful wine list brimming with interesting old-world selections, the kitchen delights long before Chef/co-owner Ryan Hardy's renowned pastas hit your plate. Think rigatoni with fennel-roasted suckling pig; or spaghetti alla carbonara formed into a ball and topped with buttery spring onions, smoked bacon, and a bright yellow duck egg.

Baby sib Pasquale Jones offers similar modern-Italian cuisine with an emphasis on Neapolitan wood-fired pizzas.

- 5 King St. (entrance on Sixth Ave.)
- Houston St
- ☎ (212) 235-7133 — **WEB:** www.charliebirdnyc.com
- Lunch & dinner daily          **PRICE: $$$**

# CHEFS CLUB 🍴○

## *Contemporary*

𝕏𝕩𝕏 | 🍸 ⬚                                          **MAP:** C2

Like a never-ending All-Star game featuring the country's best dishes, the innovative concept behind Chefs Club (by Food & Wine) is a rotating lineup of the magazine's "Best New Chefs" honorees over the years. If that isn't exciting enough, the space itself is visually stunning, featuring a state-of-the-art open kitchen with a striking blue-tile backdrop; a sensational modern bar; and lots of loud music to set the mood.

Dinner might include a cool, creamy spring pea soup dotted with pickled pearl onions and fresh herbs; or expertly smoked and seared Hudson Valley foie gras paired with sunchoke purée, apple chips, and buttermilk-thyme jam.  Squab à la plancha is then glazed with sage-honey and served over grilled confit leeks with a giblet ragout.

■ 275 Mulberry St. (bet. Houston & Jersey Sts.)
🚇 Broadway - Lafayette St
📞 (212) 941-1100 — **WEB:** www.chefsclub.com
■ Dinner nightly                                  **PRICE:** $$$$

# CICCIO 😊

## *Italian*

𝕏 | 🍷                                             **MAP:** B1

Chef/owner Giacomo Romano defines this brilliant little restaurant as an alimentaria—a place where patrons can find ever-changing temptations day or night. This may mean hearty ribollita for lunch or satisfying pasta for dinner. The sunny space is a former antique store that fashions a raw look through whitewashed brick walls and blonde wood tables.

Simple, unpretentious food is the focus here, as seen in dishes like insalata di carota, mixing sweet roasted carrots, peppery arugula, and pumpkin seeds—grab wedges of bread to soak up its citrusy vinaigrette. Fresh pasta is a must, especially the strisce alla Chiantigiana tossed with a reduction of wine, guanciale, and red onions. End with a perfect espresso or rich and oozing molten chocolate cake.

■ 190 Sixth Ave. (bet. Prince & Vandam Sts.)
🚇 Spring St (Sixth Ave.)
📞 (646) 476-9498 — **WEB:** www.ciccionyc.com
■ Lunch Mon – Fri  Dinner nightly                 **PRICE:** $$

# THE DUTCH 🍴

## *American*

🍴🍴 | 🍸 🍺 🍽 🛥

Buzzy and beloved since day one, Chef Andrew Carmellini's The Dutch quickly became a major hit and SoHo institution. Its primo corner windows open on to the sidewalk, tempting guests inside with a stocked oyster bar, cozy banquettes, and sharply dressed service staff.

The menu is just as seductive as the space, familiar but with fresh updates. Highlights include a roundabout take on the plump fried oyster po' boy, made here with mustard-pickled okra remoulade. Tasty pastas refresh the menu consistently; you might find black rigatini tossed with tender squid and spicy pork sausage, finished with fiery breadcrumbs. Desserts are divine, with fresh pies made daily, such as salted lime with passion fruit, nata de coco, and coconut sorbet.

- 131 Sullivan St. (at Prince St.)
- Spring St (Lafayette St.)
- ℘ (212) 677-6200 — **WEB:** www.thedutchnyc.com
- Lunch & dinner daily

**PRICE: $$$**

# EMILIO'S BALLATO 🍴

## *Italian*

🍴🍴 | 🍽

This unassuming Houston St. standard is an unsung hero, even if many walk past Emilio's gold- and red-etched window and write it off as some run-of-the-mill red-sauce joint. Step inside the narrow, weathered space, where owner Emilio Vitolo offers each guest a personal welcome and a genuine Italian-American experience.

The menu is filled with pasta classics like Roman cacio e pepe, tossed with sharp pecorino cheese and freshly ground black pepper. Signature specialties include pollo Emilio, a delicately breaded chicken cutlet draped in lemon-caper sauce; and plump clams oreganata speckled with garlicky breadcrumbs. Crisp cannoli shells filled with vanilla- and cinnamon-tinged ricotta cream rival any other version found from Palermo to Siracusa.

- 55 E. Houston St. (bet. Mott & Mulberry Sts.)
- Broadway - Lafayette St
- ℘ (212) 274-8881 — **WEB:** N/A
- Lunch & dinner daily

**PRICE: $$**

# ESTELA 🍴

## Contemporary

✗✗ | 🍸 🛋️                                    **MAP:** C2

This boisterous little hot spot is the perfect place to meet friends for a night of sharing small plates over a good bottle of wine. The talented duo of Chef Ignacio Mattos and Co-owner Thomas Carter have mastered exactly how to keep the vibe cozy yet festive and packed with chic crowds. Dimly lit globe lights overhead and small marble tables prevent things from feeling claustrophobic.

The bold and creative cooking features dishes like beef and sunchoke tartare, with each morsel of meat and root vegetable cut to the exact same size and faintly glistening with egg yolk and olive oil alongside country bread. An appetizing range of textures underscore the rice in squid ink sauce folded with bits of fried rice and tender squid set over romesco.

- 🔳 47 E. Houston St. (at Mulberry St.)
- 🚇 Broadway - Lafayette St
- ℰ (212) 219-7693 — **WEB:** www.estelanyc.com
- 🔳 Lunch Sat – Sun   Dinner nightly                    **PRICE: $$$**

# GIORGIONE 🍴

## Italian

✗✗ | ♿ 🏠                                    **MAP:** A1

In far west SoHo, beyond Chanel and Balenciaga, find this long-time resident cherished for its quiet location where Spring Street locals enjoy a slower pace—much like Italy itself. Founded by Dean & Deluca's Giorgio Deluca, the stylish and distinctly Italian L-shaped room focuses on straightforward pizza, outstanding pastas, and serious desserts.

You can't go wrong with the handful of pastas on the menu, such as the lovingly crafted pouches of spinach and ricotta ravioli in a light tomato sauce. Delicately grilled lamb chops with peperonata and rosemary-roasted new potatoes are simple yet beguiling. Try one (or two) noteworthy desserts, including the flaky crostata filled with rich chocolate ganache and bright green pistacchio di Bronte.

- 🔳 307 Spring St. (bet. Greenwich & Hudson Sts.)
- 🚇 Spring St (Sixth Ave.)
- ℰ (212) 352-2269 — **WEB:** www.giorgionenyc.com
- 🔳 Lunch Mon – Fri   Dinner Mon – Sat                    **PRICE: $$**

# HAROLD'S MEAT + THREE 🍴○

## Contemporary

✕✕ | ⚐ ⌂ 🍽 ⚒️                                    **MAP:** A2

This cool dude brings the global comfort food of Chef Harold Moore (formerly of Commerce) downtown to the Arlo Square Hotel dining room. With a separate bar, courtyard seating, and a modern, open layout, the vibe is au courant and family friendly.

The menu concept simply involves choosing a meat or protein along with three accompanying side dishes. However, the chef's skill and international touches mean that options include Sichuan-style pork chop, steak au poivre, or fish with green curry. Sides unveil broccoli-rice casserole or smoky campfire leeks. For a few extra dollars, diners can visit the salad bar, freshly lined with lettuces, bocconcini, and house-made dressings to snack on while they wait. It also displays tempting layer cakes for dessert.

▪ 2 Renwick St. (at Canal St.)
▪ Canal St (Varick St.)
℘ (212) 342-7000 — **WEB:** www.haroldsmeatandthree.com
▪ Lunch & dinner daily                          **PRICE:** $$

# HOUSEMAN 🍴○

## American

✕✕ | ⚐                                           **MAP:** A1

Just around the corner from the legendary Ear Inn, you'll find this amazing offering courtesy of Chef/owner Ned Baldwin. Sporting a small, but sharply designed interior by Louis Yoh, replete with schoolhouse chairs and reclaimed bowling alley wood tables, Houseman's seasonal menu isn't extensive, but each dish is extremely well-sourced—not to mention well-executed, with the help of co-chef, Adam Baumgart.

Kick things off with a grilled tomato salad, bursting with fresh herbs, salty feta and smoky shishito peppers. Then linger over a superbly fresh, slashed, and fried whole black sea bass, laced with a tarragon-forward herby sauce; or excellent, beer-braised sausage links, served with sweet caramelized onions and roasted banana peppers.

▪ 508 Greenwich St. (bet. Canal & Spring Sts.)
▪ Spring St (Sixth Ave.)
℘ (212) 641-0654 — **WEB:** www.housemanrestaurant.com
▪ Lunch Mon – Fri  Dinner nightly               **PRICE:** $$

# HIROHISA ✿

*Japanese*

XX | &

There's nothing like a discreet entrance to raise expectations—and Hirohisa is nicely concealed on Thompson Street. When you do find it, you enter into a stylish, beautifully understated and meticulously laid out room that looks like a page from Wallpaper magazine. It's run with considerable charm by an unobtrusive and very courteous Japanese team.

The two-page menu is easy to decipher with clear headings. However, you might just be better off giving in and letting the chefs decide by going for the balanced and seasonal dishes from the seven- or nine-course omakase. Two things will quickly become clear: the ingredients are exceptional and the technical skills of the chefs considerable. This is food that is as rewarding to eat as it is restorative. Standouts include the lingering, complex flavors of Kumamoto oysters wrapped in Wagyu beef carpaccio and topped with Maine sea urchin, perfectly grilled Japanese kinki, or anything with their homemade tofu.

There are tables available, but it's so much more satisfying to sit at the counter and engage with the smiling chefs—this way, you may even find that there are a few more dishes in their repertoire than they advertise.

■ 73 Thompson St. (bet. Broome & Spring Sts.)
▣ Spring (Sixth Ave.)
✆ (212) 925-1613 — **WEB:** www.hirohisa-nyc.com
■ Lunch Mon – Fri   Dinner Mon – Sat          **PRICE: $$$**

# KING 🍴

## Mediterranean

✗✗ | 🍴                                    **MAP:** B1

It's still a fresh face on the SoHo dining scene, but King boasts a rare coziness that restaurants can take ages to acquire. The popular bar area leads to an intimate rear dining space lined with blonde wood mirrors.

Chef/owners Clare de Boer and Jess Shadbolt met while working at London's esteemed River Café, then banded together with Annie Shi to open King. The talented kitchen brings a deft touch to their brief, daily-changing menu, pulled straight from the greenmarket. A tangle of warm green and wax beans are tossed with torn mint, excellent parmesan, and an exquisite extra virgin olive oil. Wildly good halibut is seasoned with restraint, then cooked to succulent perfection and plated with fresh-from-the-market wilted spinach and zucchini trifolati.

- 18 King St. (at Sixth Ave.)
- Houston St
- 𝒞 (917) 825-1618 — **WEB:** www.kingrestaurant.nyc
- Dinner Mon – Sat                          **PRICE:** $$$

# LE COUCOU 🍴

## French

✗✗✗ | ♿ 🖥 🛋                              **MAP:** C3

Chef Daniel Rose made a name for himself when he opened his popular Paris bistro, Spring. And now that France's favorite American ex-pat has returned home to work this spot with Philadelphia-based restaurateur Stephen Starr, it's only natural to find a white-hot scene. At Le Coucou, crowds linger late into the night amid plush velvet chairs, custom chandeliers, and a menu that infuses classic French food with a strong dose of cool.

A seat in the dining room with a view of the open kitchen will serve you well. From there, the carte—arranged under three headings—offers such ace items as buckwheat-fried Montauk eel plated with pickled cucumber and a warm curry vinaigrette. Set atop potato pureé, pigeon et homard with a reduced jus leaves a lasting impression.

- 138 Lafayette St. (at Howard St.)
- Canal St (Lafayette St.)
- 𝒞 (212) 271-4252 — **WEB:** www.lecoucou.com
- Lunch & dinner daily                       **PRICE:** $$$

# THE MUSKET ROOM ✿

*Contemporary*

XX | 🍸

New Zealander Matt Lambert appears to be on a mission to debunk some stereotypes and defy a few expectations about his homeland. For a chef raised in a country famous for its wild, rugged terrain and obsession with rugby, his contemporary cuisine is surprisingly subtle, thoughtful and at times even quite delicate—and if you come here expecting to find lamb on the menu, you'll probably be disappointed.

It is obvious that this is a kitchen with a mastery of all the modern culinary techniques. Don't go thinking this is all about presentation though, because the dishes really do deliver on flavour and are ridiculously easy to eat. Nothing demonstrates the ability here more than the succulent New Zealand venison accompanied by "flavors of gin" which are dots of juniper meringue, fennel, and a licorice-infused sauce. Even that antipodean classic, the pavlova, is given a new lease of life by not so much being deconstructed as being reinvented, as a subtle and delicious delicacy made with passion fruit.

The warm and inviting room fits seamlessly into the neighborhood and comes with a 20-foot walnut timbered bar and lime-washed exposed brick walls.

---

■ 265 Elizabeth St. (bet. Houston & Prince Sts.)

🚇 Broadway - Lafayette St

✆ (212) 219-0764 — **WEB:** www.themusketroom.com

■ Dinner nightly                                    PRICE: $$$

# PAOWALLA ℀○

*Indian*

✕✕ | ⊡ | ⊯                                    **MAP:** B2

Chef Floyd Cardoz, venerated and talented headliner of Danny Meyer's long-shuttered Tabla, has returned to this familiar corner with an upscale homage to India. In this kitchen, he continues in that wonderful tradition of applying Indian technique to a world of top-quality ingredients. Order the burrata and find yourself with a bowl of that wonderful yet ubiquitous cheese set in a spicy stew of heirloom peas, richer with each bite as it mixes with the cheese's creamy center.

Breads—some from the chef's native Goa—are at the center of every meal here, after being freshly baked in the wood-fired hearth at the back. The lengthy offerings may include cheddar-stuffed kulcha, sourdough naan, whole wheat roti, Tibetan tingmo, and Portuguese-inspired pao rolls.

- ▪ 195 Spring St. (at Sullivan St.)
- ▪ Spring St (Sixth Ave.)
- ✆ (212) 235-1098 — **WEB:** www.paowalla.com
- ▪ Lunch & dinner daily                        **PRICE: $$$**

# PAPATZUL ℀○

*Mexican*

✕ | ⊯                                          **MAP:** B2

Sangria and salsas are a heavenly match at SoHo's favorite cantina, where a boisterous crowd devours delightful Mexican cuisine. Decorated with masks and classic movie posters, Papatzul is abuzz with drinking buddies getting friendly with the bar's offerings and tables of friends scooping up every last drop from the signature salsa assortment—five varieties, each inspired by a different region of the country.

The talented kitchen churns out tacos and enchiladas at a steady clip. You can't go wrong with an order of enchiladas San Miguel, a creative rendition that stuffs salsa roja-soaked tortillas with sautéed kale, roasted sweet cherry tomatoes, and creamy goat cheese. If you still have room, go for the chocolate flan with cinnamon ice cream.

- ▪ 55 Grand St. (bet. West Broadway & Wooster St.)
- ▪ Canal St (Varick St.)
- ✆ (212) 274-8225 — **WEB:** www.papatzul.com
- ▪ Lunch & dinner daily                        **PRICE: $$**

# PEASANT 🍴

## *Italian*

XX | ♿                  **MAP:** C3

Year after year, Peasant hits it out of the park. From the mouthwatering Italian food and the spot-on service, to the utterly charming osteria spirit, Frank DeCarlo's ode to the Italian gathering spot is the essence of easy excellence. The décor is charmingly rustic—picture whitewashed walls, bare wood tables, and a bustling wine bar downstairs.

Kick things off with ricotta and otherworldly bread, fresh from the visible centerpiece hearth—which is the main method of cooking and sets this spot apart. But save room for house-made lasagna with braised rabbit ragù, creamy béchamel, and sweet root vegetables; tender razor clams in a fragrant white wine broth; succulent porchetta studded with garlic and rosemary; or stewed and chewy trippa alla Romana.

■ 194 Elizabeth St. (bet. Prince & Spring Sts.)
🚇 Spring St (Lafayette St.)
☏ (212) 965-9511 — **WEB:** www.peasantnyc.com
■ Dinner Tue – Sun                  **PRICE: $$**

# RAOUL'S 🍴

## *French*

XX | 🖵 🛶                 **MAP:** B1

It's the nature of all great cities to constantly change but that doesn't mean severing ties to the past. Raoul's has been around since the '70s—which alone qualifies it as an "institution"—but this is no museum piece living on past glories. Wander in on any given night and you'll see a crowd of all ages united in their fondness for French food and their ability to enjoy themselves.

The menu wouldn't necessarily entice the passer-by on content alone but the kitchen has a surprisingly delicate touch that raises dishes above the ordinary, whether that's tender octopus with chickpea purée or succulent rack of lamb with oyster mushrooms. In the stampede to find all that is new, shiny and hot we shouldn't ignore those whose sin is mere longevity.

■ 180 Prince St. (bet. Sullivan & Thompson Sts.)
🚇 Spring St (Sixth Ave.)
☏ (212) 966-3518 — **WEB:** www.raouls.com
■ Lunch Sat – Sun    Dinner nightly        **PRICE: $$$**

# REBELLE ⊛
*French*

XX | 🍸 ⛄ 🌶️ ᴖ ᴖ

French food devotees appear to have found their true calling at this chic bistro. While the bar is always full, the dining room is as dim as a cave— its palette of concrete and ebony brightened only by a white marble bar and gracious team of servers who know when they're needed and seem to disappear when they're not. Rebelle has an edgy vibe—the space was once a burlesque spot, after all. But, beneath that veneer is impressive talent delivered with a sexy French accent.

While Chef Daniel Eddy's streamlined presentations and foam flourishes have contemporary flair, rest assured that classic technique is at the root of every dish. Pan-seared chicken sausage is elegantly arranged in a shallow bowl with shaved rounds of radish. Upon presentation, the bowl is filled with an amber-colored chicken broth for a detailed study in perfect seasoning. Then exceptionally crisp and flaky hake is dressed tableside with a bit of bouillabaisse for a seasonally reimagined version of the beloved Southern French stew.

Familiar and complementary flavors abound in a dessert plate of milk gelato, chocolate mousse, and shards of toasted devil's food cake adorned with torched marshmallows.

■ 218 Bowery (bet. Prince & Spring Sts.)
🚇 Bowery
✆ (917) 639-3880 — **WEB:** www.rebellenyc.com
■ Lunch Sat – Sun   Dinner Tue – Sat                    **PRICE: $$$**

# RUBIROSA 🏮

*Italian*

XX | 🍽

**MAP:** C2

Push through the dark red velvet curtain into Rubirosa's narrow, dimly lit dining room to discover how very cool nonna can be. Although it may be loud and cramped with the requisite 80's tunes blaring overhead, this adept Italian-American kitchen is bright with classic dishes and an heirloom Staten Island pizza recipe that's 57-years-old and counting.

The classic pie balances a crispy, cracker-thin crust with tart tomato sauce and oven-browned spots of salty, melting mozzarella. And the handmade pastas are highly recommended—you can't go wrong with a bowl of chewy chittara and its three hefty and hearty meatballs. Half portions allow diners to enjoy more of the favorable cooking here, and gluten-free pasta and pizza ensures everyone can enjoy it.

■ 235 Mulberry St. (bet. Prince & Spring Sts.)
🚇 Spring St (Lafayette St.)
✆ (212) 965-0500 — **WEB:** www.rubirosanyc.com
■ Lunch & dinner daily                                **PRICE:** $$

Your opinions are important to us.
Please write to us directly at:
michelin.guides@us.michelin.com

277

# UNCLE BOONS ✿
*Thai*

XX | 🍸

Can't fit in a trip to Thailand? No problem. This transporting little gem—compliments of talented husband-wife duo Matt Danzer and Ann Redding—brings the Northern Thai experience stateside with creative cuisine and whimsical drinks—Singha beer slushies anyone?

Tucked along the eastern edge of Spring Street, the dining room is den-like. A vibrant crowd keeps the place popping through the night, as does the gentle stream of Thai pop music in the background. Though tables are mini, the kitchen feels immense in its creative vision—a window into where the magic happens offers views of a slow-rotating rotisserie and crackling embers.

Danzer and Redding's dishes are certainly rooted in this nation's cuisine, but they give each dish a unique spin thereby infusing vibrant flavor into small plates, large plates, "charcoal-grilled goodies," desserts and drinking snacks. Laab neuh gae features delicious ground lamb tossed with pickled onion, lime, and fish sauce, while a banana blossom salad with rotisserie chicken and buttery cashew nuts arrives in an appetizing coconut dressing. For an epic end, go for grilled pork jowl, topped with watermelon radish, salted duck yolk, and a shake of sawtooth herb.

■ 7 Spring St. (bet. Bowery & Elizabeth St.)
🚇 Bowery
✆ (646) 370-6650 — **WEB:** www.uncleboons.com
■ Dinner nightly

**PRICE: $$**

# TRIBECA

## DRINK AND DINE

**T**riBeCa is an established commercial center sprinkled with haute design stores, warehouses-turned-lavish lofts, and trendy drink-cum-dining destinations. Quite simply, this triangle below Canal is a cool place to eat, and its affluent residents can be seen splurging in restaurants whose reputations precede them. Of course that isn't to say that this area's famously wide, umbrella-shaded sidewalks aren't cramped with more modest hangouts.

In fact, **Puffy's Tavern** is a favored neighborhood hangout equipped with small bites, hearty sandwiches, and five flat-screens for the happy-hour crowds. Over on West Broadway, **Square Diner** is a local institution that takes you back in time via red vinyl booths and that diner counter cooking up the staples. Like every other Manhattan neighborhood, TriBeCa claims its own culinary treasures: **Bubby's** is a gem for comfort food; while **Zucker's Bagels & Smoked Fish** flaunts an updated décor

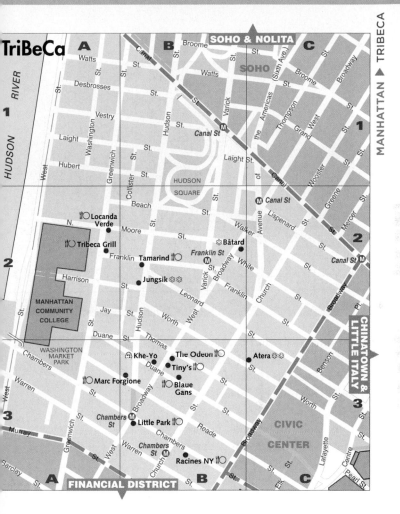

# TriBeCa

SOHO & NOLITA

SOHO

Broome St.

Watts St.

Desbrosses St.

Vestry St.

Laight St.

Hubert St.

Canal St M

Laight St.

HUDSON SQUARE

Beach St.

🍴○ Locanda Verde

🍴○ Tribeca Grill

Moore St.

M Canal St

Lispenard

Walker St.

✿ Bâtard

Franklin St M

Tamarind 🍴○

White St.

Canal St M

Franklin St.

Jungsik ✿✿

Harrison St.

Leonard St.

Franklin

Jay St.

Worth St.

Church St.

MANHATTAN COMMUNITY COLLEGE

Duane St.

Thomas St.

WASHINGTON MARKET PARK

🍴○ Khe-Yo

Duane St.

The Odeon 🍴○

Tiny's 🍴○

Atera ✿✿

Chambers

Warren St.

🍴○ Marc Forgione

🍴○ Blaue Gans

Reade St.

Murray St.

Chambers M St

● Little Park 🍴○

Chambers

CIVIC CENTER

Chambers M St

Racines NY 🍴○

CHINATOWN & LITTLE ITALY

Worth St.

and floors patrons with a taste of *bubbe*'s best. **Dirty Bird To Go** delivers fresh, all-natural chicken in its many glorious forms—join its endless line of fans to try either the buttermilk-fried bird or slow-roasted rotisserie. And over on North Moore Street, **Smith & Mills** continues to make waves as a cocoon for fantastic eats as well as spectacular drinks.

In keeping with its cutting-edge spirit, TriBeCa also offers a gourmet experience

for any palate and price tag. For instance, **Grand Banks** bobs along the Hudson River and is a summer special for seasonal oysters or a lobster roll, while winter calls for a range of first-rate vino that can be found at **Chambers Street Wines**. Adults looking to keep the party going, as well as for something to enjoy with their wine will rejoice over the events sponsored by **New York Vintners**. These might include free wine and cheese tastings, followed by a series of cooking demonstrations. Make sure to sip on a few sparkling varietals while you're at it!

## BATHS & BAKERS

**W**ork off a hangover at AIRE Ancient Baths, a luxury spa inspired by ancient civilizations and water-induced relaxation. They even offer rituals where you can soak in olive oil, cava, or red wine. The only downside? You can't drink any of it! Then, take your appetite to one of TriBeCa's numerous (and well-lauded) bakeries. **Sarabeth's** is an award-winning jam maker who turned this once humble retail store into the monstrous hit it is today. With an impressive carte of cookies, cakes, preserves, and other treats, this specialty spot knows how to play the culinary game; and keeps up with such solid competitors as **Duane Park Patisserie**, known for pastries and seasonal specialties, as well as **Tribeca Treats** popular for its plethora of decadent chocolates. Moving across to the Far East, **Takahachi Bakery** on Murray Street is a modestly decorated but must-visit treasure for Japanese refreshers. And local crowds flock here to slurp up a *matcha* latte while snacking on at least one *sakura* macaron.

## AROUND THE WORLD

**Korin** is a culinary haven that flaunts an extensive and exquisite knife collection, plus tableware and gorgeous kitchen supplies. Not only do these products shine in many fine-dining establishments, but they also bring to life the essence of food art. Chefs come here to get their blades worked on or to order a specific knife, while others may opt for the gorgeous gift sets that are sure to excite a friend or impress a colleague.

**B**efore this area became associated with top films from varying genres, director Bob Giraldi shot his mob- and food-themed movie *Dinner Rush* at famed eatery, **Gigino Trattoria**. However, thanks to the annual Tribeca Film Festival, a springtime extravaganza created by Robert DeNiro to revitalize the area after 9/11, TriBeCa is now the official home of twelve days of great films and community camaraderie. In fact, scores of locals, tourists, and film buffs collect here every year to see the movies and share their views and reviews at hot spots like **Nish Nush**, a sidewalk show-stopper incorporating authentic Israeli hummus and crispy falafel into sandwiches, hearty platters, and healthy salads. From nourishing eats to heavenly treats, **Baked** is yet another tenant in TriBeCa. While the mothership continues to flourish in Red Hook, this considerably larger venture is beloved for breakfast, coffee and other sweet treats. Carb junkies craving more bread (maybe even flatbread pizza?) but in a historic setting, should head to **Arcade Bakery**, settled on Church Street. However, for those craving crêpes, both sweet and savory selections abound at **By Suzette**—a mini counter on Chambers Street that is quickly gaining a major following. And finally, while on the topic of laudable ventures, Chef David Bouley and team have created **Bouley Botanical**, a resourceful event space, designed to entice the senses and committed to celebrating every occasion in style. This greenhouse-inspired venue is famously outfitted with state-of-the-art sound and lighting equipment, as well as an impressive exhibition kitchen.

# ATERA ✿ ✿

*Contemporary*

XX | 🍸 🍷 🍽️

MAP: C3

Counter dining can sometimes mean lots of elbows and competitive eaters who enjoy flaunting their food knowledge in front of others. Fortunately, the three-sided counter here at Atera is large enough to ensure you're sufficiently far from your fellow diners as well as a certain level of privacy while still letting you enjoy the communal, immersive experience.

Things are certainly more grown-up and a little less rock-n-roll here than in similarly styled places: there's barely a tattoo in sight and the soundtrack appears to have been chosen by someone who doesn't care that much for music. But, it is needed because there can be pauses in conversation when everyone is facing forward.

Danish chef Ronny Emborg and his multi-national team serve up a nightly menu of around 20 courses, progressing from the light and subtle to the rich and robust. There may be plenty of tweezer action from the chefs as they plate up their beguiling creations, but they know that there's nowhere to hide when food is this precise and delicate. Dishes also deliver on the promise that their beauty suggests, whether that's the creamy scallop with crisp celery or the succulent loin of lamb with snap peas.

■ 77 Worth St. (bet. Broadway & Church St.)

🚇 Chambers St (Church St.)

📞 (212) 226-1444 — **WEB:** www.ateranyc.com

■ Dinner Tue – Sat

PRICE: $$$$

# BÂTARD ✿
*Contemporary*

XX | 🐌

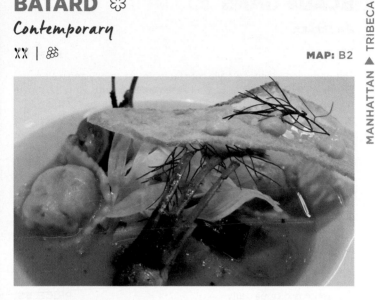

239 West Broadway will be a familiar address to those who know their restaurants as it has hosted a number of seminal establishments over the years—namely Montrachet and Corton. Drew Nieporent's Bâtard restaurant is now firmly in situ and once again we have a talented chef making waves in TriBeCa.

Chef Markus Glocker's cooking is very precise and his dishes look quite delicate on the plate. But like a good featherweight they pack more of a punch than you're expecting. You'll even notice his Austrian roots in evidence in some of the dishes, such as short rib and tafelspitz terrine, or the Granny Smith and sweetbread strudel.

The room is comfortable and neat and the atmosphere grown-up yet animated. When it comes to service though, it appears that the restaurant has mistaken informality for indifference as it lacks coordination or direction. So you may need to remind yourself that you're here primarily for the food. But that food is very good indeed.

▨ 239 West Broadway (bet. Walker & White Sts.)
🚇 Franklin St
☏ (212) 219-2777 — **WEB:** www.batardtribeca.com
▨ Lunch Fri   Dinner Mon – Sat                    **PRICE: $$$**

# BLAUE GANS 🍴○

*Austrian*

✕✕

**MAP:** B3

This unbridled Viennese-style café feels almost smoky and well-worn, but never out of touch. Its walls are papered with vintage movie posters, while banquettes and tables dominate the dining space.

Blaue Gans' strong, loyal following (an increasingly rare feat in the city) is comprised of locals engaging in familiar banter at the bar or communal table. Everyone is here for the impressive Austrian cooking, which may unveil a beautiful bibb, pumpkin seed, and shaved radish salad with a light, creamy pumpkin oil dressing. Other classic treasures include pork Jäger schnitzel with mushrooms, bacon, and herbed spätzle; or classic kavalierspitz accompanied by salty creamed spinach and sweet-tart apple horseradish. Delish desserts will have you at hello.

■ 139 Duane St. (bet. Church St. & West Broadway)
🚇 Chambers St (West Broadway)
✆ (212) 571-8880 — **WEB:** www.kurtgutenbrunner.com
■ Lunch & dinner daily                                    **PRICE: $$**

# KHE-YO 😊

*Lao*

✕✕

**MAP:** B3

This Laotian hot spot serves up vibrant family-style plates brimming with tart and spicy notes that pack a punch—make that a Bang Bang, actually, as in the house sauce of mixed chilies, cilantro, fish sauce, and garlic served to diners as a welcome, along with a basket of sticky rice.

The food is worth braving the wait and decibel levels, so sip a craft brew or cocktail before digging in. Start with a plate of wide rice noodles and bits of slow-cooked pork in a coconut-rich yellow curry garnished with herbs, bean sprouts, and slivered banana blossom. Banana leaf-steamed red snapper is another beautifully prepared item, paired with crisped artichoke hearts, Chinese broccoli, and more of that sauce. Bright and bitter grapefruit sorbet is a fitting finish.

■ 157 Duane St. (bet. Hudson St. & West Broadway)
🚇 Chambers St (West Broadway)
✆ (212) 587-1089 — **WEB:** www.kheyo.com
■ Lunch & dinner daily                                    **PRICE: $$**

# JUNGSIK ✿✿

*Korean*

XxX | 🍇 🍸 ♿ 🎏

Cool, chic, and completely urbane, Jungsik is the epitome of contemporary elegance. Inside the large, neatly partitioned space, find rich browns and ivory furnishings with flattering lighting that is just bright enough to see your food clearly. The chairs are deep and tables are well spaced, but request a plush corner banquette for maximum comfort. Even the place settings show sculptural beauty through dark pottery and white porcelain. The ambience is fairly quiet and somewhat reflective.

The modern cuisine is confident, complex, and happens to be leaning much more toward Europe than Korea of late. No matter—the cooking remains profoundly enjoyable. At the same time, the most inspired dishes are the ones that retain their heritage, as in the dome of seaweed-seasoned rice with cubes of smoked and torched yellowtail, finished with slivered lettuce. Before the red snapper arrives at the table, hot oil is poured overtop to cook the fish but also to yield incredibly crisped skin; then it is served with a brunoise of hearty greens and potatoes and rich perilla vinaigrette.

Artful desserts include black raspberry and coconut sorbet with crumbles of spinach cake, yuzu meringue, and perfect berry slices.

🔲 2 Harrison St. (at Hudson St.)
🚇 Franklin St
📞 (212) 219-0900 — **WEB:** www.jungsik.com
🔲 Dinner Mon– Sat

**PRICE: $$$$**

# LITTLE PARK ¶○

*American*

XX | 🍸 🚾 🛏 🛎

MAP: B3

Little Park flaunts that upscale downtown feel that TriBeCa seems to have trademarked. Yet Chef Min Kong delivers a personal and unique cuisine that distinguishes it from other Andrew Carmellini restaurants. Here, vegetables are often put front and center on the plate, with meat and seafood serving as accents. This means that the harmonious flavors of beet tartare with rye crumbs, dill, and smoked trout roe is just as impressive as the crisp-skinned tilefish with bok choy and black radish in toasted rice dashi. Masterful desserts include the frozen Meyer lemon "fluff" with meringue, orange sorbet, and candied ginger.

Diners take note—while the Smyth Hotel lobby bar operates at capacity early in the evening, this dining room starts buzzing at a later hour.

■ 85 West Broadway (at Chambers St.)
🔲 Chambers St (West Broadway)
☏ (212) 220-4110 — **WEB:** www.littlepark.com
■ Lunch & dinner daily          **PRICE: $$**

# LOCANDA VERDE ¶○

*Italian*

XX | 🍸 🏠 🖥 🛎

MAP: A2

This ever-trendy yet refined Italian ristorante is as much coveted for its gorgeous setting as its lineup of rustic, tasty fare. The ambience is always abuzz and everyone looks beautiful amid low lights, a long bar, and walls adorned with wine bottles.

Breakfast verges on divine—think lemon pancakes and apple cider doughnuts. Bare tables are packed throughout the day with a stylish crowd waxing poetic about crostini topped with blue crab and jalapeño. Also try terrific house-made pasta such as pappardelle with lamb Bolognese, finished with a dollop of sheep's milk ricotta, or paccheri dressed in "Sunday night ragù." No one should leave without sampling superb sweets, like the apple and concord grape crostata with rosemary hazelnut brittle and brown butter gelato.

■ 377 Greenwich St. (at N. Moore St.)
🔲 Franklin St
☏ (212) 925-3797 — **WEB:** www.locandaverdenyc.com
■ Lunch & dinner daily          **PRICE: $$$**

# MARC FORGIONE ⑪〇

*American*

✗✗ | 🍸 ♿ 🏠 🛋️          **MAP:** B3

This eponymous restaurant is dark, sexy, and attracts an endless stream of downtown denizens. Abundant candles produce more atmosphere than light for the rustic room clad in exposed brick and salvaged wood. Aloof servers dressed in black seem to disappear into the background.

The innovative American food excites with bold flavors, as in barbecued oysters sprinkled with pancetta powder. Montauk fluke en croute, set over roasted cauliflower, hazelnuts, and capers topped with a buttery panel of toast, is dressed with sauce proposal—so named because the rich brown butter and golden raisin emulsion is said to have earned the chef a few romantic offers. It is delicious, but Chef Forgione deserves equal affection for those amazing butter-glazed potato rolls.

◼ 134 Reade St. (bet. Greenwich & Hudson Sts.)
▦ Chambers St (West Broadway)
✆ (212) 941-9401 — **WEB:** www.marcforgione.com
◼ Lunch Sun   Dinner nightly       **PRICE: $$$**

# THE ODEON ⑪〇

*American*

✗✗ | 🏠 🛋️          **MAP:** B3

It's easy to see why The Odeon has been a part of the fabric of TriBeCa life for so long. Like watching a re-run of Seinfeld, it is reassuringly familiar, classically New York and, even when you know what's coming next, still eminently satisfying. The menu is a roll-call of everyone's favorites, from chicken paillard to beet salad, burgers to cheesecake. Cocktails are well made and beers carefully poured. Dishes are executed with sufficient care and portions are of manageable proportions.

The room comes with an appealing art deco feel and the terrace at the front pulls in the occasional passer-by. Service is personable and willing too, although after all this time the place could probably run itself.

◼ 145 West Broadway (at Thomas St.)
▦ Chambers St (West Broadway)
✆ (212) 233-0507 — **WEB:** www.theodeonrestaurant.com
◼ Lunch & dinner daily       **PRICE: $$$**

# RACINES NY ⅊◯

## *French*

XX | ஃ   ஃ             **MAP:** B3

The American outpost of this popular Parisian original cuts an elegant figure, with its wide marble bar and pristine flower arrangements. Throw in romantic low lighting, brick-lined walls and a tony TriBeCa address—and you have quite the operation.

The service can be a bit off-putting, which is a shame because Racines NY has an ace, even affordable, wine list that bears discussion and recommendations. As for the food, you'll pay for all that sexy ambience a little more than the cuisine currently merits—but certain dishes, like a rich chicken liver mousse served with grilled breads, make for an elegant bar snack. Paired with one of those excellent wines by the glass and a seat at that handsome bar, this is a recipe for a glam night on the town.

  ▨  94 Chambers St. (bet. Broadway & Church St.)
  ▨  Chambers St (West Broadway)
  ✆  (212) 227-3400 — **WEB:** www.racinesny.com
  ▨  Dinner Mon – Sat             **PRICE: $$$$**

# TAMARIND ⅊◯

## *Indian*

XxX | & ⌷             **MAP:** B2

Building Tamarind cost a cool five million, and it shows—every inch of this soaring space oozes with grandeur. With its classic TriBeCa edifice and gorgeous marble bar (an ideal perch for post-work indulgence), the glass-fronted behemoth draws a posh crowd of Wall Streeters and well-heeled locals.

Most impressive of all is the sleek display kitchen, outfitted with a gleaming tandoor that turns out exceptional Mughlai food like nawab shami kabab (lamb patties seasoned with ginger) and hara bhara kabab (pearl-white paneer mingled with bright emerald-green spinach). While service is mediocre at best and the kitchen may fall behind at peak times, mains like kolambi pola (prawns in a coconut-and-chili curry) make up for any gaffes and guarantee a return visit.

  ▨  99 Hudson St. (at Franklin St.)
  ▨  Franklin St
  ✆  (212) 775-9000 — **WEB:** www.tamarindrestaurantsnyc.com
  ▨  Lunch & dinner daily         **PRICE: $$$**

# TINY'S 🍴

*American*

✗ | 🖥 🍳 🔥          **MAP:** B3

The name says it all—Tiny's is indeed tiny, but in that old New York, wood-burning fire, and pressed-tin ceiling kind of way. Enter this narrow Federal-style home (c. 1810) and sidle up to the beautiful people along the pew seats that overlook a poster of the Marlboro Man. Alternatively, head on up to the suitably named Bar Upstairs.

The setting is so rich with character that one could simply be satisfied by Tiny's fine burger, featuring dry-aged rib-eye and a side of cheddar tater tots. However, this is a surprisingly ambitious kitchen turning out some very clever dishes. The wild Coho salmon for example, is grilled to specification and plated with vadouvan-spiced beurre blanc; while the vanilla flan slicked with cold caramel syrup makes a wonderful finale.

- ◼ 135 West Broadway (bet. Duane & Thomas Sts.)
- 🚇 Chambers St (West Broadway)
- ☎ (212) 374-1135 — **WEB:** www.tinysnyc.com
- ◼ Lunch & dinner daily          **PRICE: $$**

# TRIBECA GRILL 🍴

*Contemporary*

✗✗ | 🕸 ♿ 🏠 🖥        **MAP:** A2

Beckoning business titans day and night, this corner restaurant is a destination for its big, bright dining room with well-spaced tables. Wall-to-wall windows overlook two quintessential TriBeCa streets, while exposed brick, moody artwork, and a spectacular bar smack in the center of the room complete the refined vibe.

Gigantone, large tubular pasta loaded with braised short rib Bolognese beneath a dollop of fresh sheep's milk ricotta, makes a rich start to a meal. The decadence continues with seared scallops over creamy carrot risotto, topped with a truffled-Madeira vinaigrette, and brought over the top with a few fragrant shavings of black truffle. Desserts are as classic as the space; try the banana tart with malted chocolate and pecan ice cream.

- ◼ 375 Greenwich St. (at Franklin St.)
- 🚇 Franklin St
- ☎ (212) 941-3900 — **WEB:** www.myriadrestaurantgroup.com
- ◼ Lunch Sun – Fri Dinner nightly      **PRICE: $$$**

# UPPER EAST SIDE

Famously expensive and particularly charming, the Upper East Side is flanked by lush Central Park on one side and the East River on the other. If watching barges and boats bob along the river from a dense metropolis doesn't sound like a perfect paradox, know that this prime area is predominantly residential and home to iconic addresses, like Gracie Mansion. Closest to the park are posh diners catering to expats with expense accounts. But walk a few

steps east and discover young families filling the latest *sushi-ya*, artisanal pizzeria, cheese shop, or hot sidewalk spot where you can dig into salads, soup, and other types of gooey goodness—imagine panini-pressed ciabatta rolls stuffed with Iowa cheddar and locally sourced pickles, from Brooklyn, of course! Along First and Second Avenue, classic Irish pubs are packed with post-grads who keep the party alive well through happy hour and into the wee hours.

## SHOPPING CENTRAL

The most upper and eastern reaches of this neighborhood were originally developed by famous families of German descent. While here, make sure to join the queue of carnivores at **Schaller & Weber** as they hover over Austro-German specialties, including wursts for winter steaming or summer grilling as well as a plethora of pungent mustards to accompany them. This area also boasts a greater concentration of gourmet markets than any other part of town. Each of these emporiums is more packed than the next

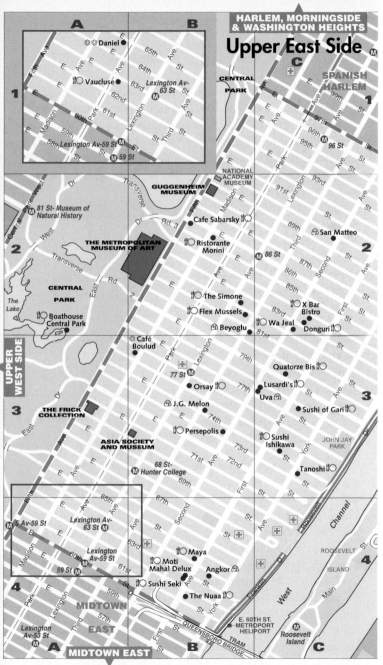

**A** **B** **C**

❋❋ Daniel ●

🍴 Vaucluse ●

Lexington Av-
63 St Ⓜ

58th Lexington Av-59 St Ⓜ

Ⓜ 59 St

CENTRAL PARK

SPANISH HARLEM

96 St Ⓜ

1

81 St- Museum of Natural History Ⓜ

GUGGENHEIM MUSEUM

NATIONAL ACADEMY MUSEUM

THE METROPOLITAN MUSEUM OF ART

Cafe Sabarsky 🍴

🍴 Ristorante Morini

86 St Ⓜ

San Matteo

CENTRAL PARK

The Lake

🍴 Boathouse Central Park

🍴 The Simone

🍴 Flex Mussels

Ⓜ Beyoglu

🍴 X Bar Bistro

🍴 Wa Jeal

Donguri 🍴

2

UPPER WEST SIDE

❋ Café Boulud

77 St Ⓜ

● Orsay 🍴

Ⓜ J.G. Melon

🍴 Persepolis ●

Quatorze Bis 🍴

Lusardi's 🍴

Uva Ⓜ

● Sushi of Gari 🍴

🍴 Sushi Ishikawa

JOHN JAY PARK

THE FRICK COLLECTION

ASIA SOCIETY AND MUSEUM

68 St-
Ⓜ Hunter College

Tanoshi 🍴

3

5 Av-59 St Ⓜ

Lexington Av-
63 St Ⓜ

Lexington Av-59 St

Ⓜ 59 St

🍴 Maya

🍴 Moti Mahal Delux

Angkor Ⓜ

🍴 Sushi Seki

● The Nuaa 🍴

Channel

ROOSEVELT ISLAND

4

MIDTOWN EAST

Lexington Av-53 St Ⓜ

E. 60TH ST. METROPORT HELIPORT

QUEENSBORO BRIDGE TRAM

Ⓜ Roosevelt Island

**MIDTOWN EAST**

**A** **B** **C**

295

and make processing long lines an art of inspired efficiency. The presence of **Fairway**, a gourmet sanctuary showcasing everything from fresh produce and glistening meats to seafood and deli delights, has made shopping for homemade meals a complete breeze. And, with such easy access to **Agata & Valentina**, a family-owned and operated food store whose famously cramped aisles are supplied with everything Italian, residents of the Upper East can't imagine residing elsewhere in the city. Outfitted with delicious gift ideas, baskets, and recipes, this epicurean haven brings an authentic European experience to the vibrant streets of Manhattan.

**A** few steps west, **Citarella** pumps out its mouthwatering aroma of rotisserie chickens to entice passersby. Prime meats and rare produce are also on offer here, and contend with the abundant goodness available at **Grace's Marketplace**. In their expanded location, this beloved bazaar boasts more space, but no lesser quality, variety, or guests at the

prepared foods counter. Such a savory spectacle is bound to leave you starving, so grab a seat at their adjoining trattoria and devour some pasta or a whole pizza. At the head of the gourmet game and celebrated as the reigning champion of

everything uptown is Eli Zabar and his ever-expanding empire. **E.A.T.** is a Madison Avenue treasure selling all things edible in its casual café. Thanks to its vast carte and appeal, other outposts (like mega-mart **Eli's**) have sprouted and continue to prosper in this quarter. Meanwhile, **Corner Café and Bakery** is a gem among nannies and mommies, who may travel with uniformed young'uns in tow for a selection of tasty salads, sammies, and fro-yo to-go. Finally, every self-respecting foodie knows that **Kitchen Arts & Letters** flaunts the largest stock of food and wine publications in the country, and founder Nach Waxman is as good a source of industry insight as any other book or blogger in town.

## SUPPER, SWEETS AND SIPS

**I**n spite of such large-scale shopping, still there are smaller purveyors to patronize here. **Lobel's** and **Ottomanelli** are among the best butchers around; while **William Greenberg** continues to bake first-rate *babka* and Gotham City's favorite black-and-white cookie. Just as **Ladurée**'s pastel-hued macarons bring a slice of the City of Lights to this glitzy enclave, **Glaser's Bake Shop** is reminiscent of everything Old World. In the same vein, **Lady M's** cakes fit perfectly into its plush setting, right off Madison Avenue. Switching from snacks to sips, thirsty revelers will appreciate **Bemelmans Bar** or **The Jeffrey**, a railcar-like space serving stellar libations and pub grub. But if in the mood for supper and a show, it doesn't get more classic than the storied hotel's **Café Carlyle**. Finally, balance things out at **Bar Pleiades**, which is yet another contemporary retreat, but just as elegantly uptown as one would expect with its quilted walls and lacquer finishes.

# ANGKOR ⊚
## *Cambodian*

XX | 🛖                                          **MAP:** B4

Connoisseurs of Southeast Asian cuisine, take note: in a city that prides itself on ethnic eats, this fresh bistro offers one of the few true places for Cambodian food in Manhattan.

Inside, the stone-accented Angkor is lined in richly-stained wood and filled with woven rattan furnishings and Buddha figurines. Owned by Minh and Mandy Truong, the husband-wife team who ran Chelsea's Royal Siam for 20 years, this menu certainly shares DNA with other Southeast Asian restaurants, offering classic items like grilled, marinated meat skewers, sour soups, spicy salads, and curries. But there are also more unique items to be explored, like delicious stir-fried specialties from Siem Reap; or nyoam, a traditional Khmer noodle dish sauced with thick red fish curry.

🔲 408 E. 64th St. (bet. First & York Aves.)
🔲 Lexington Av - 63 St
✆ (212) 758-2111 — **WEB:** www.angkornyc.com
🔲 Lunch Mon – Sat   Dinner nightly          **PRICE:** $$

# BEYOGLU ⊚
## *Turkish*

X | ♿ 🛖                                        **MAP:** B2

Upper East Siders can't get enough of the meze at cheerful Beyoglu and its enticing Turkish, Greek, and Lebanese cooking. Vibrant flavors enhanced by garlic and herbs start with chilled platters loaded with hummus, mashed eggplant spread (patlican salatasi), and salads like kisir, tabbouleh made with cracked wheat. The only other thing you'll need to fully enjoy the Beyoglu experience is a bowl of strained, house-made yogurt. The amazing flatbread is pulled straight from the hot oven only to arrive on your table seconds later, gratis and absolutely gratifying.

Tile-topped tables and pistachio-green walls displaying painted flowers accent the interior. French doors separate the dining room from the sidewalk, but during warm weather both areas fill quickly.

🔲 1431 Third Ave. (at 81st St.)
🔲 77 St
✆ (212) 650-0850 — **WEB:** N/A
🔲 Lunch & dinner daily                      **PRICE:** $$

# BOATHOUSE CENTRAL PARK 🍴○

*American*

XX | ♿ 🏠 🛎 🪑                                    **MAP:** A2

The word "touristy" is mostly used pejoratively but there's no denying that sometimes visitors to the city know a good thing when they see one. Loeb Boathouse was built in 1954 and includes an outdoor bar and a restaurant whose glass wall folds away in the summer to give every table a great view of the lake. If you want to swap the chaos of the city and its cacophony of car horns for a couple of tranquil hours, then here's where to come.

The menu is a mix of American and European classics alongside less successful dishes of a more innovative persuasion. Try the robustly seasoned linguine with Little Neck clams or Scottish salmon with chickpea purée. While brunch and lunch are year-long affairs, dinner is only served during warmer months.

▓ The Lake at Central Park (E. 72nd St. & Park Dr. North)
🚇 68 St - Hunter College
📞 (212) 517-2233 — **WEB:** www.thecentralparkboathouse.com
▓ Lunch & dinner daily                          **PRICE:** $$$

# CAFE SABARSKY 🍴○

*Austrian*

X | ♿ ☕                                         **MAP:** B2

This Museum Mile kaffeehaus is so authentic it may as well be set along Vienna's Ringstrasse. Instead, find it in a Beaux Arts mansion—which is also home to Serge Sabarsky and Ronald Lauder's Neue Galerie, replete with 20th century Austrian-and-German art and design. Located across from Central Park, this gorgeous ground-floor den is clad in dark-stained wood with diners seated along a banquette covered in Otto Wagner fabric.

Stunning cakes and pastries are displayed on a marble-topped sideboard. But first, order one of Chef Kurt Gutenbrunner's traditional specialties, including the city's best wiener schnitzel or hearty Hungarian beef goulash with creamy, herbed spätzle. When it's time for dessert, try a wedge of the chocolate, almond, and rum Sabarskytorte.

▓ 1048 Fifth Ave. (at 86th St.)
🚇 86 St (Lexington Ave.)
📞 (212) 288-0665 — **WEB:** www.kurtgutenbrunner.com
▓ Lunch Wed – Mon   Dinner Fri – Sun            **PRICE:** $$

# CAFÉ BOULUD ✿

*French*

✕✕✕ | ❀ 🍸 ♿ 🛋 💺 🍽 🔥

Taking its cue from classic French cuisine, Daniel Boulud's refined vision of food and beverage at the Surrey hotel is comprised of two spaces: the jewel box known as Bar Pleiades and this elegant, appealingly understated restaurant.

Inside, ritzy residents and in-the-know globetrotters dine in a well-groomed, secluded room furnished with plush carpeting, rich wood accents, and mirrored surfaces. Sparkling elements atop beautifully laid tables set off the spot's conviviality, and gallant, smartly-dressed servers display unwavering competence in their presentation of uniquely constructed and superb tasting compositions. Under the watch of Chef Aaron Bludorn, the kitchen makes culinary decisions that never disappoint. Classically done poulet rôti showcases evenly moist, crispy skinned chicken finished with a fragrant tarragon jus, while the Crescent Farms Pekin duck, cooked to a perfect pink and sprinkled with coarse salt, is served with currant-studded kasha for wonderful depth in flavor and texture.

For dessert, intricately layered crêpe cakes are garnished with rhubarb gelée and kissed with ricotta sorbet. Finally, warm and springy madeleines—a house signature—send satisfied diners on their way.

■ 20 E. 76th St. (bet. Fifth & Madison Aves.)

🚇 77 St

✆ (212) 772-2600 — **WEB:** www.cafeboulud.com

■ Lunch & dinner daily

**PRICE: $$$$**

# DONGURI ﹛○

*Japanese*

χ

This cozy Yorkville hideaway has endured years of non-stop construction along Second Avenue and a more recent change in ownership and chef. Yet Donguri still perseveres as a highly recommendable venue. Service has lightened up of late, reflected in the genuine smiles of the small and gracious crew, but the cuisine's ethos remains very much unaltered.

Don't expect to dine on sushi here—there's more to Japanese cuisine after all, as evidenced by their home-style cooked dishes. Nightly specials posted on the wall direct your attention to options like fried soft-shell crabs so pleasingly crispy and plump they don't need anything else. Okay, a squeeze of lemon if you must. Rice bowls topped with the likes of yellowtail and scallion are yet another specialty.

- 309 E. 83rd St. (bet. First & Second Aves.)
- 86 St (Lexington Ave.)
- ✆ (212) 737-5656 — **WEB:** www.donguriny.com
- Dinner Tue – Sun                            PRICE: $$

# FLEX MUSSELS ﹛○

*Seafood*

χχ

Presenting a focused menu of cleverly made, high-quality seafood, it's no surprise that this haven is still going strong. Inside, the setting is routinely packed to the gills, both up front where there is a bar and counter, as well as in the back dining room, adorned with an abundance of maritime-themed artwork.

Expect to taste plenty of the namesake bivalve, hailing from Prince Edward Island. Priced by the pound and steamed in no fewer than twenty globally inspired broths, they are best with some killer hand-cut skinny fries. Mussels No. 23 refers to the daily special, which may feature these mollusks in a fragrant bath of white wine, tomatillo salsa, and jalapeño for a bit of heat. When coupled with shrimp and calamari, this does indeed make for a sweet treat.

- 174 E. 82nd St. (bet. Lexington & Third Aves.)
- 86 St (Lexington Ave.)
- ✆ (212) 717-7772 — **WEB:** www.flexmusselsny.com
- Dinner nightly                              PRICE: $$

# DANIEL ✿✿

*French*

XxXxX | 😋 🍸 🍽

The stylish façade, revolving door, sound of clinking glasses—even before you reach the dining room you feel a part of something special. This bastion of contemporary French cooking epitomizes the "special occasion," but even those with money to burn treat it with respect.

Translucent Limoges-tiled chandeliers hanging from the soaring ceiling dominate the main room. If you're at one of the raised tables, you get to look down—literally rather than patronizingly—onto your fellow diners through neo-classical arches. Yet thanks to the personable staff, such grandeur never stifles the animated atmosphere.

The kitchen is as sophisticated as the setting and reflects an obvious classical education, yet remains free from the tyranny of tradition. Behold the slow-poached sea scallops served with purple potatoes and a burst of parsley vinaigrette. Bluenose grouper is arranged atop cauliflower purée, surrounded by crispy florets, and finished with a mussel-saffron sauce for a presentation that is as theatrical as delicious. For dessert, sample the divine "Illanka"—a dark chocolate and espelette crémeux with a blackberry-orange blossom sorbet that practically upstages the season's best fruit.

◼ 60 E. 65th St. (bet. Madison & Park Aves.)

🚇 68 St - Hunter College

📞 (212) 288-0033 — **WEB:** www.danielnyc.com

◼ Dinner Mon – Sat

**PRICE: $$$$**

# J.G. MELON 🐶

*American*

𝄪 | 🏛 ⑤                                          **MAP:** B3

Posterity will remember J.G. Melon as a classic and coveted New York institution. Make your way into this cave set upon a cozy Upper East corner, where the timeless vibe and cheery staff make up most of its allure. Drinks are steadily churned out at a dark wood bar, so arrive early to avoid the hordes.

The focus at this multi-generational saloon is the burger—perhaps paired with a lip-smacking Bloody Mary at brunch? The warm toasted bun topped with meat cooked on a griddle to rosy pink is coupled with onions, pickles, and crispy crinkle-cut fries. Be forewarned: you will go through the entire stack of napkins before finishing. Other simple pleasures include standards like salads, steaks, and eggs. Seal the meal with a chocolate chip-studded layer cake.

▨ 1291 Third Ave. (at 74th St.)
🚇 77 St
☏ (212) 744-0585 — **WEB:** N/A
▨ Lunch & dinner daily                    **PRICE:** 💰💰

# LUSARDI'S 🍴

*Italian*

✗✗                                              **MAP:** C3

With its pumpkin-colored walls, dark woodwork, and vintage posters, this beloved old-school mainstay offers a menu that relishes in decadent Northern Italian cooking. Picture an array of fresh pasta and veal, richly embellished with cream, authentic cheeses, or truffle-infused olive oil.

The insalata bianca is a monotone-white yet delightfully refreshing composition of shaved fennel, sliced artichoke hearts, chopped endive, and slivered hearts of palm dressed with lemony vinaigrette and Parmigiano Reggiano, all singing with black pepper freshly ground tableside. Paccheri in salsa affumicata presents large pasta tubes draped with plum tomato sauce that has been enriched with creamy smoked mozzarella and strewn with bits of roasted eggplant.

▨ 1494 Second Ave. (bet. 77th & 78th Sts.)
🚇 77 St
☏ (212) 249-2020 — **WEB:** www.lusardis.com
▨ Lunch Mon – Fri   Dinner nightly          **PRICE:** $$$

# MAYA 🍴

## *Mexican*

XX | ♿ 🛋️

Upscale Mexican dining thrives at Chef Richard Sandoval's muy popular Maya. Slick with polished dark wood furnishings, vibrant tiled flooring, and accent walls the color of a ripe mango, this is always a fun scene. Adding to the revelry is the Tequileria, Maya's bar with a serious focus on agave spirits.

Antojitos, such as squash blossom quesadillas and their trio of salsas, headline as starters. Tasty tacos are stuffed with smoked brisket and creamy chili slaw. Heartier dishes feature huitlacoche and wild mushroom enchiladas swathed in a creamy, fire-roasted poblano chile sauce. Especialidades like achiote-marinated carne asada with cactus-green bean salad and bacon-wrapped jalapeños display the kitchen's contemporary flair.

■ 1191 First Ave. (bet. 64th & 65th Sts.)
🚇 68 St - Hunter College
☏ (212) 585-1818 — **WEB:** www.richardsandoval.com
■ Lunch Sat – Sun   Dinner nightly          **PRICE: $$**

# MOTI MAHAL DELUX 🍴

## *Indian*

XX

This corner spot marks the first American location of a fine dining chain that began in Delhi and now boasts outposts throughout India. Here in NYC, Moti Mahal Delux offers two distinct seating areas: an earth-toned dining room and windowed sidewalk atrium.

Their Northern-leaning cuisine traces back to the kitchens of the Mughal Empire, which brought Muslim influences to the Indian subcontinent. Lunch is limited, while dinner is more rewarding, featuring tandoori preparations like anardana tikka—grilled chicken infused with a pomegranate and black pepper marinade. Delightful flavors abound through the brick-red mutton curry with spiced tomato, onion, and ginger; paratha dusted with dried mint; as well as the mustard seed-and curry leaf-infused lemon rice.

■ 1149 First Ave. (at 63rd St.)
🚇 Lexington Av - 63 St
☏ (212) 371-3535 — **WEB:** www.motimahaldelux.us
■ Lunch & dinner daily          **PRICE: $$**

# THE NUAA 🍴

*Thai*

XX             **MAP:** B4

The Nuaa offers a certain sultry vibe to this rather blah, trafficky stretch—it's dim and moody even in the middle of the day. Shimmering gold accents pop against the room's brown leather seating, carved woodwork, and dark palette. Fans of Thai cuisine will enjoy the pleasantly pungent notes throughout the selection of salads and noodle dishes.

Crunchy curried rice salad features deep-fried nuggets strewn with Thai sausage and lemongrass served with plenty of shallots, long beans, lettuce, and a drizzle of makrut lime-mint vinaigrette. The kanom jeen features thin rice noodles soaked in a mildly spiced coconut-rich yellow curry that is generously stocked with huge lumps of crab meat, chopped pickled mustard greens, and caper berries.

◼ 1122 First Ave. (bet. 61st & 62nd Sts.)
🚇 59 St
☏ (212) 888-2899 — **WEB:** www.thenuaa.com
◼ Lunch & dinner daily          **PRICE:** $$

# ORSAY 🍴

*French*

XX | ♿ 🛖 🖵 🍷         **MAP:** B3

Its classic art nouveau styling makes this popular French brasserie de luxe infinitely more 7th arrondissement than Upper East Side. The efficient service is overseen by managers armed with authentic French accents and highly skilled in the art of flirting and flattery—the immaculately coiffured Orcéens may be a sophisticated bunch of customers but they expect a generous side order of Gallic charm to go with their classic French cuisine.

All the favorites are here, from escargots to lobster bisque, quenelle Lyonnaise to île flottante, and the kitchen prepares them all with a healthy respect for tradition. There are also plenty of salads for those who've given up wondering how French women can eat this kind of food without ever going to the gym.

◼ 1057 Lexington Ave. (at 75th St.)
🚇 77 St
☏ (212) 517-6400 — **WEB:** www.orsayrestaurant.com
◼ Lunch & dinner daily         **PRICE:** $$$

# PERSEPOLIS 🍴

*Persian*

XX | 🏮

Silky-smooth spreads, homemade yogurt, grilled meats, and fragrantly spiced stews have solidified Persepolis' reputation as one of the city's finest Persian restaurants. Linen-draped tables, spacious banquettes, and big windows facing Second Avenue fashion a look that inspires dressing up (or not). Service is always gracious, if at times earnest.

The kitchen shines with its eggplant halim, a creamy, steaming roasted eggplant and onion dip with tender lentils and a dollop of yogurt on top. A kebab duo of saffron-tinged chicken and grilled beef are both succulent successes, served with basmati rice flecked with sour cherries. For dessert, try the tart-sweet Persian lemon ice studded with bits of rice noodles and doused in a deep red cherry syrup.

- 1407 Second Ave. (bet. 73rd & 74th Sts.)
- 77 St
- (212) 535-1100 — **WEB:** www.persepolisnewyork.com
- Lunch & dinner daily      **PRICE: $$**

# QUATORZE BIS 🍴

*French*

XX | 🛋

Savoring a meal at this ever-charming bistro is like taking a break from the constant evolution that is life in New York City, where tastes change faster than you can tweet. The red-lacquer façade, claret-velvet banquettes, and sophisticated clientele are all much the same as when Quatorze Bis opened over 25 years ago.

Though the ambience's timeless appeal is noteworthy, the traditional French cooking is their key to success. Frilly chicory, drizzled with hot bacon fat and red wine vinegar, and pocked with lardons, croutons, and shallots makes for a very hearty, très French salad. Seafood sausage is plump and studded with sweet red pepper and pine nuts. Daily specials keep the menu fresh, with dishes like striped bass served beside a creamy sorrel sauce.

- 323 E. 79th St. (bet. First & Second Aves.)
- 77 St
- (212) 535-1414 — **WEB:** www.quatorze.nyc
- Lunch Tue – Sun   Dinner nightly      **PRICE: $$**

# RISTORANTE MORINI ⅋○

*Italian*

XxX | 88 ⊡ ⤵            **MAP:** B2

Altamarea Group's prime Madison Avenue corner boasts a lively street-level lounge and second story window-lined dining room where even children in tow are properly attired for lunch. Despite the high-rent address, Ristorante Morini offers an economical lunch prix-fixe, as well as a family-style Sunday supper.

Slick Italian dining is the draw here, as demonstrated by the likes of bocconcini (chicken meatballs) infused with eggplant and fennel seed, baked with tomato sauce, and garnished with basil, breadcrumbs and more eggplant. Spaghetti vongole tossed with steamed clams, leeks, and a white wine sauce flaunts luxurious texture from a swirl of butter; while desserts like vanilla bean gelato dressed with a shot of espresso and amaro are nothing short of luxurious.

■ 1167 Madison Ave. (bet. 85th & 86th Sts.)
■ 86 St (Lexington Ave.)
✆ (212) 249-0444 — **WEB:** www.ristorantemorini.com
■ Lunch Sun – Fri  Dinner nightly            **PRICE:** $$$

# SAN MATTEO ☻

*Italian*

X | ⛩            **MAP:** C2

This tiny pizzeria has made a big splash with its panuozzo, a regional specialty hailing from Campania that's a cross between a calzone and panino. The puffy plank of tender, salted dough emerges from San Matteo's hand-built, wood-fired oven crusty and smoke-infused before being sliced and stuffed with first-rate ingredients (highlights include the ortolano's fresh, house-made mozzarella, grilled eggplant, roasted sweet peppers, and baby arugula).

The room is graciously attended to and perpetually crowded with neighborhood folks stuffing their faces. In addition to the appetizing house signature, other favorites feature fresh salads such as escarole with Gaeta olives, capers, and gorgonzola; Neapolitan-style pizza; or the day's special baked pasta.

■ 1739 Second Ave. (at 90th St.)
■ 86 St (Lexington Ave.)
✆ (212) 426-6943 — **WEB:** www.sanmatteopanuozzo.com
■ Lunch Fri – Sun  Dinner nightly            **PRICE:** ⛁

# THE SIMONE ⅏

## Contemporary

XX | 🏵

Chef Chip Smith and wife Tina Vaughn prove hospitality isn't dead at their posh dining room, where genuine service and excellent cuisine have Upper East Siders giddy. Menus ask diners to refrain from cellphone usage, proving that this is an endearingly old-school spot despite its young age. And the bonhomie present sets the perfect tone for astute cooking. Agnolotti filled with parsnip purée and garnished by crunchy hazelnuts boasts an impeccable start. Then savor a cylinder of flounder, luxuriously scented with Perigord black truffle and served alongside shaved carrots formed into a gratin-like cake and frilled with breadcrumbs.

For a true-blue finish, try the Alsatian apple tart topped with torched custard and a single scoop of prune-Armagnac ice cream.

▪ 151 E. 82nd St. (bet. Lexington & Third Aves.)
▪ 86 St (Lexington Ave.)
✆ (212) 772-8861 — **WEB:** www.thesimonerestaurant.com
▪ Dinner Mon – Sat　　　　　　　　　　**PRICE: $$$**

# SUSHI ISHIKAWA ⅏

## Japanese

XX

After honing his skills at the New York outpost of O Ya, Chef Don Pham has made his way to this quiet residential stretch of the Upper East Side, where he delivers a profoundly solid and wallet-friendly omakase each night. The new space is minimalist and very pleasant, largely thanks to the chef's charming presence, as he informs counter guests of the provenance of each morsel of fish—most often sourced from Japan.

Meals arrive primarily as a parade of nigiri, presented one piece at a time on a ceramic slab with chopped bits of pickled ginger. Highlights may reveal torched barracuda or shima-aji with a spicy dab of chilies. That procession may be broken up with delicious small plates, such as smoked bonito with shaved summer truffles and ponzu sauce.

▪ 419 E. 74th St. (bet. First & York Aves.)
▪ 77 St
✆ (212) 651-7292 — **WEB:** www.ishikawanyc.com
▪ Dinner Tue – Sat　　　　　　　　　　**PRICE: $$$$**

# SUSHI OF GARI ⭐️🍴

## Japanese

✗ | 🍶

There is a great deal that appears simple here, but there is much more that is not. The room, itself, is a minimally decorated space of pale wood, bright lights, and a few ikebana arrangements that it almost feels sterile. However, few seem to take note. It is no secret that when you make a reservation here, request the counter and go for the omakase, because precise plating, skilled knife work, and renowned sushi is where everyone's attention remains.

The kitchen's skill shines with dishes that showcase their unique creativity. Signature dishes include lean, ruby-red slices of tuna wrapped around creamy tofu dressed with spicy sesame oil, or salmon nigiri with piping hot sautéed tomato.

Dining here requires advance planning, but they also offer takeout.

🔲 402 E. 78th St. (bet. First & York Aves.)
🚇 77 St
📞 (212) 517-5340 — **WEB:** www.sushiofgari.com
🔲 Dinner Tue-Sun                                   **PRICE:** $$$$

# SUSHI SEKI 🍴

## Japanese

✗

**MAP:** B4

A local standby that doesn't actually look like much, Sushi Seki combines exceptional sushi and sashimi with a casual vibe that keeps neighborhood loyalists packed in for late-night dinners and take-out. It may seem like a simple restaurant for a very good spicy tuna roll, but their unique omakase is what makes it a worthy favorite. Dedicated itamae bring quality and creativity to each bite. Sample toro chopped with ginger that is at once tender, rich and crunchy over rice; or a slice of fatty salmon with avocado sauce. But, for a true treat, go for their signature hand roll of toasted nori surrounding chopped juicy scallop with crunchy tempura flakes, tobiko, and spicy mayo.

An expanded location in Hell's Kitchen offers an attractive array of seating options.

🔲 1143 First Ave. (bet. 62nd & 63rd Sts.)
🚇 Lexington Av - 59 St
📞 (212) 371-0238 — **WEB:** N/A
🔲 Dinner Mon – Sat                                   **PRICE:** $$

# TANOSHI ⬦

## Japanese

✕                                              **MAP:** C3

Tanoshi isn't exactly the "sushi and sake bar" that the awning lists. It is BYO, so no sake, and a clipboard posted outside the door lists reservations for their two distinct dining rooms. (The right side is nicer.)

Settle into Chef Toshio Oguma's true expression of Edomae sushi, as you forgive the lacking service and ambience. Lunch is a limited affair, so come for dinner when it is omakase-only, with the exception of a few handwritten specials. But all that is second to the sushi, which is crafted from loosely formed mounds of warm, akazu-seasoned rice and topped with perfect fish. Highlights include New Zealand king salmon that melts in the mouth, tender amberjack with marinated cherry leaf, as well as bigeye tuna crowned with wisps of kelp.

- 1372 York Ave. (bet. 73rd & 74th Sts.)
- 77 St
- ℰ (917) 265-8254 — **WEB:** www.tanoshisushinyc.com
- Lunch & dinner Mon – Sat                **PRICE: $$$**

# UVA 😊

## Italian

✕ | 🎋 🏠 🛋                                    **MAP:** C3

Perpetually packed and always pleasing, this cousin of elegant Lusardi's is a rocking, rustic good time. Votive-filled nooks and fringed sconces cast a flattering light on the inviting room furnished with straw-seat chairs and wooden tables laden with wine bar-themed small plates.

Cheeses, meats, and salads are fine ways to start. The insalata di manzo is a tasty hybrid of all three—shaved lean beef topped with peppery young arugula, nutty parmesan, and pickled mushrooms. Join the crowds at the start of the week for Meatball Mondays offering three courses revolving around...you guessed it. Sample the hearty beef meatball ravioli garnished with sliced artichoke hearts, silky smooth tomato sauce, and a drizzle of extra virgin olive oil.

- 1486 Second Ave. (bet. 77th & 78th Sts.)
- 77 St
- ℰ (212) 472-4552 — **WEB:** www.uvanyc.com
- Lunch Sat – Sun   Dinner nightly          **PRICE: $$**

# VAUCLUSE ⵊ◯

## French

𝕏ₓ𝕏 | ⌂                                               **MAP:** A1

There is no shortage of good looks in this part of town and Michael White's bold restaurant fits in nicely. It's certainly an impressive space, dressed in neutral tones. It's also a big space, with a bar that divides two dining rooms—one on the upper level that is less formal, while the lower level room has a more animated air.

The name refers to a department in France's southwest; and while service here may not be as luxe as the setting, this is proud and classical brasserie fare. There is a lot of choice on offer—bouillabaisse, grillades for those who like their food familiar, fruits de mer, and a notable selection of meat and fish. The kitchen reveals its confidence by ensuring that plates are never overcrowded. Desserts, like Paris-Brest or crème brûlée, are a highlight.

◼ 100 E. 63rd St. (at Park Ave.)
◼ 59 St
✆ (646) 869-2300 — **WEB:** www.vauclusenyc.com
◼ Lunch Sun – Fri   Dinner nightly          **PRICE: $$$**

# WA JEAL ⵊ◯

## Chinese

𝕏𝕏                                                     **MAP:** C2

This Sichuan chili house is not merely weathering the local torrent of Second Avenue subway construction; their spotless room and tasty food will make you forget that the outside world exists. The ambience is upscale and appealing, combining pale walls, prescient images of wicked-red chilies, an engaging staff, and a substantial wine list.

The chef's specialties reveal the most noteworthy cooking, as in diced fish and crispy tofu stir-fried in a reddish-brown chili sauce speckled with chili seeds and sliced green onions. Sautéed chicken with spiced miso is another pleasure, mixing crisped, boneless pieces, wok-fried with roasted red chilies and charred jalapeños. Tender baby bok choy with garlic is a refreshing contrast to such potent flavors.

◼ 1588 Second Ave. (bet. 82nd & 83rd Sts.)
◼ 86 St (Lexington Ave.)
✆ (212) 396-3339 — **WEB:** www.wajealrestaurant.com
◼ Lunch & dinner daily                       **PRICE: $$**

# X BAR BISTRO ⏧

*French*

XX

**MAP:** C2

Flaunting an intimate bar and a clutch of small tables nestled into a narrow space lined with pale walls and exposed brick, X Bar Bistro is your perfect little neighborhood date spot—elevated to Chef Danny Brown's expectations, that is.

Speaking of, you're likely to see the talented master himself toiling away in the rear kitchen. Inspired by a shuttered Parisian spot favored by the chef, which offered only two well-executed entrées, Chef Brown offers a concise but teasingly good menu here (alongside some delicious libations). Succulent, perfectly cooked duck breast is plated with roasted apricot, celery root purée, wilted mustard greens, and savory jus; while citrus-marinated seafood salad is enriched with asparagus and crushed, slow-cooked cherry tomatoes.

▨ 316 E. 84th St. (bet. First & Second Aves.)
▨ 86 St (Lexington Ave.)
✆ (646) 719-1398 — **WEB:** www.xbarnyc.com
▨ Dinner Tue – Sat

**PRICE:** $$$

Look for **red** couverts, indicating a particularly pleasant ambiance,

# UPPER WEST SIDE

The Upper West Side is the epitome of classic New York. Proudly situated between Central Park and the Hudson River, this family-friendly neighborhood is one of the Big Apple's most distinct and upscale localities that has a near-religious belief in its own way of doing things. Whether it's because these charming streets cradle some of the best cafés in town, or that life here means constantly tripping over culture vultures destined for world-renowned Lincoln Center, area residents cannot imagine living elsewhere. On the heels of this famed institution is **Dizzy's Club Coca-Cola**—one of the better places to spend a night on the town. From its alluring vibe and exceptional jazz talent, to a stellar lineup of Southern food, audiences seem entranced by this imposing home to America's creative art form. The Upper West Side is also considered

# Upper
# West Side

**A** **B** **C**

**NEW
JERSEY**

**1**

HUDSON

RIVER

COLUMBIA
UNIVERSITY

Cathedral
Pkwy (110 St)

🍴◗ **Mezzogiorno**

⚐ **Miss Mamie's
Spoonbread Too**

**Macchina** 🍴◗

Cathedral
Pkwy (110 St)

W. 103 St

🍴◗ **Noche
Mexicana II**

🍴◗ **Awadh**

96 St

**Gennaro** 🍴◗

86 St

🍴◗ **Barney
Greengrass**

**2**

**CENTRAL
PARK**

96 St

103 St

*Jacqueline
Kennedy
Onassis
Reservoir*

**3**

🍴◗ **Sushi
Yasaka**

⚘ **Dovetail**

🍴◗ **Café
Frida**

72 St

79 St

🍴◗ **Bin 71**

72 St

**81 St- Museum of
Natural History**

**AMERICAN
MUSEUM OF
NATURAL
HISTORY**

**METROPOLITAN
MUSEUM OF ART**

86 St

*The Lake*

**LINCOLN
CENTER**

66 St-
Lincoln
Center

🍴◗ **Boulud Sud**

⚘⚘ **Jean-Georges**

**Nougatine** 🍴◗

59 St-Columbus Circle

**CENTRAL

PARK**

**UPPER

EAST SIDE**

77 St

68 St-
Hunter College

72 St

**UPPER
EAST
SIDE**

**4**

*The
Pond*

5 Av-
59 St

Lexington Av-
63 St

57 St

**MIDTOWN
WEST**

an intellectual hub—cue the distinguished presence of Columbia University to the north—and coveted real estate mecca with residential high-rises freckled amid quaint townhouses. In fact, legendary co-ops like *The Dakota* speak to the area's history, while agreeable eateries like **Épicerie Boulud** nourish its affluent tenants, hungry locals, and Ivy Leaguers on the run.

## ALL IN THE FAMILY

**A**cknowledged for strolling, these sidewalks are stacked with charming diners and pre-war brownstones featuring polished parquet floors, intricate moldings, and bookish locals—arguing with equal gusto over the future of opera or if **Barney Greengrass** still serves the best sturgeon in town. One is also likely to find these deep-rooted residents browsing the shelves at **Murray's** for killer smoked fish; while more discerning palates may seek gratification at **Cleopatra's Needle**—an old-time jazz club-cum-Middle Eastern eatery named for the monument in Central Park. However, if stirring live performances and open mic (on Sunday afternoons) served with a side of Mediterranean cuisine doesn't fit the bill, then keep it easy indoors by stocking up on a selection of simple yet tasty sandwiches from **Indie Food and Wine**. Nestled inside the Elinor Bunin Munroe Film

Center, this interesting café aims to entice the palates of visitors to Lincoln Center by way of Italian sandwiches and salads, finished with American flair. Sitting within shouting distance, **The Tangled Vine** places fine wine and elegant eats under a warm and accessible spotlight. Presenting an extraordinary list of organic varietals, this boutique spot is also *the* perfect roost for a sip and small plate before heading south for a show... on Broadway, of course. But, if in the mood for familiar, old-time kitsch, find a seat at **The Cottage**, a Chinese-American standby serving nostalgic fare late into the night for area families and caffeinated scholars.

**M**igrating from the Far East and back to the Med, prepare for an evening in with *nonna* by stocking up on sips and other specialties from **Salumeria Rosi Parmacotto**. Regardless of your choice to dine-in or take-out, this Italian stallion is a guaranteed good time. Wallet-watching residents may rest easy as the price is always right at **Celeste**—known for churning out a perfect pizza as well as a regal Sunday afternoon repast. And in keeping with the value-meal theme, "Recession Specials" are all the rage at legendary **Gray's Papaya**—the politically outspoken (check the window slogans) and quintessential hot dog chain.

## BRUNCH AND BAKE

**T**his dominantly residential region also jumped on the bakery-brunch bandwagon long before its counterparts; and its paths are rarely short on calorie-rich treats. From chocolates at **Mondel** or a

trove of treasures at **Urbani Truffles**, to madeleines at **La Toulousaine**, the Upper West flaunts it all. In-the-know tenants get their sweet fix at **Levain**, where the addiction to chocolate chip cookies is only surpassed by their size.

## A MEDLEY OF MARKETS

**S**uch a "spirited" sense extends to all aspects of life in the Upper West Side—particularly food. For foodies and home cooks, the **Tucker Square Greenmarket** (anchored on West 66th and open on Thursdays and Saturdays) is popular for leafy greens and Mexican provisions—*papalo* anyone? Equally storied is the original **Fairway**, a culinary shrine to well-priced gourmet items. Intrepid shoppers should brave its famously cramped elevator to visit the exclusively organic second floor. Finally, no trip here is complete without a visit to **Zabar's**—home of all things "deli." Ogle their olives; grab some knishes to nosh on; then take the time to admire their line of exquisite kitchen supplies. But also remain assured that smaller purveyors still reside (and reign supreme) here. In fact, **Zingone Brothers**, once a fruit and vegetable stall, is now a famous, family owned-and-operated grocer that teems with conventional goodies... and treats you like a long-lost friend.

# AWADH 🍴

*Indian*

XX | ⬭

Awadh isn't an ordinary Indian spot, but one that advertises faithful flavors from Uttar Pradesh. This Northern Indian region excels in low- and slow-cooked dum pukht dishes, and the menu reads like a study in authenticity (there's no tandoori chicken in sight). Even the small room, polished and modern, is ideal for the city's well-traveled locals.

Top service and table settings further elevate the dining experience here, which begins with aloo chutney pulao or basmati rice scattered with silky potatoes and spiced peas. Couple this with nali ki nihari (perfectly pink lamb in a creamy cardamom-infused curry) or khaas chicken korma rich with nuts for a profound and regal repast. Then cool down over minty pudina raita, and just like that, you've become a regular.

■ 2588 Broadway (bet. 97th & 98th Sts.)
🚇 96 St (Broadway)
📞 (646) 861-3604 — **WEB:** www.awadhnyc.com
■ Lunch & dinner daily

PRICE: $$

# BARNEY GREENGRASS 🍴

*Deli*

X | 🎩

Bagels and bialys reign supreme in this culinary institution, set amid a culturally rich stretch dotted with synagogues and purveyors of authentic deli delights. Not all are created equal, though, and little details make all the difference inside this sturgeon king, lauded for its weathered décor featuring muraled walls, a storied past, and service that is as authentically NY as can be. It's the sort of spot families flock to for brunch—imagine a triple-decker (tongue, turkey, and Swiss cheese) on rye, paired with a pickle, of course.

Whether you take-out or eat-in, items like chopped liver with caramelized onions and boiled egg are sure to sate. Finish with a black-and-white cookie, rugelach, or rice pudding, which are all local faves and fittingly so.

■ 541 Amsterdam Ave. (bet. 86th & 87th Sts.)
🚇 86 St (Broadway)
📞 (212) 724-4707 — **WEB:** www.barneygreengrass.com
■ Lunch Tue – Sun

PRICE: 🍴

# BIN 71 ⑪○

*Italian*

🏮 | 🍸 🛏 🍷                                    **MAP:** A3

This little enoteca has been a smash-hit since day one and spawned its own cluster of knockoffs, though none have quite the same talent for pairing tasty little bites with excellent wines by the glass. The smartly designed space offers a marble U-shaped bar that makes use of every square inch but stays comfortable, especially for solo diners.

The Italian-leaning menu's small portions encourage diners to try a number of different plates. Start with gazpacho made from late-summer corn, avocado, and Jonah crab meat, or smoky tender whole grilled squid. Meatballs are a delicious surprise, seasoned with cumin and fennel, then simmered in a deep golden sauce of white wine, bay leaf, and tangy lemon with nary a tomato in sight, but plenty of bread for sopping.

■ 237 Columbus Ave. (bet. 70th & 71st Sts.)
🚇 72 St (Broadway)
℘ (212) 362-5446 — **WEB:** www.bin71.com
■ Lunch & dinner Tue – Sun                    **PRICE:** $$

# BOULUD SUD ⑪○

*Mediterranean*

XxX | 🖥 🍷                                    **MAP:** A4

Far from a chichi French affair, Chef Daniel Boulud uses this ode to Mediterranean cuisine to explore all sides of the sea—from Morocco to Italy to Turkey and back again. Packed and lively, the dining room is airy with vaulted ceilings, natural lighting, and long striped banquettes. A semi-open kitchen allows a glimpse into the creation of deftly prepared delicacies.

The menu here is light yet dense with bright flavor, from the crudo du jour (perhaps cubes of hamachi with gently braised cauliflower, pignoli, white raisins, and herbs) to a tender octopus salad with Marcona almonds, arugula, and Jerez vinegar. Huge morsels of chicken with couscous, wilted greens, and preserved lemons make a hearty dish, attractively served in a classic tagine vessel.

■ 20 W. 64th St. (bet. Broadway & Central Park West)
🚇 66 St - Lincoln Center
℘ (212) 595-1313 — **WEB:** www.bouludsud.com
■ Lunch & dinner daily                        **PRICE:** $$$

# CAFÉ FRIDA ⅃○

*Mexican*

XX | 🍽

**MAP:** B3

Festive and friendly with happy hour margaritas that flow like the Rio Grande, Café Frida is almost better than it needs to be, considering its high-traffic location across from the Museum of Natural History. Overall, it feels like a rustic and welcoming hacienda. The extensive tequila list complements the relatively economical fare, showcasing traditional moles.

Peruse the menu while delving into the guacamole served in a comal with crisp chips and fiery habanero sauce on the side. Don't miss the clear and warming sopa Azteca, a restorative consommé bobbing with chicken, cactus leaf, and abundant vegetables as well as an array of accompaniments. Finally, tlacoyos spread with a creamy fava purée and slow-cooked pork carnitas are *muy* buenas.

■ 368 Columbus Ave. (bet. 77th & 78th Sts.)
🚇 81 St - Museum of Natural History
✆ (212) 712-2929 — **WEB:** www.cafefrida.com
■ Lunch & dinner daily                    **PRICE:** $$


# GENNARO ⅃○

*Italian*

XX | 💵

**MAP:** B2

Despite its age, Gennaro hasn't lost its good looks or popularity—it still packs in hungry locals nightly who aren't deterred by its borderline gritty surrounds or no-reservations policy. Come early or risk waiting, which isn't so bad considering their bar, whose by-the-glass offerings are vast and very appealing with both familiar and unusual Italian choices.

The menu can be overwhelming considering its long list of pastas and daily specials, so trust your gut and you can't go wrong. Start with the polenta, served almost quattro stagione-style, with gorgonzola, prosciutto, and sliced portobellos; before twirling your taste buds around chewy bucatini showered with pecorino and pepper. The tiramisu is a light, creamy, and fluffy slam dunk.

■ 665 Amsterdam Ave. (bet. 92nd & 93rd Sts.)
🚇 96 St (Broadway)
✆ (212) 665-5348 — **WEB:** www.gennaronyc.com
■ Dinner nightly                          **PRICE:** $$

# DOVETAIL ✿

*American*

XxX | 🕸 ⬚

The name is apposite because this is one of those restaurants where all the elements fit together and complement each other perfectly, from the look of the room to the style of food and the tone of the service.

This large space has a chic and sophisticated feel, with pillars breaking it up into more manageable sections to ensure greater intimacy. The service is also just right: professional and structured yet undertaken with considerable warmth—you really feel as though you're being well looked after here.

What sets this restaurant apart is that vegetables are given their own moment in the limelight rather than merely playing second fiddle to meat or fish. The ingredients are from the top drawer and the dishes are quite elaborate in design but pleasingly easy to eat. Fluke crudo comes at the perfect temperature so that maximum flavor is revealed; cauliflower velouté has a remarkable depth of flavor; and the sirloin and short rib reveal a kitchen strong on technique as well as an understanding of textures and balance of flavors. It would seem churlish to end with anything other than their excellent chocolate soufflé.

---

▪ 103 W. 77th St. (at Columbus Ave.)

🚇 81 St - Museum of Natural History

📞 (212) 362-3800 — **WEB:** www.dovetailnyc.com

▪ Dinner nightly                                      PRICE: $$$

# JEAN-GEORGES ✿✿

*Contemporary*

XxxX | 😣 ♿ 🍽

The longevity of Chef Jean-Georges Vongerichten's flagship restaurant can be attributed to a combination of factors—a sumptuous dining room, polished service, a discreet atmosphere, as well as accomplished, contemporary cuisine.

Lunch is a superb option for those who don't want to break the bank. However, the best way to experience the talent of the kitchen here is to go for the prix-fixe dinner menu, where you might get a choice of seven or eight compositions per course. Classical French techniques underpin the cooking, although sometimes you'll come across subtle influences of a more global heritage, including yuzu with creamy sea urchin, or chipotle with shrimp. Desserts are more elaborate constructions and the ingredients come from the luxury end of the counter.

Like walking through Business Class on your way to First, you have to pass through the appealingly buzzy Nougatine to get to this restaurant. The low-slung chairs and large tables mean you need a certain confidence in your conversational delivery if you want to entertain your whole table. If you're here on a date, which many appear to be, you could find yourself sitting side-by-side—the new orthodoxy of dining à deux.

▪ 1 Central Park West (bet. 60th & 61st Sts.)

🚇 59 St - Columbus Circle

✆ (212) 299-3900 — **WEB:** www.jean-georgesrestaurant.com

▪ Lunch & dinner daily            **PRICE: $$$$**

# MACCHINA  🍴

*Italian*

✗✗ | ♿ 🏠 🦽
**MAP:** C1

As the name implies, Macchina combines an industrial design's raw edge and lots of iron with wood-fired Italian-American food just a stone's throw from Columbia University. A wall papered with newsprint, seasonal flower arrangements, and doors that swing open in warmer weather soften the look and feel.

Pizzas showcase quality ingredients, like fior di latte, pecorino, and cherry tomatoes over an impressively thin crust. Also try the finely tuned pastas, like carrot agnolotti "serpente" topped with amaretti and mint-hazelnut crumble in brown butter. "Al forno" items are an absolute highlight. Don't miss the cauliflower "steak," beautifully cooked in the wood-burning oven, served with the bold flavors of Castelvetrano olives, salsa verde, and sorrel.

▪ 2758 Broadway (at 106th St.)
▪ 103 St (Broadway)
✆ (212) 203-9954 — **WEB:** www.macchina.nyc
▪ Lunch & dinner daily                    PRICE: $$

# MEZZOGIORNO  🍴

*Italian*

✗✗ | 🕸 ♿ 🦽
**MAP:** B1

Locals seem to adore this beautiful Italian gift, courtesy of Lorenzo and Nicola Ansuini, the talented Italian-born brothers behind the trailblazing SoHo outpost by the same name. Here in this neighborhood, they bring their authentic food to a spacious, rustic dining room with a generous bar and enclosed front patio that might just hold some of the best seats in the house.

Kick things off with the feather-light house-made gnocchi, topped with a feisty sausage ragout; or homemade fazzoletti al rosmarino—chewy, rosemary-laced "kerchiefs" served with earthy white beans, tomato and crushed pepper. Heartier items are equally delicious, so try peposo dell'Impruneta, a classic Florentine stew of beef shank braised in red wine with black pepper and fragrant sage.

▪ 2791 Broadway (bet. 107th & 108th Sts.)
▪ Cathedral Pkwy/110 St (Broadway)
✆ (646) 895-9624 — **WEB:** www.mezzogiorno.com
▪ Lunch & dinner daily                    PRICE: $$

# MISS MAMIE'S SPOONBREAD TOO 😊

*Southern*

✗ | ♿ 🍷

**MAP:** C1

Come to Miss Mamie's and plan to indulge, Southern style. This tiny institution sports a bright, clean dining room, and is furnished with comfortable wicker chairs, roomy tables, and lots of flower arrangements. But despite its somewhat sophisticated appearance, the kitchen still embraces such tried-and-true classics as fried chicken thighs with black-eyed peas and collard greens, Louisiana catfish, and a creamy red velvet cake for dessert. Grab a fresh-squeezed lemonade and dive into the sampler, stocked with deep-fried shrimp, fall-off-the-bone beef short ribs, more fried chicken, and probably too many sides of cornbread stuffing and hoppin' John.

And if on offer, devour a wedge of the decadent and classically Southern banana pudding.

■ 366 W. 110th St./Cathedral Pkwy. (bet. Columbus & Manhattan Aves.)

🚇 Cathedral Pkwy/110 St (Central Park West)

℘ (212) 865-6744 — **WEB:** www.spoonbreadinc.com

■ Lunch & dinner daily

**PRICE:** 💰

# NOCHE MEXICANA II 🍴

*Mexican*

✗ | ♿ 🍲

**MAP:** B1

If you had a Mexican tía, you'd want her to be one of the lovely chefs pounding masa and wrapping tamales at Noche Mexicana II. This tasty corner is dominated by two veranda doors that open on to the sidewalk—a perfect setting for the specialties this talented kitchen sends out routinely. Imagine huaraches con bistec topped with tender beef and teeming with refried beans, bright tomatoes, and sour cream.

Those who venture uptown will not be met with disappointment: tomate verde mole is accented with toasted pumpkin seeds and piquant chilies that cover the tender chicken; while brick-red chilate boasts plump shrimp swimming in a spicy guajillo broth with a sprinkling of cilantro and queso fresco. A fresh flan, the only dessert on the menu, is simply excellent.

■ 842 Amsterdam Ave. (at 101st St.)

🚇 103 St (Broadway)

℘ (212) 662-6900 — **WEB:** N/A

■ Lunch & dinner daily

**PRICE:** 💰

# NOUGATINE ⅈ○

*Contemporary*

✗✗ | ♿ 🛏 🛋 🗒️                                    **MAP:** A4

Nougatine is a bright, stylish, and contemporary space on the ground floor of the Trump International Hotel—bookended by an open kitchen at one end and a huge picture window at the other. What really sets it apart, however, is the service: the restaurant is run with lots of flair and no little professionalism by a vast army of servers—this is not one of the places where you need to use semaphore to get noticed by your waiter. The food is light and current and the lunch menu, with dishes taken from the main à la carte, is a positive steal—although the immaculately coiffured clientele do not seem the sort to be overly concerned by the concept of a bargain. Dishes like veal Milanese are confidently executed and it's worth leaving room for desserts, like apple tart.

■ 1 Central Park West (at 60th St.)
🚇 59 St - Columbus Circle
☏ (212) 299-3900 — **WEB:** www.jean-georgesrestaurant.com
■ Lunch & dinner daily                              **PRICE: $$**

# SUSHI YASAKA ⅈ○

*Japanese*

✗                                                  **MAP:** A3

There are no decorative distractions at this efficient if spare sushi-ya located a few steps below street level. The simple space offers three rows of tables, unadorned white walls, a well-lit counter in the rear, and is warmed-up by enthusiastic servers. Devoted customers know the draw here is not atmosphere, but the quality and excellent value omakase.

Fish can be surprisingly luscious, especially the salmon, which has a remarkably clean finish and great salty note. The medium fatty tuna needs nothing more than a kiss of soy sauce. A 12-course omakase might also include giant clam, uni, sea eel, fluke, smelt roe, and for dessert, tamago. The kanto soba is excellent too, with a rich soy-bonito broth brimming with scallions, seaweed, and a fish cake.

■ 251 W. 72nd St. (bet. Broadway & West End Ave.)
🚇 72 St (Broadway)
☏ (212) 496-8466 — **WEB:** www.sushiyasaka.com
■ Lunch & dinner daily                              **PRICE: $$**

# THE BRONX

# THE BRONX

The only borough attached to the island of Manhattan, the Bronx boasts such awe-inspiring sights as the Bronx Zoo, Hall of Fame for Great Americans, as well as Yankee Stadium. However, it is also revered as a hotbed of culinary treasures. For instance, The New York Botanical Garden is devoted to education and hosts many garden- and food-related classes. In fact, the Botanical Garden's **Bronx Green-Up** is an acclaimed program aimed at improving inner-city areas by offering them agricultural advice and practical training.

Located along the west side, Belmont is a residential quarter marked by various ethnic and religious groups. Once an Italian hub, its population is now comprised of Hispanics (primarily Puerto Ricans), African-Americans, West Indians, and Albanians. Much of the Bronx today consists of parkland, like Pelham Bay Park with its sandy Orchard Beach. And since a day at the beach is never complete without salty eats, you'll want to step into pizza paradise—**Louie & Ernie's**—for a seriously cheesy slice. Just as home cooks and haute chefs

alike stock up on spices, herbs, and seeds from the myriad speciality stores around the way, thirsty travelers pop into **Gun Hill Brewing Co.** for an impressive bevy and more. Beyond, City Island is a gem of a coastal community teeming with seafood spots. **The Black Whale** is a local fixture frequented for its classic-meets-contemporary cuisine and quenching cocktails. Savor their offerings, either inside the quirky dining room or out in the garden. When the sun beats down, pop into **Lickety Split** for a cooling scoop of sorbet or ice cream, or both! Belmont's most renowned street, Arthur Avenue, is home to Italian food paradise—**The Arthur Avenue Retail Market**. This enclosed oasis is a culinary emporium overrun with self-proclaimed foodies as well as famed epicureans, who can be seen prowling for quality pasta, homemade sausages, extra virgin olive oil, notorious heroes, heirloom seeds, and so much more. Some begin by diving into a ball of rich, gooey mozzarella at **Joe's Deli** (open on Sundays!). Others may grab them to go, along with pistachio-studded mortadella from **Teitel Brothers** or *salumi* from **Calabria Pork Store**.

**B**eyond this venerable marketplace, find early-risers ravenously tearing into freshly baked breads from either **Terranova** or **Addeo Bakers**—the choices are plenty. Come lunchtime, find a myriad of Eastern European eats. At **Tony & Tina's Pizzeria** skip the signatures and opt for Albanian or Kosovar *burek* (flaky rolls with sweet pumpkin purée). Just as **Xochimilco Restaurant** is a playground for families with tots, South Bronxite singles revel in Ecuadorian delights like *bollon de verde* at **Ricuras**

**Panderia**. Then strolling southeast find **Gustiamo's** warehouse, which continues to flourish as a city-wide favorite for regional Italian specialties including olive oils, pastas, and San Marzano tomatoes. Similarly, the butchers at **Honeywell Meat Market** can be seen teaching newbies a thing or two about breaking down a side of beef, which always reigns as king. But over on Willis Avenue, Mott Haven's main drag, bright awnings designate a plethora of Puerto Rican diners and Mexican bodegas.

## YANKEE STADIUM

**H**ome to the "sultans of swat" (AKA the "Bronx Bombers"), **Yankee Stadium** is *the* spot for world-champion baseball. And what goes best with baseball? Big and bold bites of course, all of which may be found at the stadium's own food court. **Lobel's**, the ultimate butcher, is one such tenant and crafts perfectly marbled steak sandwiches to order. Even the Carbone-Torrisi boys have set up shop here at **Parm**, hooking fans with hearty sammies

and heavenly sweets. Refined palates will relish the farm-fresh produce from **Melissa's Farmers Market**, just as the cool kids are sure to swoon over the sips at **Tommy Bahama Bar**.

## COMFORT FOODS

**E**astchester, Wakefield, and Williamsbridge are home to diverse cultures, and ergo, each of their unique eats. Still, there are everyday vendors to be frequented here. Just as **Astor Prime Meats** proudly presents premium grade meats for every type of holiday feast, **G & R Deli** pays homage to the neighborhood's deep Italian roots by delivering authentic flavors in sausages and meat sauce sold by the quart. Then

there's **Sal & Dom's** who stick with this line of duty by serving deliciously flaky *sfogliatelle*. Over on Grand Concourse, **Bate** and **Papaye** cook up a buffet of pungent Ghanian goodies for the West African community. **Pearl's Southern Kitchen** serves up bold, bright, and flavorful cuisine along with a side of belonging, after which one may indulge in something sweet at **Kingston Tropical Bakery**. **Valencia Bakery** is yet another marvel among the Bronx's mighty Puerto Rican masses.

It is important to note that Asian food has officially arrived in the Bronx, with **Phnom Penh-Nha Trang Market** bagging a variety of Vietnamese ingredients necessary for a Southeast Asian dinner party. **Sabrosura** offers a blend of Spanish and Chinese inspiration, and even purists can't help but crave their yuca chips paired with sweet crabmeat. And over in the Castle Hill area of this vibrant borough, **Packsun Halal Chicken** packs 'em in with warm, welcoming service, as well as wonderfully wholesome meat treats. But bringing it back to the basics, the hamburger craze rages on uptown at **Bronx Alehouse**, pouring a litany of beers. Bronx beer you say? You bet. And there is an equally thrilling selection to be relished at **Bronx Brewery** over on East 136th Street.

**M**eanwhile, hosts keep the house party hoppin' and stoves turning by stocking up on pantry staples for late-night snacking from **Palm Tree Marketplace**. Also, find everything you may need here for a Jamaican-themed night. **Hunts Point Food Distribution Center** is another epicurean wonder, vital to NYC's food services industry. This expansive 329-acre complex of wholesalers, distributors, and food-processing vendors is also home to the **Hunts Point Meat Market** that sells every imaginable cut under the sun. Also housed within these grounds is the **Hunts Point Terminal Produce Market** supplying patrons with fantastic variety, as well as the famous **Fulton Fish Market**. This formidable network of

stores caters to the city's most celebrated chefs, restaurateurs, and wholesale suppliers. And such mouthwatering cruising is bound to result in a series of voracious cravings, all of which may be gratified at **Sam's Soul Food** located on the Grand Concourse, a classic joint oozing with potent doses of Bronx flavor.

## RIVERDALE

**R**iverdale is not known for its culinary distinction. However, its winning location as the northernmost tip of the city affords it incredible views, and as a result, lavish mansions. Moneyed residents mingle with curious visitors over the aromatic offerings at **S&S Cheesecake**, or freshly baked babkas at the always-primped **Garden Gourmet** on Broadway. From here, those in need of more stirring sips may head to **Skyview Wines** boasting exceptional kosher varietals. Then, finish with style and flair at **Lloyd's Carrot Cake**, which has been doling out divine slices of red velvet or German chocolate cake to the community for over a quarter-century.

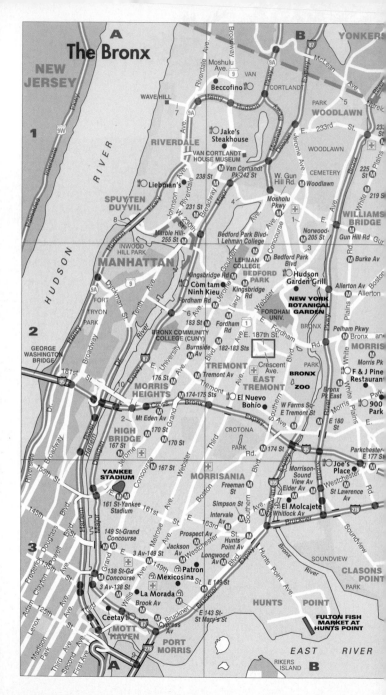

# The Bronx

**A**  **B**  YONKERS

NEW JERSEY

Moshulu Ave. VAN CORTLANDT

● Beccofino ⊓○

WAVE HILL

WOODLAWN

233rd St.

RIVERDALE  ⊓○ Jake's Steakhouse

WOODLAWN

VAN CORTLANDT HOUSE MUSEUM  Van Cortlandt Pk-242 St Ⓜ  W. Gun Hill Rd.  Woodlawn

CEMETERY

238 St

225 St Ⓜ  219 St

⊓○ Liebman's

Mosholu Pkwy Ⓜ

231 St

WILLIAMS BRIDGE

SPUYTEN DUYVIL

Marble Hill-255 St Ⓜ

Norwood-205 St Ⓜ  Gun Hill Rd Ⓜ

W. 230th

Bedford Park Blvd-Lehman College

INWOOD HILL PARK

MANHATTAN

LEHMAN COLLEGE

Bedford Park Blvd Ⓜ  Ⓜ Burke Av

BEDFORD PARK

Kingsbridge Rd Ⓜ  ⊓○ Hudson Garden Grill

FORT TRYON PARK

Kingsbridge Rd  Allerton Av Ⓜ  Allerton

⊓○ Còm tam Ninh Kieu

NEW YORK BOTANICAL GARDEN

Fordham Rd Ⓜ  FORDHAM UNIV.

183 St Ⓜ

Pelham Pkwy Ⓜ  Bronx and

GEORGE WASHINGTON BRIDGE

E. 187th St

BRONX COMMUNITY COLLEGE (CUNY)

MORRIS

Morris Pk

Burnside Av Ⓜ  182-183 Sts Ⓜ

⊓○ F & J Pine Restaurant

Crescent Ave.

181st

176 St Ⓜ  TREMONT  Tremont Av Ⓜ  EAST TREMONT  BRONX ZOO

⊓○ El Nuevo Bohío

174-175 Sts Ⓜ  W Farms Sq-E Tremont St

E 180 St Ⓜ  ⊓○ 900 Park

MORRIS HEIGHTS

Mt Eden Av Ⓜ

170 St Ⓜ  170 St Ⓜ

CROTONA PARK

Ⓜ 174 St

Parkchester Ⓜ  E 177 St

HIGH BRIDGE

167 St Ⓜ  167 St Ⓜ

⊓○ Joe's Place

YANKEE STADIUM

MORRISANIA

Morrison-Sound View Av Ⓜ  St Lawrence Av Ⓜ

161 St-Yankee Stadium Ⓜ

Freeman St Ⓜ  Elder Av Ⓜ

Simpson St Ⓜ  ⊓○ El Molcajete

149 St-Grand Concourse Ⓜ

Intervale Av Ⓜ  Whitlock Av Ⓜ

3 Av-149 St Ⓜ

Prospect Av Ⓜ  Hunts Point Av Ⓜ

138 St-Gd Concourse Ⓜ  Jackson Av Ⓜ  ⓒ Patron Mexicosina

3 Av-138 St Ⓜ  Longwood Av Ⓜ

SOUNDVIEW

La Morada

Brook Av Ⓜ

E 149 St

CLASONS POINT PARK

Ⓜ Ceetay ⊓○

HUNTS POINT

MOTT HAVEN

Cypress Av Ⓜ

PORT MORRIS

E 143 St-St Mary's St

FULTON FISH MARKET AT HUNTS POINT

RIKERS ISLAND

EAST RIVER

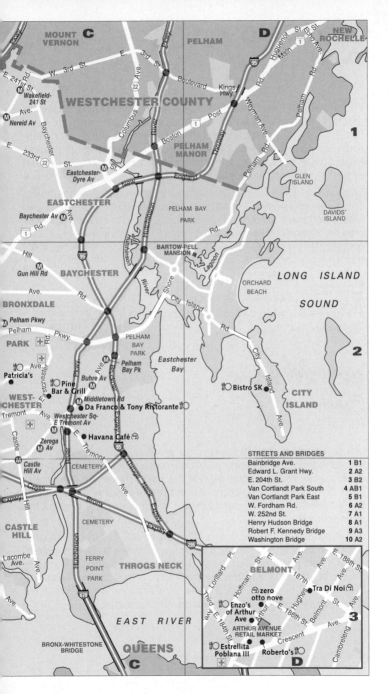

MOUNT VERNON **C** PELHAM **D** NEW ROCHELLE

WESTCHESTER COUNTY

W. 3rd. St.
E. 241st Rd.
Wakefield-241 St
Nereid Av.
E. 233rd St.
Eastchester-Dyre Av

EASTCHESTER

Baychester Av.

Gun Hill Rd
BAYCHESTER

BRONXDALE

Pelham Pkwy
PARK

Patricia's

Pine Bar & Grill
WEST-CHESTER
Tremont

Zerega Av

Havana Café

Castle Hill Av

CASTLE HILL

Lacombe Ave.

Kings Hwy

PELHAM MANOR

GLEN ISLAND

DAVIDS' ISLAND

PELHAM BAY PARK

BARTOW-PELL MANSION

Lagoon

ORCHARD BEACH

LONG ISLAND

SOUND

PELHAM BAY PARK
Pelham Bay Pk
Buhre Av

Eastchester Bay

Middletown Rd
Da Franco & Tony Ristorante
Westchester Sq-E Tremont Av

Bistro SK

CITY ISLAND

CEMETERY

CEMETERY

FERRY POINT PARK

THROGS NECK

BRONX-WHITESTONE BRIDGE

QUEENS **C**

EAST RIVER

## STREETS AND BRIDGES

| | |
|---|---|
| Bainbridge Ave. | **1 B1** |
| Edward L. Grant Hwy. | **2 A2** |
| E. 204th St. | **3 B2** |
| Van Cortlandt Park South | **4 AB1** |
| Van Cortlandt Park East | **5 B1** |
| W. Fordham Rd. | **6 A2** |
| W. 252nd St. | **7 A1** |
| Henry Hudson Bridge | **8 A1** |
| Robert F. Kennedy Bridge | **9 A3** |
| Washington Bridge | **10 A2** |

Lorillard Pl.
Hoffman St.
BELMONT
187th St.
zero otto nove
Tra Di Noi
Enzo's of Arthur Ave
Hughes Ave.
Belmont Ave.
186th St.
ARTHUR AVENUE RETAIL MARKET
Crescent Ave.
Estrellita Poblana III
Roberto's
Cambreleng Ave.
**D** **3**

# BECCOFINO 🍴○

*Italian*

🍴

Beccofino is an earnest neighborhood darling that is never taken for granted. Inside, string lights, exposed brick, and colorful, life-sized posters fashion a rustic bistro setting for indulging in their Italian-American favorites (with plenty of bread for sopping up sauces). Expect meals to be well-paced and the dedicated staff to ensure that everything is made to your liking.

Some dishes stray from being genuinely Italian but are nonetheless popular and surprisingly good, like seafood-stuffed manicotti topped with a generous amount of shrimp bisque and mild mozzarella. A crowd-pleasing chicken Milanese arrives as an insanely savory cutlet, pounded thin and sautéed, topped with broccoli rabe, chili flakes, spicy tomato sauce, and more melting mozzarella.

- 5704 Mosholu Ave. (at Fieldston Rd.)
- Van Cortlandt Park - 242 St
- (718) 432-2604 — **WEB:** www.beccofinorestaurant.com
- Dinner nightly                                          **PRICE: $$**

# BISTRO SK 🍴○

*French*

🍴 | 🏮 🛷

In a neighborhood better known for seafood, this charming bistro breaks the mold with hearty plates of French fare. The husband-wife team lures locals into a snug, dimly lit space with marvelous mahogany-hued French onion soup finished with brandy and a sultry mound of Gruyère. Particular attention to the art of service shines through the dining room.

A craving for classic Gallic dishes will surely be satisfied by cooking that is more solid than revelatory. Signatures include a tender roulade of chicken breast stuffed with spinach and mushrooms, served alongside French beans and fluffy, buttery mashed potatoes tucked with black olive for a bit of "wow!" For a finale, try the pineapple upside-down cake with a grilled ring of fruit and drizzle of caramel.

- 273 City Island Ave. (bet. Carroll & Hawkins Sts.)
- Pelham Bay Park (& Bus BX29)
- (718) 885-1670 — **WEB:** www.bistrosk.com
- Lunch Sun   Dinner Tue-Sun                            **PRICE: $$**

# CEETAY 🍴

*Asian*

🍴 | ⛩

**MAP:** A3

Its location near Hunts Point and the burgeoning South Bronx art community may have put it on the foodie trail, but Ceetay has become known for inventive Asian cooking at its best. The open kitchen offers diners a view of the race among cooks cutting, washing, and packing up an endless number of takeout orders. The tiny dining room features Mason jar fixtures, a handcrafted bar, and a wall papered with yellowing Asian newspapers.

Creative specials include a seared square of sesame-studded rice "bruschetta" topped with avocado purée, tuna tartare, and frizzled onions. But, don't miss such high-flying maki as the Kawasaki roll with a mishmash of crab, scallion, sweet glaze, and more. Traditional sushi here stands equally strong, with very nice maguro, ebi, and uni.

■ 129 Alexander Ave. (at Bruckner Blvd.)
🚇 3 Av - 138 St
☏ (718) 618-7020 – **WEB:** www.ceetay.com
■ Lunch Mon – Fri   Dinner nightly          **PRICE:** $$

# CÒM TAM NINH-KIEU 🍴

*Vietnamese*

🍴

**MAP:** B2

It's a bare bones operation at this Vietnamese joint, tucked beneath an elevated subway train and located on Jerome Avenue – but none of it will matter once you give yourself over to the amazing food. The large Vietnamese population that inhabits this pocket of the Bronx is undoubtedly in pho heaven—there are 16 varieties of the good stuff, packed with aromatic spices like star anise and coriander, and then served with a riot of Asian basil, crispy bean sprouts, chili slices and lime.

Those in the mood for a sandwich may opt for the delicious bánh mì, loaded with cilantro, jalapeño, pickled carrots, daikon radish and a dash of slow-burning chili paste. Or simply dive into the equally good bánh mì dac biet, layered with head cheese, thit nguoi and pâté.

■ 2641 Jerome Ave. (bet. Kingsbridge Rd. & 193rd St.)
🚇 Kingsbridge Rd (Jerome Ave.)
☏ (718) 365-2680 — **WEB:** N/A
■ Lunch & dinner daily          **PRICE:** ⌷

# DA FRANCO & TONY RISTORANTE ⅋○

*Italian*

XX

**MAP:** C2

There is so much to love here, where sharply dressed servers dish up equal parts warmth, hospitality, and steaming bowls of scrumptious pasta. The menu leans heavily towards that nostalgic sort of red-sauce, Italian-American cooking that is again finding more and more respect, thanks to mouthwatering dishes like merluzzo marechiaro and veal scaloppini.

The interior is lovely, which is particularly important since you're in for a bit of a wait (everything is made fresh to order). But who could complain when tender knobs of potato gnocchi arrive tossed in basil pesto with plush gorgonzola cheese and walnuts. Their chicken scarpariello is perfectly caramelized, deeply flavored, and bathed in a sinfully rich wine broth, fragrant with rosemary.

- 2815 Middletown Rd. (bet. Hutchinson River Pkwy. East & Mulford Ave.)
- Middletown Rd
- ✆ (718) 684-2815 — **WEB:** www.dafrancoandtony.com
- Lunch & dinner daily                                    **PRICE:** $$

# EL MOLCAJETE 😊

*Mexican*

X | ♿ 🚙

**MAP:** B3

This bright, cheerful Mexican gem can be found in the Soundview section of the Bronx, which was once upon a time lined with Italian flags, bakeries, and butchers. Today, you'll find a global collection of restaurants, including Mexican hot spots, pan-African grocery stores, Puerto Rican lechoneras and Dominican diners.

Breakfast at El Molcajete kicks off with delicious egg sandwiches, with a south-of-the-border twist. Lunch brings mouthwatering tacos, tortas and cemitas—served with smoky red and spicy green sauces on the side. Don't miss the sumptuous gordita, a thick masa cake filled with luscious pork and then floated with cilantro, smooth crema and serrano peppers; or the tender cabeza de res (cow head) and gamey barbacoa (barbecue goat) tacos.

- 1506-1508 Westchester Ave. (bet. Elder & Wheeler Aves.)
- Elder Av
- ✆ (917) 688-1433 — **WEB:** N/A
- Lunch & dinner daily                                    **PRICE:** 🍴

# EL NUEVO BOHÍO 🍴◯
*Puerto Rican*

🍴

**MAP:** B2

On a prominent corner, windows filled with lechòn lure passersby with mouthwatering visions of shiny-skinned roast pork. Beloved by the local Puerto Rican community, as well as a wave of newcomers, the front room is minimally adorned and filled with lines of to-go orders. Snag a seat in the back— where bright walls are flooded with photos— for friendly table service.

Begin with morcilla, a thick blood sausage with chili peppers, cilantro, and garlic before moving on to succulent pernil, pork shoulder, roasted to a luxuriously crisp exterior. Speaking of which, some 30 pigs are delivered here each week and during the holidays, you can also get an entire cooked pig to go. Close out with such complex sopas as cow's feet with yucca or asopado de carmarones.

- 791 E. Tremont Ave. (at Mapes Ave.)
- West Farms Sq - E Tremont Av
- ✆ (718) 294-3905 — **WEB:** www.elnuevobohiorestaurant.com
- Lunch & dinner daily                              **PRICE:** ⊜

# ENZO'S OF ARTHUR AVE 🍴◯
*Italian*

✗✗ | ♿

**MAP:** D3

Make your way past the front doors of this Bronx original and enter into one of two wings—either a sprawling and rustic dining room or a welcoming bar that is jam-packed on weekends. You'd be hard-pressed to find a bad word at this longstanding hearty and saucy joint, nestled into thriving Arthur Avenue. Servers whiz by, delivering glistening clams oreganata and tender fish Livornese. Enzo's affable manager is usually a step behind, checking on your table like you're one of the family.

Begin with gnocchi in tegamino, with tomato, parmesan and a kiss of sage. Then dive into juicy pork chops drenched in white wine sauce and topped with spicy pickled cherry peppers. Tender chicken breast arrives stuffed with prosciutto, mozzarella, and mushroom-cognac sauce.

- 2339 Arthur Ave. (bet. Crescent Ave. & 186th St.)
- Fordham Rd (Grand Concourse)
- ✆ (718) 733-4455 — **WEB:** N/A
- Lunch & dinner daily                              **PRICE:** $$

# ESTRELLITA POBLANA III ⅈ⅋

*Mexican*

✗ | 🎩

**MAP:** D3

The Arthur Avenue area may be known as the artery of the Little Italy of the Bronx, but a Mexican restaurant shines here with its fluffy tamales loaded with tender, fragrant corn, and so much more. The small interior is brightened with gold walls, a fuchsia ceiling, and three stars set in the coffered ceiling. Exposed brick and a semi-open kitchen complete the comfortable scene.

Conversation is common between the pleasant servers and other diners, as searing-hot sopa with shredded chicken and a nest of fideos is placed on an immaculate table. The bistec Estrellita is served with a fiery habanero sauce, topped with pico de gallo, and flanked by a side of rice and beans. Flan is a lovely finish—though that generous steak may fulfill even the heartiest appetite.

◾ 2328 Arthur Ave. (bet. Crescent Ave. & 186th St.)
🚇 Fordham Rd (Grand Concourse)
℘ (718) 220-7641 — **WEB:** www.estrellitapoblanaiii.com
◾ Lunch & dinner daily                              PRICE: ☜

# F & J PINE RESTAURANT ⅈ⅋

*Italian*

✗✗ | ⅙ ⍲ ⟳ ⿳

**MAP:** B2

This Bronx institution began as a simple storefront eatery in 1969. These days, Frankie & Johnnie's Tavern covers an entire city block, with a catering hall to boot. Locals, celebrities, Yankees and their fans alike love to roll in and pull up their sleeves in this large dining room, with its welcoming bar, visible pizza oven, backyard garden, and brass tags listing luminaries like "Rocco the Jeweler."

The Bastone family has been critical to the Bronx food scene for over 50 years now, and it shows through cooking that is as solid as it gets. No one is reinventing the wheel, but gargantuan portions of beloved Italian-American classics like stuffed pork chops, delicious pizzette, tender stuffed artichokes, and fresh seafood pastas more than hit the spot.

◾ 1913 Bronxdale Ave. (bet. Matthews & Muliner Aves.)
🚇 Bronx Park East
℘ (718) 792-5956 — **WEB:** www.fjpine.com
◾ Lunch & dinner daily                              PRICE: $$

# HAVANA CAFÉ 😊
*Latin American*

XX | 🛖 🍶             **MAP:** C2

This bumping Latin café straddles a corner of the Schuylerville section, and when the weather permits, grab a seat in its palm tree-shaded sidewalk retreat. Inside, you'll find a friendly bar, ceiling fans and tropical fronds. The partners behind this operation have deep roots in the Bronx, and they've hit upon a great formula here—so much so, they've opened a second spot nearby called Cabo. The classic Cuban-American black bean soup, frijoles negro, gets a zesty kick from lime-spiked crème fraîche. Then tender palomilla is topped with caramelized onions and paired with yucca fries; while coconut rice pudding empanadas are filled with sweet dates and sided by a vanilla dipping sauce.

If here on a Tuesday night, follow the conga drums on E. Tremont, where a dance party awaits.

◼ 3151 E. Tremont Ave. (at LaSalle Ave.)
✆ (718) 518-1800 — **WEB:** www.bronxhavanacafe.com
◼ Lunch & dinner daily        **PRICE: $$**

# HUDSON GARDEN GRILL 🍴
*American*

XX | ♿ 🛖 🍶           **MAP:** B2

There are many reasons why this is such an exciting partnership between The New York Botanical Garden and Chef Julian Alonzo, not the least of which is the idyllic setting. It is situated within sight of the landmarked Haupt Conservatory, open and airy, where huge arched windows overlook the manicured lawns.

The menu is polished, makes the most of locally sourced ingredients, and exceeds expectations with delicious cooking that is as beautiful as the surroundings. Start with chewy, savory monkey bread served with honey butter in a cast-iron pan, then move on to tender and buttery crab cakes with pickled cucumbers, sea beans, and mustard seeds.

The only disappointment maybe that it keeps the same hours as the NYBT, so this is a lunch-only treat.

◼ 2900 Southern Blvd. (in New York Botanical Garden)
🚇 Bedford Pk Blvd
✆ (646) 627-7711 — **WEB:** www.nybg.org/visit/hudson-garden-grill.php
◼ Lunch Tue – Sun        **PRICE: $$$**

# JAKE'S STEAKHOUSE ⅃○

*Steakhouse*

XX | ⬭ ⌂

**MAP:** B1

This bustling and upscale restaurant is one of the borough's best steakhouses. Duck inside the limestone facade and you'll find a clubby, multi-level space with lots of private nooks, a lively, well-stocked bar, flat-screens displaying the latest games, and an upstairs wall of windows overlooking Van Cortlandt Park.

A true American steakhouse ought to have a substantial shrimp cocktail, and at Jake's this classic starter arrives fresh and plump with the sweetness of the shrimp offset by a tangy cocktail sauce. Any steak on the menu can be topped with Gorgonzola and a thatch of frizzled fried onions, though a succulent and well-marbled T-bone seared to rosy pink perfection begs for little beyond a fork, knife and good conversation.

◾ 6031 Broadway (bet. Manhattan College Pkwy. & 251st St.)
🚉 Van Cortlandt Park - 242 St
℘ (718) 581-0182 — **WEB:** www.jakessteakhouse.com
◾ Lunch & dinner daily        **PRICE: $$$**

# JOE'S PLACE ⅃○

*Puerto Rican*

X | ♿ ⬭ ⌂

**MAP:** B3

From abuelas to niños, locals know to come to this "place" for solid Puerto Rican food. A glance at the wall of politicos and celebrities who have dined here proves how well-loved it truly is. The space is divided into two very different areas: a classic lunch counter also serving takeout, and a dark wood dining room.

A wonderful Nuyerican accent can be heard at gathering family tables and tasted in classic dishes like mofongo al pilon de bistec (savory shredded beef over mashed plantains) or pernil con arroz y gandules (roasted pork with pigeon peas and rice). Prices become even more reasonable when you realize that dishes are big enough to be split three ways. Daily sopas are a highlight, but end meals with a hot and flaky cheese-filled pastelito.

◾ 1841 Westchester Ave. (at Thieriot Ave.)
🚉 Parkchester
℘ (718) 918-2947 — **WEB:** www.joesplacebronx.com
◾ Lunch & dinner daily        **PRICE: $$**

# LA MORADA 🐶

## Mexican

🍴                **MAP:** A3

Tucked among the many Willis Avenue bodegas, this sweet spot stands out for its authentic Oaxacan food. It's a homey, no frills sort of place that welcomes everyone, and the owner loves to chat about the traditions behind this region's cooking—or history or art as evidenced by the impromptu lending library that has emerged in the comfy back seating area.

This part of Mexico is known for its incredible moles, so sample a wonderfully complex red pumpkin seed version (pipián rojo de pepitas) with pork spare ribs. Another, the glossy mole Oaxaqueño, arrives fragrant with cloves, tomatillos, plantains, peanuts and chocolate, served over chicken. Don't miss the wildly fresh tamales either, filled with silky chicken, spices and covered with a rich tomatillo sauce.

🔲 308 Willis Ave. (bet. 140th & 141st Sts.)
🚇 3 Av - 138 St
✆ (718) 292-0235 — **WEB:** www.lamoradanyc.com
🔲 Lunch & dinner Mon – Sat        **PRICE:** 💰

# LIEBMAN'S 🍴

## Deli

🍴 | 🎩             **MAP:** A1

Some things never change (phew!) and thankfully this iconic kosher deli is still stuffing sandwiches and ladling matzoh ball soup (reputed for its healing powers), just as it has for over 50 years. Residents wax poetic about the place: a true-blue deli with a neon sign in the front window, the grill slowly roasting hot dogs, and meat-slicing machines churning out endless piles of pastrami.

Soulful classics include stuffed veal breast, potato latkes, and tongue sandwiches with tangy pickles. Some order to-go, but a hearty Reuben stacked with mounds of hot corned beef, sauerkraut, and Russian dressing is more enjoyable when freshly plated and served in a comfortable booth. End with a perfect little rugelach filled with chocolate and ground nuts.

🔲 552 W. 235th St. (bet. Johnson & Oxford Aves.)
🚇 231 St
✆ (718) 548-4534 — **WEB:** www.liebmansdeli.com
🔲 Lunch & dinner daily        **PRICE:** 💰

# MEXICOSINA 😊
## *Mexican*

✕ | ♿︎

The light-filled interior of this Mexican powerhouse sitting on a quiet corner is a busy amalgam of rustic artifacts, wolf taxidermy, and the Virgin Mother in all her glory with flowers and votives at her feet. And those huge jars of jamaica, horchata, and the agua fresca del dia are just as tasty and refreshing as they are decorative.

If they have the tlayuda, order it. Its crunchy paper-thin base is smothered in a veritable fiesta of refried black beans, chicharrón, lettuce, queso Oaxaca, crema and much, much more. Other equally terrific specials have included chivo, a rich goat stew in an intense habanero-spiked consommé, or tender and fatty lamb barbacoa tacos. Cold accompanying salsas are so divine one could skip the chips and just eat them—with a spoon.

🔲 503 Jackson Ave. (at E. 147th St.)
🔲 E 149 St
✆ (347) 498-1339 — **WEB:** www.mexicosina.com
🔲 Lunch & dinner daily

PRICE: 😊

# 900 PARK 🍴
## *Italian*

✕✕ | ♿︎ 🏠 🖥 🛋 🍽

Neither fancy nor innovative, there is a certain heartwarming quality that makes this an easy place to return to time and again. Couples often settle in the lounge near the fireplace, while larger groups gather in the elevated dining room for platters of hot antipasti. White leather chairs, cotton panels, and rustic tables lend a breezy feel.

Italian and Italian-American classics span the wide menu—from grilled calamari with a tomato sauce topped with peppers and olives, to ridged tubes of manicotti stuffed with ricotta, pecorino, and cooked in a meaty Bolognese, finished with rich béchamel. Brick-oven pizzas are always worthy orders, especially the Calabrese decked with spicy soppressata and a few dollops of mozzarella.

🔲 900 Morris Park Ave. (at Bronxdale Ave.)
🔲 Bronx Park East
✆ (718) 892-3830 — **WEB:** www.900park.com
🔲 Lunch & dinner daily

PRICE: $$

# PATRICIA'S 🍴◯

## *Italian*

✗✗ | 🎱 ♿ 👋     **MAP:** C2

Much more than a neighborhood staple, Patricia's is an elegant restaurant committed to the convivial spirit of Southern Italy. Its seasonal fare is served in a gracious, brick-lined dining room among white tablecloths, chandeliers, and the warmth of a wood-burning oven.

That brick oven churns out pleasing pizzas with lightly charred crusts, like the Regina simply adorned with buffalo mozzarella, torn basil, and a drizzle of excellent olive oil. Spaghetti Frank Sinatra is a stain-making bowl of slippery pasta loaded with shrimp, clams, olives, and capers in chunky tomato sauce.

A light touch is seen in the grilled vegetables, topped with paper-thin cremini mushrooms. Don't miss the flaky and gently poached baccalà alla Livornese in a sharp, tangy sauce.

◻ 1082 Morris Park Ave. (bet. Haight & Lurting Aves.)
◻ Morris Park (& Bus BX8)
☎ (718) 409-9069 — **WEB:** www.patriciasnyc.com
◻ Lunch & dinner daily     **PRICE:** $$

# PATRON 👻

## *Mexican*

✗     **MAP:** A3

This fantastic Mexican jewel is proof you don't need a lot of flash to produce honest, authentic food. The décor is simple, but Patron takes its food quite seriously, and the fragrant, bustling open kitchen lends it a wonderfully homey, informal vibe. Next door, a full-fledged market offers some of the best mangos in the Bronx, amongst other treasures.

Daily specials on the board complement the short (but sweet) menu: think aromatic pipián verde paired with tender braised chicken; or brick-red caldo de res, a comforting beef soup served with fresh corn tortillas. Come fall, don't miss the impressive chiles en nogada, a bright green poblano with walnuts, fruit-laced picadillo, and a beautiful cream sauce studded with tart and juicy pomegranate seeds.

◻ 835 E. 152nd St. (bet. Union & Prospect Aves.)
◻ Jackson Av
☎ (347) 590-0570 — **WEB:** N/A
◻ Lunch & dinner daily     **PRICE:** ⬤

# PINE BAR & GRILL ЇО
*Italian*

XX | ᕕ 🛱 ⛶ 🔦

Between this outpost and their popular sister restaurant, F & J Pine, the Bastone family has become a fixture on the Bronx restaurant scene, and their eateries thrive for good reason. Pine Bar & Grill, with its lovely muted yellow walls and black-and-white photos depicting the hometown borough, is, at heart, a red sauce joint of the old school variety. Yet the menu reflects the neighborhood's sizable Latin-American population in dishes like pernil and coconut shrimp paella; or a tender trio of empanadas.

Don't miss the mouthwatering pizzette (especially good when Frankie's around); eggplant rollatini, stewed in a fragrant tomato sauce and drizzled with basil aïoli; or a juicy center-cut pork chop, finished with sweet and hot cherry peppers.

▨ 1634 Eastchester Rd. (at Blondell Ave.)
▨ Westchester Sq - Tremont Av
🕾 (718) 319-0900 — **WEB:** www.pinebargrill.com
▨ Lunch & dinner daily                    **PRICE: $$**

# ROBERTO'S ЇО
*Italian*

XX | ᕕ ⛶

You can't miss this storied Italian-American favorite whose design falls somewhere between a cozy farmhouse and Mediterranean villa. In fact, Roberto's bright coral façade lets you know right away there's allegria to be had at this hopping respite.

This space is as ideal for big groups as it is for romantic evenings. Inside, you'll find a cozy, carved-wood bar and roomy farmhouse tables lit by candlelight. In addition to the regular menu (think wonderful, fun shapes of pasta al cartoccio as well as other classic entrées like grilled pork chop), it's always worth a look at the chef's delicious daily specials. Of course, save the best for last as evidenced by the sbriciolata crumb cake with amaretto, chunks of chocolate, ricotta and almonds.

▨ 603 Crescent Ave. (at Hughes Ave.)
▨ Fordham Rd (Grand Concourse)
🕾 (718) 733-9503 — **WEB:** www.roberto089.com
▨ Lunch & dinner Mon – Sat                **PRICE: $$**

# TRA DI NOI 😊
*Italian*

✗                                                          **MAP:** D3

Decked out with crimson walls and red checkered tablecloths, this is the kind of place where diners feel like they're in on a delicious secret—and that's no coincidence, as Tra Di Noi is Italian for "between us."

Responsible for the success behind this tiny spot is Chef/owner Marco Coletta, who directs the front and back of house with the precision of an air traffic controller and the passion of an Italian nonno.

This sincerity shines through in the cooking, from the ethereally light gnocchi di patate in a rich lamb ragù to the quickly pan-fried fillet of sole Francese nestled in a creamy lemon sauce with shrimp, parsley, and white wine. Only a few desserts are on offer, and all are made in house. For a classic finale, go with the ricotta cheesecake.

🔲 622 E. 187th St. (bet. Belmont & Hughes Aves.)
🚇 Fordham Rd (Grand Concourse)
📞 (718) 295-1784 — **WEB:** www.tradinoi.com
🔲 Lunch Tue – Fri   Dinner Tue – Sun                **PRICE:** $$

# ZERO OTTO NOVE 😊
*Italian*

✗✗ | ♿                                                    **MAP:** D3

This Arthur Avenue favorite is easily recognized by the powder-blue FIAT parked outside, but is better appreciated for the wood-burning dome oven. Brick and cement archways, high ceilings, and a second-floor dining terrace strive to keep that oven—and its wares—within each table's line of vision.

The menu showcases Salerno-style cooking with pizzas, baked pastas, and wood-fired entrées. In fact, any dish that is "al cartoccio" (in parchment) is sure to please. Open up this pouch to try the pitch-perfect al dente radiatori baked with porcini, cherry tomatoes, breadcrumbs, and loads of deliciously spicy sausage. The ragù Salernitano is a gut-busting triumph of stewed braciole, sausage, and tender meatballs. The Nutella calzone makes a sweet, rich finish.

🔲 2357 Arthur Ave. (at 186th St.)
🚇 Fordham Rd (Grand Concourse)
📞 (718) 220-1027 — **WEB:** www.roberto089.com
🔲 Lunch Tue – Sat   Dinner Tue – Sun                **PRICE:** $$

# BROOKLYN

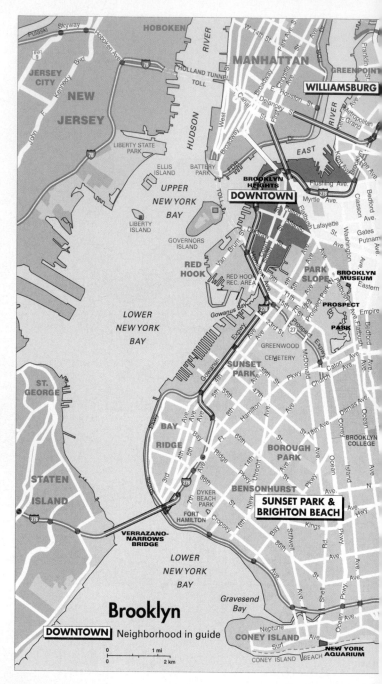

MANHATTAN

HOBOKEN

GREENPOINT

**WILLIAMSBURG**

**DOWNTOWN**

BROOKLYN
HEIGHTS

NEW
JERSEY

JERSEY
CITY

HUDSON RIVER

EAST RIVER

UPPER
NEW YORK
BAY

LIBERTY STATE
PARK

ELLIS
ISLAND

BATTERY
PARK

LIBERTY
ISLAND

GOVERNORS
ISLAND

RED
HOOK

RED HOOK
REC. AREA

**PARK
SLOPE**

**BROOKLYN
MUSEUM**

**PROSPECT
PARK**

LOWER
NEW YORK
BAY

Gowanus Bay

GREENWOOD
CEMETERY

**SUNSET
PARK**

ST.
GEORGE

**BAY
RIDGE**

**BOROUGH
PARK**

BROOKLYN
COLLEGE

**BENSONHURST**

STATEN
ISLAND

DYKER
BEACH
PARK

FORT
HAMILTON

**SUNSET PARK &
BRIGHTON BEACH**

**VERRAZANO-
NARROWS
BRIDGE**

LOWER
NEW YORK
BAY

Gravesend
Bay

# Brooklyn

**DOWNTOWN** Neighborhood in guide

| 0 | | 1 mi |
| --- | --- | --- |
| 0 | 2 km | |

**CONEY ISLAND**

**NEW YORK
AQUARIUM**

CONEY ISLAND BEACH

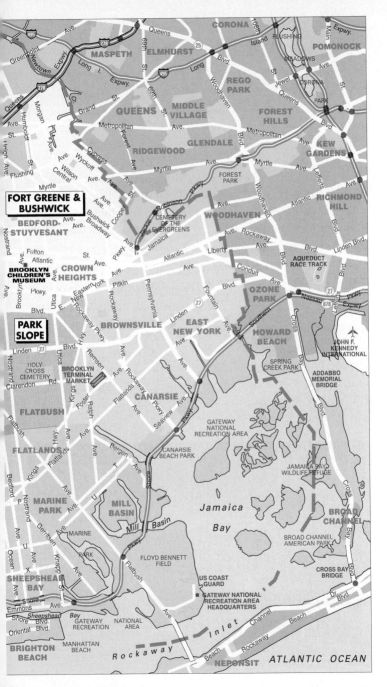

# DOWNTOWN

The Brooklyn Navy Yard may be a hub for commercial business and houses over 200 vendors, but the most impressive tenant remains the expansive **Brooklyn Grange Farm**. This leading green-roof consultant and urban farm is responsible for promoting healthy communities by providing them with fresh and locally sourced vegetables and herbs. After admiring DUMBO's stunning views, stroll down cobblestoned Water Street. Then make like every proud local and walk straight into **Jacques Torres** for a taste of chocolate bliss.

If savory is more your speed, be sure to spend an afternoon in Carroll Gardens, a historically Italian neighborhood that offers shoppers a spectrum of family-owned butchers and bakers along Court Street. Also set along this commercial paradise is **D'Amico**, an old-time haunt dealing in specialty roasted coffees and teas.

Step inside for a rewarding whiff, before heading over to **Caputo's Fine Foods** for more substantial sustenance— including *salumi*-packed sandwiches, lard bread, and fresh mozz. Folks may also favor **G. Esposito & Sons** for sausages, *sopressata*, arancini, and other Italian-American fun.

**O**therwise, rest your weary heels at **Ferdinando's Focacceria**, an age-old establishment famous for cooking up the classics, which taste as if they were transported straight from *nonna's* kitchen in Palermo and onto your plate. And for the perfect finale, stop by **Court Pastry** for such exceptional sweets as cannoli, marzipan cookies, and Italian ice.

**A**s Court Street blends into family-friendly Cobble Hill, find **Staubitz Market**—the most sociable butcher in town—blending the best of the old and the new by way of top-quality chops, cheeses, and charcuterie. But those with tots in tow or groups looking for a change in mood (and food) should shift "hills" from Cobble to Boerum to feast on Middle Eastern hits at **Sahadi's** or **Damascus Bakery**—each lauded for outrageously good pitas, spreads, and pastries.

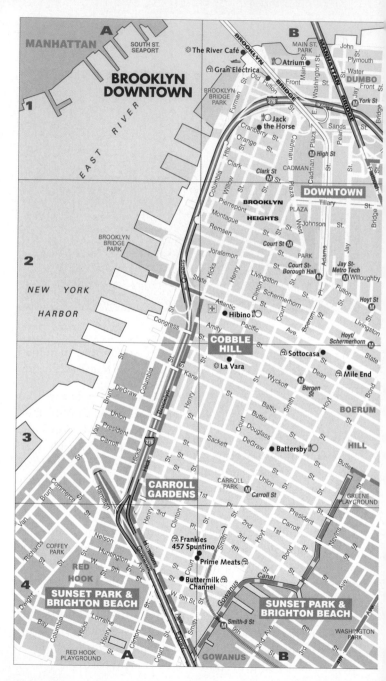

A

South St.
Seaport

⊕ The River Café

🚋 Gran Eléctrica

**BROOKLYN
DOWNTOWN**

B

MAIN ST.
PARK

John
St.

Plymouth
St.

Water
St.

🍴○ Atrium

**DUMBO**

Front
St.

BROOKLYN
BRIDGE
PARK

Old
Fulton
St.

Front
St.

Washington

St.

Main
St.

Adams

Jay
St.

🚇 York St

E A S T   R I V E R

1

BROOKLYN
BRIDGE
PARK

278

🍴 Jack
the Horse

Cranberry
St.

Orange
St.

Columbia
Hts.

Willow
St.

Clark
St.

Cadman

Pearl
St.

Sands
St.

Plaza

🚇 High St

Clark St 🚇

CADMAN

St.

St.

Jay

St.

St.

Pearl

Adams

Cadman
Plaza

**DOWNTOWN**

2

**NEW YORK
HARBOR**

BROOKLYN
BRIDGE
PARK

Pierrepont

Montague
St.

Remsen
St.

Joralemon

State

Henry

Hicks

Congress

Amity

St.

Clinton

St.

St.

St.

**BROOKLYN
HEIGHTS**

PLAZA

Court St 🚇

Court St-
Borough Hall 🚇

Livingston

Schermerhorn

St.

Tillary

Johnson

Fulton

Jay St-
Metro Tech 🚇

St.

St.

PARK

Adams

Jay

St.

St.

Bridge

St.

St.

Willoughby

Hoyt St 🚇

Livingston
St.

🏥

● Hibino 🍴○

Atlantic
St.

Pacific
Ave.

Court

Boerum

St.

Ave.

Schermerhorn

Hoyt
St.

Hoyt/
Schermerhorn 🚇

**COBBLE
HILL**

⊕ La Vara

🚋 Sottocasa ●

Clinton

Kane

Henry

St.

St.

St.

Wyckoff

St.

● Mile End

State
St.

Bond

3

278

DeGraw

Union

President

Carroll

Brunt

Columbia

Hicks

Henry

St.

St.

St.

St.

St.

St.

Sackett

Baltic

Butler

Douglass

DeGraw

St.

St.

St.

Court

Smith

Bergen
St 🚇

● Battersby 🍴○

Dean
St.

St.

St.

**BOERUM
HILL**

Butler
St.

GREENE
PLAYGROUND

CARROLL
GARDENS

CARROLL
PARK

Carroll St 🚇

1st

Union

St.

Pl.

St.

Smith

Court

Clinton

Henry

3rd

1st

2nd

3rd

4th

St.

St.

St.

St.

President

Carroll

1st

Hoyt

Bond

Newns

St.

4

**SUNSET PARK &
BRIGHTON BEACH**

Van

Richards

COFFEY
PARK

RED
HOOK

Commerce
St.

Nelson

Huntington

W.
9th

St.

Hamilton

Columbia

Clinton

Court

🚋 Frankies
457 Spuntino

● Prime Meats 🚋

● Buttermilk
Channel

St.

Smith

Gowanus

Smith-9 St 🚇

Canal

2nd

Ave.

**SUNSET PARK &
BRIGHTON BEACH**

WASHINGTON
PARK

Dwight

Bay

Columbia

Hicks

Lorralne

Henry

Clinton

St.

RED HOOK
PLAYGROUND

W. 9th
St.

Ave.

Smith

9th

Court

**GOWANUS**

2nd Ave.

6th

3rd

A

B

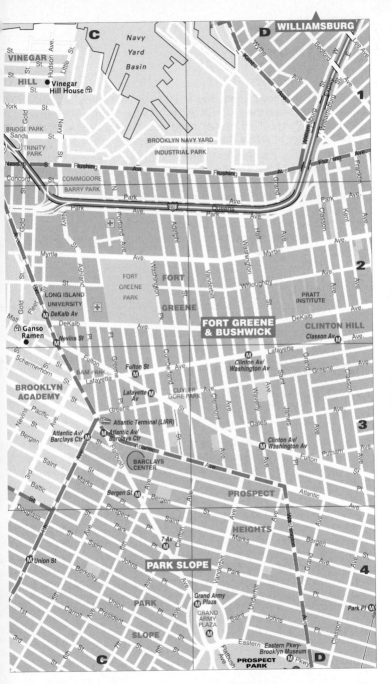

# ATRIUM 🍴⊙
*Contemporary*

✕✕ | 🍸 🍷 ♿ 🛏

**MAP:** B1

This industrial bi-level space has a rather iconic setting along the waterfront, between the Brooklyn and Manhattan bridges. Dark wood dominates the light-filled interior, amid metal accents and walls that sprout greenery to soften the room.

The food may have a farm-to-table focus, but a contemporary tilt is clear in everything that emerges from Atrium's bustling open kitchen. Elegant "baby greens" arrive as enticingly charred root vegetables over peppery arugula coulis; whereas crisply seared red snapper served over wild rice with dashi-simmered baby turnips, meaty mushrooms, and finished with a rich fumet makes the chef's (Laurent Kalkotour) French heritage abundantly clear. The chocolate-dipped crème fraîche and quark cheesecake is deservedly popular.

■ 15 Main St. (bet. Plymouth & Water Sts.)
🚇 York St
📞 (718) 858-1095 — **WEB:** www.atriumdumbo.com
■ Lunch & dinner daily  **PRICE: $$$**

# BATTERSBY 🍴⊙
*Contemporary*

✕

**MAP:** B3

This intimate Smith Street stunner is the domain of Co-chefs Joseph Ogrodnek and Walker Stern. The tiny kitchen at the back of the minimally decorated room belies the abundance of brilliance delivered by the short and sweet menu.

Caserecci tossed with petite, al dente cauliflower florets, briny capers, sweet currants, and a showering of crunchy breadcrumbs is a treat. Choosing the smaller portion size allows for more room to enjoy the lamb duo—rare seared loin and slow-braised belly—composed with a chickpea-and-piquillo pepper stew slicked with delicious lamb jus. For dessert, the chocolate mille-feuille with mint ganache and Fernet Branca whipped cream is like a Thin Mint made by some very talented and very sophisticated Girl Scouts.

■ 255 Smith St. (bet. Degraw & Douglas Sts.)
🚇 Bergen St (Smith St.)
📞 (718) 852-8321 — **WEB:** www.battersbybrooklyn.com
■ Dinner Tue – Sat  **PRICE: $$**

# BUTTERMILK CHANNEL 😊

*American*

✗ | ♿ 🛋                                    **MAP:** A4

Buttermilk Channel is the sort of joint we'd all like to have at the end of our street. It's warm and relaxed, run with care and attention, offers an appealing menu for all occasions—and has prices that encourage regular attendance. The name may refer to the tidal strait but also evokes feelings of comfort and cheer in a place that's already cute and where the close-set tables and large bar both add to the animated atmosphere.

The kitchen seeks out worthy suppliers and with no little skill imbues each dish with that little extra something, be it the cod with Littleneck clams, the fresh linguini with beets or indeed the buttermilk-fried chicken. This care is even evident at weekend brunches on standouts like short rib hash.

■ 524 Court St. (at Huntington St.)
🚇 Smith - 9 Sts
℘ (718) 852-8490 — **WEB:** www.buttermilkchannelnyc.com
■ Lunch & dinner daily                    **PRICE: $$**

# FRANKIES 457 SPUNTINO 😊

*Italian*

✗ | ⛱ 🛋                                    **MAP:** B4

Frank Castronovo and Frank Falcinelli (collectively known as the Franks) have built a small empire for themselves based on delicious, seasonal Italian fare served in rustic little haunts. Frankies 457 Spuntino, a charming, brick-lined space with bare wood tables and a quiet, shady backyard strung with twinkling bistro lights, is a classic example of their easy Brooklyn style.

Seem familiar by now? Well, these guys wrote the book. Service is laid-back and unpretentious, perhaps because they know the food does the talking here: a wildly fresh fennel, celery root, and parsley salad arrives with aged pecorino and a delicate lemon vinaigrette; while a tender tangle of linguini is laced with a fresh tomato broth studded with fava beans and garlic.

■ 457 Court St. (bet. 4th Pl. & Luquer St.)
🚇 Smith - 9 Sts
℘ (718) 403-0033 — **WEB:** www.frankies457.com
■ Lunch & dinner daily                    **PRICE: $$**

# GANSO RAMEN 😳

*Japanese*

🍴

A welcome sight amidst the sneaker stores and pizza joints of commercial Fulton Mall, this friendly and comforting ramen-ya is a sure sign that things are changing in downtown Brooklyn. Inside, wood booths and tables sit atop sleek stone floors while buzzing chefs are visible through encased glass.

Cookbook author and owner Harris Salat ensures that these steaming bowls of springy noodles remain a notch above those slurp shops opening throughout the city. Nightly specials are deftly executed, including a Mongolian lamb ramen in chili-sansho broth, topped with slices of lamb, fried onions, garlic chives, and ajitama egg. Also try the pillowy steamed buns stuffed with roasted pork belly and kimchi or crunchy shrimp tempura and cabbage.

■ 25 Bond St. (bet. Fulton & Livingston Sts.)
🚇 Nevins St
☎ (718) 403-0900 — **WEB:** www.gansonyc.com
■ Lunch & dinner daily

PRICE: ⸿

# GRAN ELÉCTRICA 😳

*Mexican*

🍴🍴 | 🍴 🛋

Looking to market ingredients and a California-style approach to Mexican cuisine, this chic yet comfortable restaurant impresses with its lovely décor and lively vibe. Servers are engaged and enthusiastic about the menu's pleasures. An ideal visit starts with a margarita at the bar and moves to the garden as strings of lights flicker to life.

Mexico and Brooklyn are in balance on a menu that includes small plates such as memelitas de frijoles, a masa disc topped with mashed black beans, spicy salsa verde, queso fresco, and crema. Flavor is bright in the deliciously untraditional poblano chile relleno stuffed with Havarti, roasted tomato-jalapeño salsa, and tortillas. Try the frijoles de la olla (black beans topped with avocado) on the side.

■ 5 Front St. (bet. Dock & Old Fulton Sts.)
🚇 High St
☎ (718) 852-2700 — **WEB:** www.granelectrica.com
■ Lunch Sat – Sun   Dinner nightly

PRICE: $$

# HIBINO 🍴

*Japanese*

🍴

The team at this demure retreat isn't constrained by a menu. Instead, diners are greeted by servers bearing blackboards that list the day's offerings. The list of obanzai (Kyoto-style tapas) are enticing and include marinated, fried chicken thigh with tartar sauce, grilled pork sausage, or roasted oysters with spicy gazpacho. The kitchen's regional dedication is also evident in its offering of Osaka's traditional hako sushi. This box-pressed preparation might be served as a layering of quality rice, shiso, kanpyo (preserved gourd), and salmon. Meanwhile, lunch is a concise affair that reveals either a bento box or platter of nigiri accompanied by a neatly stuffed futomaki.

Of course, if lunch seems limited, come back for dinner when the kitchen truly shines.

◼ 333 Henry St. (at Pacific St.)
🚇 Borough Hall
📞 (718) 260-8052 — **WEB:** www.hibino-brooklyn.com
◼ Lunch Mon – Fri   Dinner nightly                   PRICE: 🍝

# JACK THE HORSE 🍴

*American*

XX | 🍸 ♿ 🛋                               **MAP:** B1

A Brooklyn Heights favorite, this sleepy American tavern is a consistent spot in a neighborhood that lacks a variety of serious eats. However, exposed brick walls covered with old-fashioned clocks set a cozy tone, and have regulars returning for the well-stocked bar, complete with myriad bitters.

Slurp a few bivalves at the Oyster Room next door before settling into a table, or if thirst beckons, sip an Old Fashioned with barrel strength Bourbon while perusing the menu. Some locals head straight for the burger—focaccia layered with Gruyère, caramelized Bourbon onions, and a juicy beef patty. Though ricotta and butternut squash ravioli, tossed in sweet brown butter and topped with crumbled smoky bacon, is a fine alternative.

◼ 66 Hicks St. (at Cranberry St.)
🚇 High St
📞 (718) 852-5084 — **WEB:** www.jackthehorse.com
◼ Lunch Sun   Dinner nightly                   PRICE: $$

# LA VARA ✿

*Spanish*

XX | 🏠 🖫

Chef Alex Raij knows her tapas. She helped kickstart the craze in Manhattan when she opened her beloved Tía Pol years ago. From there, she moved on to the equally popular El Quinto Pino. And in 2012, she brought her beloved style to Brooklyn via La Vara, which she co-owns with her husband, Eder Montero. It's been a hit since day one.

La Vara bills itself as "cocina casera" or home cooking, but this tapas den elevates the humble cuisine to such impressive levels that it's well worth the cab trip for non-Brooklynites. Product quality is excellent, and the playful spirit at work in the lineup of cold and hot small plates is the definition of creative cooking. Think crunchy fried sea anemone served in a chilled purée of almonds, bread, and garlic, drizzled with huitlacoche oil; or tender rabbit loin puddled in delicious sweet onion vinaigrette.

Tucked into a charming brownstone-lined enclave of Cobble Hill, this small, slender space is chic and cozy, with red brick walls and a little white marble counter lined with glossy, high-backed chairs. A curved tan leather booth and small white tables dot the room. It's an atmosphere meant to put you at ease, with a menu guaranteed to wow.

■ 268 Clinton St. (at Verandah Pl.)
🚇 Bergen St (Smith St.)
✆ (718) 422-0065 — **WEB:** www.lavarany.com
■ Lunch Sat – Sun   Dinner nightly                    **PRICE:** $$

# MILE END 🐧

*Deli*

✗ | 🍺 🍴 🥢          **MAP:** B3

Boerum Hill's most bodacious deli serves up killer smoked meat and so much more. The tiny space gets lots of traffic, and those who can't find a seat along the counter or trio of communal tables can feast at home with takeout procured from the sidewalk window.

Now for the food: a cured and charred brisket sandwich, stacked onto soft rye bread and smacked with mustard, is the stuff that dreams are made of. The smoked mackerel sandwich heaped with fennel slaw, avocado, and chunky tartar sauce is an eclectic take on the deli theme, which also reveals poutine and a Middle East-inspired falafel platter. Don't overlook the hand-rolled, wood-fired Montreal-style bagels from owner and Montreal native Noah Bernamoff's SoHo offshoot, Black Seed Bagel shop.

⬛ 97A Hoyt St. (bet. Atlantic Ave. & Pacific St.)
🚇 Hoyt - Schermerhorn
📞 (718) 852-7510 — **WEB:** www.mileenddeli.com
⬛ Lunch & dinner daily          PRICE: 👛

# PRIME MEATS 🐧

*European*

✗✗ | 🍸 🥢          **MAP:** B4

Prime Meats stands tall and proud as a true original and local gem for German eats set to American beats. The booths in front are bright and snug, while bentwood chairs and net curtains tied into a knot add to that brasserie feel. A warm vibe and cheery servers complete the picture.

Hand-crafted sausages and burgers are all the rage here. Nibble away on homemade pretzels while perusing the lunch menu, which may be simple and sandwich-focused, but always showcases a gutsy edge. Bold flavors shine through in a creamy roasted squash soup; jagerwurst, a lightly charred, delicately smoky, and meaty sausage with red cabbage casserole; or Jen's German potato salad tossing waxy potato slices, chopped herbs, and thick bacon lardons in a pickled dressing.

⬛ 465 Court St. (at Luquer St.)
🚇 Smith - 9 Sts
📞 (718) 254-0327 — **WEB:** www.frankspm.com
⬛ Lunch & dinner daily          PRICE: $$

# SOTTOCASA 😳
*Pizza*

✗ | 🏠                                    **MAP:** B3

Located just below street level on frenetic Atlantic Avenue, a nondescript façade holds a quiet den of serious Neapolitan pizza magic. Enter and you'll find a simple, narrow, wood-paneled room with whitewashed brick walls; a little bar showcasing a handful of wines; an enormous, two-ton clay oven (imported directly from Naples); and a little patio out back for alfresco dining.

The mood is decidedly relaxed, and while there are delicious salads, antipasti, and desserts to be tried at Sottocasa, the name of the game here is undoubtedly their wickedly good pizza, served folded, bianche or rosse (with—hurrah!—a gluten-free option as well). Regulars adore the Diavola pie, which comes laced with excellent mozzarella, fresh basil, black olives, and hot sopressata.

■ 298 Atlantic Ave. (bet. Hoyt & Smith Sts.)
🚇 Hoyt - Schermerhorn
✆ (718) 852-8758 — **WEB:** www.sottocasanyc.com
■ Lunch Sat – Sun   Dinner nightly              **PRICE:** $$

# VINEGAR HILL HOUSE 😳
*American*

✗ | 🍸 🏠 🍴 ⚓                              **MAP:** C1

This local standout is situated in a waterfront neighborhood that feels not only charming but utterly untouched by time. The original carriage house was a butcher shop before becoming Vinegar Hill House—a lineage that seems apropos of such steady and perfectly delicious cooking.

From the kitchen, diners may expect such rustic and enchanting wood-fired fare as a wintry fennel salad dressed in lemony olive oil and arranged with fronds over a swipe of burnt onion crème (think of the best onion dip you've ever had). Then, dig into a roasted half chicken with copious jus and a splash of snappy sherry vinegar served in a cast-iron skillet. Dark and impossibly moist chocolate Guinness cake is outrageously good, beneath a thick layer of cream cheese frosting.

■ 72 Hudson Ave. (near Water St.)
🚇 York St
✆ (718) 522-1018 — **WEB:** www.vinegarhillhouse.com
■ Lunch Sat – Sun   Dinner nightly              **PRICE:** $$

# THE RIVER CAFÉ ✿
*Contemporary*

XxX | 🍽️ 🎩 🍷 ✍️

Thanks to its enviable location and stunning skyline vistas, this waterside favorite more than lives up to its reputation as one of the dreamiest escapes in town. Delicate details like fresh, fragrant flowers, beautifully set tables, and cozy rattan chairs make for romantic environs—and though the tight space has a way of turning intimate whispers into public displays of affection, all will be forgiven after a bite or two of Chef Brad Steelman's solid-as-ever cuisine.

Launch into plump wild shrimp smothered in creamy Hollandaise and served with crunchy white asparagus for added texture; or the perfectly crisped crab cake arranged with decadent uni, avocado, and a light herb salad. Pearly white halibut with roasted maitakes is a testament to the kitchen's focus on simplicity and supreme freshness, while a glistening rack of mint- and mustard seed-glazed lamb—charred on the outside with an evenly pink interior—exemplifies its artistry.

Enjoy dessert, as the mouthwatering offerings (think milk chocolate soufflé with melted marshmallow, or dark chocolate marquise topped with a replica of the nearby Brooklyn Bridge) are a veritable education in soigné presentations and sumptuous flavors.

🔲 1 Water St. (bet. Furman & Old Fulton Sts.)
🔲 High St
📞 (718) 522-5200 — **WEB:** www.therivercafe.com
🔲 Lunch Sat – Sun  Dinner nightly               **PRICE: $$$$**

**B**rooklyn is particularly big on international cuisines, and its every nook overflows with enticing eats. Set in the northwest corner and right across from Lower Manhattan lies Fort Greene, famous for West Indian and African communities (and cooking). **Bati** is a traditional retreat for Ethiopian home food with a focus on vegetarian options. Since 1999, **Madiba** (named for the late-great Nelson Mandela) has amassed a cult-like following for faithfully conceived South African dishes. But, if good old-fashioned Caribbean food is what fits your mood, then get in line at **Gloria's Caribbean** for excellent roti, oxtail, jerk chicken, and more. Otherwise, simply imbibe the vibe and feel the love at the annual West Indian Day parade—a veritable riot of color and flavor.

Then follow the culinary trail further east to Bedford-Stuyvesant. Here in Bed-Stuy (as locals commonly refer to it), carb-junkies gather at **Clementine Bakery** for its nostalgic scene and addictive listing, while others who wish to plan a Southen-themed evening should stock up on wares from **Carolina Country Store**. Bringing crave-worthy signatures straight from the namesake states, this food truck sensation is every carnivore's fantasy. Meanwhile, Mexico makes its presence known at old-timey **Tortilleria Mexicana Los Hermanos**, a bona fide factory turning out some terrific tortillas in Bushwick. Similarly, **Cesar's Empanada Truck** is mobbed for its cheesy renditions of the eponymous treat. And, if all's well that ends well, then be sure to seal the deal over the 200-plus flavors found at **Dun-Well Doughnuts**. In the same vein, **Berg'n** in Crown Heights is a big and boisterous beer hall pouring myriad drafts or popping bottles of local brew that pair perfectly with a menu of light bites from **Ramen Burger**.

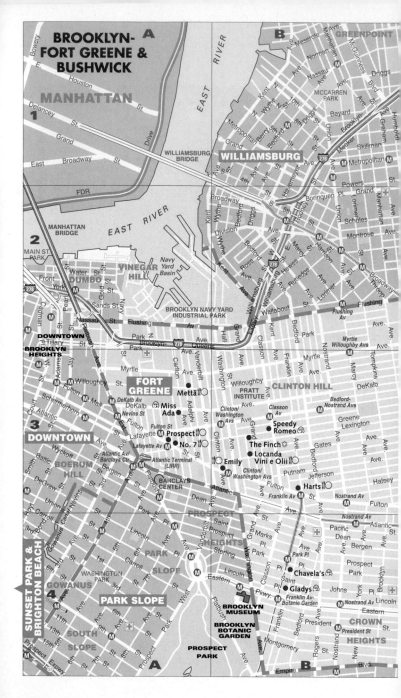

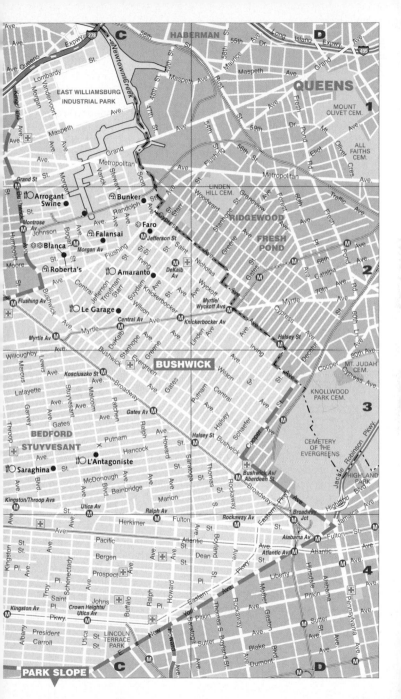

# AMARANTO 🍴

*Mexican*

✗ | 🏠                                                    **MAP:** C2

Named for the staple grain of the Aztecs and emblazoned with a mural of Quetzalcoatl, this tidy but truly caliente restaurant makes its love of its homeland clear from first glance. Adding to the lure, the father-son duo delivers their own unique take on Mexican cuisine, which is irresistible at best.

Most dishes here, from enchiladas to tamales, are sure to incorporate their excellent masa. Memelitas may begin with griddled dough layered with crispy chorizo, vegetables, pinto beans, and more. Then, superb tortillas are folded with shredded chicken and draped with dark and luscious mole poblano enriched with cacao, almonds and spices. A range of other moles include pipian verde that dresses deliciously tender short ribs in a pool of nutty richness.

▪ 887 Hart St. (bet. Knickerbocker & Irving Aves.)
▪ DeKalb Av
☎ (718) 576-6001 — **WEB:** www.amarantobklyn.com
▪ Lunch & dinner daily                          **PRICE: $$**

# ARROGANT SWINE 🍴

*Barbecue*

✗ | 🍺 ♿ 🏠                                            **MAP:** C2

A boon to this otherwise industrial warehouse neighborhood, Arrogant Swine's whitewashed brick walls and rows of picnic tables steadily fill with hungry patrons. Striking exterior wall murals and the aroma of sweet smoke both impress from the approach. Heat lamps extend the season for savoring slow-cooked pork outdoors, with rock music and a smoke-fueled barbecue buzz in the background.

Whole hog barbecue is the specialty here—smoked slow and whole over live embers, resulting in tender, glistening meat. The loin, shoulder, jowl, and more are then chopped or pulled and tossed with a Carolina-style vinegar sauce. Sides complete the downhome experience, especially their traditional cornpone (savory cornbread in an iron skillet with bacon drippings and slaw).

▪ 173 Morgan Ave. (bet. Meserole & Scholes Sts.)
▪ Morgan Av
☎ (347) 328-5595 — **WEB:** www.arrogantswine.com
▪ Lunch & dinner Tues – Sun                     **PRICE:** 🐷

# BLANCA ✿ ✿

*Contemporary*

XX

If you're lucky enough to score a seat at Blanca, you'll first pass through Roberta's corrugated metal façade, beyond the scent of a wood-burning pizza oven, and buzzing outdoor garden filled with tattooed urbanites and millennials. Because deep within that compound—which first helped elevate seedy Bushwick into a haute foodie 'hood—lays this gleaming kitchen for serious eaters. Here, products and dishes take inspiration from around the world, while warm, fluid service keeps the mood friendly among the small group.

Blanca serves a carefully conceived 20-course tasting menu that promises immense creativity and an artist's ability to weave an unforgettable experience. This is dinner theater, with all eyes fixed on the open kitchen and its focused, muted chefs quietly tweezing each morsel of food into perfection.

Menus aren't presented until the end of the meal, but list dishes like sunflower seed "milk" topped with Pink Lady apple cubes and a mouth-coating grating of foie gras, tied together with chili and salt flakes. Fantastic pasta includes thick noodles "carbonara" with crisp and tender bits of lamb. Fragrant Makrut lime makes coconut ice and cashew ice cream refreshing and delicious.

▪ 261 Moore St. (bet. Bogart & White Sts.)

🚇 Morgan Av

📞 (347) 799-2807 — **WEB:** www.blancanyc.com

▪ Dinner Wed – Sat                    PRICE: $$$$

# BUNKER 😊

*Vietnamese*

✗

**MAP:** C2

Chef Jimmy Tu could cook his killer Vietnamese street food out of a box, and the masses would still line up. But lucky for us, he and partner/brother Jacky Tu have found bigger and better digs to park their beloved Bunker. Tucked into an industrial Bushwick block, this fun and fresh space features colorful cinder block walls, a bamboo wood bar lined with Crayola-bright metal stools, and ample seating for their fans.

And oh, is that fandom deserved. Think caramelized wild shrimp with heritage pork and basil; or fragrant grass-fed oxtail stew. Don't miss the bánh xèo either, which is a crispy, turmeric-laced Vietnamese crêpe tucked with heritage bacon and wild prawns, served over crunchy bean sprouts and paired with Thai basil, red lettuce, and mint.

■ 99 Scott Ave. (at Randolph St.)
🚇 Jefferson St
☎ (718) 386-4282 — **WEB:** www.bunkernyc.com
■ Lunch & dinner Tue – Sun

**PRICE: $$**

# CHAVELA'S 😊

*Mexican*

✗✗ | 🍃 🛋

**MAP:** B4

Look for the light blue dome and wrought-iron doors to enter Chavela's and discover an absolute riot of color inside. From the bar's Mexican tiles to the wall of ceramic butterflies, this room is an explosion of artistic sensibilities.

Mexico City native, Chef Arturo Leonar, is the man behind this menu and his guacamole—traditional or creative with smoked trout, pico de gallo, and morita chile salsa—is just as pleasing as the setting. Crisp taquitos de cangrego filled with the perfect balance of sweet crabmeat, salsa verde, and crema Mexicana are irresistible; while a thick, deliciously tender pork short rib stew named costilla en salsa verde is studded with nopales and served with a mountain of yellow rice and refried black beans for a wonderful finale.

■ 736 Franklin Ave. (at Sterling Pl.)
🚇 Franklin St
☎ (718) 622-3100 — **WEB:** www.chavelasnyc.com
■ Lunch & dinner daily

**PRICE:** 🍃

# EMILY ⑩

## *Pizza*

✗                                                    **MAP:** B3

This charming Fort Greene trattoria arrives courtesy of Matt Hyland—a graduate of the Institute of Culinary Education and a former partner at Sottocasa. Named for his wife, this is a cozy, intimate reprieve from bustling Fulton Street, with a simple décor and small back bar where you can catch a glimpse of the kitchen's wood-fired pizza oven. The rustic tables bustle with young families from the neighborhood.

The menu is concise, creative, and often curious in the best possible way. Try Asian small plates like sticky-spicy Korean-style wings, tender Szechuan pork ribs, and comfort classics like grass-fed, dry-aged burgers.

Lip-smacking pizzas are categorized as The Reds, Pinks (vodka sauce), Whites (sauce-free), and Greens (tomatillo sauce).

■ 919 Fulton St. (bet. Clinton & Waverly Aves.)
▣ Clinton - Washington Avs
✆ (347) 844-9588 — **WEB:** www.pizzalovesemily.com
■ Lunch Sat – Sun   Dinner nightly                **PRICE:** $$

# FALANSAI ☺

## *Vietnamese*

✗ | ♿ ⌂                                              **MAP:** C2

Just say yes should someone invite you to sample the amazing food at Falansai. Bay Area food enthusiasts might recognize Chef/owner Henry Trieu from his days cooking at the popular Slanted Door; here at Falansai, a pretty little nook that feels miles from the gritty streets surrounding it, Trieu elevates the already complex Vietnamese cuisine to the next level. The results will knock your socks off—honestly, you might never look at a bánh mì the same way again.

Don't miss the tender shrimp fritters, enveloped by mashed cassava and chilies; fresh papaya salad laced with mint leaves, sweet poached shrimp, and crushed toasted peanuts; or a surprisingly complex and special coconut curry bobbing with sweet kabocha squash, Thai eggplant, and tender carrots.

■ 112 Harrison Pl. (at Porter Ave.)
▣ Morgan Av
✆ (347) 599-1190 — **WEB:** www.falansai.com
■ Lunch Tue – Fri   Dinner Tue – Sun              **PRICE:** $$

# FARO ✿

*American*

XX | &

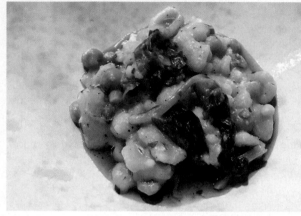

There is an undeniable air of sophistication here, making Faro much more of a destination than neighborhood stop. The space looks like a cover shoot for an interior design magazine. Every wall, from the painted brick dining room to the back of the open kitchen, is covered in glossy white to complement the metal-framed seating and wood plank floor.

The smell of the kitchen's wood-burning fire perfumes everything here, acting as a savory prelude to the cuisine and reminding guests of their motto: "Earth, Wheat, Fire."

Chef Kevin Adey's worthy exploration of pasta begins with a traditional Southern Italian frascatelli, made with irregular bits of semolina dough mixed with tender peas and shoots dressed in bright mint oil. Offerings go on to include candy-shaped caramelle filled with ricotta, then tossed with bacon, charred ramps, and airy potato cream. From the carte, dry-aged duck breast is cooked to rosy perfection and fanned over green wheat and roasted kabocha squash, with orange squash purée and a drizzle of savory-sweet Thai caramel. Crushed feuilletine add a crunchy note to textbook-perfect golden sable crust filled with chocolate custard and sliced bananas topped with butterscotch syrup.

▦ 436 Jefferson St. (bet. St Nicholas & Wyckoff Aves.)
🚇 Jefferson St
☏ (718) 381-8201 — **WEB:** www.farobk.com
▦ Dinner nightly

PRICE: $$

# THE FINCH ✿

*American*

XX

If you've ever had Brooklyn envy, buckle your seatbelt. Tucked among rows of brownstones straight off the set of a movie, The Finch's charming location pulls at your heart strings long before Chef Gabe McMackin's outrageously good food warms your soul.

Duck behind the bright blue façade, and things get even better: a warm staff welcomes you to a charming, rustic décor, replete with wood beam ceilings and farmhouse chairs. At the heart of this expansive space, which sprawls out into a series of cozy nooks, is an open kitchen where the chef extraordinaire guides his team to excellence before an audience of diners seated at a Carrara marble counter.

Modern yet comforting, McMackin's dishes mix skill and personality. The food is well-executed, satisfying and carefully sourced—from tender shishito peppers, blistered to perfection, with a squirt of lemon and crunchy sea salt, to shaved lamb tongue with fennel, green olives, orange and chili. Chewy cavatelli with yellow foot chanterelles, broccoli rabe, nettles and smoked yolk is yet another highlight, while slices of spot-on Berkshire pork fanned over Calypso beans, littleneck clams, chicory and a sumptuously spicy broth is a fine way to end the affair.

■ 212 Greene Ave. (bet. Cambridge Pl. & Grand Ave.)

🚇 Classon Av

☎ (718) 218-4444 — **WEB:** www.thefinchnyc.com

■ Dinner Mon – Sat                                    PRICE: $$

# GLADYS 🐶
*Caribbean*

✗ | 🍽️

Ready to live the Caribbean dream? All it takes is a few sips of a rum cocktail at Chef/owner Michael Jacober's festive café. This turquoise-tinted destination is where locals come together for Happy Hour libations (the comprehensive list features bottles from Jamaica, Trinidad, and Barbados) as well as for flavor-packed dishes at budget prices.

The kitchen is liberal with Jamaica's signature jerk seasoning, a magical blend of allspice, Scotch bonnet pepper, and citrus that's applied to chicken, pork, seitan, and even whole lobsters. The latter are kept fresh in a tank and a thrown onto a pimento wood-fired grill. Save room for the succulent bowl of curry goat with chunks of potatoes and carrots, best enjoyed with a side of coconut-scented rice and peas.

- 788 Franklin Ave. (at Lincoln Pl.)
- Franklin Av
- (718) 622-0249 — **WEB:** www.gladysnyc.com
- Lunch & dinner daily                                    **PRICE:** $$

# HART'S 🍴
*Contemporary*

✗ | 🍽️

Tucked behind the elevated Franklin Avenue subway stairs, this intimate little Mediterranean venue has been causing quite a stir. A pretty slate-blue façade directs you to a small space containing whitewashed brick walls, blonde wood tables, and a skylight. A handful of seats at the low marble counter face a wall of shelved liquor bottles and offer a view into the mini kitchen.

However, there is nothing mini about Chef Nick Perkins' culinary skills. In fact, he is the master of working magic out of a small kitchen. An heirloom tomato salad, laced with olive oil and crushed dried red chili, is paired with escabeche-style mussels; while a generous plate of golden pork Milanese is plated with sliced cucumber and shaved fennel for a bit of fun and flair.

- 506 Franklin Ave. (bet. Fulton St. & Jefferson Ave.)
- Franklin Av
- (718) 636-6228 — **WEB:** www.hartsbrooklyn.com
- Lunch Sat – Sun   Dinner Tue – Sun                     **PRICE:** $$

# L'ANTAGONISTE 🍴⃝

## French

**✕✕** | 🏠 🛋️                                    **MAP:** C3

From the razor-sharp service staff and its charming décor (think elegantly set wood tables and banquettes), to the killer but notably traditional French menu, everything about this buzzing hangout in burgeoning Bed-Stuy is bang-on. The fact that it is surrounded by bodegas and a fast food joint simply adds to the overall intrigue.

Owner Amadeus Broger is the master of operations here and appears to have just one, single formula in mind—and that is to churn out serious food in a fun and convivial setting. Don't miss the soufflé au fromage, rendered light and frothy with nutty Comté; the tournedos Rossini, tender filet mignon over a potato pancake, topped with foie gras medallions and finished with Madeira; or the perfectly executed duck a l'orange.

- 🟦 238 Malcom X Blvd. (at Hancock St.)
- 🚇 Utica Av
- ☏ (917) 966-5300 — **WEB:** www.lantagoniste.com
- 🟦 Lunch Sat – Sun   Dinner nightly          **PRICE: $$$**

# LE GARAGE 🍴⃝

## French

**✕✕** | 🛋️                                       **MAP:** C2

As the name implies, this chic Bushwick address once housed a garage. Nowadays, you'll find a bright and cheerful space boasting whitewashed brick walls, sleek blonde wood, and sunny yellow accents. The walls are hung with old black-and-white photographs of co-owner Catherine Allswang's previous restaurants in Paris. Now, with Le Garage, she partners with her daughter Rachel to bring a contemporary French menu to Brooklyn.

Classic dishes like leeks vinaigrette are cooked to silky perfection, and served chilled with finely diced hard-boiled egg. However, their heartier options are just as impressive: imagine the likes of slow-cooked pork cheek dressed with savory pan juices, pink grapefruit segments, braised radicchio, and peppery watercress.

- 🟦 157 Suydam St. (bet. Central & Wilson Aves.)
- 🚇 Central Av
- ☏ (347) 295-1700 — **WEB:** www.legaragebrooklyn.com
- 🟦 Lunch Sat – Sun   Dinner Tue – Sun          **PRICE: $$**

# LOCANDA VINI E OLII ⑪○

*Italian*

Ⓧ | 🍸 ⌂

While regulars at this beloved Clinton Hill trattoria know just where to go, the uninitiated may be surprised to find it tucked underneath a sign that reads Lewis Drug Store. Old-school without feeling hyper-designed, the ambience at this re-purposed apothecary is truly special. Envision lace-covered windows, a penny-tile floor, and ladder-fronted shelves filled with vintage glassware and cookbooks.

Tuscany influences the cooking here, where the diverse list of antipasti includes tripe alla Fiorentina, and the pasta is expertly prepared, like a luscious tangle of chitarra con le sarde. Salads follow entrées on the menu, but no one will raise an eyebrow if you order the baby spinach with roasted beets and pecorino before the charred poussin al mattone.

- 129 Gates Ave. (at Cambridge Pl.)
- Clinton - Washington Avs
- ℰ (718) 622-9202 — **WEB:** www.locandany.com
- Dinner nightly                           **PRICE: $$**

# METTĀ ⑪○

*Contemporary*

ⓍⓍ | 🍸

This kitchen has made its mark with distinguishing open-fire cooking, searing its way through hot-off-the-grill food. Occupants inside the snugly arranged room may start with a cool bluefish tonnato, served as a dip with radishes and other market vegetables, as if in preparation for the smoky flavors that are to come. Then, grilled steaks make their arrival with chimichurri and wilted greens to combat the richness of the meat. Pair them with bronzed carrots, enriched with an herbaceous oil and farmers cheese, for a fine balance. Finish on a high note with lovage ice cream accompanied by parsnip cake.

Set on a quiet corner of Fort Greene, this fire-hot spot centers around a big-as-life kitchen that can be observed by every one of its pretty patrons.

- 197 Adelphi St. (at Willoughby Ave.)
- Fulton St
- ℰ (718) 233-9134 — **WEB:** www.mettabk.com
- Dinner Tue – Sun                         **PRICE: $$**

# MISS ADA ☺
## *Middle Eastern*

XX | ☂ ☞

Middle Eastern eateries are popping up faster than you can say labne, but Miss Ada stands apart from the pack. This Fort Greene charmer delivers a one-two punch of good looks and great food. Rustic chic meets urban cool in the dining room, but wait, what's that out back? It's only the most darling backyard patio and garden beseeching you to plant yourself and stay a while.

Chef Tomer Blechman puts his own stamp on the ancient cuisine of the Middle East with hit after delicious hit. Even items that seem basic—creamy, smooth hummus and the fluffy cloud-like pita—are elevated here. Smoky octopus, so tender and fragrant, is ramped up with grassy Castelvetrano olives, while hanger steak is bathed in a charred onion tahini that has you begging for more.

▦ 184 DeKalb Ave. (bet. Carlton Ave. & Cumberland St.)
▦ Clinton - Washington Avs
✆ (917) 909-1023 — **WEB:** www.missadanyc.com
▦ Dinner Tue – Sun          **PRICE: $$**

# NO. 7 ⅃O
## *American*

XX | ☞

With its worn-in good looks, it's no surprise that No. 7 is this neighborhood's favorite hangout—a place where a cool crowd sip at the lively bar and sink into the dining room's sumptuous, horseshoe-shaped banquette. Add to that a menu so intriguingly original, it started a movement (the brand now includes kiosks serving sandwiches and veggie burgers), and you've got a recipe for success.

A delicious alchemy is at work in this open kitchen creating the likes of braised pork shoulder-stuffed cabbage paired with grilled stone fruit panzanella. Starters and dessert here are every bit as fun as the main event. The proof is in the perfectly ripe avocado topped with smoked trout, tobiko, and jalapeño oil, followed by the decadent brandy Alexander tiramisu.

▦ 7 Greene Ave. (bet. Cumberland & Fulton Sts.)
▦ Lafayette Av
✆ (718) 522-6370 — **WEB:** www.no7restaurant.com
▦ Lunch Sat – Sun   Dinner Tue – Sun          **PRICE: $$**

# PROSPECT 🍴

*American*

XX

**MAP:** A3

This Fort Greene standout offers delicious cooking and just so happens to be pretty cool, too. The beverage menu features riffs on the Negroni cocktail—one for instance substitutes reposado tequila for gin. Walls are lined with reclaimed planks of the Coney Island boardwalk, and genuinely hospitable service tames the packed house.

Quality trumps quantity in the streamlined selection of product-driven creations. A neatly arranged row of silver dollar-sized kimchi pancakes, topped with tender strands of pulled pork make an enticing starter; while toothsome and tender house-made gnocchi is plated with snap peas, sautéed wild mushrooms, and sweet peas for a springtime treat. Finish with a contemporary take on banana cake enhanced with coconut cream foam.

■ 773 Fulton St. (bet. Oxford & Portland Aves.)
🚇 Lafayette Av
✆ (718) 596-6826 — **WEB:** www.prospectbk.com
■ Dinner Mon – Sat                    **PRICE:** $$

# ROBERTA'S 😋

*Contemporary*

X | 🍴 🛋

**MAP:** C2

Entering through this (now) iconic red door is like a trip through the looking glass and into Bushwick's foodie wonderland. The city's love affair with Roberta's seems stronger each year, and for good reason. Everything from the industrial space to the underground Bohemian vibe epitomizes Brooklyn-chic. A new takeaway option has been added to the compound, so when the wait for a table is too long, snag a porchetta sandwich to-go.

Queens native Carlo Mirarchi leads a talented kitchen and its menu of beautifully prepared pasta, vegetables, and more. Many diners stick to the creatively named, less than purely Italian pizza, like the Speckenwolf, with freshly dried oregano, house-made mozzarella, thinly sliced speck, red onion, and roasted cremini mushrooms.

■ 261 Moore St. (bet. Bogart & White Sts.)
🚇 Morgan Av
✆ (718) 417-1118 — **WEB:** www.robertaspizza.com
■ Lunch & dinner daily                    **PRICE:** $$

# SARAGHINA 🍴

*Italian*

🍴 | 🛋 🗜 👜 💵               **MAP:** C3

If you build it, they will come: and sure enough, from the moment Saraghina opened its doors to a just-burgeoning Bed-Stuy, diners have flooded this cool, multi-room restaurant decorated in garage-sale knickknacks, old butcher signs, and marmalade jars. It's downright adorable. But, it's the delicious food that fills these seats.

Still best known for their irresistible pizzas, blistered to puffy perfection, the menu offers all kinds of heavenly dishes not to miss, like the fried calamari and shrimp, served with tangy lemon and aïoli; or a wood fire-roasted side of cauliflower mixed with creamy mascarpone, tart labneh cheese, and Marcona almonds.

Just around the corner, at 433 Halsey, a sister bakery serves up fresh pastries and a mean espresso all day.

▪ 435 Halsey St. (at Lewis Ave.)
🚇 Utica Av
📞 (718) 574-0010 — **WEB:** www.saraghinabrooklyn.com
▪ Lunch & dinner daily           **PRICE:** $$

# SPEEDY ROMEO 😊

*American*

🍴 | 👜               **MAP:** B3

Named for a racehorse and just as focused and quick, Speedy Romeo is in for a successful run. Part tavern, part roadside grill, its kitschy décor and modern touches transform this former automotive shop into a surprisingly attractive spot.

The owner benefited from years at Jean-Georges' empire, and that intelligence and experience is conveyed through the smart accents and whimsical menu that begins with Italian ingredients. Look to the wood-burning oven for smoky, meaty artichoke halves topped with lemon aïoli, sourdough crumbs, mint, and peppery arugula. Take a chance on the non-traditional but utterly fantastic pizza combinations, such as the St. Louis, layering a proper crust with meats, pickled chillies, and Midwestern Provel cheese.

▪ 376 Classon Ave. (at Greene Ave.)
🚇 Classon Av
📞 (718) 230-0061 — **WEB:** www.speedyromeo.com
▪ Lunch & dinner daily           **PRICE:** $$

**B**ordering Prospect Park, historic Park Slope brags of fancy trattorias and chic cafés perpetually crammed with stroller-rolling parents. Set in the heart of the 'hood, **The Park Slope Food Coop** is a veteran member-operated and owned purveyor of locally farmed produce, grass-fed meat, and free-range poultry. Lauded as the largest of its kind in the country, membership is offered to anyone willing to pay a small fee and work a shift of less than three hours each month. The like-minded **Grand Army Plaza Greenmarket**, held every Saturday at Prospect Park, is a shopping haven among area residents craving organic, farm-fresh produce as well as cooking programs and demonstrations to boot.

**C**lose at hand on Flatbush Avenue, **Bklyn Larder** is an artisanal provisions store that sells every imaginable type of cheese, meat, snack, beverage, and sweet. Devoted locals line up outside **The Ploughman**—a South Slope boutique—for an impressive bevy of beers,

even more cheese, and over 20 varieties of cured meats. Favoring something sweet? Find it at **The Chocolate Room** where desserts are exclusively hand-crafted and composed of pure, all-natural ingredients. From myriad boxes and bars of chocolate, to cakes, cocoa, coffees, and teas, this is every sugar fiend's reverie. Over in Windsor Terrace, **Brancaccio's Food Shop** is a serious dine-in and take-out treat that keeps the crowds returning for more Italian-American eats (think caponata and meatballs) or even breakfast specials starring eggs, potatoes, cheese, and meats. Ramen is another wildly popular comfort food here, so on those cold, wintry

days, head to **Chuko's** in Prospect Heights for an impressive selection with vegetarian options that are bound to stun. Further south, Ditmas Park residents make the pilgrimage to **Olympic Pita** for fresh, handmade bread or arguably the most perfect falafel in town. Finally, go big or go home—with a bold cup of tea (or coffee) at **Qathra Cafe**.

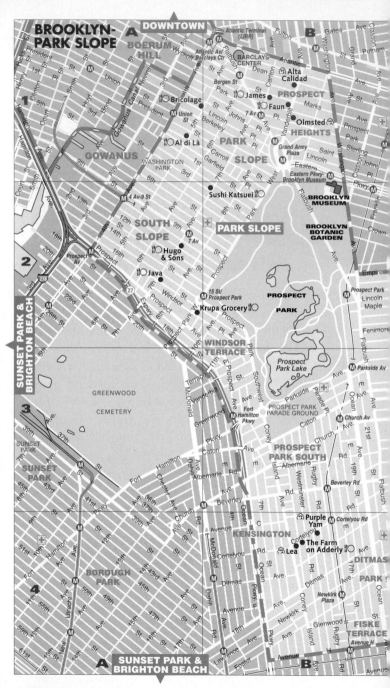

# BROOKLYN–PARK SLOPE

A

B

BOERUM HILL

Atlantic Terminal (LIRR)

Fulton

Gates

Ave.

Classon

Putnam

Ave.

Washington

Grand

BARCLAYS CENTER

Atlantic Avl Barclays Ctr

Atlantic

Ave.

Dean

St.

Alta Calidad

Bergen St

Park

Pl.

Marks

PROSPECT

Bricolage

Bergen St

James

St. Johns

Faun

7 Av

Pl.

Olmsted

HEIGHTS

Union St

Lincoln

Berkeley

Pl.

Vanderbilt

Prospect

Sterling

Johns

Al di Là

Carroll

St.

Grand Army Plaza

Lincoln

Saint

GOWANUS

WASHINGTON PARK

Garfield

1st

3rd

6th

PARK

SLOPE

Eastern Pkwy-Brooklyn Museum

Eastern

Crown

Sushi Katsuei

4 Av-9 St

9th

St.

8th

St.

Park

Pl.

BROOKLYN MUSEUM

12th

14th

St.

SOUTH

SLOPE

7 Av

PARK SLOPE

BROOKLYN BOTANIC GARDEN

Prospect

Ave.

Empire

Prospect Ave

16th

6th

St.

Hugo & Sons

15 St/ Prospect Park

Lincoln

Maple

Java

Windsor

Krupa Grocery

PROSPECT PARK

Fenimore

Flatbush

WINDSOR TERRACE

Prospect Park Lake

Parkside Av

GREENWOOD CEMETERY

Terrace

Fort Hamilton Pkwy

Southwest

Parkside

PROSPECT PARK PARADE GROUND

SUNSET PARK

Caton

Ave.

Church Av

Church

Ave.

PROSPECT PARK SOUTH

SUNSET PARK

Albemarle

Rd.

Beverley Rd

Beverley

Purple Yam

Cortelyou Rd

KENSINGTON

Lea

The Farm on Adderly

DITMAS PARK

BOROUGH PARK

Cortelyou

Rd.

Ditmas

Ave.

Newkirk Plaza

FISKE TERRACE

Glenwood

Avenue H

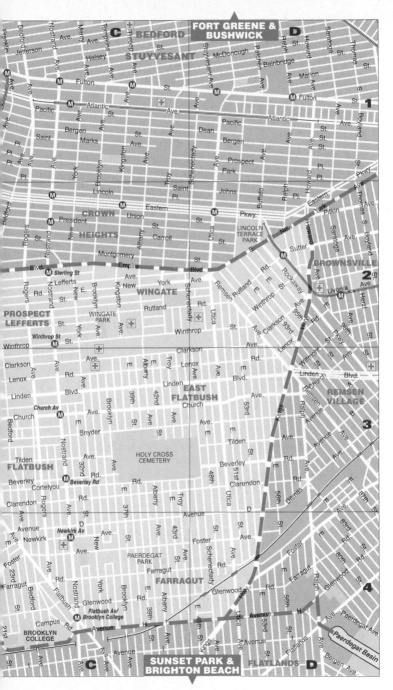

# AL DI LÀ ○||○

*Italian*

X | ⊯

When Al di Là opened nearly twenty years ago, it was a forward-thinking husband-and-wife operation serving rustic food to a gentrifying neighborhood. Today, it is every local's favorite spot for soul-satisfying pasta. This is a kitchen for that special kind of diner—one which is ruled by energy and ease. Lunches may bring a duo of insalata di farro tossed with roasted beets, red onion, spinach, goat cheese, and toasted pistachios paired with a daily panino such as pork belly with pickles, horseradish mayo, and salsa verde. Tables are laden with hearty and chewy ricotta cavatelli with smoky and enticingly charred cauliflower, anchovies, chili, and tomato sauce finished with grated pecorino.

The room may show wear, but consider that part of its charm.

■ 248 Fifth Ave. (at Carroll St.)
🚇 Union St
📞 (718) 783-4565 — **WEB:** www.aldilatrattoria.com
■ Lunch & dinner daily                    PRICE: $$

# ALTA CALIDAD 😀

*Mexican*

XX | ♿ ⊯

What's in a name? Well, at Akhtar Nawab's contemporary Mexican restaurant, it's "high quality." Literally.

This supremely talented chef takes thoroughly Mexican dishes and shakes them up just enough for a satisfying surprise. His creativity is boundless but never veers out of focus. Case in point? Crispy skate tacos smothered with smoky salsa and pickled ramps or the pumpkin blossom quesadilla. Other standouts include the oh-so-tender lamb ribs, shellacked in Coca-Cola for that glorious hint of caramel, as well as the meaty fluke ceviche enhanced by habanero and mandarin. Like Nawab's creativity at the burner, the menu is seemingly limitless, offering an array of plates you'll want to sample. Bring a friend, or three, to justify ordering more.

■ 552 Vanderbilt Ave. (at Dean St.)
🚇 Bergen St (Flatbush Ave.)
📞 (718) 622-1111 — **WEB:** www.altacalidadbk.com
■ Lunch & dinner daily                    PRICE: $$

# BRICOLAGE 🍴

## *Vietnamese*

✗ | 🏠 🛋️

This delicious Vietnamese gem is overseen by the team behind San Francisco's popular Slanted Door. Tucked into a simple, wood-and-exposed-brick space in family-friendly Park Slope, the restaurant's open kitchen bustles with energy as diners huddle together in lively conversation. Bricolage bills itself as a gastropub (and the creative cocktails are certainly fantastic), but make no mistake—this is modern, next-level Vietnamese bar food.

Crispy, golden imperial rolls are routinely churned out of the kitchen and arrive stuffed with glass noodles, crunchy cabbage, earthy mushrooms, and minced pork. Then look forward to "Unshaking Beef," laced in a salty-sweet marinade, seared to tender, juicy perfection, and served alongside a peppery watercress salad.

■ 162 Fifth Ave. (bet. Degraw & Douglass Sts.)
🚇 Union St
✆ (718) 230-1835 — **WEB:** www.bricolage.nyc
■ Lunch & dinner daily                    **PRICE:** $$

# THE FARM ON ADDERLEY 🍴

## *American*

✗✗ | ♿ 🏠 🖥️ 🛋️

It's easy to fall in love with The Farm on Adderley with its cozy bar, enclosed back garden, and softly lit dining room, which oozes bonhomie. And then of course, there's the farm-to-table food: neighborhood regulars and borough-hopping gastronomes pack this charmer night and day for irresistible dishes that may include fluffy cheddar omelets. Brunch is a standout as well, but really, any meal here is bound to sate.

Kick things off with a bright green salad, dotted with pickled red onion, thick slices of heirloom tomato and plump red raspberries. Then, try a tender nest of spaghettini laced with fresh tomato, briny capers, anchovies, and breadcrumbs; or opt for sizzling pork paired with sunchoke confit and crunchy pistachios.

■ 1108 Cortelyou Rd. (bet. Stratford & Westminster Rds.)
🚇 Cortelyou Rd
✆ (718) 287-3101 — **WEB:** www.thefarmonadderley.com
■ Lunch & dinner daily                    **PRICE:** $$

# FAUN 🍴

## Contemporary

XX | 🍸 🛖

**MAP:** B1

Chef Brian Leth, who wooed many a culinary heart at Vinegar Hill House, takes the helm at this delicious Prospect Heights restaurant. Dressed in a pale palette with marble surfaces and an open kitchen, the space feels welcoming, intimate and tranquil, complete with a long bar for socializing and the kind of charming backyard diners clamor for on warm days.

Dig into crisp, homemade focaccia with good olive oil; or delicately fried fry pepper tucked beside strands of meaty blue crab, cubes of cantaloupe, and crushed peanuts over a cool crème fraîche. Homemade mezze maniche is tossed with a ground pork ragù, laced with tomato, herbs and freshly grated pecorino. Wagyu coulotte is served over braised rainbow chard with a spicy horseradish cream.

◼ 606 Vanderbilt Ave. (bet. Prospect Pl. & St. Marks Ave.)
🚇 Bergen St (Flatbush Ave.)
☏ (718) 576-6120 — **WEB:** www.faun.nyc
◼ Dinner Tue – Sun                    **PRICE: $$$**

# HUGO & SONS 🍴

## Italian

XX | 🛋

**MAP:** A2

Hugo & Sons may contain every requisite detail that conjures the look of rustic Italian hospitality straight from the heart of Park Slope, thanks to exposed brick, penny-tiled floors, and wood planters. Yet this is a special little family-focused place, where the skilled chef/owner, Andrea Taormina, is attentive and hands-on.

The simple and uncomplicated cooking highlights the best of each ingredient. Crispy Brussels sprouts are true to their name, with loose and lightly charred outer layers, tender and moist within, finished with a zing of lemon zest, parsley, and aïoli. Heartier courses are thoroughly delicious, especially the pork braciole lined with breadcrumbs, pine nuts, raisins, and hard-cooked egg, then seared and served in a chunky tomato sauce.

◼ 367 Seventh Ave. (at 11th St.)
🚇 7 Av (9th St.)
☏ (718) 499-0020 — **WEB:** www.hugoandsons.com
◼ Lunch Sat – Sun   Dinner nightly        **PRICE: $$**

# JAMES 🍴

*American*

✗✗ | 🛋

This romantic restaurant holds a nostalgic sort of charm, as though it's been a fixture on the corner for a hundred years. It hasn't, of course, but its pressed-tin ceilings, silver bowls filled with bright citrus, whitewashed exposed brick walls and tufted leather banquettes lend it an old-school sort of sophistication.

Chef/co-owner Bryan Calvert and his co-owner wife, Deborah Williamson, live just above the restaurant, pulling most of the herbs used in the kitchen's dishes straight from their rooftop garden. Items wander from sautéed Carolina shrimp over creamy "polenta" to crispy honey-glazed pork belly—all of it divine. The restaurant holds a popular burger night every Monday, with an expanded burger menu and happy hour prices all night.

- 🟦 605 Carlton Ave. (at St. Marks Ave.)
- 🚇 7 Av (Flatbush Ave.)
- ✆ (718) 942-4255 — **WEB:** www.jamesrestaurantny.com
- 🟦 Lunch Sat – Sun   Dinner nightly   **PRICE: $$**

# JAVA 🍴

*Indonesian*

✗

Java's corner in Park Slope has been an enduring first choice for the exotic eats of Indonesia since 1992. Tiny yet tidy, this dark wood-furnished space is brightened by tall windows covered in golden drapery, native artwork, and the smiles of a friendly staff wearing batik aprons.

A nibble from the bevy of fried appetizers is certainly recommended. Begin with bakwan or golden-fried corn fritters, but don't forget about the mouthwatering sate—charred skewers of chicken, beef, or seafood brushed with kecap manis and topped with diced tomato and crispy fried shallots. The array of saucy, simmered options includes sambal goring udang: excellent batter-fried shrimp doused in turmeric-tinted coconut milk infused with lemongrass, ginger, and basil.

- 🟦 455 Seventh Ave. (at 16th St.)
- 🚇 7 Av (9th St.)
- ✆ (718) 832-4583 — **WEB:** N/A
- 🟦 Dinner nightly   **PRICE:** 🍴

# KRUPA GROCERY 🍴○

*American*

XX | ♿ 🛋 🍽 ⬛

**MAP:** A2

Since its arrival on the scene, Krupa Grocery has been a hit that makes you want to become a regular right out of the gate. Owner Peter Cooke's food is so simple and perfectly calibrated, it's hard to miss. Get things started with country toast, served alongside delicious spreads like smashed pea and fava bean with pecorino, tarragon vinaigrette, and pea leaves; or whipped lardo with radish, caper salad, and parsley. For dinner, try buttermilk-fried skate set over cracked hominy with basil seeds and salsa verde. Brunch is also a slam dunk here and is alone worth a visit.

Designed with a long industrial bar that's ideal for solo eating or lingering couples, the interior is effortlessly cool, but the place to be come summer is undoubtedly the gorgeous backyard.

◼ 231 Prospect Park West (bet. 16th St. & Windsor Pl.)
🚇 15 St - Prospect Park
✆ (718) 709-7098 — **WEB:** www.krupagrocery.com
◼ Lunch Wed – Mon  Dinner nightly          **PRICE:** $$

# LEA 😊

*Italian*

XX | 🛋 ⬛

**MAP:** B4

Italian is the name of the game at this stylish restaurant, where diners tuck into refined versions of the country's favorite dishes—try the tender eggplant, baked to silky perfection with fragrant basil, milky mozzarella and chunky tomato sauce. Don't miss a plate of chewy grilled squid, served over sheep's milk yogurt and cucumbers; or soft meatballs pocked with pine nuts and raisins in a mouthwatering sauce. A sublime, tart-like cheesecake is sure to seal the deal.

Settled on a prime corner location with sidewalk seating and a sexy, all-glass façade, Lea is a head-turner. The interior is fitted with unique accents (dismantled water tower "art," anyone?) while the overall vibe is breezy, stylish and welcoming.

◼ 1022 Cortelyou Rd. (at Stratford Rd.)
🚇 Cortelyou Rd
✆ (718) 928-7100 — **WEB:** www.leabrooklyn.com
◼ Lunch & dinner daily          **PRICE:** $$

# OLMSTED 😳
## *Contemporary*

✕✕ | 🍸 ♿ 🏠

This lively neighborhood restaurant serves a light-hearted cuisine that flaunts the technical skill of Chef Greg Baxtrom. The setting is quintessentially Brooklyn, with a long marble dining counter, bare wood tables, and mismatched ceramics.

The food is first and foremost delicious, featuring the freshest of ingredients plucked straight from their picturesque garden. Dishes also highlight notable skill, especially as seen in the guinea hen roulade of beautifully cooked breast meat stuffed with ramp mousse and served alongside a bowl of thigh meat confit as well as black trumpet mushrooms à la Grecque. Finally, versatility is at the center of the delicate and shining chawanmushi topped with maitake mushrooms, smoked trout roe, and a shaving of bottarga.

■ 659 Vanderbilt Ave. (bet. Park & Prospect Pls.)
🚇 Grand Army Plaza
☏ (718) 552-2610 — **WEB:** www.olmstednyc.com
■ Dinner nightly                                    **PRICE:** $$

# PURPLE YAM 😳
## *Asian*

✕ | ♿ 🏠 🛏

Owners Amy Besa and Romy Dorotan mix and match Southeast Asian dishes in such an appealing way at this neighborhood café, you'll have trouble figuring out what not to order. So follow the lead from the crowd—a smart, urbane mix of neighborhood types and savvy gourmands—and try a little bit of everything by sharing. Begin with pa jun, a delicious Korean scallion-and-shrimp pancake, and then move on to tender oxtail kare-kare, braised in peanut sauce and loaded with adobo, root vegetables and fermented fish paste. Other hits include the deliciously tangy and garlicky chicken adobo served with a refreshing green mango salad.

The décor is simple and comfortable—a long, narrow dining room lined with art leads to a pretty backyard garden.

■ 1314 Cortelyou Rd. (bet. Argyle & Rugby Rds.)
🚇 Cortelyou Rd
☏ (718) 940-8188 — **WEB:** www.purpleyamnyc.com
■ Lunch Sat – Sun   Dinner nightly          **PRICE:** $$

# SUSHI KATSUEI 🍴○

*Japanese*

🍴

**MAP:** B2

Sushi Katsuei does Park Slope proud with some of the borough's best sushi, expertly seasoned and sliced. In fact, this Brooklyn spot is now staking its claim in Manhattan with an outpost in the West Village.

Populated with locals and their kids, the mood is upbeat and warm, as regulars crowd the counter for the best seats. The chefs know their stuff and they showcase quality fish, but the menu is equally well suited to those who just want a spicy tuna roll or a cooked dish. Stray from the pedestrian and surrender to the omakase, where you will be rewarded with a parade of remarkably fresh sushi and sashimi. Tempura dishes are just as enticing, especially the naturally sweet roasted pumpkin.

The prices are fantastic for such high quality food.

- 210 Seventh Ave. (at 3rd St.)
- 7 Av (9th St.)
- (718) 788-5338 — **WEB:** www.sushikatsuei.com
- Lunch Sat – Sun   Dinner nightly

**PRICE:** $$

The sun is out — let's eat
alfresco! Look for 🏠.

# SUNSET PARK
# & BRIGHTON BEACH

**R**ed Hook rests on Brooklyn's waterfront, where diligent locals and responsible residents have transformed the area's aged piers and deserted warehouses into cool breweries, bakeries, and bistros. Following suit, the **Red Hook Lobster Pound** is a popular haunt for seafood fans, but if sugar is what you favor, then **Baked** is best, followed by **Steve's Authentic Key Lime Pie**. Close the deal at **Cacao Prieto**, widely cherished for family farm-sourced chocolates and spirits. Just as **Red Hook Village Farmer's Market** (open on Saturdays) brings pristine produce from its Community Farm to the locality, trucks and tents in **Red Hook Ball Fields** cater to natives in the know with *delicioso* Central American and Caribbean cuisine. Dining destinations in their own right, these diners-on-wheels may only be parked on weekends from May through October, but leave an impression that lasts through the year. Meanwhile, carnivores

on a mission venture east to Gowanus where **Fletcher's Brooklyn Barbecue** proffers tons of variety and quality; while Bensonhurst best-seller **Bari Pork Store** sticks to perfecting the pig. Foodies can also be found scouring the shelves of **G & S Salumeria and Pork Store** for cold cuts to be stuffed into delicious sandwiches. But, even flesh fiends need a break—perhaps at **Four & Twenty Blackbirds**—a bakeshop with *the* best black bottom oatmeal pie in town. Others may look for **Raaka Chocolate** showcasing beans in all their glory, while ensuring a healthy relationship with the environment. Pair these sweets with cherries from **Dell's Maraschino** and know you're in for a tantalizing treat. An afternoon in Sunset Park is a must, especially for mouthwatering Mexican flavors. Some take their tacos to this nabe's namesake park for one-of-a-kind views of the Manhattan skyline. But if gentrification is more your speed, then opt for a perfectly pulled espresso accompanied by a fresh-baked pastry from corner cafe, **Parkette**. Then cool off with an original ice pop (*paleta*) at **Sley Deli**—an authentic grocer booming with business in Borough Park. Of course, die-hard butter cookie fans can't imagine going a day without a whiff from **St. Anthony's Bakery**. Across from Maimonides Medical Center, **Fei Long Market** is a giant emporium flooded with Asian foodies in search of dried squid, eel, and other such exotic things. Slightly south, where Mexico meets China, sidewalks teem with vendors steaming tofu and fishmongers purveying wonderfully offbeat eats—bullfrog anyone? More mainstream but equally tasty is **Ba Xuyên**, a modest storefront revered for its deliciously crusty *bánh mì*. Moving from the Far East to a flock of kosher restaurants, **Di Fara** is a popular pizzeria with a mini offshoot (**MD Kitchen**) in Midwood. **Totonno's Pizza** is another sought-after haunt for Neapolitan-style pies; and **Joe's of Avenue U** is divine for crispy chickpea panelle.

At the southernmost end of Brooklyn is Brighton Beach, best known for its borscht and blintzes. This dominantly Russian quarter cradles a number of restaurants that churn out staples for its patrons packed within. But for a true alfresco snack to tote, **Gold Label International**

**Food** remains unrivaled. If a stroll along the Coney Island boardwalk doesn't trigger a sense of nostalgia for summers by the beach, an all-beef hot dog from the original

**Nathan's Famous** hot dog stand is a piece of Americana everyone can relate to. Couple these with juicy kielbasa from **Jubilat Provisions** for a real deal feast.

Customs, traditions, and cuisine come alive in culinary bastion **Moldova**, while over at **Octopus Garden** the wistful vibe is never-ending—with Italian regulars stocking up on goods for the Christmas Feast of the Seven Fishes. Also set within this Eastern European enclave is **Mansoura**, a Syrian institution proudly preparing savories and pastries. **Le Sajj** dishes up Lebanese food with live tunes (on Saturdays); and across the way, local sensation, **Lindenwood Diner** is loved for its liberally spiced Caribbean-Latin cooking. And while there is no confusing the Chesapeake with Sheepshead Bay, **Randazzo's Clam Bar** promises to provide you with a superior seafood experience. However, don't ever forget that beef is always king here, and there are big, bold flavors to be had at **Brennan & Carr**—where the menu doesn't change, but New Yorkers love it all the same.

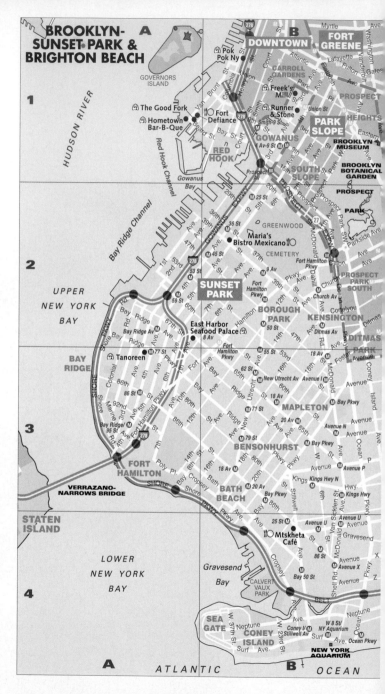

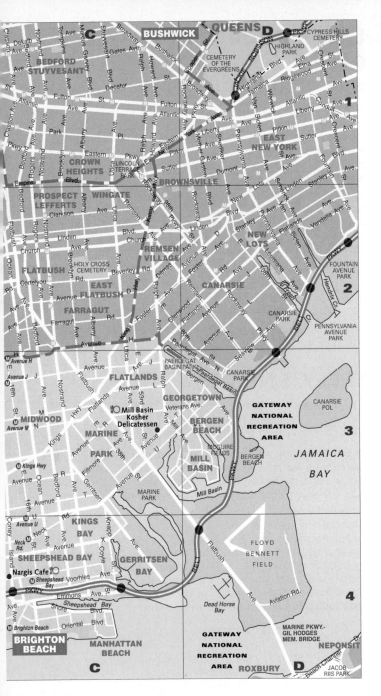

# EAST HARBOR SEAFOOD PALACE 😳

*Chinese*

XX | ♿ 🚇 🍴 🥢

**MAP:** A2

Dim sum is a well-orchestrated dance at this boisterous hall, where small crowds wait for a spot at one of the large round tables for an indulgent weekend brunch. Steaming carts roll by and waiters ferry trays briskly into the red dining room with shiny gold accents. Service is quick but helpful; the constant clatter of chopsticks and rollicking groups are part of the fun.

Eyes can guide the ordering when it comes to the dim sum carts, stocked with authentically prepared bites. Try the plump shrimp siu mai followed by rice noodles wrapped around crunchy whole shrimp and doused in a sweet-salty soy sauce. Snappy, stir-fried green beans are addictively crunchy. Don't miss the Singapore mei fun, a mound of vermicelli noodles with shrimp, pork, and scallions.

🔲 714-726 65th St. (bet. Seventh & Eighth Aves.)
🚇 8 Av
📞 (718) 765-0098 — **WEB:** N/A
🔲 Lunch & dinner daily

**PRICE:** $$

# FREEK'S MILL 😳

*American*

XX | 🍸 🥢

**MAP:** B1

This contemporary American small plates restaurant calls an industrial stretch of Gowanus home. Inside, you'll find a cozy, intimate space with exposed brick walls, filament light bulbs, as well as a wood-burning oven in the back of the dining room—it's that Brooklyn feel we've come to know and love, and Freek's Mill does it just so.

The cuisine is seasonal, light, and fresh, with each plate delivering something unique and unexpected. Try the fried soft-shell crab—its streak of cashew butter balanced by a sweet and spicy sambal and chopped baby bok choy; or the deliciously caramelized barbecue kohlrabi with buttery grits and wilted mustard greens. Close out with a beautifully aged duck breast coupled with refried cranberry beans and a rosemary-honey glaze.

🔲 285 Nevins St. (at Sackett St.)
🚇 Union St
📞 (718) 852-3000 — **WEB:** www.freeksmill.com
🔲 Lunch Sat – Sun   Dinner Tue – Sun

**PRICE:** $$

# THE GOOD FORK 😊

## *Contemporary*

✗ | 🏠 🛋                **MAP:** A1

The Good Fork is a perfect neighborhood restaurant with a serious local following. Located on the food-centric Van Brunt Street near the Red Hook Waterfront, this inviting spot swaps New York pretense for pure passion—it's the dream of a married couple who built the restaurant from scratch, literally. Co-owner Ben Schneider crafted the space, while his classically trained wife, Chef Sohui Kim, helms the kitchen.

Her cuisine emphasizes Korean and other global flavors, as well as a commitment to locality. Homemade dumplings are filled with nicely seasoned pork, crisped, and served with black vinegar dipping sauce. Market-fresh bluefish is not only superbly cooked but creatively served with buttery taro root mash, citrus sauce, and pickled radish.

◼ 391 Van Brunt St. (bet. Coffey & Van Dyke Sts.)
◼ Smith - 9 Sts (& Bus B61)
✆ (718) 643-6636 — **WEB:** www.goodfork.com
◼ Lunch Sat – Sun   Dinner Tue – Sun        **PRICE:** $$

# HOMETOWN BAR-B-QUE 😊

## *Barbecue*

✗ | &#9855;                **MAP:** A1

Texas-style barbecue has come to Brooklyn, even if this 'cue begins in an 18-foot smoke pit located a few blocks away. And yet this kitchen remains focused on creamy mac n' cheese, whiskey sour pickles, and mayo-mustardy potato salad. Meats arrive tender enough to have a caramel crunch— for instance, coated in a blackened peppery bark, the beef rib is obscenely large, deliciously moist and mighty popular.

Sausages snap and explode with juice and chili-spiced bite (each is sold by the plump quarter-pound link), while desserts are less provocative and may feature a simple banana cream pudding.

The warehouse-like space is clad in repurposed wood with communal picnic tables lending an intimate and friendly vibe. Water Taxi is the easiest way here from Manhattan.

◼ 454 Van Brunt St. (entrance on Reed St.)
◼ Smith - 9 Sts (& Bus B61)
✆ (347) 294-4646 — **WEB:** www.hometownbarbque.com
◼ Lunch & dinner Tue – Sun        **PRICE:** $$

# MARIA'S BISTRO MEXICANO ¶O

*Mexican*

X | 🏠 🛏

In a vibrant pocket of Brooklyn, locals flock to this timeworn façade for generous portions of fresh, well-priced, and tasty Mexican cuisine. Complete with a backyard, the décor of this quirky neighborhood staple is distinctly Mexican, from its bright woven textiles and vibrant pink walls, to lava rock molcajetes that top each table.

Start your meal with a delicious and filling chorizo taco topped with onion, tomato, and cilantro. Crepas de elote are stuffed with bits of tender onion, juicy corn, and poblano peppers. The chile poblano is a house specialty that satisfies with its one-two punch: the first is plumped with a savory combination of cheeses, while the other is stuffed with a beguiling mixture of chicken, almonds, diced plantain, and crunchy apple.

🟦 886 Fifth Ave. (bet. 38th & 39th Sts.)
🚇 36 St
☏ (718) 438-1608 — **WEB:** N/A
🟦 Lunch & dinner daily
                                                    PRICE: $$

# MILL BASIN KOSHER DELICATESSEN ¶O

*Deli*

X | ♿

This middle-aged Brooklyn treasure is as old-school as it gets, and though it's a bit of a trek to Mill Basin, anyone looking for a true-blue Jewish deli won't think twice. Part deli counter, part artsy dining room, and part party hall, Mark Schachner's beloved spot serves up all the classics—from beef tongue sandwiches to gefilte fish.

The wildly overstuffed sandwiches (all served with homemade pickles and coleslaw) are a home run, as in soft rye bread with pastrami, which is steamed not once but twice, leaving the meat juicy yet hardly fatty. Then dive into a heap of thin latke chips that are fried until golden-brown, crunchy on the outside, tender and chewy on the inside. Garnished with a mound of shiny caramelized onions, this is a sweet treat indeed.

🟦 5823 Avenue T (bet. 58th & 59th Sts.)
☏ (718) 241-4910 — **WEB:** www.millbasindeli.com
🟦 Lunch & dinner daily
                                                    PRICE: $$

# MTSKHETA CAFÉ ⅈ⦿

## Central Asian

✗

Deep in the heart of Brooklyn bordering Bath Beach, Mtskheta Café pumps out Georgian classics in a green-hued, faux-brick dining room, complete with paper napkins, a campy jungle mural, and television looping foreign music videos. While the décor may be lacking, the service and food excel, setting this impossible-to-pronounce restaurant apart from the nearby bodegas and elevated subway tracks.

Whether or not you can deduce what's on the Cyrillic menu, friendly servers stand by, directing guests to native dishes like badrijani, an almost overwhelming helping of eggplant stuffed with fluffy walnut purée. It's light compared to the mutton bozbashi, though—a heady soup of tarragon, cilantro and lamb fat that adds a layer to any blustery day.

■ 2568 86th St. (bet. Bay 41st St. & Stillwell Ave.)
▣ 25 Av
℘ (718) 676-1868 — **WEB:** N/A
■ Lunch & dinner Thu – Tue                    PRICE: ⊜

# NARGIS CAFE ⅈ⦿

## Central Asian

✗✗ | ⌂

This industrial strip is ground zero for Central Asian hot spots, where Nargis Cafe endures as a real treat. Composed of a front bar area and larger, brighter dining room, the entire space is brought together with marvelous Persian rugs and exotic pierced-metal sconces.

Nargis hits a strong stride among the locals for its convivial vibe and unique repertoire of dishes that may include a bojon salad of smoky eggplant tossed with garlic, peppers, carrots, and cucumber. Kebabs are taken seriously here, so try the succulent lamb with chopped onion and dill. Uzbek plov studded with chickpeas, lamb, and raisins is simple but imperative. For dessert, the honey-sweet chak-chak is fried but surprisingly light and exquisitely indulgent.

■ 2818 Coney Island Ave. (bet. Kathleen Pl. & Avenue Z)
▣ Sheepshead Bay
℘ (718) 872-7888 — **WEB:** www.nargiscafe.com
■ Lunch & dinner daily                    PRICE: $$

# POK POK NY 😊

*Thai*

𝗫 | 🍸 🕍

It takes a special talent to bridge the gap between Brooklyn and Northeast Thailand, but Chef Andy Ricker does so deftly, having dedicated his life to the study of Northern Thai cuisine. Pok Pok Ny is the delicious manifestation of that education, along with his ongoing travels.

Tucked into the Columbia St. waterfront district, this casual spot offers seating along a bar and at little tables covered in colorful plastic. Service is equally laid-back as servers mill about in chambray shirts, while Thai pop music wafts overhead. On a good day, you'll get dishes loaded with sweet, sour and spicy flavors, highlighted best in the grilled boar collar dressed with a dangerously good garlic-fish sauce and balanced by a side of coconut rice in khao man som tam.

- 117 Columbia St. (at Kane St.)
- Carroll St
- 📞 (718) 923-9322 — **WEB:** www.pokpokny.com
- Lunch Sat – Sun   Dinner nightly

**PRICE: $$**

# RUNNER & STONE 😊

*Contemporary*

𝗫𝗫 | 🛋

This ambitious Gowanus operation has a clear sense of purpose. Its name refers to the two stones used to grind grain; the location is just blocks from where the city's first tide-water grist mill once stood; and a Per Se alum heads the fantastic bakery. Inside, the theme continues with walls constructed of concrete blocks shaped like flour sacks.

Lunchtime sandwiches showcase their beloved array of house-baked breads, like whole wheat pain au lait grilled with cheddar and pickled peppers, or falafel-inspired broccoli fritters swaddled in a warm pita with shots of harissa and walnut-yogurt sauce. Come dinnertime, try impressive house-made pastas or the crowd-pleasing fish of the day, like a monkfish fillet that is seared golden and buttery inside.

- 285 Third Ave. (bet. Carroll & President Sts.)
- Union St
- 📞 (718) 576-3360 — **WEB:** www.runnerandstone.com
- Lunch & dinner daily

**PRICE: $$**

# TANOREEN 😋
*Middle Eastern*

XX | ♿

One of the city's finest Middle Eastern experiences is tucked into an unassuming Bay Ridge corner and run by Chef/owner Rawia Bishara and her daughter.

Meals graciously commence with pickled vegetables and za'atar-dusted flatbread and are followed by a tableful of unique plates brimming with flavors and colors. Turkish salad is actually a bright red tomato spread, shot with harissa and dressed with bits of diced cucumber and a drizzle of excellent olive oil. Appetizers are numerous, but try to fit in the chicken fetti: an entrée of basmati rice pilaf studded with toasted, broken vermicelli and topped with spicy bits of chicken, slivered toasted almonds, a generous drizzle of yogurt-tahini sauce, and chopped parsley for a fresh, final note.

- 🟦 7523 Third Ave. (at 76th St.)
- 🚇 77 St
- ✆ (718) 748-5600 — **WEB:** www.tanoreen.com
- 🟦 Lunch & dinner Tue – Sun

**PRICE:** $$

**Look for the symbol 🍽 for a brilliant breakfast to start your day off right.**

# WILLIAMSBURG

## GREENPOINT

Williamsburg—traditionally an Italian, Hispanic, and Hasidic hub—is now a mecca for hipsters and artists. Here in Billyburg, creative culinary endeavors abound and include several, small-scale stores preparing terrific eats—imagine the artisan chocolate line crafted at **Mast Brothers Chocolate** and you'll start to get the picture. Bring an appetite or posse of friends to **Smorgasburg**, where sharing is crucial for a true gustatory thrill. This open-air market is held on the waterfront from spring through fall and headlines everything from beef sliders and brisket, to *bulgogi* and *chana masala*. Less interested in eating and more so in cooking? Sign up for a class at **Brooklyn Kitchen**, where home cooks can keep up with haute chefs by learning how to pickle, bake, and ferment... even kombucha! Over on Metropolitan Avenue, cute takeout shop **Saltie** serves a tempting list of sammies and sweets; while **Pies 'n' Thighs** soothes the soul with down-home goodness. And, there's no going wrong with a cup of joe from **Toby's Estate** or **Blue Bottle Coffee Co.** on Berry Street. In need of a different type of pick-me-up?

**Maison Premiere** is perfect. The vague signage may be of little help, but the line out the door is enough of a clue that this boîte is *the* spot for stellar sips. Within its distressed walls, freshly shucked oysters are washed down with absinthe, icy juleps, and other skillfully made libations. Inspired by the art of butchery, **Marlow & Daughters** is adored for regionally sourced meat, house-made sausages, and dry goods. Locals who live and breathe by meat and cheese make routine trips to **Best Pizza**, a destination that delivers on what its name proclaims. In keeping with the vibe of the 'hood, the interior is disheveled by design, but that doesn't keep peeps from coming in for a slice of "white." Tried and true **Fette Sau** brings rudimentary comfort with roadhouse-style barbecue to residents; just as the falafel at Palestinian-owned **Oasis** has been winning over hearts for a while now.

Greenpoint bakeries offer stacks of traditional Polish pastries, but for a change of pace head to **Ovenly**, just steps away from WNYC Transmitter Park, for a slice of pitch-dark Brooklyn blackout cake.

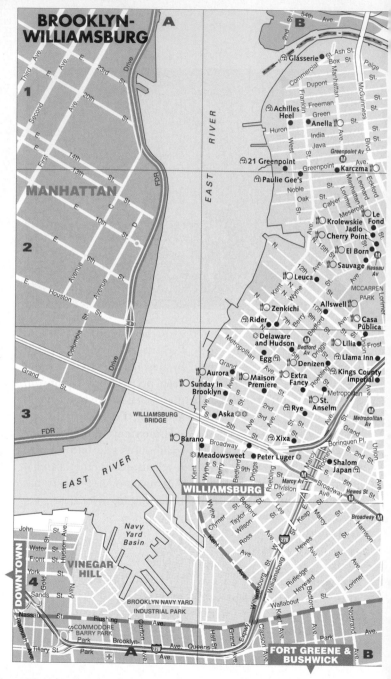

# BROOKLYN-WILLIAMSBURG

A

B

## 1

Third Ave.
Second Ave.
E. 23rd St.
E. 20th St.
Drive

54th Ave.
2nd St.
Ash St.
Box St.
Paige St.
McGuinness Blvd.

Glasserie

Commercial St.
Dupont St.
Manhattan Ave.
Franklin St.
Freeman St.
Green St.
Huron St.
India St.
Java St.

Achilles Heel

Anella

## MANHATTAN

EAST RIVER

FDR

Greenpoint Av

21 Greenpoint

Greenpoint Av.
West St.

Paulie Gee's

Noble St.
Oak St.
Calyer St.

Karczma

Leonard St.
Eckford St.
Manhattan Ave.

Meserole Av.

Le Fond
Jadlo

## 2

E. 14th St.
E. 13th St.
E. 10th St.
E. Houston St.
Avenue D
Avenue C
6th St.

Krolewskie
Cherry Point
N. 15th St.

El Born

Sauvage

Nassau Av

Leuca

12th St.

Wythe Ave.
Kent Ave.

Allswell

MCCARREN PARK

N. St.

## 3

Grand St.
FDR

Zenkichi

Rider

7th St.
Berry St.
9th St.
Bedford Av.
Roebling St.

Casa Pública

Delaware
and Hudson

Metropolitan Av.

Egg

Lilia

Frost St.

Denizen

Llama Inn

Aurora

Grand Ave.

Maison
Premiere

Extra
Fancy

Kings County
Imperial

Sunday in
Brooklyn

S. 1st St.

Metropolitan Av.

Aska

S. 2nd St.
S. 3rd St.

Rye

St.
Anselm

Metropolitan Av.

WILLIAMSBURG
BRIDGE

Barano

Broadway

Xixa

Borinquen Pl.
Union Ave.

Meadowsweet

Peter Luger

Grand St.

Shalom
Japan

Kent Ave.
Wythe Ave.
Berry St.
Bedford Ave.
9th St.
Driggs Ave.

EAST RIVER

Marcy Av

Division Ave.

Broadway

Hewes St St.

## WILLIAMSBURG

Roebling St.

Broadway

## 4

John St.
Water St.
Front St.
York St.
Sands St.
Nassau St.
Tillary St.

Hudson Ave.

Navy
Yard
Basin

VINEGAR
HILL

Clymer St.
Taylor St.
Wilson St.
Ross St.
Kent Ave.

Lee Ave.
Keap St.

Marcy Ave.
Hewes St.

Harrison Ave.

Broadway

DOWNTOWN

Gold St.

Navy St.

BROOKLYN NAVY YARD
INDUSTRIAL PARK

Flushing Ave.
COMMODORE
BARRY PARK

Carlton Ave.

Park Ave.

Brooklyn-Queens Expy.

Hall St.

Rutledge St.
Heyward St.
Wallabout St.

Williamsburg St.

Classon Ave.
Bedford Ave.
Nostrand Ave.
Lorimer St.

Park Ave.

FORT GREENE &
BUSHWICK

B

— 408

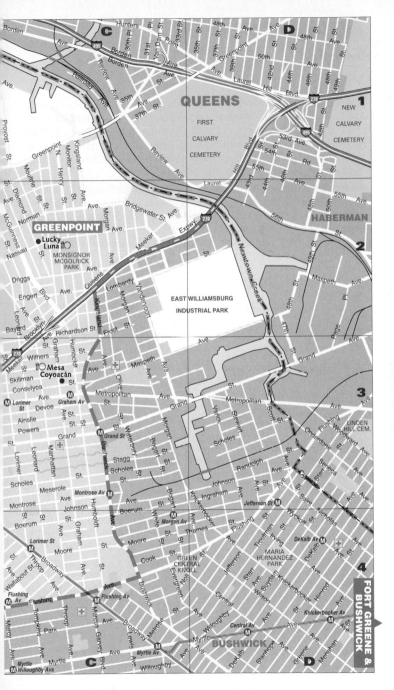

# ACHILLES HEEL 😊

*Gastropub*

✗ | 🍸

**MAP:** B1

Ace restaurateur Andrew Tarlow (of Diner, Marlow & Sons, The Reynard and more) brings next-level bar food to a tavern in Greenpoint—and the result is predictably spectacular. Located near the East River, Achilles Heel is beautifully worn, with big windows and an authentic dockside tavern warmth. Chef Lee Desrosiers heads the tiny kitchen, where the menu is succinct but surprise dishes are common.

A crisp three-bean salad is paired with thick aïoli and soft-crumb sourdough; while lobster mushrooms are pooled in a perfect tomato dashi. Don't miss the Hell Chicken (served on Sundays only)—an otherworldly chicken extravaganza that's smoked, grilled, braised, then grilled again, and served with chicken jus, chicken schmaltz and garlicky miso.

🔳 180 West St. (at Green St.)
🚇 Greenpoint Av
☏ (347) 987-3666 — **WEB:** www.achillesheelnyc.com
🔳 Lunch Sat – Sun   Dinner nightly

**PRICE:** $$

# ALLSWELL 🍴

*Gastropub*

✗ | 🏠 🛋

**MAP:** B2

For remarkably good food and drinks, head to this rustic, farm-to-table favorite with the soul of a time past. The simple interior reflects the straightforward pleasure of this gastropub fare.

Burgers are popular, but the cooking here is thoroughly delicious. Start with potato-ricotta gnocchi tossed with walnuts, wild mushrooms, and finished with rosemary oil for a smart and pleasing interplay of flavors. The veal piccata is also excellent, pounded thin and served in a marvelous lemon-caper sauce splashed with white wine, alongside artichoke hearts and green fava beans. An intensely chocolate-y tart with buckwheat crust is brought to an entirely new level with taste bud-tingly anise ice cream. Their always-changing frittatas are a brunchtime highlight.

🔳 124 Bedford Ave. (at N. 10th St.)
🚇 Bedford Av
☏ (347) 799-2743 — **WEB:** www.allswellnyc.com
🔳 Lunch & dinner daily

**PRICE:** $$

# ANELLA ¶⃝

*American*

✗ | 🍴 〰️

Tucked into the renovated landscape of upper Franklin Street, Anella charms locals and visitors alike with their beautifully composed fare. The owners, also involved in nearby Jimmy's Diner, know their audience well—the space is all weathered wood planks, sepia-toned mirrors and creaky floors; and while a darling bar springs to life come happy hour, teetotalers are bound to delight in their list of loose-leaf teas. The food is light and well-executed, with a lunch menu featuring a BLT on ciabatta with beefsteak tomatoes, crispy bacon and spicy remoulade. Then savor a vibrant tomato soup with thyme and white cheddar, before moving on to seared striped bass with lentils and cauliflower.

Close with an apple crémeux accompanied by almond cake and rum ice cream.

- 222 Franklin St. (bet. Green & Huron Sts.)
- Greenpoint Av
- ℘ (718) 389-8100 — **WEB:** www.anellabrooklyn.com
- Lunch & dinner daily                          PRICE: $$

# AURORA ¶⃝

*Italian*

✗ | 🍴 〰️                                        **MAP:** B3

A waning sun over the twinkling East River; a chilled glass of Italian white in an ivy-covered garden: these are the details that set your heart in motion at this beloved little neighborhood trattoria. And, that's long before you sink your teeth into their homemade dishes laced with pristine seasonal ingredients. La vita é bella, indeed.

Aurora takes Italian cooking back to its rustic roots with simply dressed market greens; impeccably executed pastas; and beautifully seasoned meats and whole fish. A lovely plate of fave e pecorino arrives bursting with fresh fava beans, sharp pecorino, and springy additions like fennel, pea shoots and mint; while a thick tangle of al dente spaghetti is paired with plump shrimp, chili and a touch of mullet roe.

- 70 Grand St. (at Wythe Ave.)
- Bedford Av
- ℘ (718) 388-5100 — **WEB:** www.aurorabk.com
- Lunch & dinner daily                          PRICE: $$

# ASKA ✿✿

*Scandinavian*

XXX | 🍸 ♿ ⛺

A dramatic space in a former warehouse is made even more theatrical by clever lighting: the darkness of the dining room is juxtaposed with the brightness of the open kitchen, which sits on one side of the room like a stage. Tablecloths are black; the uniforms of the waitstaff are black but your eyes are drawn inexorably towards the white-jacketed chefs as they go about their work with quiet efficiency.

Eating here may be a serious business, but happily the place isn't blighted by a monastic atmosphere—a contented buzz fills the room, helped along by the chefs who deliver the dishes themselves and describe them with contagious enthusiasm.

Expect around 19 courses—that may seem daunting but each one, whether a squid tart or meltingly soft dry-aged ribeye, is small and exquisitely formed. Swedish chef Fredrik Berselius and his team use a myriad of techniques from fermenting and pickling to curing, smoking and preserving. This is new Nordic cuisine that celebrates man's relationship with nature and the changing seasons. It's clever without being self-congratulatory, original without being gimmicky, and complex without being complicated—a kitchen shimmering with intelligence.

▪ 47 S. 5th St. (bet. Kent & Wythe Aves.)

🚇 Marcy Av

☏ (929) 337-6792 — **WEB:** www.askanyc.com

▪ Dinner Tue – Sat

**PRICE: $$$$**

# BARANO 🍴

*Italian*

XX | &

Hot off the success of his time at Rubirosa in SoHo, Chef Al Di Meglio brings his distinctive take on the cooking of Ischia to Barano. The stylish stallion sits at the base of a new residential development, just a stone's throw from the East River. Inside, you'll find a smart décor featuring sepia mirrors, polished tables, and columns lined in pearly mosaic tiles. The vibrant bar, fully open kitchen, and wood-burning oven add to its appeal.

Everything here is executed with great care, but the pasta and pizza are particularly noteworthy. Sensational nettle tortellini are tucked with mushrooms and bathed in a purée of mild spring garlic ramps and sweet peas; while tender bucatini are twirled with an irresistible rabbit ragù.

- 26 Broadway (bet. Kent & Wythe Aves.)
- Marcy Av
- (347) 987-4500 — **WEB:** www.baranobk.com
- Dinner nightly                    PRICE: $$$

# CASA PÚBLICA 🍴

*Mexican*

XX | 🍸 &    **MAP:** B3

This breezy Williamsburg restaurant will transport you to sunny Mexico in a flash. Tucked into a multi-room space boasting floor-to-ceiling windows, an ample bar, and gorgeous imported floor tiles, Casa Pública is like a modern-day hacienda filled with well-crafted small plates and dreamy cocktails. Here, tequila is a food group of its own.

Everything on Casa Pública's menu is executed with care, but this kitchen is so talented you should try venturing outside your comfort zone. Aguachile ceviche arrives wildly fresh, chockablock with tender sea scallops, serrano chilies, and crunchy jicama. For dinner, try the carne encebollada, a sizzling platter of Creekstone ribeye topped with sweet, melted ramps, meco chilies, and smoky bone marrow.

- 594 Union Ave. (at Richardson St.)
- Bedford Av
- (718) 388-3555 — **WEB:** www.casapublicabk.com
- Dinner nightly                    PRICE: $$$

# CHERRY POINT 🍴

## *American*

XX | 🍷                                        **MAP:** B2

This charming Greenpoint restaurant used to be a butcher shop, as evidenced by the glass-enclosed meat case built into the end of a lively and very stylish bar. The rustic space now houses a buzzing open kitchen, great music, and jumbo windows that look out over the neighborhood, offering prime people-watching. Most importantly, though, Cherry Point is home to some luscious cooking compliments of Chef Julian Calcott.

Speaking of which, tender grilled oysters are laced in an excellent, smoky Hollandaise with roasted and blackened lime. Then crispy and supremely fresh local baby greens are elevated to noteworthy salad status with pristine anchovies. Close out over a nightly pork chop special, rubbed with koji and accompanied by chimichurri.

■ 664 Manhattan Ave. (bet. Bedford & Norman Aves.)
🚇 Nassau Av
📞 (718) 389-3828 — **WEB:** www.cherrypointnyc.com
■ Lunch Sat – Sun   Dinner Tue – Sun          **PRICE:** $$$

# DENIZEN 🍴

## *American*

XX | 🍇 🍸 🍷                                  **MAP:** B3

Exceptionally good, next-level cheese is the star of this Williamsburg gem, whether it's a spruce-wrapped Harbison from Jasper Hill in Vermont, or French goat milk blue from La Ferme de La Tremblaye. But the menu doesn't stop at fromage—and Denizen's sophisticated small plates are delicious enough to merit a proper dinner.

French onion toast is topped with braised oxtail ragout and soft ribbons of Timberdoodle; butter-poached tile fish bobs in a 'nduja broth over braised sunchokes and cabbage; and burrata plated with broccoli pesto, white anchovies, and sunflower oil is served with crisp rye toast. The modern, tavern-like space is small, so you can expect a wait—but that's not necessarily a bad thing with such an impressive wine list to peruse.

■ 88 Roebling St. (at N. 7th St.)
🚇 Bedford Av
📞 (929) 337-6412 — **WEB:** www.denizenbrooklyn.com
■ Lunch Sat – Sun   Dinner nightly              **PRICE:** $$

# DELAWARE AND HUDSON ✿

*American*

✗✗ | 🍴

**MAP:** B3

Chef Patti Jackson can almost always be found in her kitchen—and that's the first sign you're in for a treat at this *bijou* of a restaurant, where her exceptional Mid-Atlantic fare is the name of the game. This kitchen boasts deep ties to some of the tri-state area's most beloved farms, orchards, and fisheries, adding quality and authenticity to every dish.

The prix-fixe menu offers diners a handful of appetizers to share, including Jackson's famous pretzel roll, followed by a first course and entrée. The starting lineup might feature creamy chestnut soup; golden crab cake paired with purslane and Hollandaise; or green tomato pie with molasses and brown sugar. Pillowy farmer's cheese dumplings tossed with apple schnitz, ham, and Brussels sprouts could be next. And to follow, a fragrant porchetta paired with cider-braised root vegetables and spinach. Dessert, always a delicious affair, is usually hand-delivered by Jackson herself.

The space is small and polished, with flowers sitting pretty on the tables and vivid photographs brightening steely sea-foam walls. If a relaxed, abbreviated tour of the menu is more your speed, head next door to the Tavern for impressive à la carte options.

◼ 135 N. 5th St. (bet. Bedford Ave. & Berry St.)

🚇 Bedford Av

📞 (718) 218-8191 — **WEB:** www.delawareandhudson.com

◼ Lunch & dinner Tue – Sun                    **PRICE: $$$**

# EGG 😊

*American*

✗ | 🍳 🥢

MAP: B3

Breakfast is served all day at this popular Williamsburg spot, which has a second outpost in Tokyo. The setting is industrial but inviting—flushed with light bouncing off concrete floors, plain wood tables and light-colored brick walls.

The star of the show are the fantastic buttermilk biscuits, fresh-baked beauties that are split and smothered with pork sausage-studded sawmill gravy. These may then be stacked with country ham, house-made fig jam, and Vermont cheddar cheese; or simply accompanied by molasses, honey, or jelly. A plump fried oyster sandwich appears laced with a mustard-pickled okra remoulade. Much of the produce is sourced locally—a good part of it provided by Goatfell Farm (located on the northern edge of the Catskills mountain range).

🔲 109 N. Third St. (bet. Berry St. & Wythe Ave.)
🔲 Bedford Av
📞 (718) 302-5151 — **WEB:** www.eggrestaurant.com
🔲 Lunch daily

PRICE: 🍴

# EL BORN 🍴

*Spanish*

✗✗ | 🍤 🥢

MAP: B2

Named for a trendy neighborhood in Barcelona, this Greenpoint tapas den has a decidedly urban feel. Make your way inside to discover a glossy space, featuring a neon squiggle suspended from the ceiling, red Shaker-style chairs, as well as a long bar with twelve contemporary (but comfy!) stools for perching.

Over in the kitchen, the chefs slide effortlessly between Andalusia, Catalonia, and Castilla-La Mancha, giving each of their dishes a dusting of contemporary flair. Warm goat cheese croquetas are served with apple compote; while shaved summer squash straddles sweet-salty perfection with jamon Ibérico, blueberries, and padrón pepper vinaigrette. For a flavor-packed finale, go for stone-grilled octopus seasoned with olive oil, thyme, and paprika.

🔲 651 Manhattan Ave. (bet. Nassau & Norman Aves.)
🔲 Nassau Av
📞 (347) 844-9295 — **WEB:** www.elbornnyc.com
🔲 Lunch Sat – Sun   Dinner nightly

PRICE: $$

# EXTRA FANCY ⁂⚬
*Seafood*

🍴 | 🛋

Williamsburg's restaurant scene may be awash in excellence, yet this guy still manages to find its own niche. Their particular bag is fresh seafood, rendered in an inventive American fashion, and served in a charming, rustic dining room dressed with warm woods and nautical lighting fixtures. Out front, you'll find a lively, packed bar; toward the back, cozy seating and a truly welcoming service staff.

Pristine dorade ceviche arrives bursting with crisp onion and bright cilantro; while a lovingly constructed lobster roll teems with sweet, fresh meat. Wild-caught King salmon confit is paired with smoked crème fraîche, dill and toasted bagel crumbs. Don't miss the superb Jonah crab bucatini with tender Littleneck clams, lemon and parsley.

◼ 302 Metropolitan Ave. (at Roebling St.)
🚇 Bedford Av
✆ (347) 422-0939 — **WEB:** www.extrafancybklyn.com
◼ Dinner nightly                          **PRICE:** $$

# GLASSERIE 😋
*Middle Eastern*

⁂⁂ | 🏮 | 🛋

Housed in an old glass factory, the beautiful Glasserie is colorful, rustic and industrial, with lots of original details, a welcoming bar, and a small door that peeks into the bustling kitchen. Add to this lovely setting a straight-up delicious Middle Eastern menu from a wildly talented kitchen, and you begin to understand why the crowds are flocking to this hot spot.

Manning the kitchen is Eldad Shem Tov, a talented chef who favors organic and locally sourced ingredients. Highlights may include the table-shared mezze feast—served with ten or so incredible small dishes—or the rabbit taco, spiked with harissa and folded into a thin kohlrabi "taco" with herbs and radish. The silky chicken liver mousse, served with arak, is a crowd-pleaser and fittingly so.

◼ 95 Commercial St. (bet. Box St. & Manhattan Ave.)
🚇 Greenpoint Av
✆ (718) 389-0640 — **WEB:** www.glasserienyc.com
◼ Lunch Sat – Sun   Dinner nightly       **PRICE:** $$

# KARCZMA ¶○

*Polish*

¶ | &

Located in a slice of Greenpoint that still boasts a sizeable Polish population, Karczma offers a lovely old-world ambience that perfectly matches its very traditional and budget-friendly menu. The kitchen has been known to turn out a host of hearty offerings, including peasant-style lard mixed with bacon and spices, or even a plate of the nation's specialties piled high with pierogies (three varieties, steamed or fried, topped with onions and butter), kielbasa, potato pancakes and stuffed cabbage. Grilled plates can be prepared for two or three, while others like the roasted hocks in beer, could easily feed an army.

The quaint, farmhouse-inspired interior is efficiently staffed with smiling servers in floral skirts and embroidered vests.

■ 136 Greenpoint Ave. (bet. Franklin St. & Manhattan Ave.)

▣ Greenpoint Av

✆ (718) 349-1744 — **WEB:** www.karczmabrooklyn.com

■ Lunch & dinner daily                          **PRICE:** ⌘

# KINGS COUNTY IMPERIAL ☺

*Chinese*

¶ | ☕ ☕

While this 'hood has enjoyed a rush of good restaurants in recent years, Kings County Imperial created a stir within the stir. The décor is nothing to write home about—though it's cute and disheveled in all the right ways and boasts a mean "backyard." But, their pan-Chinese dishes have certainly set tongues a wagging.

Think juicy white broiler chicken dumplings laced with cinnamon-red oil and Kings County Soy Works (carried on tap, fresh from the Pearl River Delta in Southern China); or creamy kung pao sweet potatoes paired with silky king trumpet mushrooms. A salt-and-pepper pork chop features outstanding quality meat; while tender tea-smoked moo shu duck, marinated for 48 hours, is paired with soft homemade wheat pancakes.

■ 20 Skillman Ave. (at Meeker Ave.)

▣ Lorimer St - Metropolitan Av

✆ (718) 610-2000 — **WEB:** www.kingscountyimperial.com

■ Dinner nightly                          **PRICE:** $$

# KROLEWSKIE JADLO ¶O

*Polish*

✗

**MAP:** B2

Krolewskie Jadlo ("king's feast" in Polish) sits in a Greenpoint enclave that was once home to a large number of Polish immigrants. Although the size of the community has decreased through the years, the area still thrives with a distinct Eastern European soul.

The room is pleasant and routinely packed with crowds basking in the enjoyable authenticity. The Polish plate brings all one could hope for in a hearty old-world platter: cabbage rolls stuffed with ground beef and braised in tart tomato sauce; pan-fried potato pierogis; and a link of smoky kielbasa. Other items are just as tasty, like the pounded pork shoulder steak, grilled and brushed with honey, and served with pickled cabbage and beets.

Known for their dessert make sure to end on a sweet note.

■ 694 Manhattan Ave. (bet. Nassau & Norman Aves.)
▣ Nassau Av
✆ (718) 383-8993 — **WEB:** www.krolewskiejadlo.com
■ Lunch & dinner daily                    PRICE: ⬝

# LE FOND ¶O

*French*

✗ | 🛋

**MAP:** B2

Chef-owner Jake Eberle's cute corner restaurant shows us that not every dish needs reimagining and not every recipe requires reinterpretation. He's a French-trained chef whose cooking is crisp, clean, and comfortingly classic—and his well-balanced menu includes words like "roulade" and "blancmange" that here seem curiously reassuring. That's not to say his food doesn't pack a punch: the rich, meaty cassoulet could keep an army on the march for days.

Globe lights hang from the ceiling to illuminate a sea-blue room with bespoke wooden furniture. The acoustics can be bouncy and those lacking the necessary padding will find the seating a little numbing. But, there is honest toil and earnest endeavor happening here and it deserves support.

■ 105 Norman Ave. (at Leonard St.)
▣ Nassau Av
✆ (718) 389-6859 — **WEB:** www.lefondbk.com
■ Lunch Sun  Dinner Tue – Sun              PRICE: $$

# LEUCA 🍽

*Italian*

XX | 🍸 ⛄ ♿ 🏠 🛏

This well-curated addition to the booming local scene arrives courtesy of NoHo Hospitality Group with the talented Andrew Carmellini at the helm. Named for the charming maritime town in the southernmost region of Puglia, Italy, Brooklyn's Leuca is tucked into the gorgeous William Vale Hotel, a stone's throw from the East River.

The lovely space features a bright and airy dining room with yellow leather chairs and marble-topped tables, as well as a second elegant nook fitted out with wood paneling and oversized black-and-white photographs.

Dinner might unveil tender lemon chicken for two, fragrant with spices and strung with blistered peppers; or a delicious tangle of spaghetti and sea urchin topped with succulent crab and spicy chili flakes.

▪ 111 N. 12 th St. (bet. Berry St. & Wythe Ave.)
🚇 Nassau Av
☎ (718) 581-5900 — **WEB:** www.leuca.com
▪ Lunch Mon – Fri  Dinner nightly          **PRICE: $$$**

# LILIA 🍽

*Italian*

XX | 🍸 ♿

Who's not happy to see Missy Robbins back on the culinary scene, whipping up pastas that could bring the savviest diner to their knees? Tucked amongst the mish-mash of shiny new condos and the roar of the BQE that make up this part of Williamsburg, sleek Lilia occupies an old corner auto shop. The transformation is dramatic, replete with iron casement windows, unique tiling, and contemplative artwork.

Most of the dishes at Lilia ooze authenticity, made all the better by a warm, knowledgeable service staff who are happy to elaborate on details. Dinner might begin with cured sardines laid over a thick slice of sourdough, dotted with dill and capers; or chewy rigatoni diavola in a chunky tomato-based salsa humming with chili pepper and salty pecorino.

▪ 567 Union Ave. (at N. 10th St.)
🚇 Lorimer St - Metropolitan Av
☎ (718) 576-3095 — **WEB:** www.lilianewyork.com
▪ Dinner nightly          **PRICE: $$$**

# LLAMA INN 😊

*Peruvian*

XX | 🍸 🍺 ♿ 🛋️                    **MAP:** B3

Upbeat, modern, and cool, the Llama Inn pays respect to all styles of Peruvian cooking, but with the technical flair of a chef who has trained in New York's top restaurants. The result is a fresh, fun, and spontaneous cuisine that aims to elevate Peruvian food.

Fish courses are notable, and nowhere is that more clear than in the fresh and expertly cut raw sea bream tiradito with persimmon, ginger, yuzu, and nutty poppy seeds. Fluke ceviche is just as memorable, served in a bit of dashi with lime, onion, cilantro, aji, and wonderfully spicy leche de tigre. Then move on to devour decadent little skewers of pork belly brushed with Chinese five-spice, soy, garlic, and barbecue sauce. Excellent desserts include airy coffee mousse with chocolate and lucuma.

■ 50 Withers St. (bet. Lorimer & Union Sts.)
🚇 Lorimer St - Metropolitan Av
📞 (718) 387-3434 — **WEB:** www.llamainnnyc.com
■ Lunch Sat – Sun   Dinner nightly                    **PRICE:** $$

# LUCKY LUNA 🍽️

*Fusion*

X | 🍸                    **MAP:** C2

There's no other restaurant around like Lucky Luna. Seriously. Their delicious menu is a hybrid of Taiwanese and Mexican cuisine. The pizzazz on the plate is served in a simple yet tidy assemblage of glossy black tables, and an ambitious beverage program makes the small bar a total draw.

Mom's sweet-and-sour cucumber salad, flavored with ginger and garlic, is a bracing start for Peking duck confit bao spread with hoisin mayonnaise, garnished with crispy duck chicharrònes and duck fat popcorn dusted with Chinese five spice. Another hit: the taco of "reverse" carnitas is a pile of succulent pork shoulder that's been seared, then braised in a broth of beer, oranges, and tomatoes, and finally topped with crunchy bits of radish and spicy pickles.

■ 167 Nassau Ave. (at Diamond St.)
🚇 Nassau Av
📞 (718) 383-6038 — **WEB:** www.luckyluna-ny.com
■ Lunch Thu – Sun   Dinner Tue – Sun                    **PRICE:** $$

# MAISON PREMIERE 🍴

*Seafood*

X | 🍸 ⌂ 🛋

This ultra-retro tavern may feel dark and old-timey, like a watering hole where the Founding Fathers would have stopped for fortification before fending off the British. But, the massive, U-shaped bar is particularly coveted, so arrive early or prepare to wait for your absinthe drip.

To accompany the stellar sips, a vast selection of oysters, clams, and group-friendly seafood plateaux seem to pop up on every table. The kitchen's talent is equally clear in such preparations as luscious sea urchin served in a chilled shellfish consommé with fragrant lemongrass and thin slices of sweet grapes. Heartier appetites will delight in a thick, juicy pork Porterhouse, glazed with jus, served alongside braised kale, roasted beets, and finished with zippy horseradish cream.

■ 298 Bedford Ave. (bet. S. 1st & Grand Sts.)
🚇 Bedford Av
☏ (347) 335-0446 — **WEB:** www.maisonpremiere.com
■ Lunch & dinner daily          **PRICE: $$$**

# MESA COYOACÁN 🍴

*Mexican*

X | ♿ 🛋

Mexico City native, Chef Ivan Garcia is at the helm of this Brooklyn hot spot, where wolfish appetites are sated with richly flavored cooking. Fronted by windows that open up on to bustling Graham Avenue, the long space is outfitted with patterned wallpaper, snug banquettes, and communal tables.

The kitchen's spirited presentations are simply a joy. Partake in tacos featuring hand-crafted tortillas, like the suadero for instance, stuffed with beef brisket and avocado salsa; or torta tinga de pollo, packed with shredded chipotle-braised chicken, mashed black beans, pickled jalapeños, and a toasted roll to sop up that delish sauce. Reposado and diced mango enhances the pastel tres leches—and to keep the tequila flowing, hit up nearby Zona Rosa.

■ 372 Graham Ave. (bet. Conselyea St. & Skillman Ave.)
🚇 Graham Av
☏ (718) 782-8171 — **WEB:** www.mesacoyoacan.com
■ Lunch Wed – Sun   Dinner nightly          **PRICE: $$**

# MEADOWSWEET ✿

*Mediterranean*

✕✕ | 🍸 🍺 ♿ 🏠 🍴

Tucked next to the steely skeleton of the Williamsburg Bridge, Meadowsweet cuts a stylish industrial figure with its glass-fronted façade, whitewashed brick walls, and original mosaic-tiled floors. Leather banquettes line the wall, and pendant bulbs illuminate one of several beautiful oil paintings of a meadow. Inside, the restaurant jumps with Williamsburg's finest—along with more than a few bridge-hoppers from Manhattan and beyond. And that's on a slow night.

The fuss is quite merited. Despite ample competition in this section of town, Chef/owner Polo Dobkin and wife, Stephanie Lempert, manage to elevate the kitchen's dishes into next level territory, and they do so in a lovely, urbane setting with loads of charm and friendly service.

The inventive American menu gets a lift from Mediterranean accents: a bowl of deliciously chewy squid ink "fettuccine" arrives with Spanish octopus, chorizo, hot chili and breadcrumbs. Tender duck finds its match in braised red cabbage, poached Seckel pear, and roasted pear-and-black currant coulis. There's an impressive list of cocktails and wine; not to mention a globetrotting beer selection ranging from Austrian lagers to Japanese ales.

■ 149 Broadway (bet. Bedford & Driggs Aves.)

🚇 Marcy Av

✆ (718) 384-0673 — **WEB:** www.meadowsweetnyc.com

■ Lunch Thu – Sun   Dinner Wed – Mon          **PRICE: $$**

# PAULIE GEE'S 😋

*Pizza*

🍴 | ♿

MAP: B2

Owner Paul Giannone, aka Paulie Gee, channeled a lifelong love of pizza into this charmingly delicious spot that feels as if it has been around forever. Rustic in appearance, the room's cool concrete and brick are warmed by the glow of the wood-burning oven imported from Naples. From here, Giannone and his son work their magic.

The addictive crust is beguilingly moist and chewy, perfumed with smoke, and adroitly salted. Killer wood-fired pies dominate the menu with tempting combinations, excellent ingredients, and whimsical names. Offerings may include the Harry Belafontina—fontina, tomatoes, beefy meatballs, cremini mushrooms, and golden raisins. Vegans get equal respect here, with an added menu of vegan cheese and house-made vegan sausage.

◼ 60 Greenpoint Ave. (bet. Franklin & West Sts.)
◼ Greenpoint Av
✆ (347) 987-3747 — **WEB:** www.pauliegee.com
◼ Dinner nightly

PRICE: 😑

# RIDER 😋

*Contemporary*

🍴🍴 | 🏮 🍱 🥢

MAP: B2

Some may think this hip, bi-level eatery is an offshoot of the Brooklyn performance space National Sawdust, but in fact Rider vies for top billing. Downstairs, you'll find an industrial vibe outfitted with concrete flooring, exposed brick walls, and comfy banquettes; upstairs is polished, low-lit and moodier.

Patrick Connolly has put together an exciting menu designed for sharing, with a refreshing focus on vegetables. The execution and flavors transcend the trendiness of the space, offering unfussy, timeless dishes that may be considered small plates, but are generously portioned. Try gemelli bathed in mushroom ragù with crisp breadcrumbs, or grilled mortadella on sourdough with ricotta, toasted sunflower seeds and a nasturtium "pesto."

◼ 80 N. 6th St. (at Wythe Ave.)
◼ Bedford Av
✆ (718) 210-3152 — **WEB:** www.riderbklyn.com
◼ Lunch daily   Dinner Tue – Sat

PRICE: $$

# PETER LUGER ⌘

*Steakhouse*

🍴 | 🖥 | 🈴 | 💵

More than just an icon of the New York dining scene—Peter Luger is an idolized classic. Run on wheels by a team of gloriously forthright waiters, this munificent paean to beef doesn't just serve legendary steaks, it provides a side helping of history too. The wood paneling and beer-hall tables tell of family gatherings, friends united, deal making, success celebrated and stories swapped. It's evocative and unforgettable. It's also unapologetically old-school—computerization and credit cards remain fanciful futuristic concepts, so you'll need to come with a few Benjamins tucked into your wallet.

Start with a thick slice of bacon to get your taste buds up to speed before the steak arrives. These slabs of finely marbled Porterhouse are dry-aged in-house for around 28 days, which means there's tenderloin on one side of the bone and strip steak on the other. They are then broiled to perfection, sliced before being brought to the table, and served with their own sauce as well as a host of sides, which range from their version of German fried potatoes to creamed spinach.

If you can still feel a pulse after that, there's always cheesecake served with their equally famous "schlag" to finish you off.

■ 178 Broadway (at Driggs Ave.)
🚇 Marcy Av
☎ (718) 387-7400 — **WEB:** www.peterluger.com
■ Lunch & dinner daily                    **PRICE:** $$$$

# RYE 🐶

*American*

🍴 | 🍸 🍴

MAP: B3

Rye's Classic Old Fashioned—a carefully crafted swirl of liquid amber—is the perfect personification of Chef Cal Elliott's beloved gastropub: strong and comforting. Anchored by a reclaimed mahogany bar, this speakeasy is accented accordingly with plank flooring, a pressed-tin ceiling, and exposed filament bulbs. Killer bar snacks such as oysters and cheeses lead to a succinct lineup of cooking that is bound to satisfy on every level. Highlights include the glazed meatloaf sandwich with duck, veal, and pork stuffed inside a hoagie roll and served with crisp-fried onion rings. For dessert, the warm and fudgy molten chocolate cake is another classic Rye gets just right.

For live tunes and libations on the late night, drop by casual counterpart—Bar Below Rye

🔲 247 S. 1st St. (bet. Havemeyer & Roebling Sts.)

🔳 Marcy Av

📞 (718) 218-8047 — **WEB:** www.ryerestaurant.com

🔲 Lunch Sat – Sun   Dinner nightly                **PRICE: $$**

# SAUVAGE 🍴

*Contemporary*

🍴🍴 | 🎛 🍸 🎚 🍴

MAP: B2

Sauvage means "wild and natural" in French, and that's a perfectly apt description for this handsome restaurant with a thoughtful list of naturalist wines. Select one of the organic, biodynamic offerings; then sit back, relax and take in the leather booths, walnut bar, hand-blown glass chandeliers and tropical plants.

But enough about drinks and décor, because the kitchen happens to be whipping up dishes that absolutely thrill. Highlights include roasted cauliflower served with anchovy and peppercorn; or even Japanese fingerlings dressed with beef fat-vinaigrette. Pooled in a vinegar swirl, crispy sweetbreads are delivered with mushrooms and watercress. Pan-seared rabbit with turnip purée and a mustard seed-honey "broth" makes for a hearty and fragrant finale.

🔲 905 Lorimer St. (at Nassau Ave.)

🔳 Nassau Av

📞 (718) 486-6816 — **WEB:** www.sauvageny.com

🔲 Lunch & dinner daily                          **PRICE: $$$**

# SHALOM JAPAN 😊

*Fusion*

✗ | 🍴 🛋

**MAP:** B3

The curious moniker of this sweet spot refers to the backgrounds of its husband-and-wife team, Chefs Aaron Israel and Sawako Okochi. Each has an impressive resume, and together the result is a unique labor of love.

Nightly specials are displayed via a wall-mounted blackboard with small plates progressing to a handful of entrées. Monkfish hot pot features ankimo-enriched miso broth, ground shrimp balls, glass noodles, and a heap of fragrant herbs. The house-baked sake kasu challah with raisin butter is a highly recommended start. But, it may also turn up as toro toast smeared with scallion, wasabi cream cheese, and topped with finely chopped, smoked lean tuna belly. Still craving more? Experience it once again in the warm chocolate bread pudding.

■ 301 S. 4th St. (at Rodney St.)
🚇 Marcy Av
☏ (718) 388-4012 — **WEB:** www.shalomjapannyc.com
■ Lunch Sat – Sun   Dinner nightly                    PRICE: $$

# ST. ANSELM 🍴

*American*

✗ | 🍷

**MAP:** B3

Step through the heavy wood-framed glass door and let the smell of charred meat and grassy notes from chimichurri greet you. The low ceiling is shingled with distressed wood to lend a rustic note to the room. Its open floor plan accentuates the bright flames from the sizzling grill, visible through the kitchen.

Settle down at the bar to sample offbeat wines and cocktails. A genuine sense of contentedness fills the packed room, as guests enjoy small plates of monster prawns, grilled quickly in their steaming shells, finished with garlic, parsley, and a hint of spice. Sweet tea-brined young Bobo chicken served with head and feet intact may seem like it isn't for everyone, but it should be. Perfectly moist and whole-roasted, it is a pure, hands-on pleasure.

■ 355 Metropolitan Ave. (bet. Havemeyer & Roebling Sts.)
🚇 Bedford Av
☏ (718) 384-5054 — **WEB:** N/A
■ Lunch Sat – Sun   Dinner nightly                    PRICE: $$

# SUNDAY IN BROOKLYN 🍴

## *American*

XX | ⚐ 🛋 🍽 ⚒

**MAP:** B3

With all due respect to Monday through Saturday, the best day may be Sunday in Brooklyn. That is if grooving to old-school hip hop with a well-made cocktail in one hand and freshly baked sourdough slathered with beer butter in another is your kind of thing. This café is free of that formulaic hipster décor and instead flaunts a rustic Med villa-meets-ski cabin look.

Those warm, gooey sticky buns are sinfully delicious and no one skips the breads. The kitchen also deserves praise for brunch, which is on everyone's mind. However, it's far from the only game here, where the chef curries favor with diners all day long. A $4 Dark and Stormy can be a fine tonic against inclement weather. Don't miss the market for goodies like smoked fish and irresistible pastries.

■ 348 Wythe Ave. (at S. 2nd St.)
🚇 Bedford Av
✆ (347) 222-6722 — **WEB:** www.sundayinbrooklyn.com
■ Lunch & dinner daily     **PRICE:** $$$

# 21 GREENPOINT 😋

## *American*

XX | 🍹 ⚒

**MAP:** B1

A big and bright red wood-burning oven is not merely a visual centerpiece at 21 Greenpoint, it is also the soul of their thoroughly pleasing American fare. This is where those fresh breads and pizze are baked just as meats and a tantalizing array of root vegetables are roasted.

The menu changes daily and the kitchen is notably accommodating, so vegan/vegetarian variations are easily made. Don't miss the Sunday night prix-fixe, offering six excellent courses like a frittata, peppery pork shoulder soup with foraged mushrooms, and more for a mere $21. Nowhere else can you find this level of delicious American cooking at such a price. This may be a relative newcomer, but it has a familiar feel with plank floors, colorful mosaics, and pleasantly disheveled walls.

■ 21 Greenpoint Ave. (bet. the East River & West St.)
🚇 Greenpoint Av
✆ (718) 383-8833 — **WEB:** www.21greenpoint.com
■ Lunch Sat – Sun   Dinner Tue – Sun     **PRICE:** $$

# XIXA 😋

## Mexican

🍴 | 🍸                     **MAP:** B3

Thanks to the trademark style of Chef Jason Marcus, this lovely Mexican favorite draws those chill, relaxed Williamsburg crowds into its slender space. Everything seems to glow beneath etched brass ceiling pendants, as servers carefully place course after well-paced course on those tiny tables.

A delicious alchemy is at work here, as evidenced in the remarkably delicate corn flan tamal, topped with buttery roasted corn, set over garlic-poblano cream, and tucked with pickled trumpet mushrooms. Tacos are also absolute standouts, thanks to soft, warm tortillas folded with roasted bone marrow, chorizo marmalade, and charred lime. Like the menu, the beverage listing is loads of fun, with wines whimsically arranged under headings of iconic women.

- 241 S. 4th St. (bet. Havemeyer & Roebling Sts.)
- Marcy Av
- (718) 388-8860 — **WEB:** www.xixany.com
- Dinner Wed – Sun                  **PRICE:** $$

# ZENKICHI 🍴

## Japanese

🍴 | 🍶                     **MAP:** B2

Though this Japanese standby might have seemed more novel a few years ago, Zenkichi still retains plenty of magic. The atmosphere is relaxed but focused, and the omakase is surprisingly well-priced for this neighborhood. Secluded booths offer a sexy vibe for date night, where couples can ring a bell for service. And Akariba, a cool little cash-only bar next door that is connected to the restaurant, serves up such treats as oysters and sake.

In addition to the à la carte and dessert menus, this kitchen also offers three variations on omakase: traditional, vegetarian, and wheat-free. But unlike the typical omakase, there's something here for everyone, and the pre-determined dishes may unveil Saikyo miso cod or a heap of summer vegetables in Tosazu gelée.

- 77 N. 6th St. (at Wythe Ave.)
- Bedford Av
- (718) 388-8985 — **WEB:** www.zenkichi.com
- Dinner nightly                    **PRICE:** $$

# QUEENS

# QUEENS

Nearly as large as Manhattan, the Bronx, and Staten Island combined, Queens covers 120 square miles on the western end of Long Island. Reputedly the most ethnically varied district in the world, its diversified nature is reflected in the numerous immigrants who arrive here each year for its affordable housing, strong sense of community, and cultural explosion. Such a unique convergence of cultures results in this stately borough's predominantly global and very distinctive flavor. Though Superstorm Sandy was especially damaging to the Rockaways, these streets continue to prosper with amazing and affordable international eats even today.

## GLOBE-TROTTING

Begin your around-the-world feast in Astoria, a charming quarter of old-world brick row houses and Mediterranean groceries. Discover grilled octopus bookended by baklava at one of the many terrific

Greek joints. Then, prolong your culinary spree over juicy kebabs at Little Egypt on Steinway Street; or chow on equally hearty Czech *tlac'enka* at the popular **Bohemian Hall & Beer Garden**. On lazy days, brew buffs can be found at Astoria's hottest beer havens—**Sweet Afton**—for an intimate setting with a serious selection, or equally sublime **Studio Square** for the ultimate alfresco experience. Showcasing equally exquisite beverages alongside beautiful baked goods, **Leli's Bakery** may be a relatively young member of Astoria's dining scene, but hooks its troops with age-old roots—their commercial kitchen in the Bronx has been supplying fine-dining establishments with a wealth of sweetness since time immemorial. Founded in 1937, **La Guli** is an Italian *pasticceria* whose expert talent has been feeding families with rich, creamy cakes and cookies. And staying true to tradition, **The Lemon Ice King of Corona**, brought to you by the Benfaremo family, is a nostalgic ode to Italian ice complete with sugar-free selections for health-embattled hordes. But, for an unapologetically potent treat, **To Laiko** is the area's favorite for a delicious frappe.

**S**ojourning south and then to the east, **La Boulangerie** brings a slice of France to Forest Hills by way of fresh-baked loaves of white bread and crusty baguettes. Of course, cheese couples best with bread, and the choices are abundant at **Leo's Latticini**

in Corona. Surprisingly, eating in **Terminal C** at La Guardia Airport is now considered a gastronomic delight with wonderful food and beverage outposts churned out by star chefs like Andrew Carmellini and Michael Lomonaco. Hopping airports, JFK's **Delta**

**Terminal 4** is also becoming known as a culinary emporium in its own right, replete with such acclaimed offerings as **Shake Shack** courtesy of restaurateur Danny Meyer, and **Uptown Brasserie** from the much raved-about chef, Marcus Samuelsson. Frequent flyers with refined palates

will also appreciate Dave Cook's *Eating in Translation*, a daily newsletter citing fantastic food finds at unusual locations—including airports! Speaking of which, **M. Wells Dinette** which is housed inside MoMA PS 1, delivers insanely inventive items to curious visitors and the lucky locals of Long Island City. Offering an imaginative blend of diner signatures, Quebecois favorites, and "are you serious!?" combos, this sequel to the original, outstanding diner continues to charm crowds by simply doing their thing.

**W**hile biding time in this neighborhood, feel the sass and spirit at MoMA PS 1's "Warm Up"—one of Gotham City's greatest summer soirées, featuring a DJ, turntables, and all that jazz. Need something sweet to combat the heat? Look out for the **Doughnut Plant** housed in the historic Falchi Building and boasting an outré selection, crafted from the best ingredients in town—tres leches doughnuts anyone? And what goes best with dessert? Coffee of course, with a crowning range of roasted beans available at **Vassilaros and Sons**. Enhancing this quarter's global repute is **Güllüoglu**, a Turkish bakery and café whose elegant space and tasty bites bring Istanbul to life. But if Pakistani flavors are a particular fave, then **Bundu Khan** is worth a trip for every type of grilled delight. Close out these global eats at cozy **Norma's Corner Shoppe**—a hot spot for homey, comfort fare.

## ASIA MEETS THE AMERICAS

**F**lushing still reigns as Queens' most vibrant Asian haven and NY'ers are always dropping in for dim sum, Henan specialties, or a bowl of *pho* like you'd find streetside in Saigon. Food vendors at Flushing's mini-malls offer foods from far flung corners of China that are light on the pockets but big on flavor. Of both local note and city-wide acclaim, **New World Mall Food Court** is a clean, airy space serving excellent Asian eats. You'll find everything at these inviting stalls from hand-pulled noodles (at **Lang Zhou**) to Taiwanese shaved ice for the end of the night.

On Saturdays, when the weather warms and the sun sets, grazers and shoppers flock to **The Queens International Night Market** at the New York Hall of Science in Flushing Meadows Corona Park. Their tempting array of inexpensive Asian and Latin

American snacks further celebrates the rich diversity of this borough's population. But the offerings don't stop here. Over on Main Street, vegans feel the love and care at **Bodai Vegetarian** where such kosher-friendly dishes as vegetarian duck and seaweed-sesame rolls keep the crowds

returning for more. These same health food fans as well as epicureans from all walks may then trek east to arrive at **Queens County Farm Museum**, considered one of the largest working farms in the city that supports sustainable farming, farm-to-table meals, and is rife with livestock, a greenhouse, and educational programs.

From Flushing to Floral Park, **Real Usha Sweets & Snacks** cooks India's favorite street eats, which also make for excellent dinner party treats. Think c*hana chor*, *papadi*, and banana chips—a Kerala specialty. Also reminiscent of flavors from the subcontinent, **Singh's Roti Shop and Bar** prepares Caribbean delicacies like curry chicken, saltfish, and *aloo pie* to gratify its contiguous community. Shifting gears from south to Central Asia, as many as 40,000 immigrants traveled to New York after the fall of the Soviet Union. They staked their claim in Forest Hills, and **King David Kosher Restaurant** remains a paragon among these elder statesmen and their large families

for Bukharian specialties. Energy and variety personify Elmhurst, the thriving hearth of settlers primarily from Latin America, China, and Southeast Asia. The Royal Kathin, a celebration that occurs at the end of Thailand's rainy season, pays homage to the spirit of Buddhist monks. While Elmhurst's adaptation of this festival may lack the floods, it certainly proffers a bounty of authentic Thai bites. Whitney Avenue is home to a booming restaurant row with an array of small Southeast Asian storefronts. Indulge a *gado gado* craving at **Upi Jaya** before getting your *laksa* on at **Taste Good**. Elmhurst spans the globe, so if the pungent flavors of Southeast Asia don't fit the bill, relocate from Asia to the Americas by way of thick, creamy Greek yogurt at **Kesso Foods**. This mini shop is a gem among locals, while **Cannelle Patisserie**'s carb-o-licious goodies keep the entire borough abuzz.

Jackson Heights is home to a large South Asian community. Take in the bhangra beats blaring from cars rolling along 74th Street. This dynamic

commercial stretch is dotted with numerous Indian markets, Bengali sweet shops, and Himalayan-style eateries serving all types of *tandoori* specialties, spicy curries and steaming Tibetan *momos*.

In keeping with the fact that Latin Americans also make up a large part of the demographic here, Roosevelt Ave. swarms with taquerias, aromatic Colombian coffee shops, and sweet Argentinean spots to sate their vast range of assorted tastes.

## WANDERING THROUGH WOODSIDE

**T**ake this thriving thoroughfare west to Woodside, where Irish bars mingle with Thai restaurants. Once home to an enormous Irish population, Woodside now shares its streets with Thai and Filipino communities—even if the kelly green awnings of decades-old pubs scatter these blocks and clover-covered doors advertise in Gaelic. Set alongside **Donovan's**, an age-old Irish respite grilling up one of the best burgers in town, is **Little Manila**— an eight-block stretch of Roosevelt Avenue where you can stock up on Filipino groceries galore. Also find folks join the line outside **Jollibee**, a fast-food chain serving up flavors from home. If Filipino cooking sounds far too funky for your liking, rest assured as **Piemonte Ravioli** carries every choice of fresh pasta for an Italian *cena con la famiglia*. And of course, down south in Sunnyside, you may also eat your way through Romania, Turkey, Mexico, Korea, China and more.

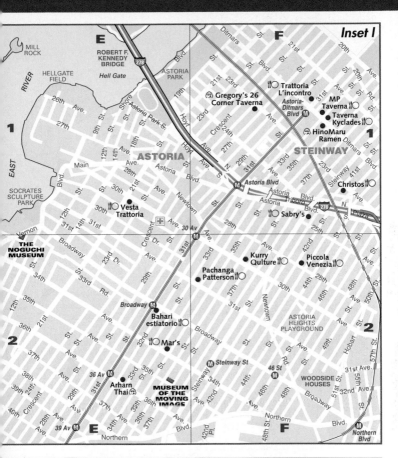

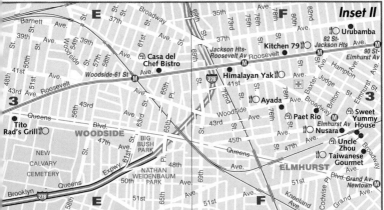

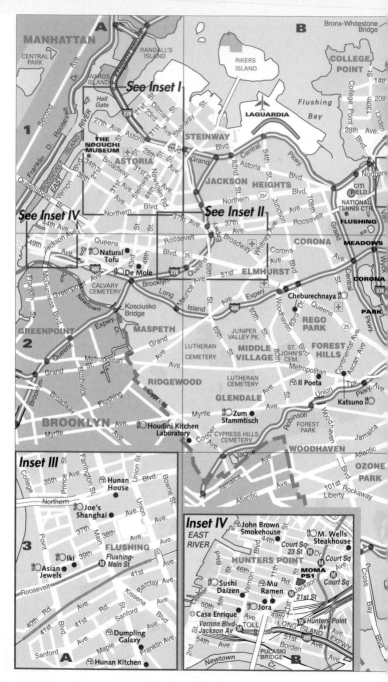

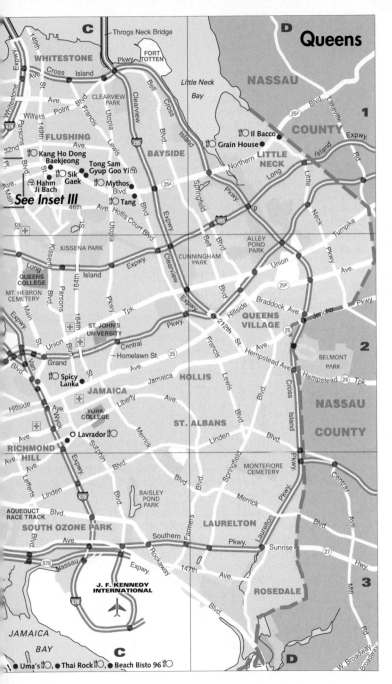

# Queens

**C**

Throgs Neck Bridge

WHITESTONE

FORT TOTTEN

Cross Island Pkwy.

Little Neck Bay

**D**

NASSAU

CLEARVIEW PARK

COUNTY

Willets Point Blvd.

FLUSHING

BAYSIDE

Il Bacco ●

Grain House ●

LITTLE NECK

Kang Ho Dong Baekjeong

Tong Sam Gyup Goo Yi

Sik Gaek

Hahm Ji Bach

Mythos

Tang

Northern Blvd.

*See Inset III*

46th

Hollis Court Blvd.

KISSENA PARK

CUNNINGHAM PARK

ALLEY POND PARK

Union Ave.

QUEENS COLLEGE

MT. HEBRON CEMETERY

Long Island Expwy.

ST. JOHN'S UNIVERSITY

Hillside

Braddock Ave.

Jericho

QUEENS VILLAGE

BELMONT PARK

Central

Homelawn St.

HOLLIS

Hempstead Ave.

NASSAU

Spicy Lanka

JAMAICA

YORK COLLEGE

Liberty Ave.

ST. ALBANS

COUNTY

Lavrador ○

RICHMOND HILL

MONTEFIORE CEMETERY

BAISLEY POND PARK

AQUEDUCT RACE TRACK

SOUTH OZONE PARK

LAURELTON

J. F. KENNEDY INTERNATIONAL

ROSEDALE

JAMAICA BAY

**C**

Uma's ● Thai Rock ● Beach Bisto 96

**D**

441

# ARHARN THAI 😳

*Thai*

χ

The look here may be demure with its pale pink walls and gilded artwork, but this gem serves up a bounty of bold, northern-leaning specialties. And though tables are draped in embroidered linen, glass tops encourage diners to partake in the flavor-packed cooking as lustily as they please.

A shelf of snacks is the extent of the restaurant's retail component, but these will be the last thing on your mind after consuming their excellent gai yang sided by sweet chili sauce; or nua nam tok, a warm salad of grilled steak tossed with roasted rice powder, red onion slivers, and fragrant herbs. The yum woon sen combines glass noodles with stir-fried ground pork, fresh chilies, and a liberal amount of bright dressing redolent of lime and fish sauce.

■ 32-05 36th Ave. (bet. 32nd & 33rd Sts.)
🚇 36 Av
📞 (718) 728-5563 — **WEB:** www.thaiastoria.com
■ Lunch & dinner daily

PRICE: 😞

# ASIAN JEWELS 🍴

*Seafood*

χχ | 🍽️ 🎿

Arguably the best dim sum in Flushing, this spectacular gem is an absolute must for anyone seeking serious seafood and very authentic Cantonese cooking. A longtime resident of 39th Avenue, the expansive dining room is outfitted with round, banquet-style tables, bamboo plants, and ornate chandeliers.

Let the feasting begin with memorable crab-and-pork soup dumplings, before moving on to the thrill-inducing dim sum carts. Taste the likes of steamed rice rolls with honey-roast pork; pork spareribs with rice starch and black beans; chicken and ham wrapped in yuba; and poached jellyfish with scallions and sesame. The signature Dungeness crab—steamed and stir-fried with ginger and green onions, served with Japanese eggplant and garlic—is simply outstanding.

■ 133-30 39th Ave. (bet. College Point Blvd. & Prince St.)
🚇 Flushing - Main St
📞 (718) 359-8600 — **WEB:** www.asianjewelsseafood.com
■ Lunch & dinner daily

PRICE: $$

# AYADA 🍴

*Thai*

✗

A bright green sign leads the way to little Ayada, where the décor's a bit plain but the food is anything but. Inside the popular Thai restaurant, guests are greeted with a smattering of tables; a simple, but homey setting; and a warm, family-focused staff to walk them through the menu.

And what a menu it is, with dishes like the crispy catfish salad, paired with green mango and laced with a perfectly balanced lime dressing; a whole, deep-fried snapper, served with shredded green mango and tamarind sauce; a bowl of chewy drunken noodles sporting crisp green beans and tender chicken in a fragrant chili-garlic sauce; or fresh ripe mango and sticky rice, steamed to pearly, translucent perfection and carrying flavors of sweetened coconut milk.

- 77-08 Woodside Ave. (bet. 77th & 78th Sts.)
- Elmhurst Av
- (718) 424-0844 — **WEB:** N/A
- Lunch & dinner daily                                    PRICE: $$

# BAHARI ESTIATORIO 🍴

*Greek*

✗

Astoria is awash in good Greek food, but Bahari estiatorio still sets itself apart. Hiding behind an unassuming façade, the dining room is clean, generously sized and simple—think exposed red brick, white walls, and tables draped with paper placemats featuring the Greek Isles. Service is friendly and knowledgeable.

Everything on the menu here is a temptation, but a collection of traditional casserole dishes under the mageirefta portion of the menu offers the coziest of baked Greek dishes. One example, saganaki methysmeno, arrives bubbling with caramelized kefalograviera cheese and a tomato-red wine sauce. Papatsouki, or tender roasted eggplant stuffed with ground beef and a layer of fluffy caramelized béchamel, is deliciously decadent.

- 31-14 Broadway (bet. 31st & 32nd Sts.)
- Broadway
- (718) 204-8968 — **WEB:** www.bahariestiatorio.com
- Lunch & dinner daily                                    PRICE: $$

# BEACH BISTRO 96 🍴O

*Brazilian*

🍴

Helmed by Brazilian-born chef Carlos Varella and his wife, former model Andressa Junqueira, this tiny orange shack perched on the edge of the Atlantic feels more like Bahia than Rockaway Beach. Once an outer borough no-man's land in steady state of decline, the seaside Queens nabe—now a summertime destination for surfers and hipsters alike—is finally having its day in the sun.

Beach Bistro 96 is basking in that glow with a decidedly laid-back vibe, walls lined in banana leaf print paper, and pristine, simple food that celebrates Brazil in all of its delicious glory. Don't head back to the surf without sampling the feijoada, a stew-like specialty bursting with pork and black beans; or the pasteis, golden-fried empanadas filled with tasty ground beef.

■ 95-19 Rockaway Beach Blvd. (at Beach 96 St.)
🚇 Beach 98 St
✆ (718) 474-6000 — **WEB:** www.beachbistro96.com
■ Lunch & dinner Tue – Sun                    PRICE: 🍴🍴

# CASA DEL CHEF BISTRO 😊

*Contemporary*

🍴 | ⑤

Heart, passion, and skill—this inviting bistro embodies the spirit of its dedicated owners. Chef Alfonso Zhicay earned his stripes at some of New York's finest, including Blue Hill at Stone Barns; his daughter is the one-woman show behind the personal, warm service. In a cozy room with large glass windows, elegant (and often vegetable-driven) dishes comfort and surprise.

The four-course prix-fixe is a remarkable value, perhaps beginning with a mushroom confit tart showcasing meaty strips of portobellos, mushroom purée, and truffle oil. Move on to savory pasta courses like orzo folded with seasonal vegetable ragout, topped with parmesan foam. Chocolate-hued braised short ribs sit among braised savoy cabbage, buttery potatoes, and hits of citrus horseradish.

■ 39-06 64th St. (bet. 39th & Roosevelt Aves.)
🚇 69 St
✆ (718) 457-9000 — **WEB:** www.casadelchefny.com
■ Dinner nightly                    PRICE: $$

# CASA ENRÍQUE ✿

*Mexican*

XX | 🏠 🛋

**MAP:** B3

Chiapas. Puebla. San Luis Potosí. One can literally taste the regions and cities that Chef Cosme Aguilar's amazingly complex menu explores— including his own childhood recipes to honor his mother's memory. A steady stream of hungry diners seek out this rather small, tasteful dining room for friendly yet professional service and soul-warming fare. Aim for the large, fantastic communal table.

Start your meal with hearty rajas con crema, combining none-too-spicy poblanos with sweet, fresh corn, Mexican sour cream, and cheese served alongside a stack of fresh and slightly toasty tortillas. This kitchen's tender chicken enchiladas with mole de Piaxtla may induce swooning, thanks to a sauce that is unexpectedly sweet yet heady with bitter chocolate, raisins, almonds, cloves, cinnamon, chilies, garlic, sesame, and so much more, with incomparable results. It's the kind of food that thrills palates (and tempts wanton thoughts). Expect the chamorros de borrego al huaxamole to arrive falling off the bone and redolent of epazote, allspice, and pulla chilies. Its fruity-spicy broth is drinkable.

Every bit of every spongy and buttery layer of the cow and goat's milk pastel tres leches is absolutely worth the indulgence.

■ 5-48 49th Ave. (bet. 5th St. & Vernon Blvd.)
🚇 Vernon Blvd - Jackson Av
📞 (347) 448-6040 — **WEB:** www.henrinyc.com
■ Lunch Sat – Sun   Dinner nightly                    **PRICE:** $$

# CHEBURECHNAYA 🍴

## Central Asian

🍴 | ♿

This may be a kosher spot with no bagel in sight, but one look at its counter loaded with layers of bowl-shaped noni toki bread and you quickly realize that a meal here is a dining adventure. Specializing in Bukharian (Central Asian) cuisine, longstanding Cheburechnaya has been a neighborhood pioneer.

The focused menu is more engrossing than the décor, and it's easy to want every cumin- and paprika-laced item on it. Bring your own vodka and start with the house specialty, chebureki, an empanada-like deep-fried wrap stuffed with either hand-cut lamb seasoned with cumin, chili, cilantro, and paprika; or fennel-sparked cabbage. It may serve as the perfect complement to smoky lamb fat, tender quail, veal heart, and seared beef sweetbread kebabs.

◼ 92-09 63rd Dr. (at Austin St.)
🚇 63 Dr - Rego Park
✆ (718) 897-9080 — **WEB:** www.cheburechnaya1.com
◼ Lunch Sun – Fri   Dinner Sat – Thu          **PRICE:** 🍴

# CHRISTOS 🍴

## Steakhouse

🍴🍴 | 🍴

This beloved Astoria steakhouse has a lot going for it, but its cause for celebration is that authentic Greek accent that imbues everything here. Excellent quality beef, as in the signature prime "wedge" for two, is dry-aged in-house, charbroiled to exact specification, and finished with sea salt and dried oregano. Vibrant starters and sides underscore the Aegean spirit at play with pan-fried vlahotyri cheese, charred octopus with roasted peppers and red wine dressing, and smoked feta mashed potatoes.

Christos has a commanding presence on a quiet tree-shaded corner just off bustling Ditmars Blvd. Mixing shades of brown, the cozy and elegant dining room has a separate bar area and is lined with fish tanks stocked with live lobsters.

◼ 41-08 23rd Ave. (at 41st St.)
🚇 Astoria - Ditmars Blvd
✆ (718) 777-8400 — **WEB:** www.christossteakhouse.com
◼ Dinner nightly                              **PRICE:** $$$

# DE MOLE ♪○
*Mexican*

✗                                **MAP:** A2

If the words sweet, competent, clean, and authentic come to mind, you're most likely thinking of this heart-warming haunt for delightful Mexican. Albeit a tad small, with a second dining room in the back, rest assured that De Mole's flavors are mighty, both in their staples (burritos and tacos) and unique specials—seitan fajitas anyone?

This delightful pearl rests on a corner of low-rise buildings where Woodside meets Sunnyside, yet far from the disharmony of Queens Boulevard. Fans gather here for hearty enchiladas verdes con pollo, corn tortillas smeared with tomatillo sauce and queso blanco. Crispy chicken taquitos are topped with rich sour cream; steamed corn tamales are surprisingly light but filled with flavor; and the namesake mole is a must.

◼ 45-02 48th Ave. (at 45th St.)
◼ 46 St - Bliss St
✆ (718) 392-2161 — **WEB:** www.demolenyc.com
◼ Lunch & dinner daily                **PRICE:** ☯

# DUMPLING GALAXY ☺
*Chinese*

✗ | ♿                           **MAP:** A3

Neon bounces off all the new, shiny surfaces at Dumpling Galaxy, inside the Arcadia Mall. Navigate beyond the phone retailers and stalls to find this huge, modern space full of red booths and hanging red lights. Spiffy and inviting, this establishment is lauded for crafting scores of dumpling variations, plus comforting entrées that shouldn't be ignored.

Fill your table with a dumpling feast, stuffed chock-full of duck and mushroom, spicy-sour squash, or lamb and celery redolent of lemongrass and spices. Larger dishes are equally memorable; those cold, thick, slurp-inducing green bean noodles soaked in heady, tart black vinegar with raw white sesame seeds, cilantro, cucumbers, and wood-ear mushrooms will have you coming back for more...and then some more.

◼ 42-35 Main St. (in Arcadia Mall)
◼ Flushing - Main St
✆ (718) 461-0808 — **WEB:** www.dumplinggalaxy.com
◼ Lunch & dinner daily                **PRICE:** ☯

# GRAIN HOUSE 🍴⦿

*Chinese*

🍴

**MAP:** D1

It may be situated at the eastern edge of Queens, but a meal at Grain House is worth the trek to Little Neck. The room is amiably attended to and minimally adorned, with blue-and-white ceramic pieces lending a distinct Chinese tone to the otherwise staid but comfortable room.

Grain House brings joy to enthusiasts of Chinese cookery with a menu representing the many regions of the country's culinary map. "Homestyle" specialties include the salted, tea-smoked duck—which is, in a word, perfection—and Sichuan dishes factor prominently, as in a platter of impossibly crispy, fried tofu smacked with ground cumin and dried chilies. Succulent, soothing, and braised in a clay pot, the cabbage casserole proves this kitchen knows how to wow with subtlety, too.

■ 249-11 Northern Blvd. (bet. 249th St. & Marathon Pkwy.)
🚇 Little Neck
☎ (718) 229-8788 — **WEB:** N/A
■ Lunch & dinner daily

**PRICE:** $$

# GREGORY'S 26 CORNER TAVERNA 👻

*Greek*

🍴

**MAP:** F1

Judge a book by its cover and miss the rustic pleasures found within this old-fashioned Greek taverna. Disheveled charm fills the tiny two-room interior, festooned with Greek flags, bunches of artificial grapes, and framed countryside scenes. The bare tables are topped with butcher paper and the service is slow as molasses, but the cooking is honest and intensely flavorful.

Begin with tirokafteri, a spicy, satisfying spread of thick feta blended with pickled red chili peppers and served with hot pita points. A stuffed green horn pepper might be next, over a bed of fried squash slices and a well of garlicky scordalia. The seafood combo offers the simple pleasures of stuffed clams, mussels, lobster, and shrimp with lots of butter, lemon, and parsley...Greek style!

■ 26-02 23rd Ave. (at 26th St.)
🚇 Astoria - Ditmars Blvd
☎ (718) 777-5511 — **WEB:** N/A
■ Lunch & dinner daily

**PRICE:** $$

# HAHM JI BACH 😳
## Korean

✕✕                                    **MAP:** C1

This beloved Queens institution enjoys fine digs where they serve popular and praise-worthy Korean food. The contemporary dining room is spacious and airy, with the warm, always informative, staff buzzing from table to table. It's not uncommon for the manager to roll up her own sleeves when the pace elevates—and elevate it does, for this is not your average Korean barbecue.

It's hard to go wrong on Hahm Ji Bach's delightful menu, but don't miss the samgyeopsal, tender slabs of well-marinated pork belly sizzled to crispy perfection tableside for you to swaddle in crisp lettuce with paper-thin daikon radish, spicy kimchi, and bright scallions; or the mit bachan, a hot clay pot with soft steamed eggs, kimchi, tofu, pickled cucumbers, and spicy mackerel.

- 40-11 149th Pl. (bet. Barclay & 41st Aves.)
- Flushing - Main St
- (718) 460-9289 — **WEB:** www.hahmjibach.com
- Lunch & dinner daily                 **PRICE:** $$

# HIMALAYAN YAK 🍴
## Tibetan

✕ | ♿                                  **MAP:** F3

Broadly appealing yet truly unique, Himalayan Yak transports diners from Jackson Heights to Central Asia for a hybrid of Nepalese, Tibetan, and Indian cuisines. The room is a bit worn—a testament to its long-standing popularity—but orange walls invoke mountain sunsets; carved dark wood and colorful fabrics create a far-flung ambience.

Start with an order of momo: these steamed minced meat-filled dumplings are seasoned with scallions, cilantro, and ginger. Then sample yak in the form of sausage, stew, or cheese. Labsha is a beef and daikon curry served with tingmo, a multi-layered steamed bun for sopping up the mildly spiced sauce, which simply must not be missed. And finally the lassi, a traditional yogurt-based drink, is the perfect complement to every meal.

- 72-20 Roosevelt Ave. (bet. 72nd & 73rd Sts.)
- 74 St - Broadway
- (718) 779-1119 — **WEB:** www.himalayanyak.net
- Lunch & dinner daily                 **PRICE:** $$

449

QUEENS

# HINOMARU RAMEN ☻

*Japanese*

✗ | ♿︎                                           **MAP:** F1

What this simple spot lacks in décor, it makes up for in charming details (think friendly service, an energetic open kitchen, and a chalkboard menu). Order a Sapporo on tap and a small plate like shrimp nikuman, shrimp tempura wrapped in a steamed bun, and prepare for the main event: truly remarkable ramen. The menu lists several slurp-worthy varieties, including a to-die-for Hakata-style tonkatsu. This pork bone distillation is vigorously simmered to produce a creamy broth infused with bone marrow and stocked with straight noodles, char siu, nori, and fishcake. Equally delicious is the vegetarian variety, a soy milk base teeming with carrots, ginger, and broccoli.

For Manhattan residents, Lucky Cat, an offshoot, sits on busy East 53rd Street.

▪ 33-18 Ditmars Blvd. (bet. 33rd & 34th Sts.)
▪ Astoria - Ditmars Blvd
✆ (718) 777-0228 — **WEB:** www.hinomaruramen.com
▪ Lunch & dinner daily                    **PRICE: $$**

# HOUDINI KITCHEN LABORATORY ¶◯

*Pizza*

✗✗ | ⛲ ⬚                                       **MAP:** B2

Located in an industrial stretch of Ridgewood, this inventive pizzeria more than lives up to its creative name. Taking residence in a repurposed brewery built in the late 1800s, the red brick structure sits near the borough's massive cemeteries where this establishment's namesake has been laid to rest. While the "lab" isn't especially large, it feels cavernous nonetheless thanks to immensely high ceilings, a sparse arrangement of tables with views of the cement dome oven, and an ample covered terrace.

This kitchen whips up a small but selective menu of salads and wood-fired pies that includes the Houdini Green—a chewy crust spread with quality sauce and topped with fresh mozzarella, creamy knobs of goat cheese and flame-kissed veggies.

▪ 15-63 Decatur St. (at Wyckoff Ave.)
▪ Halsey St
✆ (718) 456-3770 — **WEB:** N/A
▪ Dinner Tue – Sun                         **PRICE:** ⬚

# HUNAN HOUSE 😃

*Chinese*

✗                                          **MAP:** A3

Located along quiet Northern Boulevard in Flushing, Hunan House offers a delicious reprieve from the street. The interior is crisp and sophisticated, with dark, ornately carved wood and thick linen tablecloths. But, the real draw here is the wonderfully authentic Hunanese fare, with its myriad fresh river fish; flavorful preserved meats; complex profiles; and mouth-puckering spice.

Hunan House's menu is filled with exotic delights, but don't miss the wonderful starter of sautéed sour string beans featuring minced pork, chilies, ginger, and garlic; smoky dried bean curd with the same preserved meat; or spicy sliced fish-Hunan style, perfectly cooked and served in a delicious pool of fiery red sauce and plated with tender bulbs of bok choy.

■ 137-40 Northern Blvd. (bet. Main & Union Sts.)
▣ Flushing - Main St
✆ (718) 353-1808 — **WEB:** www.hunanhouseflushing.com
■ Lunch & dinner daily                    **PRICE:** ⊜

# HUNAN KITCHEN 😃

*Chinese*

✗                                          **MAP:** A3

As New York's Sichuan renaissance continues apace, this pleasant and unpretentious Hunanese spot has popped up on Flushing's Main Street. The look here is tasteful and uncomplicated; the cooking is fiery and excellent.

The extensive menu of Hunan specialties includes the likes of the classic regional dish, pork "Mao's Style" simmered in soy sauce, Shaoxing wine, oil, and stock, then braised to tender perfection. Boasting heat and meat in equal amounts, the spicy-sour string beans with pork expertly combines rich and savory aromatics, vinegary beans, and fragrant pork with tongue-numbing peppercorns. The barbecue fish Hunan-style is a brilliant menu standout.

Smaller dishes, like winter melon with seafood soup, round out an expertly prepared meal.

■ 42-47 Main Street (bet. Blossom & Franklin Aves.)
▣ Flushing - Main St
✆ (718) 888-0553 — **WEB:** N/A
■ Lunch & dinner daily                    **PRICE:** ⊜

# IKI 🍴⭘

*Japanese*

✕✕ | ♿ 🛋 ⬜

MAP: A3

While One Fulton Square hasn't quite caught on, this upscale gem tucked into the Hyatt Place Hotel is a worthy anchor and addition to the local scene. Duck inside the modern glass façade and you're greeted with curving leather booths and beautiful blonde flooring. You've seen this before, you think to yourself, but this is a curious outlier— think Queens in high heels.

Diners can opt for omakase or à la carte. While the former might begin with a chilled bowl of soft tofu topped with creamy uni; the latter showcases cool kanpachi, shima aji, tai, and kinmedai nigiri. Then, tender-cooked rice, cooked in an earthenware pot, is tinted with the addition of dashi, topped with maitakes, and folded with flakes of salmon for a bright assortment.

▪ 133-42 39th Ave. (bet. College Point Blvd & Prince St.)
▪ Flushing - Main St
☏ (718) 939-3388 — **WEB:** www.ikicuisuine.com
▪ Lunch & dinner daily

PRICE: $$$

# IL BACCO 🍴⭘

*Italian*

✕✕ | ♿ 🛋 ⬜

MAP: D1

With its striking Mediterranean façade, crimson awnings, and rooftop garden, Il Bacco is hard to miss. This local favorite offers a stylish Little Neck-by-way-of-Tuscany setting for enjoying their thoughtfully crafted classics with top-notch ingredients. A seasoned staff guides patrons through the many menu temptations.

The kitchen dutifully honors Italian-American staples with skill. The pizza oven is a beauty, churning out perfect pies, while tables pile up with salads of fennel, red radicchio, pitted olives, and orange, as well as pastas like house-made spinach fettuccine with peas, cream, mushrooms, and parmesan. Portions are generous but do not sacrifice quality, which is clear in the hefty rack of lamb with brandy sauce and simple roasted potatoes.

▪ 253-24 Northern Blvd. (bet. Little Neck Pkwy & Westmoreland St.)
☏ (718) 224-7657 — **WEB:** www.ilbaccoristorante.com
▪ Lunch & dinner daily

PRICE: $$

# IL POETA 👓
## *Italian*

✗✗                                          **MAP:** B2

Queens is teeming with family-owned Italian restaurants dishing up the red sauce, and yet Il Poeta manages to carve out a unique place among its competitors by cooking real classics that locals can't help but enjoy. Perched on a quaint corner of Forest Hills, the fresh décor is simple but elegant, with a suited staff and vibrant pieces of art lining the walls.

Chef Mario di Chiara knows a thing—or ten—about Italian fare: you can't miss with items like cannelloni gratinati al profumo di tartufo, a homemade pasta plump with veal and carrot, baked in buttery béchamel, and kissed with truffle oil; or pollo spezzatino alla pizzaiola con salsiccia, a rustic chicken stewed in a light-as-air tomato sauce pocked with sweet porky sausage and roasted peppers.

■ 98-04 Metropolitan Ave. (at 69th Rd.)
℘ (718) 544-4223 — **WEB:** www.ilpoetarestaurant.com
■ Lunch & dinner Tue – Sun                  **PRICE:** $$


# JOE'S SHANGHAI ⅙◯
## *Chinese*

✗ | 💲                                       **MAP:** A3

Diners at this venerable Flushing institution are greeted with menus and a dish of black vinegar dipping sauce, as it's practically a given that you'll be ordering their famous xiao long bao here. Despite stiff competition, these soup dumplings—soft and delicate with perfectly spiraled shoulders and a mouthful of lip-smacking golden broth wrapped inside—still stand a head above the rest. In fact, these chefs have made it their mission to ensure biting into them is a sensual experience.

But there are other pleasures to be had here, too, such as steamed cabbage in light broth scattered with dried shrimp, or the popular Shanghainese lion's head meatballs. Made from ground pork, the latter are incredibly light and lacquered with a dark, savory glaze.

■ 136-21 37th Ave. (bet. Main & Union Sts.)
🚇 Flushing - Main St
℘ (718) 539-3838 — **WEB:** www.joeshanghairestaurants.com
■ Lunch & dinner daily                      **PRICE:** $$

# JOHN BROWN SMOKEHOUSE 🐷

*Barbecue*

✗ | 🍴 🏠

Regional barbecue has arrived in the city, but John Brown continues his reign as the true "bawss" for Kansas-style bites. The décor is minimal with a front area plating infinite orders, but find a seat in the back and settle in for a serious shindig. Amid sepia-toned photos and a flat-screen showing football (a religion here), find famished city folk ordering perfectly done proteins served with a thick and rich barbecue sauce.

Rib tips and burnt ends are juicy, tender, and sumptuous when paired with baked beans studded with bits of smoked meat or killer mac-and-cheese that is appropriately bright orange, creamy, and sparked by black pepper. An order of the corn pudding is a must, and nicely caps off a meal here. Fingerlicking is an inevitable end.

🔲 10-43 44th Dr. (bet. 10th & 11th Sts.)

🚇 Court Sq - 23 St

☎ (347) 617-1120 — **WEB:** www.johnbrownseriousbbq.com

🔲 Lunch & dinner daily

**PRICE: $$**

# JORA 🍴

*Peruvian*

✗✗ | ♿

Peruvian pottery and tapestries set a casually elegant scene at this neighborhood gem, which is quickly earning a loyal following for its frothy pisco sours and dishes full of spice and flavor. Beyond the limestone façade, the deep, narrow dining room is filled with light from arched windows and boasts a wall covered in river stones as well as a relaxed bar with striking artwork.

The diversity of Peruvian cuisine is on tasty display here, from classic items like ceviche mixto with crunchy red onion, oversized kernels of corn and sweet potato, to chupe de camarones—a thick, restorative soup of rice, seafood, and gently poached eggs. A juicy skirt steak with sautéed onions, peppers, cilantro, and sweet plantains on the side will satisfy carnivores.

🔲 47-46 11th St (at 48th Ave.)

🚇 Vernon Blvd - Jackson Av

☎ (718) 392-2033 — **WEB:** www.jorany.com

🔲 Lunch Fri – Sun   Dinner nightly

**PRICE: $$**

# KANG HO DONG BAEKJEONG ㏘

*Korean*

✗✗

The Korean barbecue of the moment is a short LIRR trip away, and well worth the ride. This was the first East Coast branch of (Korean wrestler and TV personality) Kang Ho Dong's growing empire—and it is among the best in the city. A younger sib now resides in midtown.

The menu is focused, the space is enormous, the air is clean, and the service is friendly. Start your grill off with steamed egg, corn, cheese, and more to cook along the sides while marbled pork belly or deeply flavorful marinated skirt steak strips sizzle at the center. Bibimbap is a classic rendition, mixing beef seasoned with gochujang, vegetables, sesame, nori, and crisp sprouts in a hot stone bowl—so hot that it sears the bottom rice to golden while cooking the raw egg on top.

- 152-12 Northern Blvd. (bet. 153rd & Murray Sts.)
- Flushing - Main St (& Bus Q13)
- (718) 886-8645 — **WEB:** N/A
- Lunch & dinner daily

PRICE: $$

# KATSUNO ㏘

*Japanese*

✗

To find Katsuno, look for the white lantern and those traditional noren curtains. Featuring less than ten tables, what this Japanese jewel lacks in size it makes up for in flavor and attitude. The owner's wife greets each guest at the door, while Chef Katsuyuki Seo dances around the miniscule kitchen crafting precise Japanese dishes from top-quality ingredients.

His elegant plating of sashimi may reveal the likes of amberjack topped with a chiffonade of shiso, luxurious sea urchin, translucent squid crested with needle-thin yuzu zest, as well as supremely fresh fluke, tuna, and mackerel. Meanwhile, carb fans will enjoy a warm bowl of soba in duck broth with tender duck breast; or the fantastically brothy inaniwa udon, served only on special nights.

- 103-01 Metropolitan Ave. (at 71st Rd.)
- Forest Hills - 71 Av
- (718) 575-4033 — **WEB:** www.katsunorestaurant.com
- Dinner Wed – Sun

PRICE: $$

# KITCHEN 79 🍴

*Thai*

XX | &. 🍤

Shiny black subway tiles and glowing fixtures set a dateworthy tone at this new Thai standout. Patient, helpful servers assist in exploring the menu, focused mainly on dishes of southern Thailand. Patrons can choose to be as adventurous as the sometimes familiar yet authentic and funky menu allows.

Thick green curry (gaeng kiew warn) is packed with tender shrimp, bamboo shoots, eggplant, Chinese long beans, and holy basil simmered in coconut milk with pleasantly restrained spicing. A whole flounder (pla neung ma nao) is brilliant, distinct, and steamed to perfection with sour and spicy notes from garlic, minced ginger, and a Thai hot sauce. Flat noodles (ka nom jeen gang tai pla) with pumpkin, mackerel, and curry paste is a powerful, spicy dish.

■ 37-70 79th St. (bet. Roosevelt & 37th Aves.)
🚇 82 St - Jackson Hts
✆ (718) 803-6227 — **WEB:** www.kitchen79nyc.com
■ Lunch & dinner daily

PRICE: ∞

# KURRY QULTURE 🍴

*Indian*

XX | 🍤

Noted Chef Hemant Mathur and owner Sonny Solomon bring their considerable talents to this contemporary collaboration set on a busy stretch of Astoria. Inside, the vibe is friendly and casual, in an attractive room that extends from a front bar to brick-lined dining room and open back patio.

The regional (and sub-regional) Indian cooking is both tasty and high achieving, beginning with mirchri ka salan featuring a complex peanut- coconut and sesame seed-base spiced with fresh-ground tamarind, curry leaf, and fenugreek. More notable is the fact that this may be a mere accompaniment to a very interesting South Indian riff on vegetarian biryani, made wonderfully fragrant with fluffy rice and jackfruit. The slow-cooked bhuna gosht is silky, gamey excellence.

■ 36-05 30th Ave. (bet. 36th & 37th Sts.)
🚇 30 Av
✆ (718) 674-1212 — **WEB:** www.kurryqulture.com
■ Lunch Sat - Sun   Dinner nightly

PRICE: $$

# M. WELLS STEAKHOUSE ¶○

*Gastropub*

XX | 🍸 ら 🛋   **MAP:** B3

First impressions can be deceiving at this hip Queens gastropub. From the outside, M. Wells Steakhouse looks like the old auto body garage it's housed in, but step inside and the interior is all gloss and swagger. The dining room is a dark, sultry space—from its gold-and-black wallpapered ceiling and crystal chandeliers, to its sexy red walls, stunning bar area, and open, wood-burning kitchen. Of course, the service is just as polished as the design.

Though the kitchen bills itself as a steakhouse, you can't go wrong with the excellent raw bar, creative fish entrées (maybe the "trout no trout" composed with potatoes and cabbage?), and unique appetizers. Of course desserts, like pouding chômeur topped with maple syrup, remain as outstanding as ever.

■ 43-15 Crescent St. (bet. 43rd Ave. & 44th Rd.)
🚇 Court Sq - 23 St
☏ (718) 786-9060 — **WEB:** www.magasinwells.com
■ Dinner Wed – Sat    **PRICE:** $$$$

# MAR'S ¶○

*Seafood*

X | 🍸 🛋 ⬛   **MAP:** E2

Oh, Astoria, fine—you're finally the coolest kid on the culinary block. Mar's, a charming oyster bar plucked out of another century, is a good example of why: with its weathered seaside tavern décor, whitewashed walls, and curving bar, you'll feel dropped into a sun-bleached, turn-of-the-century photo.

Most of the menu is given over to raw seafood and New England classics; part, to Mediterranean tavern small plates like sweetbreads and steak tartare. Kick things off with the excellent Mar's chowder, bobbing with briny clams, tender potatoes, bacon, and thyme. Then move on to sautéed sweetbreads with buttery fingerlings, pickled onion, and a swirl of balsamic reduction; or the house lobster roll kicked up with salty batons of Granny Smith apple.

■ 34-21 34th Ave. (at 35th St.)
🚇 Steinway St
☏ (718) 685-2480 — **WEB:** www.lifeatmars.com
■ Lunch Sat – Sun   Dinner nightly    **PRICE:** $$$

# MP TAVERNA ⅋○
*Greek*

✗✗ | 🍺 ♿ ⛲ 🛶

MAP: F1

Just in case you still weren't convinced of Astoria's hopping dining scene, enter MP Taverna—courtesy of Greek food God, Michael Psilakis. No one owns the modern Greek kitchen like this beloved author, chef, and local who manages to keep his food authentic and uniquely refined. And here he does it again, this time in a fun, tri-level space boasting a cool, industrial feel with wood paneling, iron chairs, and an impressive patio for warmer months.

For a more intimate feel, head to the second floor decked with leather chairs and chandeliers, or better yet, the rooftop terrace. Any place you land, be prepared for delicious fare: a perfectly cooked fillet of sole arrives stuffed with spinach, feta, and dill, and is finished in a wine-caper sauce.

▪ 31-29 Ditmars Blvd. (at 33rd St.)
▪ Astoria - Ditmars Blvd
☏ (718) 777-2187 — **WEB:** www.michaelpsilakis.com
▪ Lunch & dinner daily

PRICE: $$

# MU RAMEN 😄
*Japanese*

✗ | 🍺

MAP: B3

What began as a pop-up found an insanely popular home behind an unmarked door in this industrial yet residential nook of Long Island City. Lines never cease; arrive early if possible. A thick wood block serves as a communal table in the dining room, where slurpers can witness the focus and dedication of chefs working within an open kitchen in the back.

The kitchen's methodical devotion results in a superior bowl of ramen. In the spicy miso ramen, springy noodles (from Sun Noodle) are nested in a red miso- and pork-based soup of rich bone broth that slowly simmers for over 24 hours. Topped with scallion, ground pork, sesame, and chili oil, it is one of many rewarding bowls. Okonomiyaki are ethereally light, with smoked trout and shaved bonito.

▪ 12-09 Jackson Ave. (bet. 47th Rd. & 48th Ave.)
▪ Vernon Blvd - Jackson Av
☏ (917) 868-8903 — **WEB:** N/A
▪ Dinner nightly

PRICE: $$

# MYTHOS ⅋○
## Greek

XX | ♿ ⌂        **MAP:** C1

A gathering place for Greeks and non-Greeks alike, this family-run and friendly restaurant tempts with impeccably fresh fish, cooked over charcoal and basted simply with olive oil, lemon juice, and herbs. Beyond the whitewashed exterior and dark blue awning is a large dining room with rows of neat tables for indulging in Hellenic pleasures, from zesty appetizers to boisterous conversations.

Settle into an array of pikilia; cold appetizers such as melitzansalata, eggplant whipped with herbs and olive oil. Chargrilled fish, priced by the pound, has a delightfully smoky essence and moist flesh. Whole smelts are a rare and traditional treat, simply pan-fried with a lemony herb dressing. Finish with a choice of authentic, nutty, and syrup-soaked pastries.

▪ 196-29 Northern Blvd. (bet. 196th St. & Francis Lewis Blvd.)
☏ (718) 357-6596 — **WEB:** www.mythosnyc.com
▪ Lunch & dinner daily        **PRICE: $$**


# NATURAL TOFU ⅋○
## Korean

X        **MAP:** A2

This is the sort of place you've walked by a hundred times and never noticed, but look up, because the house-made tofu here is unrivaled. The space may be more functional than cozy, but this staff knows how to treat their customers—from welcoming each table with a succulent assortment of banchan to happily adjusting a dish's spice level.

They also clearly know the many secrets of tofu: the kitchen makes its own, on view at the front of the restaurant, then deploys it in a series of silken soondubu (soft bean curd stews). Served scalding hot in a ddukbaegi or glazed earthenware cauldron, this bubbling piquant broth contains your choice of pork, seafood, or even beef intestine—but kimchi, the funky favorite, is the hands-down winner.

▪ 40-06 Queens Blvd. (bet. 40th & 41st Sts.)
🚇 40 St
☏ (718) 706-0899 — **WEB:** N/A
▪ Lunch & dinner daily        **PRICE: $$**

# NUSARA 🍴⊙
## Thai

🍴

Despite its less-than-impressive strip mall surroundings, this Thai kitchen—a haven of soft pink walls and cordial servers—is nothing short of wonderful. Bypass the small selection of snacks available for purchase, and instead settle in to a table to peruse the menu and prepare for the aromatic and savory feast ahead.

Begin with the som tum Lao-style, a traditional green papaya salad made less so with the stimulating addition of salty anchovies. Then crispy pork may top the pick-your-protein options for noodles and entrées. Additionally, those deep-fried bits of pork belly are a treat when thrown into creamy red chili- and coconut-based chu chee curry. And as an ideal accompaniment to any of the curries, look no further than the salted fish fried rice.

▪ 82-80 Broadway (at Whitney Ave.)
▣ Elmhurst Av
℘ (718) 898-7996 — **WEB:** www.nusarathaikitchen.com
▪ Lunch & dinner daily

PRICE: $$

# O LAVRADOR 🍴⊙
## Portuguese

XX | ⊡

This throwback pleases with rib-sticking Portuguese fare and an attention to hospitality. Choose between two experiences: the long, well-worn bar (which may be rowdy with soccer fans) or the spacious dining room, reached through lovely arches. Seasoned servers know how to charm and keep customers patient, as dishes are made to order and can take time.

Zoom in on anything with bacalhau here, a superior air-dried fish (not salt-cured) with excellent flavor and texture. The bacalhau à pescador sates with a stew of clams, mussels, shrimp, calamari, and potatoes. Another appealing soup is caldo verde full of meaty collards and smoky chorizo. Round out this elaborate feast with feijoada de mariscos, a slurry of white beans, seafood, and of course, more chorizo.

▪ 138-40 101st Ave. (bet. Cresskill & Sanders Pls.)
▣ Sutphin Blvd - Archer Av - JFK Airport
℘ (718) 526-1526 — **WEB:** www.olavradorrestaurant.com
▪ Lunch & dinner daily

PRICE: $$

# PACHANGA PATTERSON 🍴○

*Mexican*

🍴 | 🍸 🏠 🛶                                    **MAP:** F2

This unassuming spot for tasty Mexican food with a twist has been a smash from the start, offering much more than guacamole with chips and a margarita (though these happen to be excellent here).

Floor-to-ceiling windows, fairy lights, and quirky artifacts adorn the space while enhancing the feel-good, neighborhood vibe.

The fuchsia-painted kitchen brims with bold flavors, skill, and creativity that incorporate worldly influences. Try tacos that fold crisp and faintly honeyed pig's ear with pickled onion and none-too-spicy habanero mayo into soft, warm tortillas. Earthenware-baked enchiladas are a particular treat, perhaps rolled with shredded bits of braised lamb in rich and luscious mole coloradito, topped with a delicately set fried egg.

◼ 33-17 31st Ave. (at 34th St.)
🚇 30 Av
☏ (718) 554-0525 — **WEB:** www.pachangapatterson.com
◼ Lunch Sat – Sun   Dinner nightly                **PRICE:** $$

# PAET RIO 😊

*Thai*

🍴                                              **MAP:** F3

With so many Thai places around, it's easy to get lost in this exceptional concentration; just be sure to find yourself at Paet Rio. The design of this long and inviting room may elevate the experience, but it is their spicy and unusual cooking that makes everything shine.

The menu here is a dance of sensations—tart, spicy, sour, fresh—as seen in Chinese broccoli leaves (miang kha-na) with pork, chilies, peanuts, garlic, and lime. Grilled squid (pla muek yang) has an addictive fiery sauce, while fermented pork and sticky rice sausage (sai krok Isan) is pleasurably sour with cabbage, chili, and peanuts. End this steamy affair over noodles sautéed with pork, squid, and soy sauce (kua gai); or khao phat pla kem featuring a tasty twist on the tired fried rice.

◼ 81-10 Broadway (bet. 81st & 82nd Sts.)
🚇 Elmhurst Av
☏ (917) 832-6672 — **WEB:** N/A
◼ Lunch & dinner daily                          **PRICE:** ☺☺

# PICCOLA VENEZIA ⅋○

*Italian*

XX | 🎴 🛋 ✋                                    **MAP:** F2

This old-time idol deserves its landmark status as it has been going strong since opening in 1973. With Italian-American cooking so rampant in the city, it's wholly refreshing to happen upon a classic of such welcoming comfort. The décor is outdated, but white tablecloths are clean and crisp, and glasses gleam at the prospect of great wine varietals.

With a trio of pasta, you needn't choose between fusi swirled in a grappa- mushroom- and Grana-sauce; squid ink taglierini; or maltagliati in a roasted tomato and basil sauce with a touch of cream. Spiedini alla Romana sees thick slabs of focaccia and mozzarella dredged and fried, served with an anchovy and caper sauce, and pork osso buco is of the falling-apart-tender variety—perfect with the velvety polenta.

▪ 42-01 28th Ave. (at 42nd St.)

🚇 30 Av

✆ (718) 721-8470 — **WEB:** www.piccola-venezia.com

▪ Lunch Mon – Fri   Dinner nightly                **PRICE:** $$$$

# SABRY'S ⅋○

*Seafood*

X | 🛖                                           **MAP:** F1

There are no distractions at this authentic Egyptian café. The look is simple and alcohol isn't offered since this is a strictly Muslim establishment, but friendly service provides the small space with just enough ambience.

Seafood is without a doubt the star attraction here. Whole fish are pulled from their icy display and thrown onto a sizzling flattop to be barbecued Egyptian-style (blackened and sprinkled with spices and chopped herbs); and the fried shrimp are also a very popular option. But, no matter what main you decide on, a platter of cool and creamy spreads is the only accompaniment you'll need—especially since it's served with pillows of wonderfully chewy pita that arrives so hot you might burn your fingers ripping into it.

▪ 24-25 Steinway St. (bet. Astoria Blvd. & 25th Ave.)

🚇 Astoria Blvd

✆ (718) 721-9010 — **WEB:** N/A

▪ Lunch & dinner daily                            **PRICE:** $$

# SIK GAEK 🍴

## Korean

✗ | ♿ 🎨                                          **MAP:** C1

There may be glitzier Korean spots in town, but insanely delicious, exceedingly simple Sik Gaek assures a good time, every time. Dressed in silly costumes, the staff is always having a blast in this seasonally decorated shack-like dining room featuring corrugated metal roofs, street lights, buckets for shells, and walls papered in dollar bills. Booths along the edge are filled with noisy regulars.

The kitchen serves the ocean's bounty, starting with a deliciously crisp and gargantuan pancake, pajeon, studded with seafood and kimchi begging to be dipped in enticingly salty soy-sesame sauce. A cloudy soup bobbing with tofu arrives piping hot, boasting that sharp, nutty, telltale flavor of fermented bean curd, and seems to have its own restorative powers.

▪ 161-29 Crocheron Ave. (bet. 161st & 162nd Sts.)
▪ Flushing - Main St (& Bus Q12)
☎ (718) 321-7770 — **WEB:** N/A
▪ Dinner Tues – Sun                          **PRICE:** $$

# SPICY LANKA 🍴

## Sri Lankan

✗                                             **MAP:** C2

It's worth the trek to this far-out Jamaica restaurant for its veritable explosion of hip-hop beats, brightly colored murals of palm trees, and an unbridled enthusiasm for heat and colliding Sri Lankan flavors.

The heady aroma of spices that fills the dining room can be attributed to any number of specialties. Find a blast of flavor on the plate by way of the biryani, which is steamed for hours in a blend of cardamom, nutmeg, bay leaves, and star anise, then tossed with garlic- and ginger-marinated chicken and okra. String hoppers are another fragrant specialty, featuring rounds of steamed rice flour noodles meant to be drenched in a host of spicy embellishments, like dried chili-speckled dhal, coconut sambal, or fish curry infused with Ceylon cinnamon.

▪ 159-23 Hillside Ave. (bet. 160th St. & Parsons Blvd.)
▪ Parsons Blvd
☎ (718) 487-4499 — **WEB:** N/A
▪ Lunch & dinner daily                       **PRICE:** 🍝

# SUSHI DAIZEN 🍴🅞

*Japanese*

💥💥

The staff is upbeat, and the room is attractively minimal in design, but what really stands out here is the adoration of this little sushi-ya's devoted clientele. The mood is light and engaging as everyone digs into their omakase, with options to add sashimi or a small list of à la carte pieces.

Start your meal with a cool appetizer of enoki mushrooms in soy and dashi broth, or crisp green beans over creamy tofu. A knob of pickled ginger freshly sliced before your eyes signals the beginning of your sushi course, a progression of neatly trimmed, hand-formed morsels of fish. Highlights include excellent poached tiger shrimp, Santa Barbara sea urchin, and kawa kawa from Japan. A fatty tuna hand roll at the end of your meal serves a perfect finale.

■ 47-38 Vernon Blvd. (bet. 47th Rd. & 48th Ave.)

🚇 Vernon Blvd - Jackson Av

📞 (718) 729-1297 — **WEB:** www.sushidaizen.com

■ Dinner Tues – Sun

**PRICE: $$$$**

# SWEET YUMMY HOUSE 😊

*Chinese*

🍴

This tiny, impeccably clean dining room is drawing diners left and right to Elmhurst these days. But wait, you argue—isn't this just another Chinese joint along a stretch of Broadway filled with such Chinese joints? Not quite. In fact, Sweet Yummy House is a diamond in the rough for those hunting down authentic spice levels and Taiwanese specialties they've never heard of.

A meal might kick off with a duo of sautéed cabbages, one cooked in a delicate Taiwanese style, the other in the Shanghai tradition, sporting fiery oil. Then move on to tender, crispy chicken and pickled turnips in a nose-twitching spicy sauce; before lingering over deep and dark cold jelly, rendered Chengdu-style, with slippery mung bean noodles and lip-numbing Sichuan peppercorns.

■ 83-13 Broadway (bet. Cornish & Dongan Aves.)

🚇 Elmhurst Av

📞 (718) 699-2888 — **WEB:** N/A

■ Lunch & dinner daily

**PRICE: $$**

# TAIWANESE GOURMET ¶○

*Chinese*

✗ | 〔$〕      **MAP:** F3

A truly local spot, Taiwanese Gourmet puts diners in the mood with its semi-open kitchen (a rarity for Chinese restaurants) and tasty food. Natural light floods the walls, which showcase an impressive collection of ancient warrior gear, all beautifully framed as if museum-ready. Menu descriptions are minimal but the staff is happy to elaborate.

Excellent technique shines through the Taiwanese specialties, notably in strips of "shredded beef" sautéed in a dark, meaty paste, and tossed with dried tofu that balances complex flavors with fresh Chinese celery—a hands down winner on the menu. Likewise, the stir-fry of wonderfully briny clams and basil offers a perfect balance of sweet and salty flavors with oyster sauce, soy, rice wine, and red chilies.

■ 84-02 Broadway (at St. James Ave.)
🚇 Elmhurst Av
✆ (718) 429-4818 — **WEB:** N/A
■ Lunch & dinner daily      **PRICE:** ⊜

# TANG ¶○

*Korean*

✗✗ | ♿ 🖐      **MAP:** C1

When craving authentic Korean specialties, Tang is an absolute must-visit. The restaurant's impeccably cool style extends from its angled exterior ablaze in beams of yellow light to its sleek interior with exposed brick walls and bare wood tables. The attractive art gallery next door is attached and doubles as a private dining space.

Meals begin with an unending supply of wonderfully crisp and mild house kimchi. Also try the hearty bibimbap of marinated beef strips, root vegetables, and mushrooms alongside a bowl of ox-bone broth. The main attraction is the sensational jeon, traditional Korean pancakes grilled to order (weekend dinners only). Round out the meal with steamed pigs feet accompanied by Tang's special fiery, salty, shrimp-based dipping sauce.

■ 196-50 Northern Blvd. (at Francis Lewis Blvd.)
✆ (718) 279-7080 — **WEB:** N/A
■ Lunch & dinner daily      **PRICE:** $$

# TAVERNA KYCLADES ᵞ⃝

*Greek*

𝖄

Forget the no-frills surroundings and focus instead on the fantastically fresh fish. This beloved Greek spot (with a second location in the East Village) has folks happily dining elbow to elbow in a tiny yet lively space where the bustling kitchen is in view and seafaring scenes paint the walls. Quick, straightforward servers may address you in Greek if you look the part—that's just how local it gets here.

Grab a seat on the enclosed patio for some serenity and get things going with garlicky and bubbling hot crab-stuffed clams; or the cold, classic trio of powerful skordalia, cooling tzatziki, and briny taramosalata served with toasted pita triangles. Order a side of horta (steamed escarole and dandelion) to accompany a plate of sweet and delicate mullets, served with a side of lemon potatoes.

▪ 33-07 Ditmars Blvd. (bet. 33rd & 35th Sts.)

▪ Astoria - Ditmars Blvd

℘ (718) 545-8666 — **WEB:** www.tavernakyclades.com

▪ Lunch & dinner daily

**PRICE:** ⊜⊜

# THAI ROCK ᵞ⃝

*Thai*

𝖄 | ♿ 🏠

The "rock" in Thai Rock is not just a reference to the restaurant's location in the beachside Rockaways, but a nod to the live music that takes over after the sun dips down. Inside, you'll find tightly packed wooden tables and comfortable high-backed chairs, but the large uncovered patio overlooking the bay is certainly the place to be come summer.

The menu covers the usual Thai standards—think pad Thai, curries, and various stir fries—as well as a few Northern Thai specialties, with aplomb. Don't miss the plump and tender dumplings stuffed with crunchy turnips, peanuts, and fragrant garlic; refreshing chicken larb gai, laced with a bright and zesty lime sauce featuring mint and scallion; or the delicious and very savory Issan sausage.

▪ 375 Beach 92nd St. (at Beach Channel Dr.)

▪ Beach 90 St

℘ (718) 945-5111 — **WEB:** www.thairock.us

▪ Lunch & dinner daily

**PRICE:** $$

# TITO RAD'S GRILL ⅉ◐

*Filipino*

XX | 💼          **MAP:** E3

This eclectic grill seduces with its perfectly encapsulated fusion of the Malay, Spanish, Chinese, and Japanese flavors that typify the wholly unique cuisine of the Philippines. Cozy touches accent the décor and a mix of light stone with dark wood strikes just the right balance between contemporary and familiar.

Bold and generously portioned, the authentic specialties here have amassed a devout following. Highlights from the extensive pork- and seafood-dominated menu might include binagoongang baboy, tender chunks of pork cooked in a shrimp paste-sparked sauce made rich with melted fat; and adobo fried rice studded with crunchy and delicious bits of pork belly skin. If it's on offer, be sure to opt for the inihaw na panga or grilled tuna jaw.

🔲 49-10 Queens Blvd. (bet. 49th & 50th Sts.)
🚇 46 St - Bliss St
✆ (718) 205-7299 — **WEB:** www.titorads.com
🔲 Lunch & dinner daily        **PRICE:** 🍝

# TONG SAM GYUP GOO YI 😊

*Korean*

X | ⓢ          **MAP:** C1

Murray Hill is no stranger to Korean food, but this prized, pig-loving barbecue destination is always packed. Inside, the bright room's décor forgoes all frills to focus on regional specialties. Smiling servers are earnest and hospitable.

Begin with the usual but very exquisite banchan-like pickled turnips, fermented bean paste soup, and specially aged house kimchi—funky, garlicky, and a total pleasure. Bowls of glassy naengmyun noodles dancing in a chilled broth with kimchi are just as popular. Yet what makes this place unique is that barbecue grill on each table, used for sizzling slices of flavorful duck with miso, garlic cloves, and bean sprouts; spicy, tender bits of octopus; and sweet, fatty pork with soy sauce, red chili paste, and scallions.

🔲 162-23 Depot Rd. (bet. Northern Blvd. & 164th St.)
🚇 Flushing - Main St (& Bus Q13)
✆ (718) 359-4583 — **WEB:** N/A
🔲 Lunch & dinner daily        **PRICE:** $$

# TRATTORIA L'INCONTRO ⭐○

*Italian*

✗✗ | ♿ ⌴ 🍽

A litany of delights sets the stage for an entertaining evening at this beloved institution of Italian-American pleasure. Frescoes of tranquil Italian scenes adorn coral walls in the unfussy dining room, complete with white-clothed tables spread at an ample distance. Service is relaxed, professional, and even theatrical in their performance of reciting special upon special.

Flavors are classic and robust, from eggplant rollatini stuffed with ricotta and herbs to the ravioli golosi, filled with both ground filet and veal, then topped with a sauce of mushrooms and sausage. Tender veal scaloppini is gently dredged and pan-fried, then bathed in a silky sauce of wine, butter, garlic, and lemon. Crunching through crisp cannoli is a divine finale.

■ 21-76 31st St. (at Ditmars Blvd.)
🚇 Astoria - Ditmars Blvd
✆ (718) 721-3532 — **WEB:** www.trattorialincontro.com
■ Lunch & dinner Tue – Sun

**PRICE: $$**

# UMA'S ⭐○

*Central Asian*

✗ | ♿

Thanks to a warm, unpretentious vibe, ukulele tunes, and the talented husband-and-wife team at its helm, this Far Rockaway haven of central Asian cuisine is as easy and breezy as its unique surf town environs.

Uma's unique interplay of flavors guarantees a delightful meal that's as hearty and fragrant as it is unpretentious: shredded Korean-style carrot salad is dressed with chili flakes and aromatic herbs, and the signature butternut squash manti—here topped with caramelized onions—are an utterly satisfying vegetarian take on the typically meat-stuffed dumplings. Daily specials are always a treat, and may reveal succulent braised lamb seasoned with cumin and rosemary, plated with sundried apricots as well as a fluffy mound of kasha.

■ 92-07 Rockaway Beach Blvd. (bet. Beach 92nd & 94th Sts.)
🚇 Beach 90 St
✆ (718) 318-9100 — **WEB:** N/A
■ Lunch & dinner daily

**PRICE: $$**

# UNCLE ZHOU ⊛

*Chinese*

X | ⌐S⌐

**MAP:** F3

Gifted cooks have been setting up in Elmhurst to show off their skills, but the chef/visionary of this modestly decked, massively popular Henanese gem has been a fixture from the start. Seat yourself inside the butterscotch-hued room, surrender to the affable staff, and await a memorable feast.

Opening this culinary show are pickled cucumbers and briny bamboo shoots with mushrooms, followed by pan-seared lamb dumplings or hugely fortifying "Dial oil" noodles sautéed with dried red chilies. For the consummate finale, pre-order "Taosibao," an impressive showpiece of rice-stuffed quail inside a squab, inside a chicken, inside a duck. Not only is this trumped-up version of turducken technically superb, but every element is flavored by an aromatic broth.

■ 83-29 Broadway (at Dongan Ave.)
🚇 Elmhurst Av
✆ (718) 393-0888 — **WEB:** N/A
■ Lunch & dinner Wed – Mon          PRICE: ⊛

# URUBAMBA ⑪⃝

*Peruvian*

X | ⅖ 🍽

**MAP:** F3

Named for Peru's intensely beautiful river, the Rio Urubamba, this hacienda-inspired space features indigenous paintings and artifacts that echo the rustic fare pouring out of the kitchen.

On weekends, the eatery serves traditional desayuno, a gut-busting feast of chanfainita beef stew and other hearty favorites. Here, tamales are a broad and flat banana leaf wrapped and stuffed with chicken and olives—a tasty contrast to the familiar Meso-American counterpart. For ultimate comfort, go for the seco de cabrito, a fantastically tender lamb and aji panca stew served with chunks of cassava and extra sauce in a tiny clay kettle. The dense alfajor cookie sandwich filled with dulce de leche and crema volteada flan is a perfectly decadent ending.

■ 86-20 37th Ave. (at 86th St.)
🚇 82 St - Jackson Hts
✆ (718) 672-2224 — **WEB:** N/A
■ Lunch & dinner daily          PRICE: $$

# VESTA TRATTORIA 🍴

*Italian*

✗ | 🛋

Ever-changing daily specials and a respectable wine list—celebrated with a weekday happy hour—have fostered the favorable reputation of Astoria's favorite trattoria. Local foodies fill the wee room, a moderately dressed space with sage-green banquettes and a wall-mounted blackboard displaying the names of farms and producers sourced for the menu's array of contemporary Italian food.

To that end, tender meatballs are braised in a serrano chili-sparked tomato sauce; and free-range chicken Milanese is plated with a swipe of roasted lemon purée. For dessert, la torta del piccolo bambino Gesu Cristo reveals a block of excellent sticky toffee pudding cake that arrives warm, caramel-soaked, and capped with a refreshing scoop of crème fraîche sorbet.

🔲 21-02 30th Ave. (at 21st St.)

🚇 30 Av

🖋 (718) 545-5550 — **WEB:** www.vestavino.com

🔲 Lunch Sat – Sun   Dinner nightly          PRICE: $$

# ZUM STAMMTISCH 🍴

*German*

✗

Family owned and operated since 1972, this unrelenting success story has expanded over the years and welcomed Stammtisch Pork Store & Imports next door.

Zum Stammtisch hosts a crowded house in a Bavarian country inn setting where old-world flavor is relished with whole-hearted enthusiasm. The goulash is thick and hearty, stocked with potatoes and beans, but that's just for starters. Save room for sauerbraten, jägerschnitzel, or a platter of succulent grilled sausages that includes bratwurst, knockwurst, and hickory-smoked krainerwurst served with sauerkraut and potato salad. The Schwarzwälder Kirschtorte (classic Black Forest cake) layers dense chocolate sponge with Kirsch-soaked cherries and cream, and is absolutely worth the indulgence.

🔲 69-46 Myrtle Ave. (bet. 69th Pl. & 70th St.)

🖋 (718) 386-3014 — **WEB:** www.zumstammtisch.com

🔲 Lunch & dinner daily          PRICE: $$

# STATEN ISLAND

# STATEN ISLAND

Staten Island may be the least populated borough of New York City, but the building of the Verrazano-Narrows Bridge ended its once bucolic existence. This fact is especially fitting because one of the strongest, most accurate simplifications is that this "island" is home to a large Italian-American population, and no self-respecting foodie visits here without picking up a calamari pizza from **Joe &** **Pat's**, or a slice from **Nunzio** and **Denino's Pizzeria &** **Tavern**. In fact, anyone with preconceived notions about this "forgotten borough" can leave them at the ferry door. Though deemed at one time the largest landfill in the world, Staten Island is currently being transformed into a verdant and very vast public park.

## CULINARY CORNUCOPIA

While it is revered as an Italian-American hub, Staten Island's shores, marinas, and waterfronts continue to surprise visitors and tourists alike with its ethnically diverse enclaves. During your time here, take a culinary tour of the Mediterranean by way of the island's numerous Italian establishments proffering such Old Country classics as pizzas, pastas, calzones, and so much more. Alternatively, stop by those popular old-time Polish delis that seem to comfortably thrive on their takeout business and homemade jams alone.

## Staten Island

Spice heads will rejoice at the fantastic Sri Lankan food finds in the area surrounding Victory Boulevard. A spectrum of restaurants (think storefronts) reside here, including **New Asha** serving the same nation's fiery cuisine. Of course, **Lanka Grocery** is an epicurean's dream featuring a riot of colorful, authentic ingredients Staying within South Asia— its cuisine and culture—this borough is also home to Jacques Marchais Museum of Tibetan Art, an institution aimed at advancing Tibetan and Himalayan art. Steps from these subcontinent gems, discover authentic taquerias and a large Liberian outdoor market in the vicinity of Grasmere, where a small but

special selection of purveyors supply West African staples and other regional treats. Take these to enjoy at home; or cook up a globally inspired feast with locally farmed produce from **Gerardi's** farmer's market in New Brighton or **St. George Greenmarket**, open on Saturdays. Historic Richmond Town pays homage to the sustainable food movement here by organizing the family-focused festival **Uncorked!**, which features the best in homemade cuisine and wine. They even offer recipes for traditional American classics. For rare and more mature varietals, **Mission Fine Wines** is top-notch, but if yearning for more calorie-heavy (heavenly) eats, **The Cookie Jar** is way above par. Opened in 2007, this youngest sibling of **Cake Chef**, a beloved bakeshop up the road and **Piece A Cake** further south on New Dorp Lane, not only incites its audience with a range of sweets but savory focaccias and soups galore.

## FOOD, FUN & FROLIC

**G**iven its booming culinary scene and cultural merging, it should come as no surprise that the Staten Island of the future includes plans for a floating farmer's market, aquarium, and revamped waterfronts, giving residents and tourists another reason to sit back and savor a drink at one of the bars along Bay Street. Couple these sips with abundant small plates at **Adobe Blues**, a cantina preparing sumptuous Southwestern food and prettified with a fireplace, clay walls, and collectibles depicting the island's... yee-haw...rodeo days! Residents and locals of course adore this neighborhood hangout for its modest demeanor and gratifying grub, and will probably continue to flock to it until the end of time.

After dawdling on Lafayette Avenue, drive through some of the city's wealthiest zip codes, featuring mansions with magnificent views of Manhattan and beyond. Whether here to glimpse the world's only complete collection of rattlesnakes at the zoo, or seek out the birthplaces of such divas as Christina Aguilera and Joan Baez, a visit to Staten Island is nothing if not interesting.

# BIN 5 ⫻○

## Contemporary

XX | 🛖

At this intimate bistro in Rosebank, dinner comes with a view of the Manhattan skyline. Complete with teardrop chandeliers and exposed brick, Bin 5's romantic setting has long drawn locals seeking good food and quiet conversation (plus that fantastic panorama!).

The playful menu—complete with solid daily specials—may reveal a perfect pan-seared and golden-brown pork loin, set atop slices of pickled red and green peppers and surrounded by a generous amount of pan sauce made from prosecco and vinegar. Then, cauliflower florets are pulsed to form couscous-like beads and cooked in the style of fried rice, studded with veggies and seasoned by soy. A tall wedge of pistachio-walnut cake dusted with powdered sugar is a light, fluffy and fitting finale.

◾ 1233 Bay St. (bet. Maryland & Scarboro Aves.)

🚆 Bus S51, S81

📞 (718) 448-7275 — **WEB:** www.bin5nyc.com

◾ Dinner Tue – Sun                    **PRICE:** $$

# ENOTECA MARIA 😊

## Italian

X | ⑤

No need to venture far on Staten Island for excellent Italian. Enoteca Maria is just blocks from the St. George Terminal and brought to you by Jody Scaravella, whose cookbook Nonna's House has been earning him (and this tiny gem) much applause. With its Carrara marble and lively vibe, most foodies flock here for a certain authenticity that is rarely sacrificed.

Each night, the menu changes depending on which nonna is presiding over the kitchen, as in Nina from Belarus, who might serve a salat Odessa mingling grilled eggplant, red onion, tomato and parsley. Lasagna de Adelina arrives as an inspired layering of zucchini, basil pesto and cream cheese, all topped with parmesan. And for a bit of sweet, try the torta di vaniglia di Melissa served with whipped cream.

◾ 27 Hyatt St. (bet. Central Ave. & St. Marks Pl.)

📞 (718) 447-2777 — **WEB:** www.enotecamaria.com

◾ Lunch Wed – Fri   Dinner Wed – Sun       **PRICE:** $$

# GIULIANA'S 🍴

*Italian*

✗✗ | ♿ ⬚

Staten Island may swarm with Italian-American eateries, but this festive classic does a masterful job in keeping its kitchen distinct and the patrons loyal. Guiliana's is the queen bee amid shops, catering halls, and ample competition. The interior is modest and charming, with framed pictures of smiling patrons and a fully stocked bar.

Hearty stracciatella is loaded with spinach and a comforting sauce of eggy parmesan, finished with a generous shower of black pepper. Seek out the perciatelle con sarde, a Sicilian-style pasta tossed in a powerful blend of fennel, saffron, raisins, sardines, anchovy paste, and a crunch of toasted breadcrumbs. A trio of gelatos—pistachio, chocolate, and bitter almond, served with biscotti—is a divine ending.

■ 4105 Hylan Blvd. (at Osborn Ave.)
🚍 Bus S54, S78, S79
☎ (718) 317-8507 — **WEB:** www.giulianassi.com
■ Lunch & dinner Tue – Sun **PRICE:** $$

# LAKRUWANA 🍴

*Sri Lankan*

✗ | ⓢ **MAP:** B2

Prepare for a sensory overload the moment you set foot into Lakruwana—the Sri Lankan hot spot is covered from floor-to-ceiling in murals, sculptures, flags, and more. The bright kaleidoscope of textures and colors is a welcome sight in an otherwise downtrodden part of the borough, as is the energetic owner who drifts from table to table.

Those familiar with Indian food will love Lakruwana's abundance of curries, green chili-spiked kuttu roti, as well as refreshingly salty-and-sour lassi. But their flavorful fare is considerably spicier, packing heat into everything from fiery red chili lunu miris chutney to deviled chicken. Loaded with ginger and garlic, this stellar tomato-based chicken specialty comes with cooling raita and tangy vegetable curry.

■ 668 Bay St. (at Broad St.)
🚍 Bus S51, S76
☎ (347) 857-6619 — **WEB:** www.lakruwana.com
■ Lunch Fri – Wed  Dinner Tue – Sun **PRICE:** ☜

# PHIL AM KUSINA ⅋○

*Filipino*

Ⅹ | ♿                                           **MAP:** B2

This charming dining room is located amidst a mostly residential neighborhood blocks away from busy Bay Street. The peaked-roof interior is brightened by skylights and pale peach walls, and the jovial vibe is amplified by genuinely gracious service.

The menu offers a wide range of Filipino specialties including fried delights, noodle preparations, and simmered specialties like humba—a lusciously tender and fatty pork shank slow-simmered with soy sauce and pineapple. A side of crispy garlic-flecked rice is the perfect accompaniment to this sweet-and-salty treat. Inspired to whip something up in the comfort of your own kitchen? Just head across the street, where a long-standing Filipino grocery store shares the same name and family ownership.

▪ 556 Tompkins Ave. (bet. Clifton Ave. & Hylan Blvd. )
▪ Bus S53
✆ (718) 727-3672 — **WEB:** www.philamkusina.com
▪ Lunch & dinner Thu – Tue                    **PRICE:** ⊜

# SAN RASA 😊

*Sri Lankan*

Ⅹ                                              **MAP:** B2

A little excursion to Staten Island is a must for knock-your-socks-off Sri Lankan food. Life is short, and honestly so is that charming ferry ride, which deposits you on this local island destination. Then step inside the bright and large San Rasa only to find sleek wood accents and vessels lined up for their popular Sunday lunch buffet.

Their food is prepared fresh to order, offering the perfect excuse to nurse a cold, salty lassi while you wait. Dinner may begin with a starter of string hoppers or crispy little pancakes laced in a rich fish curry carrying hints of clove, fennel, and cardamom; and then move on to the lampri, a succulent little bundle of beef curry wrapped in banana leaf with nutty yellow rice, eggplant, and cashews.

▪ 226 Bay St. (bet. Hannah & Minthorne Sts.)
▪ Bus S51
✆ (718) 682-1653 — **WEB:** www.sanrasa.com
▪ Lunch & dinner Wed – Mon                    **PRICE:** ⊜

# VIDA

*American*

X | $

All the locals love Vida, where popular Chef/owner Silva Popaz has created a cozy little restaurant with a firm commitment to simple, but well-executed, dishes. Inside the café-like atmosphere, you'll find unique artwork lining brightly painted walls, and a smattering of tables surrounding a long communal wood table in the center.

The charming Popaz travels quite often, and the flavors she picks up along her journeys tend to make their way back into her menu at Vida. The "Mexican Duo"—her most popular dish—features pulled pork- and chicken-stuffed tortillas, topped with a vibrant Chimayo chile and tangy cheese sauce, and paired with tender stewed beans sporting bright green onion; while a delicate bread pudding arrives puddled in creamy vanilla ice cream.

▦ 381 Van Duzer St. (bet. Beach & Wright Sts.)

▦ Bus S78

✆ (718) 720-1501 — **WEB:** www.vidany.com

▦ Dinner Tue – Sat                    **PRICE:** $$

The ✿ symbol indicates
a private dining room option.

MICHELIN
IS CONTINUALLY
INNOVATING
FOR SAFER, CLEANER,
MORE ECONOMICAL,
MORE CONNECTED
AND BETTER ALL
AROUND MOBILITY.

*Tires wear more quickly on short urban journeys.*

**?** **TRUE!**

You tend to accelerate and brake more often when driving around town so your tires work harder!
If you are stuck in traffic, keep calm and drive slowly.

*Tire pressure only affects your car's safety.*

**?** **FALSE!**

Driving with underinflated tires (0.5 below recommended pressure) doesn't just impact handling and fuel consumption, it will take 8,000 km off tire lifespan.
Make sure you check tire pressure about once a month and before you go on vacation or a long journey.

If you only encounter **winter weather from time to time** - sudden showers, snowfall or black ice - **one type of tire** will do the job.

**?**

**TRUE!**

The revolutionary **MICHELIN CrossClimate** - the very first summer tire with winter certification - is a practical solution to keep you on the road whatever the weather.

Fitting **2 winter tires** on my car guarantees maximum safety.

**?**

## FALSE!

In the winter, especially when temperatures drop below 44.5°F, to ensure better road grip, all four tires should be identical and fitted at the same time.

**2 WINTER TIRES ONLY =** risk of compromised road grip.

**4 WINTER TIRES = safer handling** when cornering, driving downhill and braking.

If you regularly encounter rain, snow or black ice, choose a **MICHELIN Alpin tire**. This range offers you sharp handling plus a comfortable ride to safely face the challenge of winter driving.

MICHELIN

# MICHELIN
# IS COMMITTED

▶ MICHELIN IS THE **GLOBAL LEADER IN FUEL-EFFICIENT TIRES** FOR LIGHT VEHICLES.

▶ **EDUCATING YOUNGSTERS ON ROAD SAFETY FOR BIKES**, NOT FORGETTING TWO-WHEELERS. LOCAL ROAD SAFETY CAMPAIGNS WERE RUN IN **16 COUNTRIES** IN 2015.

# QUIZ

### 1 TIRES ARE BLACK SO WHY IS THE MICHELIN MAN WHITE?

Back in 1898 when the Michelin Man was first created from a stack of tires, they were made of natural rubber, cotton and sulphur and were therefore light-colored. The composition of tires did not change until after the First World War when carbon black was introduced. But the Michelin Man kept his color!

### 2 HOW LONG HAS MICHELIN BEEN GUIDING TRAVELERS?

Since 1900. When the MICHELIN guide was published at the turn of the century, it was claimed that it would last for a hundred years. It's still around today and remains a reference with new editions and online restaurant listings in a number of countries.

### 3 WHEN WAS THE "BIB GOURMAND" INTRODUCED IN THE MICHELIN GUIDE?

The symbol was created in 1997 but as early as 1954 the MICHELIN guide was recommending "exceptional good food at moderate prices." Today, it features on the MICHELIN Restaurants website and app.

If you want to enjoy a fun day out and find out more about Michelin, why not visit the l'Aventure Michelin museum and shop in Clermont-Ferrand, France:
**www.laventuremichelin.com**

# Tell us what you think about our products.

## Give us your opinion
**satisfaction.michelin.com**

# INDEXES

# ALPHABETICAL LIST OF RESTAURANTS

# RESTAURANTS BY CUISINE

## JAMAICAN

## JAPANESE

# CUISINES BY NEIGHBORHOOD

# STATEN ISLAND ___

# STARRED RESTAURANTS

# BIB GOURMAND

# CREDITS